Challenges and Opportunities for SMEs in Industry 4.0

Noor Hazlina Ahmad
Universiti Sains Malaysia, Malaysia

Qaisar Iqbal
Universiti Sains Malaysia, Malaysia

Hasliza Abdul Halim
Universiti Sains Malaysia, Malaysia

IGI Global
DISSEMINATOR OF KNOWLEDGE

A volume in the Advances in Business Strategy and Competitive Advantage (ABSCA) Book Series

Published in the United States of America by
IGI Global
Business Science Reference (an imprint of IGI Global)
701 E. Chocolate Avenue
Hershey PA, USA 17033
Tel: 717-533-8845
Fax: 717-533-8661
E-mail: cust@igi-global.com
Web site: http://www.igi-global.com

Library of Congress Cataloging-in-Publication Data

Names: Ahmad, Noor Hazlina, 1974- editor. | Iqbal, Qaisar, 1986- editor. | Halim, Hasliza Abdul, 1975- editor.
Title: Challenges and opportunities for SMEs in industry 4.0 / Noor Hazlina Ahmad, Qaisar Iqbal, and Hasliza Abdul Halim, editors.
Description: Hershey, PA : Business Science Reference, [2020] | Includes bibliographical references and index. | Summary: "This book explores the challenges and opportunities for small and medium enterprises in Industry 4.0"-- Provided by publisher.
Identifiers: LCCN 2019042259 (print) | LCCN 2019042260 (ebook) | ISBN 9781799825777 (hardcover) | ISBN 9781799825784 (paperback) | ISBN 9781799825791 (ebook)
Subjects: LCSH: Small business. | Industrial management.
Classification: LCC HD2341 .C42 2020 (print) | LCC HD2341 (ebook) | DDC 658.4--dc23
LC record available at https://lccn.loc.gov/2019042259
LC ebook record available at https://lccn.loc.gov/2019042260

This book is published in the IGI Global book series Advances in Business Strategy and Competitive Advantage (ABSCA) (ISSN: 2327-3429; eISSN: 2327-3437)

British Cataloguing in Publication Data
A Cataloguing in Publication record for this book is available from the British Library.

All work contributed to this book is new, previously-unpublished material. The views expressed in this book are those of the authors, but not necessarily of the publisher.

For electronic access to this publication, please contact: eresources@igi-global.com.

Advances in Business Strategy and Competitive Advantage (ABSCA) Book Series

Patricia Ordóñez de Pablos
Universidad de Oviedo, Spain

ISSN:2327-3429
EISSN:2327-3437

Mission

Business entities are constantly seeking new ways through which to gain advantage over their competitors and strengthen their position within the business environment. With competition at an all-time high due to technological advancements allowing for competition on a global scale, firms continue to seek new ways through which to improve and strengthen their business processes, procedures, and profitability.

The **Advances in Business Strategy and Competitive Advantage (ABSCA) Book Series** is a timely series responding to the high demand for state-of-the-art research on how business strategies are created, implemented and re-designed to meet the demands of globalized competitive markets. With a focus on local and global challenges, business opportunities and the needs of society, the **ABSCA** encourages scientific discourse on doing business and managing information technologies for the creation of sustainable competitive advantage.

Coverage

- Ethics and Business Strategy
- Strategy Performance Management
- Differentiation Strategy
- Globalization
- Joint Ventures
- Value Chain
- Innovation Strategy
- Foreign Investment Decision Process
- Value Creation
- Strategic alliances

IGI Global is currently accepting manuscripts for publication within this series. To submit a proposal for a volume in this series, please contact our Acquisition Editors at Acquisitions@igi-global.com or visit: http://www.igi-global.com/publish/.

The Advances in Business Strategy and Competitive Advantage (ABSCA) Book Series (ISSN 2327-3429) is published by IGI Global, 701 E. Chocolate Avenue, Hershey, PA 17033-1240, USA, www.igi-global.com. This series is composed of titles available for purchase individually; each title is edited to be contextually exclusive from any other title within the series. For pricing and ordering information please visit http://www.igi-global.com/book-series/advances-business-strategy-competitive-advantage/73672. Postmaster: Send all address changes to above address.

Titles in this Series

For a list of additional titles in this series, please visit: http://www.igi-global.com/book-series/advances-business-strategy-competitive-advantage/73672

Handbook of Research on Approaches to Alternative Entrepreneurship Opportunities
José Guilherme Leitão Dantas (CARME, School of Technology and Management, Polytechnic of Leiria, Portugal) and Luísa Cagica Carvalho (Institute Polytechnic of Setúbal, Portugal & CEFAGE, University of Évora, Portugal)
Business Science Reference • © 2020 • 512pp • H/C (ISBN: 9781799819813) • US $295.00

Reshaping Entrepreneurship Education With Strategy and Innovation
Ayansola Olatunji Ayandibu (University of Zululand, South Africa)
Business Science Reference • © 2020 • 300pp • H/C (ISBN: 9781799831716) • US $205.00

Implementing Knowledge in Organizations for Improved Performance Outcomes Emerging Research and Opportunities
Michael J. Gravier (Bryant University, USA) and Ted Farris (University of North Texas, USA)
Business Science Reference • © 2020 • 260pp • H/C (ISBN: 9781799824879) • US $195.00

CSR and Socially Responsible Investing Strategies in Transitioning and Emerging Economies
Anetta Kuna-Marszałek (University of Łódź, Poland) and Agnieszka Kłysik-Uryszek (University of Łódź, Poland)
Business Science Reference • © 2020 • 346pp • H/C (ISBN: 9781799821939) • US $235.00

Handbook of Research on the Strategic Management of Family Businesses
Jesús Manuel Palma-Ruiz (Universidad Autónoma de Chihuahua, Mexico) Ismael Barros-Contreras (Universidad Austral de Chile, Chile) and Luca Gnan (Università degli Studi di Roma "Tor Vergata", Italy)
Business Science Reference • © 2020 • 539pp • H/C (ISBN: 9781799822691) • US $275.00

Utilizing Gamification in Servicescapes for Improved Consumer Engagement
Miralem Helmefalk (Linnaeus University, Sweden) and Leif Marcusson (Linnaeus University, Sweden)
Business Science Reference • © 2020 • 319pp • H/C (ISBN: 9781799819707) • US $225.00

Cases on Strategic Management Issues in Contemporary Organizations
Mona Rashidirad (University of Brighton, UK)
Business Science Reference • © 2020 • 300pp • H/C (ISBN: 9781799816300) • US $195.00

Competitive Drivers for Improving Future Business Performance
Carlos Martins (Lusiada University - North, Portugal) and Paula Rodrigues (Lusiada University - North, Portugal)
Business Science Reference • © 2020 • 360pp • H/C (ISBN: 9781799818434) • US $225.00

IGI Global
DISSEMINATOR OF KNOWLEDGE

701 East Chocolate Avenue, Hershey, PA 17033, USA
Tel: 717-533-8845 x100 • Fax: 717-533-8661
E-Mail: cust@igi-global.com • www.igi-global.com

Table of Contents

Preface xiv

Acknowledgment xix

Section 1
Challenges and Opportunities in Industry 4.0

Chapter 1
Chinese SMEs in Industry 4.0: Analysis and Future Trends 1
Hu Shi, Universiti Sains Malaysia, Malaysia
Qaisar Iqbal, Universiti Sains Malaysia, Malaysia

Chapter 2
Challenges for Pakistani SMEs in Industry 4.0: Applications of Disruptive Technologies 12
Qaisar Iqbal, Universiti Sains Malaysia, Malaysia
Noor Hazlina Ahmad, Universiti Sains Malaysia, Malaysia

Chapter 3
The Effect of Artificial Intelligence on Management Process: Challenges and Opportunities 22
Mustafa Sundu, Beykent University, Turkey
Sebnem Ozdemir, Istinye University, Turkey

Section 2
Sustainability and SMEs in Industry 4.0

Chapter 4
Sustainability of SMEs and Health Sector in a Dynamic Capabilities Perspective 43
Bülent Akkaya, Manisa Celal Bayar University, Turkey
Sema Üstgörül, Manisa Celal Bayar University, Turkey

Chapter 5
Sustainable Performance of Tunisian SMEs in Industry 4.0 65
Abdullah Abdulaziz Alhumaidan, Universiti Sains Malaysia, Malaysia
Noor Hazlina Ahmad, Universiti Sains Malaysia, Malaysia

Section 3
Resources and SMEs in Industry 4.0

Chapter 6
Innovation Capability for SME Biomass Industry Performance: Perspectives of HRM, OC, KMC in Industry 4.0 79
Teoh Ming Fang, Universiti Sains Malaysia, Malaysia
Lee Heng Wei, UOW Malaysia KDU Penang University, Malaysia
Rajendran Muthuveloo, Universiti Sains Malaysia, Malaysia

Chapter 7
Health 4.0: Learning, Innovation, and Collaboration of Small and Medium Private Hospitals in India 104
Sahrish Ahmad, Universiti Sains Malaysia, Malaysia
Hasliza Abdul Halim, Universiti Sains Malaysia, Malaysia
Mohammad Jamal Khan, Saudi Electronic University, Saudi Arabia
Noor Hazlina Ahmad, Universiti Sains Malaysia, Malaysia

Chapter 8
The Labour, Machine, and Material as Sources of Value-Addition for SMEs: An Empirical Evidence From India 123
Mokhalles Mohammad Mehdi, Tezpur University, India
Tridib Ranjan Sarma, Tezpur University, India

Chapter 9
Employer's Role Performance Towards Employees' Satisfaction: A Study of SME Industry 4.0 in Malaysia 140
Siti Noorjannah Abd Halim, Universiti Sains Malaysia, Malaysia
Siti Noorhaslina Abd Halim, Universiti Teknologi MARA, Malaysia

Chapter 10
Cultural Elements in Spanish SME Websites and Social Media: From Localization to Transcreation? 155
Celia Castillo Rodríguez, University of Granada, Spain
María Dolores Olvera-Lobo, University of Granada, Spain
Elena Moya-Molina, University of Granada, Spain

Section 4
Strategic Management in Industry 4.0

Chapter 11
Strategic Management in SMEs in the Context of Clustering 183
Mustafa Atilla Arıcıoğlu, Necmettin Erbakan University, Turkey
Büşra Yiğitol, Konya Food and Agriculture University, Turkey

Chapter 12
Strategic Management in SMEs in Industry 4.0 205
Mustafa Atilla Arıcıoğlu, Necmettin Erbakan University, Turkey
Büşra Yiğitol, Konya Food and Agriculture University, Turkey

Compilation of References 228

About the Contributors 265

Index 270

Detailed Table of Contents

Preface xiv

Acknowledgment xix

Section 1
Challenges and Opportunities in Industry 4.0

Chapter 1
Chinese SMEs in Industry 4.0: Analysis and Future Trends 1
Hu Shi, Universiti Sains Malaysia, Malaysia
Qaisar Iqbal, Universiti Sains Malaysia, Malaysia

Small and medium enterprises (SMEs) play a vital role in the economic development of the People's Republic of China. SMEs contribute to the total of 60% gross domestic product (GDP) and 80% employment. Chinese SMEs contribute to the more than 50% of the country tax. In 2015, China released the Made-in-China 2025 plan to response to the German Industry 4.0, which focuses on knowledge-, innovation-, and quality-intensive manufacturing for cutting-edge technology, new materials, key parts of major products. The chapter aims to explore the challenges and opportunities faced by SMEs in China in the context of Industry 4.0 and Made-in-China 2025. This chapter has used SWOT analysis to explore the challenges and opportunities of Chinese SMEs. Presently, SMEs are facing limited credit facilities, low innovative human capital, sustainable performance as a challenge, and ineffective performance appraisal. This chapter has presented as internationalization, coastal outsourcing, rising middle-class (high consumption), 'one belt, one road' opportunities for SMEs in Industry 4.0 context.

Chapter 2
Challenges for Pakistani SMEs in Industry 4.0: Applications of Disruptive Technologies 12
Qaisar Iqbal, Universiti Sains Malaysia, Malaysia
Noor Hazlina Ahmad, Universiti Sains Malaysia, Malaysia

Small and medium enterprises (SMEs) play a vital role in the development of any economy. The disruptive technologies of the fourth industrial revolution have ignited the flexibility and dynamic nature of the market. Industry 4.0 requires firms to deliver highly customized and high-quality products at low price and on time. However, the SMEs sector is not performing up to the standard, which is quite disturbing in the current economic situation of the country. This chapter has elaborated the application of advanced information and communication technologies of Industry 4.0 in the context of SMEs. Based on the requirements of Industry 4.0, this chapter has also explored the challenges faced by SMEs in Pakistan.

The SMEs in Pakistan are presently coping the challenges such as limited access to finance, the undue compliance and excessive paperwork imposed by regulators, lacking mechanism of talent management, lacking skilled workforce, absence of networking and collaboration, mismanagement of raw material, and insufficient infrastructure.

Chapter 3
The Effect of Artificial Intelligence on Management Process: Challenges and Opportunities 22
Mustafa Sundu, Beykent University, Turkey
Sebnem Ozdemir, Istinye University, Turkey

Artificial intelligence has started to dominantly affect every sector in Industry 4.0. However, the adaptation of the concept to managerial processes are closely related to the concepts of data science and digital transformation. Because artificial intelligence applications being developed are within the scope of artificial narrow intelligence (ANI), that situation requires the company to have a digital transformation policy in order to use artificial intelligence in managerial processes. In addition, to avoid biased artificial intelligence applications, the learning set of artificial intelligence requires a highly rigorous design. This necessitates the establishment of a data science department within the company. In this chapter, digital transformation processes in managerial perspective and the surrounded effect of artificial narrow intelligence on management are discussed.

Section 2
Sustainability and SMEs in Industry 4.0

Chapter 4
Sustainability of SMEs and Health Sector in a Dynamic Capabilities Perspective.............................. 43
Bülent Akkaya, Manisa Celal Bayar University, Turkey
Sema Üstgörül, Manisa Celal Bayar University, Turkey

In Industry 4.0, enterprises have economic, social, and environmentally sustainable policies, and the implementation of these policies may lead to raising the national economy and society welfare. It can be achieved by firms' dynamic capabilities. Therefore, structuring of the activities of enterprises, especially SMEs and health sector organizations within the framework of sustainability and establishing standards by establishing control mechanisms, plays an important role in the development of the country. One of the most important responsibilities of managers in these sectors in implementing sustainable policies is to utilize the dynamic capabilities of the organization. In this context, it is necessary to have knowledge about what dynamic capabilities are and their relationship with sustainability. This study discusses the relationship between dynamic capabilities and sustainability of SMEs and the firms in health sector.

Chapter 5
Sustainable Performance of Tunisian SMEs in Industry 4.0 65
Abdullah Abdulaziz Alhumaidan, Universiti Sains Malaysia, Malaysia
Noor Hazlina Ahmad, Universiti Sains Malaysia, Malaysia

The research aims to know the impact of sustainability orientation on sustainable performance. The data has been collected through a survey and the probability-random sampling technique has been employed. The study sample is micro and small enterprises in Tunisia. The organizational level is the unit of analysis, which are the owners of these enterprises. It has been concluded that managers' orientations have an influence on environmental and social performance, but their orientations towards sustainability did not impact economic performance. The study has suggested that future research could investigate different organizations irrespective of their size and industry that would make it easy to generalize results.

Section 3
Resources and SMEs in Industry 4.0

Chapter 6
Innovation Capability for SME Biomass Industry Performance: Perspectives of HRM, OC, KMC in Industry 4.0 79
Teoh Ming Fang, Universiti Sains Malaysia, Malaysia
Lee Heng Wei, UOW Malaysia KDU Penang University, Malaysia
Rajendran Muthuveloo, Universiti Sains Malaysia, Malaysia

Industry 4.0 exerts great pressure on the organization today to innovate its business model in order to stay competitive. This study examines the positive and indirect effect of human resource management, organizational culture, knowledge management capabilities on organizational performance, with the mediating effect of organizational innovation capability among small and medium-sized enterprise (SME) in biomass industry in Malaysia. In addition, this study integrates resource-based view (RBV) and dynamic capabilities theories to investigate how the organization utilize its resources and capabilities to enhance organizational performance. Data were collected using survey questionnaire from biomass SMEs located in Malaysia. Structural equation modelling (Smart PLS 3.0) was used to test and analyze the data. The findings reveal that knowledge management capability and organizational culture exert a positive influence on organizational innovation capabilities. Similarly, organizational innovation capabilities also found to positively affect organizational performance.

Chapter 7
Health 4.0: Learning, Innovation, and Collaboration of Small and Medium Private Hospitals in India 104
Sahrish Ahmad, Universiti Sains Malaysia, Malaysia
Hasliza Abdul Halim, Universiti Sains Malaysia, Malaysia
Mohammad Jamal Khan, Saudi Electronic University, Saudi Arabia
Noor Hazlina Ahmad, Universiti Sains Malaysia, Malaysia

In the new era of Industry 4.0 and on the basis of current knowledge about innovation in Industry 4.0, it has become a pretty clear that Industry 4.0 had a major impact on the manufacturing sector. At its origin, this industry is evolving from manufacturing to service providers. This chapter explains how innovation of new digital services such as Industry 4.0 integrates towards the healthcare system such as Health 4.0 in India. Although innovation is significant among the manufacturing sector, the practice of this concept is still lacking among the service sector such as hospitals. This study will investigate the impact of organizational learning on horizontal technology collaboration and vertical technology collaboration. The study is designed as a quantitative study and the non-probability purposive sampling technique was used. The data was collected from the doctors of small and medium private hospitals. The findings of data analysis reveal that organizational learning has significant positive impact on horizontal technology collaboration and vertical technology collaboration.

Chapter 8
The Labour, Machine, and Material as Sources of Value-Addition for SMEs: An Empirical Evidence From India 123
Mokhalles Mohammad Mehdi, Tezpur University, India
Tridib Ranjan Sarma, Tezpur University, India

Value addition is a process of changing (converting) input into output with an investment of optimum resources. The present study aims to identify the variables of value addition among MSMEs and its performance in an economy. The study is based on a review of literature from various published sources and analyses to uncover the required variables. Past reviews highlighted that SME performance can be categorized into financial and non-financial characteristics. The previous studies have identified that SME performance depends on the financial factors, marketing factors, production factors, operation activities, and human resources of the enterprises. A survey was conducted among four MSMEs in district industries and commerce centre (DIC), Jorhat (Assam), India using a structured questionnaire constructed from the variables found in past studies. The survey findings highlighted the growth indicators and the challenges that MSMEs faced.

Chapter 9
Employer's Role Performance Towards Employees' Satisfaction: A Study of SME Industry 4.0 in Malaysia 140
Siti Noorjannah Abd Halim, Universiti Sains Malaysia, Malaysia
Siti Noorhaslina Abd Halim, Universiti Teknologi MARA, Malaysia

The wave of the Fourth Industrial Revolution (IR4.0) is a phenomenon in which one or more technologies are replaced by another technology in a short amount of time. In small and medium-sized enterprises (SMEs), some internal and external problem are occurring that suggest change from classical to technological approach. Thus, this chapter aims to establish the relationship between the employees' satisfaction toward their employer's role performance. Based on the power-dependence and agency theories, this study contributes to the SMEs industry in Malaysia and will involve IR4.0 by offering a much more comprehensive theoretical perspective to aid understanding and prepare for the revolution internally. The sample of this study comprises of employees who are working in various sectors of the SMEs industry. G-power technique was employed to find the minimum sample size in this study. Meanwhile, the SPSS and PLS will be used to analyse the data. The practical implication of this research concerns the factors that can enhance employee satisfaction if their company jumps into the IR4.0. Thus, the employer should play the right role to make sure the employees are ready and well prepared for the revolution despite there being environmental uncertainty happening in the process.

Chapter 10
Cultural Elements in Spanish SME Websites and Social Media: From Localization to Transcreation? 155
Celia Castillo Rodríguez, University of Granada, Spain
María Dolores Olvera-Lobo, University of Granada, Spain
Elena Moya-Molina, University of Granada, Spain

The establishment of a professional online corporate presence is an indispensable step for most companies. However, this online presence must consider linguistic, cultural, and technical differences, as well as variations in user expectations across markets. The language industry has responded to these needs by offering two services, namely localization and transcreation, which may act as valuable tools for the adaptation of corporate communications and whose benefits may be particularly advantageous for smaller companies. This study analyzes the application of localization and transcreation processes and strategies in the corporate context, with a focus on Spanish SMEs and English-speaking markets. Results suggest that the signs of the application of these activities in the corporate online field are still scarce. Furthermore, the online presence of both Spanish SMEs and large US corporations show numerous deficiencies, such as partial translations, typos, a non-updated use of social media, and little adaptation to the addressed markets.

Section 4
Strategic Management in Industry 4.0

Chapter 11
Strategic Management in SMEs in the Context of Clustering 183
Mustafa Atilla Arıcıoğlu, Necmettin Erbakan University, Turkey
Büşra Yiğitol, Konya Food and Agriculture University, Turkey

Nowadays, the effects of global dynamics are directive on enterprises. Competitiveness is triggered by these dynamics and determine the efficiency of enterprises. Therefore, not only the local and national dimension, but also the global actors have a say on the viability of enterprises and their competitiveness. In such an ecological environment, it is possible to come across many strategies for gaining competitiveness and skills. Porter points out that the national resources should be used optimally and that each country should specialize in specific areas and build clusters through these areas and thus use the resources effectively. Therefore, it draws attention to "the importance of clustering," which is one of the instruments effective in competitiveness with global dynamics. In this study, strategic management processes of small and medium-sized enterprises in the context of clustering will be discussed. In addition, the contribution of cluster studies to SMEs in Industry 4.0 digitalization process will be briefly mentioned.

Chapter 12
Strategic Management in SMEs in Industry 4.0 205
Mustafa Atilla Arıcıoğlu, Necmettin Erbakan University, Turkey
Büşra Yiğitol, Konya Food and Agriculture University, Turkey

It is envisioned that the fourth industrial revolution contains many concepts such as modern automation and production systems, data collection, data processing, analysis, and data transfer and consists of intelligent factory applications such as augmented reality, the internet of things, cyber physical, and cyber security systems. It reveals the fact that a new era awaits enterprises in the relationship between technology and production due to these predictions for future changes. SMEs are one of the important segments that these triggers, which are the precursors of structural change, will affect. So how will SMEs experience the Industry 4.0 process? What do unmanned factories mean for SMEs? Which countries/ SMEs will have the Industry 4.0 technology and Industry 4.0 infrastructure which require high capital, Which of them will create opportunities? In this chapter, the problems that SMEs will face in the digital transformation process and the political and strategic approaches that can be developed to deal with these problems will be evaluated.

Compilation of References 228

About the Contributors 265

Index 270

Preface

This book, *Challenges and Opportunities for SMEs in Industry 4.0*, is proposed for both academia and practitioners in the field of small and medium enterprises (SMEs) in a highly dynamic market. Chapters of this book were categorized into four sections. The first section, titled "Opportunities and Challenges in Industry 4.0," presents a general overview of the SME's business. This section contains three chapters that will familiarize the readers about the challenges, opportunities, business performance, artificial intelligence, a Turkish perspective and positions of SMEs in Pakistan and China. The second section, titled "Sustainability and SMEs in Industry 4.0," discusses the dynamic capability and sustainable orientation about the sustainable performance of SMEs in industry 4.0. The second section consists of two chapters representing sensing, seizing, and reconfiguring as three categories of dynamic capabilities influencing sustainable performance in the health sector, and investing the impact of sustainable orientation on the individual three dimensions such as social, economic, and environmental of sustainable performance in the context of Tunisian SMEs. The third section, titled "Resources and SMEs in Industry 4.0," examines various resources namely human resource management, organizational culture, knowledge management capabilities, organizational learning, Spanish SME Websites and Social Media, employee's satisfaction as potential influencers on the performance of SMEs. The five chapters of this section deliberate on the role of organizational learning on horizontal technology collaboration and vertical technology collaboration among doctors of small and medium private hospitals in India by using non-probability sampling, human resource management, organizational culture, knowledge management capabilities on organizational performance, with the mediating effect of organizational innovation capability among small and medium-sized enterprise (SME) in biomass industry in Malaysia, by explaining growth indicators of MSMEs in district industries and commerce center (DIC), Jorhat (Assam), India using a structured questionnaire, establishing the relationship between the employees' satisfaction with their employer's role performance in the presence of the environmental uncertainty as a moderator taking its cue from the Power-Dependence and Agency Theories, and by revealing numerous deficiencies, such as partial translations, typos, a non-updated use of social media and little adaptation to the addressed markets in the Spanish SMEs and large US corporations. The final section focuses on the application of strategic management in the clustering and industrial fourth revolution. This section comprises of two chapters where authors have tried to elaborate the nature of competitiveness, efficiency of enterprises, importance of clustering, global dynamics in 4IR, and the problems that SMEs will face in the digital transformation process and the political and strategic approaches that can be developed to deal with these problems will be evaluated.

We hope that the publication n of this book will enhance the spread of ideas and good practices among SMEs within the context of industry 4.0 revolution. This book will enrich knowledge and assist researchers or practitioners in the field of SMEs concerning the fourth industrial revolution to comprehend and solve the challenges and issues associated with SMEs.

SECTION 1: CHALLENGES AND OPPORTUNITIES IN INDUSTRY 4.0

Chapter 1, "Chinese SMEs in Industry 4.0: Analysis and Future Trend," by Hu Shi and Qaisar Iqbal of Universiti Sains Malaysia from Malaysia, has explored the challenges and opportunities faced by SMEs in China in the context of Industry 4.0 and Made-in-China 2025. This chapter has used SWOT analysis to explore the challenges and opportunities of Chinese SMEs. Presently, SMEs are facing limited credit facilities, low innovative human capital, sustainable performance as a challenge, and ineffective performance appraisal. This chapter has presented as internationalization, coastal outsourcing, rising middle-class (high consumption), 'One belt, one road' opportunities for SMEs in industry 4.0 context.

Chapter 2, "Challenges for Pakistani SMEs in Industry 4.0: Applications of Disruptive Technologies," by Qaisar Iqbal and Noor Hazlina Ahmad of Universiti Sains Malaysia from Malaysia, has elaborated the application of advanced information and communication technologies of industry 4.0 in the context of SMEs. Based on the requirements of industry 4.0, this chapter has also explored the challenges faced by SMEs in Pakistan. The SMEs in Pakistan are presently coping the challenges such as limited access to finance, the undue compliance and excessive paperwork imposed by the regulator, lacking mechanism of talent management, lacking skilled workforce, absence of networking and collaboration, mismanagement of raw material, and Insufficient infrastructure. The government agencies, regulators and management of SMEs are emphasized to effectively develop strategies and initiative programs to cope with these issues so that this sector could deliver at its possible potential.

Chapter 3, "The Effect of Artificial Intelligence on Management Process: Challenges and Opportunities," by Mustafa Sundu of Beykent University from Turkey and Sebnem Ozdemir, of Istinye University from Turkey, has explained the obstacles in the way of application of artificial intelligence. As artificial intelligence applications being developed are within the scope of artificial narrow intelligence (ANI) this situation requires the company to have a digital transformation policy to use artificial intelligence in managerial processes. Besides, to avoid biased artificial intelligence applications, the learning set of artificial intelligence requires a highly rigorous design. This necessitates the establishment of a data science department within the company. In this section, digital transformation processes in managerial perspective and the surrounded effect of artificial narrow intelligence on management are discussed.

SECTION 2: SUSTAINABILITY AND SMES IN INDUSTRY 4.0

Chapter 4, "Sustainability of SMEs and Health Sector in Dynamic Capability Perspective," by Bülent Akkaya and Sema Üstgörül of Manisa Celal Bayar University from Turkey, has elaborated the relationship of dynamic capabilities in the shape of sensing, seizing, and reconfiguring with the sustainable performance of SMEs in the health sector. Enterprises exist in a very fast-changing environment. Enterprises must sense incoming and outcoming opportunities and threats created by the changing environment in a market place to be able to adapt these changes. This is called dynamic capabilities in literature. It has three dimensions namely sensing, seizing and reconfiguring. In the Industry 4.0 term, enterprises have economic, social and environmentally sustainable policies and the implementation of these policies may lead to raising the national economy and social welfare. It can be achieved by firms' dynamic capabilities. Therefore, structuring the activities of enterprises, especially Small and Medium Enterprises and health sector organizations within the framework of sustainability and establishing standards by establishing control mechanisms, play an important role in the development of the country. One of the most important responsibilities of managers in these sectors in implementing sustainable policies is to utilize the dynamic capabilities of the organization.

Chapter 5, "Sustainable Performance of Tunisian SMEs in Industry 4.0," by Abdullah Abdulaziz-Alhumaidan and Noor Hazlina Ahmad of Universiti Sains Malaysia from Malaysia, aims to know the impact of sustainability orientation on sustainable performance. The data has been collected through a survey and probability- random sampling technique has been used. The study sample is micro and small enterprises in Tunisia. The organizational level is the unit of analysis, which are the owners of these enterprises. It has been concluded that enterprises managers' orientations have an influence on environmental and social sustainable performance, but their orientations towards sustainability did not impact economic sustainable performance. The study has suggested that future research could investigate other sectors and other sizes of organizations because they might provide other views than micro and small manufacturers' owners.

SECTION 3: RESOURCES AND SMES IN INDUSTRY 4.0

Chapter 6, "Innovation Capability for SME Biomass Industry Performance: Perspectives of Human Resource Management, Organizational Culture, and Knowledge Management Capabilities in the Context of Industry 4.0," by Teoh Ming-Fang of Universiti Sains Malaysia from Malaysia, Lee Heng Wei of KDU Penang University College from Malaysia and Rajendran Muthuveloo of Universiti Sains Malaysia from Malaysia, examines the positive and indirect effect of human resource management, organizational culture, knowledge management capabilities on organizational performance, with the mediating effect of organizational innovation capability among small and medium-sized enterprise (SME) in biomass industry in Malaysia. Also, this study integrates a resource-based view (RBV) and dynamic capabilities theories, to investigate how the organization utilizes its resources and capabilities to enhance organizational performance. Data were collected using a survey questionnaire from biomass SMEs located in Malaysia. Structural equation modeling (Smart PLS 3.0) was used to test and analyze the data. The findings reveal that knowledge management capability and organizational culture exert a positive influence on organizational innovation capabilities. Similarly, organizational innovation capabilities also found to positively affect organizational performance.

Chapter 7, "Health 4.0: Learning, Innovation, and Collaboration of Small and Medium Private Hospitals in India," by Sahrish Ahmad, Hasliza Abdul Halim of Universiti Sains Malaysia from Malaysia, Mohammad Jamal Khan of Saudi Electronic University from Saudi Arabia, and Noor Hazlina Ahmad of Universiti Sains Malaysia from Malaysia, explains how the innovation of new digital services such as industry 4.0 integrates the healthcare system such as health 4.0 in India. Although innovation is significant among the manufacturing sector, the practice of this concept is still lacking among the service sector such as hospitals. This study will investigate the impact of organizational learning on horizontal technology collaboration and vertical technology collaboration. The study is designed as a quantitative study and the non-probability purposive sampling technique was used. The data was collected from the doctors of small and medium private hospitals in India. The findings of data analysis revealed that organizational learning, have a significant positive impact on horizontal technology collaboration and vertical technology collaboration.

Chapter 8, "The Labour, Machine, and Material as a Source of Value-Addition for SMEs: An Empirical Evidence From India," by Mokhalles Mohammad Mehdi and Tridib Ranjan Sarma of Tezpur University from India, aims to identify the variables of value addition among MSMEs and its performance in an economy. The study is based on a review of literature from various published sources' and analyzed to uncover the required variables. Past reviews highlighted that SMEs' performance can be categorized into financial and non-financial characteristics. The previous studies have identified that SMEs' performance depends on the financial factors, marketing factors, production factors, operation activities and human resources of the enterprises. A survey was conducted among four MSMEs in district industries and commerce center (DIC), Jorhat (Assam), India using a structured questionnaire constructed from the variable of past studies. The survey findings highlighted the growth indicators and the challenges that MSMEs in faced.

Chapter 9, "Employer's Role Performance Towards Employees' Satisfaction: A Study of Malaysian SMEs in Industry 4.0," by Siti Noorjannah Binti Abd Halim of University Sains Malaysia from Malaysia and Siti Noorhaslina Binti Abd Halim of Universiti Teknologi MARA Malaysia from Malaysia, aims to establish the relationship between the employees' satisfaction with their employer's role performance in the presence of the environmental uncertainty as a moderator. Taking its cue from the Power-Dependence and Agency Theories, the study contributes to the SME industry in Malaysia from the perspective of IR4.0 by offering a much more comprehensive theoretical perspective to aid understanding and prepared for the revolution on an internal basis. Practically, this study explores the factors that can enhance the employee's satisfaction when their company operate in the IR4.0. Thus, the employers should play the right role to make sure the employees ready and well prepared for the revolution even though there is environmental uncertainty happen in between the process.

Chapter 10, "Cultural Elements in Spanish SME Websites and Social Media: From Localization to Transcreation?" by Celia Castillo Rodríguez, María Dolores Olvera-Lobo and Elena Moya-Molina of University of Granada from Spain analyzes the application of localization and transcreation processes and strategies in the corporate context, with a focus on Spanish SMEs and the English-speaking markets. Nowadays, the establishment of a professional online corporate presence is an indispensable step for most companies. However, this online presence must consider linguistic, cultural and technical differences, as well as variations in user expectations across markets. The linguistic industry has responded to these needs by offering two services, namely localization, and transcreation, which may act as valuable tools for the adaptation of corporate communications and whose benefits may be particularly advantageous for smaller companies. Results suggest that the signs of the application of these activities in the corporate online field are still scarce. Furthermore, the online presence of both Spanish SMEs and large US corporations shows numerous deficiencies, such as partial translations, typos, a non-updated use of social media and little adaptation to the addressed markets.

SECTION 4: STRATEGIC MANAGEMENT AND INDUSTRY 4.0

Chapter 11, "Strategic Management in SMEs in the Context of Clustering," by Mustafa Atilla Arıcıoğlu of Necmettin Erbakan University from Turkey and Büşra Yiğitol of Konya Food and Agriculture University from Turkey, has discussed the strategic management process in the context of clustering. In this age, the effects of global dynamics are directive on enterprises. Competitiveness is triggered by these dynamics and determines the efficiency of enterprises. Therefore, not only the local and national dimensions but also the global actors have a say on the viability of enterprises and their competitiveness. In such an ecological environment, it is possible to come across many strategies for gaining competitiveness and skills. Porter (1998) points out that the national resources should be used optimally, and that each country should specialize in specific areas and build clusters through these areas and thus use the resources effectively. Therefore, it draws attention to "the importance of clustering", which is one of the instruments effective in competitiveness with global dynamics.

Chapter 12, "Strategic Management in SMEs in Industry 4.0," by Mustafa Atilla Arıcıoğlu of Necmettin Erbakan University from Turkey and Büşra Yiğitol of Konya Food and Agriculture University from Turkey, has evaluated the problems faced by organizations and talked about the political and strategic approaches in the same domain. It is envisioned that the fourth industrial revolution contains many concepts such as modern automation and production systems, data collection, data processing, analysis, and data transfer, and consists of intelligent factory applications such as augmented reality, the Internet of Things, cyber-physical and cybersecurity systems. It reveals the fact that a new era awaits enterprises in the relationship between technology and production due to these predictions for future changes. Especially SMEs are one of the important segments that these triggers, which are the precursors of structural change, will affect. So how will SMEs experience the industry 4.0 process? What do unmanned factories mean for SMEs? Which countries / SMEs will the industry 4.0 technology and industry 4.0 infrastructure, which require high capital, create opportunities? In this section, the problems that SMEs will face in the digital transformation process and the political and strategic approaches that can be developed to deal with these problems will be evaluated.

Acknowledgment

We are highly obliged to the authors and reviewers for their support and insightful comments - without their input, this book could not have been accomplished. Special thanks go to the practitioners that granted us their expertise, Ms. Sana Zia, Mrs. Xi Zhang, and to our colleagues who provided their manifold contributions and reviews, especially Ms. Nurhayati Samad and Mr. Ahmad Yar Khan. Finally, we thank our families and friends for standing by us through this still exploratory journey into the world of digital marketing.

Noor Hazlina Ahmad
School of Management, Universiti Sains Malaysia, Malaysia

Qaisar Iqbal
School of Management, Universiti Sains Malaysia, Malaysia

Hasliza Abd Halim
School of Management, Universiti Sains Malaysia, Malaysia

Section 1

Challenges and Opportunities in Industry 4.0

Chapter 1
Chinese SMEs in Industry 4.0:
Analysis and Future Trends

Hu Shi
Universiti Sains Malaysia, Malaysia

Qaisar Iqbal
https://orcid.org/0000-0002-6619-7243
Universiti Sains Malaysia, Malaysia

ABSTRACT

Small and medium enterprises (SMEs) play a vital role in the economic development of the People's Republic of China. SMEs contribute to the total of 60% gross domestic product (GDP) and 80% employment. Chinese SMEs contribute to the more than 50% of the country tax. In 2015, China released the Made-in-China 2025 plan to response to the German Industry 4.0, which focuses on knowledge-, innovation-, and quality-intensive manufacturing for cutting-edge technology, new materials, key parts of major products. The chapter aims to explore the challenges and opportunities faced by SMEs in China in the context of Industry 4.0 and Made-in-China 2025. This chapter has used SWOT analysis to explore the challenges and opportunities of Chinese SMEs. Presently, SMEs are facing limited credit facilities, low innovative human capital, sustainable performance as a challenge, and ineffective performance appraisal. This chapter has presented as internationalization, coastal outsourcing, rising middle-class (high consumption), 'one belt, one road' opportunities for SMEs in Industry 4.0 context.

INTRODUCTION

China is regarded as the largest emerging economy in the world with the largest population. China is a leader in world manufacturing areas and the products cover from high-tech goods to daily consumer goods. In 2013 German as a world advanced industrialized nation prompted the initiation and concept of 'Industry 4.0', which means the new industrial revolution. In 2015, China released 'Made-in-China 2025' plan to respond to German Industry 4.0', which focuses on the knowledge, innovation, and quality of intensive manufacturing for cutting-edge technology, new materials, key parts of major products (Li,

DOI: 10.4018/978-1-7998-2577-7.ch001

2018; Iqbal & Nawaz, 2019). Industry 4.0 refers to the fourth industrial revolution in the world and puts forward the conception of cyber-physical systems (CPS) with the integration of automation, data exchange, 3D printing and cloud computing advanced technologies (Iqbal, Yang, Nawaz & Iqbal, 2019). 'Industry 4.0' is the integration of physical basic systems and software systems (Kosacka-olejnik & Pitakaso, 2019). One of the similarities for German Industry 4.0 and Made-in-China 2025 is the automation acceleration and collaborative industrial robots. Another point is the time of the goal achievement for Industry 4.0 and Made-in-China 2025 set a similar time duration between ten years to fifteen years. Manufacturing digitalization, CPS, artificial intelligence and big data will be the future trend and 'Made-in-China' will transform to 'Design-in-China'.

The concentration of this chapter is the opportunities and challenges faced by Chinese SMEs in the trend of Industry 4.0 and Made-in-China 2025. This chapter is organized as follows. The first section is the introduction and Made-in-China 2025. Moreover, the next section follows the current situation of Chinese SMEs and government policies. Then the opportunities and challenges of Chinese SMEs are discussed in detail. SWOT analysis is summarized at the end of the chapter. The last section is the conclusion, which focuses on the trend of Chinese SMEs.

THE DEFINITION OF SMEs IN CHINA

SME is a crucial part of the Chinese economy. SMEs comprise 99.81% of total firms in China. The definition of SME varies with the category of the industry in China. SME is defined based on the number of employees, total assets, and total annual revenue of an enterprise. The SME Promotion Law of China (2003) has provided guidelines to define Small and medium-sized enterprises (SMEs) by replacing the old criteria of 1998 and the supplementary criteria of 1992.

Table 1. Definitions of SMEs in China

Size category	Industries	Employment-based	Total assets	Business revenue
Small	Industry	<300	< ¥ 40 million	< ¥ 30 million
	Construction	< 600	< ¥ 40 million	< ¥ 30 million
	Hotel & Restaurant	<400		< ¥ 30 million
Medium	Industry	300-2000	¥ 40 million-400 million	¥ 30 million-300 million
	Construction	600-3000	¥ 40 million-400 million	¥ 30 million-300 million
	Hotel & Restaurant	400-800		¥ 30 million-150 million

Regarding the above criterions, Small enterprises must fulfill at least one criterion. In the case of Medium enterprises, the firm must meet all three conditions. An industrial SME in China may have up to 2,000 employees where a small enterprise has less than 300 and medium-sized business have a number of employees in between 301 and 2,000.

CURRENT SITUATION OF CHINESE SMEs AND GOVERNMENT POLICIES

In China, SMEs play an overwhelming role in economic development and employment as more than 60% percent of GDP contribution and more than 50 % of the country tax. SMEs represent 99.6% of Chinese total enterprises and attract more than 80 percent of the employment with more than 70 percent of the patent's contribution (Chen, 2011). According to the Law of the People's Republic of China on the Promotion of Small and Medium-sized Enterprises (2017), (SME Promotion Law) SMEs are referred to as the companies that have a relatively small size in personnel and scope of business. Moreover, the standards for identifying SMEs are stipulated by the relevant departments of the State Council. The classification of a company that should be micro, small or medium-sized based on the belonging industry, operating income, total assets and a number of employees. Compared with the definition of SMEs from other countries the recognition of SMEs mainly depends on the belonging industry, enterprise assets, number of staff and business incomes (Li, 2018).

Legal supports by SME Promotion Law in China aim to protect the rights of Chinese SMEs. Both of public financing and private financing for SMEs are prompted by the Chinese governments. However public financing is more prevalent and common as private financing includes more high-risk investments and low-return. Public financing from state-owned commercial banks in China has increased 30% of loans for SMEs. At the same time for medium and small banks, the RRR (Required Reserve Ratio) has reduced and lefts out money for funding the SMEs. Moreover, SMEs in China are also encouraged to issue bonds and equality in the National Equities Exchange and Quotation (NEEQ) as a channel of funding. Moreover, to reduce the tax burden Chinese SME Promotion Law stipulates that business with a monthly sales volume between CNY20,000 and CNY 30,0000 is exempted from VAT (value-added tax) from 1st January 2018 to 31st December 2020. The tax policies for Chinese SMEs also cover corporate income tax (Centre, 2019).

Challenges for SMEs in China

State-owned enterprises (SOEs) in China benefit from Chinese government policy and dominated the Chinese economic although accounts for no more than 1% of the number of total enterprises with strong support from the Chinese government and stay as monopoly status in China.

Lack of Credit Facilities

The biggest challenge that SMEs meet in China is a financial burden and liquid capital. Cash flow is very vital for SMEs' continuous operation and development. However, the channel of finance is often limited due to the reliability of its operation. The main financing source for SMEs is the bank institutions while due to the small size of the operation and instable profits the criteria for a loan sometimes become extremely hard to comply with (Centre, 2019). Lack of financing is big trouble for Chinese SMEs. Compared with state-owned companies SMEs often face financial problems and support. To release the stress of SMEs in China in the financial area Chinese governments implement a serious of friendly policies to SMEs in China. SMEs as the main contributors to Chinese economic development sufficient attention is gained from the Chinese government. Facing the pressure from the US trade threaten Chinese governments to devote greater efforts to develop SMEs to improve the total business circumstance on China (Chen, 2011).

Lack of Innovative Human Capital

In 2019, there are about 8.34 million graduate college students, which brings a huge pressure for Chinese employment. Employees are the competitive advantages and cannot be replaced easily in an organization. There are tangible and intangible resources in an organization. The competence of human resources is an intangible resource in an organization. Therefore, the competencies of human resources are a vital element to improve the whole performance of SMEs. SMEs are the driving power for economic growth, enterprise structure and the creation of employment opportunities in a country (Centre, 2019). Employee competence not only refers to professional job skills but also soft skills such as communication skills and problem-solving skills. Nevertheless, due to the scale and capability of SMEs talents attraction seems extremely hard for SMEs especially innovative talents. Compared with large enterprises and foreign enterprises the pay packets and incentives are not attractive to talents. Based on the role of SMEs which contributes to more than 90% of the employment in China Chinese government encourage talent acquisition project for senior and technical talents for high-technology SMEs with more incentives and subsidiaries (Centre, 2019). Human capital cannot be easily replaced and replicated in an enterprise and belongs to the unique assets to the enterprise. Not only the ability of employees is important for SMEs development but also the ability of entrepreneurs. The conception and stagey of entrepreneurs in SMEs play a vital role which reflects the mission and vision of an enterprise and the way of decision-making (Tsai, Wang & Yuan, 2015).

Sustainable Performance as a Challenge

Another obvious challenge for Chinese SMEs is the balance between operating costs and environmental protection. Now the Chinese government prompted cleaner production and sustainable development for Chinese enterprise. SMEs must strictly comply with environmental regulations and rules. Chinese enterprises integrate both economic development and environmental protection to achieve energy efficiency and environmentally friendly. As SMEs on one hand, profits need to be achieved with low cost at the

Figure 1. Number of ISO 14001 Certificates Trend (1999-2015)
Source: (Pesce, M. et al.,2018)

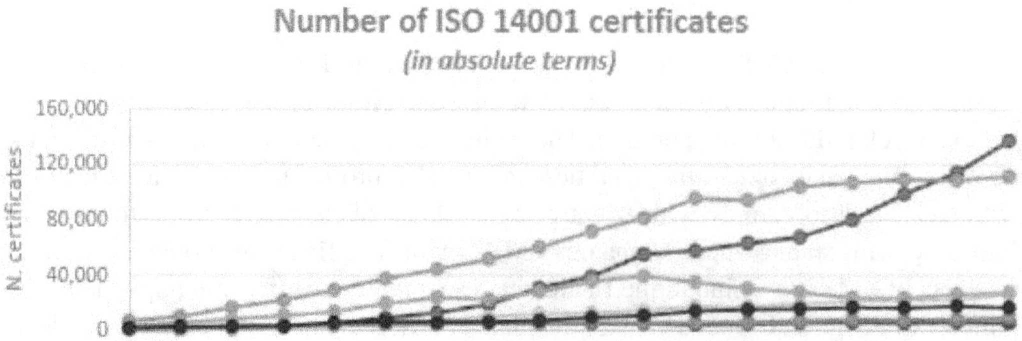

same time green supply chain and green operation should be ensured. China has the largest number for ISO14001, which is a certificate that combines sustainable management and environmental protection (Pesce, M. *et al.*,2018).

From Figure 1 the conclusion could be got that the number of ISO 14001 certificates in China increased largely from 1999 to 2015. In 2015 the number of ISO 14001 certificates owned by China exceeded the European Union and ranked the first position in the world in 2015. That reflects the trend of Chinese focus on sustainable development and green production. By the way among them electronic and electric equipment accounted for 52% in 2015 with the most occupation of ISO 14001 certificates.

Lack of Effective Performance Appraisal

Nowadays strategic human resource management is widely recognized by the organizations, which covers the areas of human resource planning, job analysis, recruitment, training and development, performance management, compensation management, and employee relationship management. Performance management is the key factor to determine compensation and performance appraisal for employees in an organization. Moreover, performance management could identify the potential advantages of employees for further development and disadvantages for employee further improvements (Tsai, Wang, & Yuan, 2015). However, there exist some problems in performance management of Chinses SMEs such as not scientific performance indicators, lack of skillful performance appraisal methods, insufficient communication during the performance appraisal process, not enough training and only focus on the performance appraisal process (Chen, 2011).

OPPORTUNITIES FOR SMES in CHINA

In 2025, China is going to become a powerful manufacturing nation with high technology and high-speed automation. To extend Chinese SMEs' business range 'go global' policy is initiated to utilize the competitive advantages of SMEs. Some Chinese SMEs choose to escape from Chinese policy obstacles and venture abroad with low resource commitment, which adopts internationalization as its development strategy. Exporting and licensing are the two main competitive entry modes (Wu & Deng, 2019). However, geographic relocation needs to evaluate the resources in a targeted market, non-discriminate policy treatment, uncertainty and risks in host countries. Upwards internalization refers to the entry to the developed countries and downwards internationalization means the entry to the developing countries. Mostly upwards internationalization implies enterprises could sell products and services in certain developed countries while downwards internationalization refers to the achievement of the low cost of labor and production (Piantoni, Baronchelli & Cortesi, 2012). Dynamics of internationalization in the foreign market can be achieved by opportunity identification and social capital occupation that means pre-internationalization preparation is vital to SMEs. Comparison of the social, economy and culture differences between home country and host country SMEs need to consider thoroughly before internationalization based on knowledge, information, and relevant social capital. The main concept of SMEs internationalization is utilized advantages and opportunities in the host country and reduce the risks, which could help them create more value (Anna, Y. *et al.*,2017).

As shown in figure 2 before the internationalization of enterprises four stages should go through. They are international opportunity unawareness, international opportunity visualization, international

Figure 2. Pre-Internationalization Stage of Stage Model
Source: Anna, Y. et al., (2017)

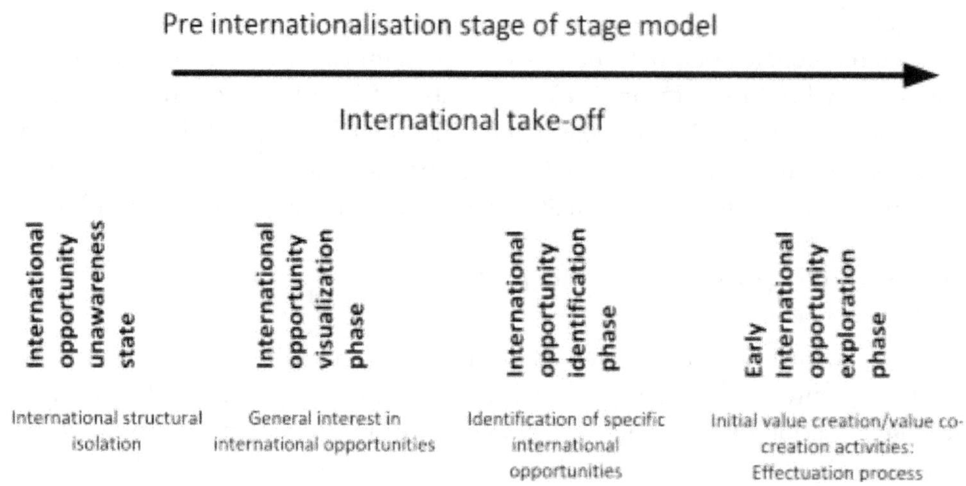

opportunity identification, and early international opportunity exploration. 'The Belt and Road' involves 65 countries around the route and 13 Chinese land provinces with another name 'The Silk Road Economic Belt' and '21st Century Maritime Silk Road' which was promoted by the Chinese chairman Xi Jinping in 2013. This project takes advantage of the ancient Chinese silk road and actively cooperates with the countries around the road line and increases cooperation in many areas including the business area (Ferdinand, 2016). This increases the opportunities for Chinese SMEs to find more opportunities and cooperate with SMEs in other countries. Some Chinese SMEs, which are located in the Chinese southeast coastal province conduct offshore service outsourcing business to foreign countries by utilizing their location and competitive advantages. By the location and labor cost advantages, coastal SMEs can play a role as outsourcing providers for development. India is famous for its outsourcing in the IT area. Outsourcing could be achieved by some coastal Chinese SMEs with their competitive advantages in certain areas, which could contribute to more employment, entry to foreign markets and add higher value to their products. Outsourcing provides big potential for Chinese SMEs to go global especially for high technology Chinese SMEs and is a proper way to go globalization (Yue & Yu, 2008). The factors, which could have an impact on SMEs outsourcing by foreign countries such as technology, labor cost, labor skills, product quality, host country infrastructure, physical location, and economic development.

Another opportunity for Chinese SMEs is the increasing number of Chinese middle class, which has a big influence on Chinese consumption. The Purchasing Power Parity (PPP) has been more than the US since 2014. As the number of Chinese middle-class increased and millions of people gets out of poverty. It is predicted that the amount of Chinese middle class will be around 275 million by 2020. The characteristics of a new Chinese middle class could be identified by the annual income (75,000-280,000 yuan) and is mainly clustered in urban areas and about 80% of this group have their property and housing. The rising number of Chinese middle class indicates that the standards of living of Chinese residents are improving and the ability of consumption arises (Morreale, Costa & Villada, 2018). This provides more opportunities for Chinese SMEs to develop their business and discover more opportunities to satisfy the needs of the middle-class. From figure 3., the information could be gained that the PPP of China

Figure 3. Purchasing Power Parity (Unit: trillion dollars)
Source: Morreale, Costa & Villada, (2018)

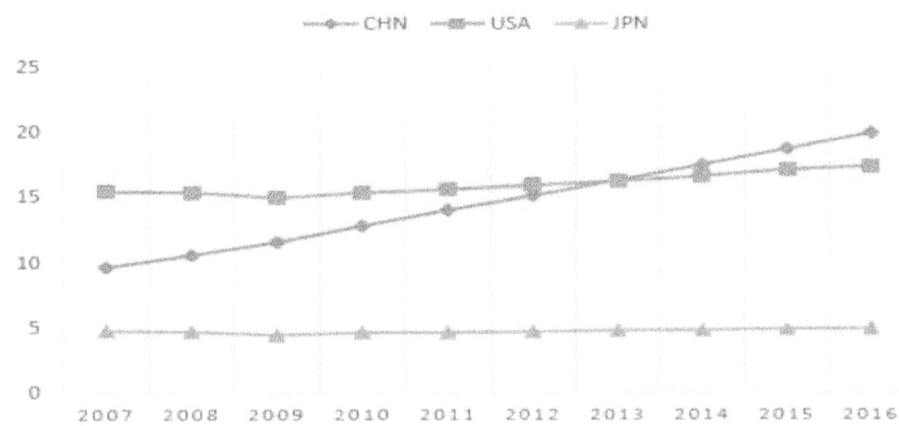

has increased quickly from 2007 to 2016. Moreover, the PPP of China has exceeded the US in 2014 and the number was around 20 trillion dollars in 2016. This phenomenon provides huge opportunities for Chinese SMEs to develop different types of business.

Purchasing Managers' Index (PMI) is an index for understanding the economic trend of manufacturing and service sectors which is a diffusion index that reflects the market conditions based on five major indicators: new orders, inventory levels, production, supplier deliveries, and employment. PMI could range from 0 to 100. Above 50 means there is an expansion compared with the last month while below 50 means there is a contraction. PMI is an excellent way to provide current and future business information for company decision-making (Investopedia, 2019). PMI for SMEs in China is closed to 50 and among the five sub-indices composing PMI, the production index, new orders index and supplier distribution time index were higher than the threshold, while raw materials inventory index and employment index were lower than the threshold. That means the economic trend of Chinese SMEs is prosperous (National Bureau of Statistics of China, 2019).

Internet development provides another opportunity for Chinese SMEs such as B2B electronic commerce for Chinese SMEs. By electronic platform, the cost of operation could be reduced and increase business efficiency with more flexibility. For example, Alibaba.com has offered more opportunities for SMEs to find a business chance and conduct their business online. With the development of B2B Chinese SMEs could choose more channels to conduct their business to achieve efficiency and lower the cost to gain more revenues (Chong, Shafaghi, & Tan, 2011).

Figure 4. Chinese Manufacturing PMI in 2018
Source: National Bureau of Statistics of China (2019)

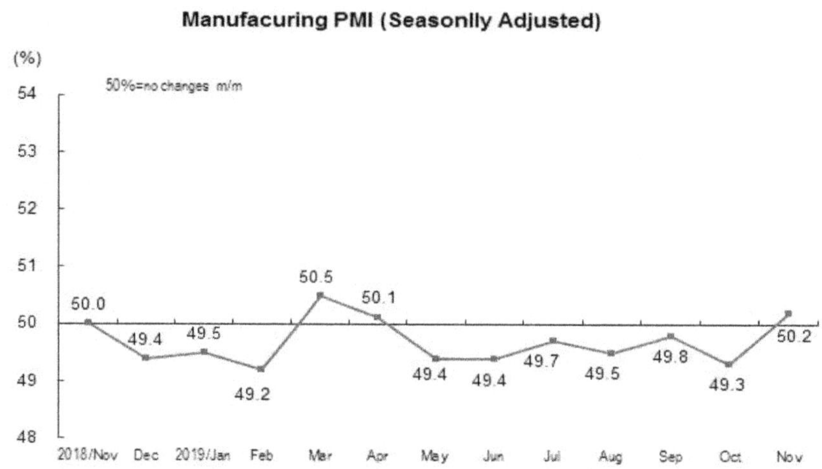

FUTURE TREND AND CHINESE SMEs

Now China ranks the 17th among total 126 countries for total innovation score based on the latest GII (Global Innovation Index). Moreover, the expenditure of R&D (Research and Development), researchers' numbers, patents, and publications rank the 1st and 2nd position in the world. Innovation and internationalization will be the future trend for SMEs and cites such as Beijing and Shanghai are the pioneering cities belonging to the top 10 Global Startup Ecosystems. AI (Artificial Intelligence) develops very quickly in China, which becomes the future trend in technological areas (Centre, 2019). In China, SMEs are encouraged to develop technology and IT companies with the Chinese government support for the reduction of an administrative and financial burden especially for high-technological companies (Li, 2018). The Chinese government has initiated the 'One Belt and One Road' project more and more enterprises are encouraged to take part in while some incentives are provided for Chinese governments such as favorable tax policies, independent IP protection and financial burden reduction (Centre, 2019). In the future, the Chinese government will focus on the SMEs with innovation and improve the IP protection so SMEs with innovation can use its IP as a movable property to get a loan. Many SMEs choose to translate the nature of the business to high technology to meet the demands of Chinese market growth and maintain competitive status in the Chinese market (Alqahtani, 2016). Innovation and technology development is very essential for Chinese SMEs' future development. With the high seed of industry 4.0 and the development of technology, SMEs have to keep learning new skills consistently. Learning means the identification of new trends and seeks for more opportunities. Besides, innovation will be the target for the enterprises to achieve. Moreover, learning also implies gain lessons from failure (Wei, *et al.*, 2016).

Table. 2 SWOT Analysis

Strengths	Weakness
Flexibility **A large Amount of Human Capital** **Government Policy Supports (SME Promotion Law)**	Lack of credit facilities Lack of innovative human capital Sustainable performance as a challenge Lack of effective performance appraisal
Opportunities	**Threats**
Internationalization & E-commerce **Coastal Outsourcing** **Increasing Number of Middle-class (Large Consumption) & Prosperous economic trend** **'One belt, one road' project prompted more cooperation**	SOEs (State-owned Enterprise) still dominate the Chinese market Talent attraction and retention

RECOMMENDATION

From the SWOT Analysis for this chapter, we could get the conclusion that Chinese SMEs face both challenges and opportunities. How to grasp the government policies and economic trend seem to be essential for the survival of Chinese SMEs. In this high-speed development, world innovation is always the main strain for SMEs to become competitive. At the same time how to balance the operation cost and sustainable development is another obstacle that SMEs need to overcome. Chinese SMEs can gain competitiveness by extending to internationalization. However, pre-internationalization and evaluation must be prepared first. How to attract and retain the talents will be the most vital factor for SMEs to consider as human capital is unique and core competitiveness to an enterprise. In the future high-end and cutting-edge SMEs with innovation could go further.

REFERENCES

Alqahtani, K. M. (2016). *Challenges of Innovation for Chinese Small and Medium-sized Enterprises: Case Study in Beijing*. DOI: .v9n12p165 doi:10.5539/ibr

Anna, Y. (2017). The interplay between social capital and international opportunities: A processual study of international "take-off" episodes in Chinese SMEs. *Industrial Marketing Management*. Doi:10.1016/j.indmarman.2017.07.006

Chen, D. (2011). *Research on Performance Management of Chinese SME*. DOI: .v6n4p263 doi:10.5539/ijbm

Chong, W. K., Shafaghi, M., & Tan, B. L. (2011). *Development of a business-to-business critical success factors (B2B CSFs) framework for Chinese SMEs*. Doi:10.1108/02634501111153700

EUSME Centre. (2019). *SMEs in China: Policy Environment Report*. Author.

Ferdinand, P. (2016). *Westward ho — the China dream and "one belt, one road": Chinese foreign policy under Xi Jinping*. Academic Press.

Iqbal, Q., & Nawaz, R. (2019). Rife information pollution (infollution) and virtual organizations in industry 4.0: within reality causes and consequences. In *Big Data and Knowledge Sharing in Virtual Organizations* (pp. 117–135). IGI Global. doi:10.4018/978-1-5225-7519-1.ch005

Iqbal, Q., Yang, S., Nawaz, R., & Iqbal, K. (2019). A multi-dimensional construct of perceived information pollution in the era of rife infollution. *VINE Journal of Information and Knowledge Management Systems*, *49*(2), 162–180. doi:10.1108/VJIKMS-10-2018-0093

Kosacka-olejnik, M., & Pitakaso, R. (2019). Industry 4.0: State of the Art and Research Implications. *Log Forum, 15*(4), 475–485.

Li, L. (2018). Technological Forecasting & Social Change China's manufacturing locus in 2025: With a comparison of "Made-in-China'. *Technological Forecasting & Social Change*, *135*, 66–74. Doi:10.1016/j.techfore.2017.05.028

Morreale, J. C., Costa, A., & Villada, M. (2018). *China's rising middle class: A case study of Shanghai college students*. Doi:10.14254/2071-8330.2018/11-2/1

Pesce, M. (2018). *SWOT Analysis of the Application of International Standard ISO 14001 in the Chinese Context: A Case Study of Guangdong Province*. Doi:10.3390u10093196

Piantoni, M., Baronchelli, G., & Cortesi, E. (2012). The recognition of international opportunities among Italian SMEs: Differences between European and Chinese markets. *International Journal of Entrepreneurship and Small Business*, *17*(2), 199. doi:10.1504/IJESB.2012.048847

Purchasing Managers Index for November 2019. (2019). *National Bureau of Statistics of China*. Retrieved from: http://www.stats.gov.cn/english/PressRelease/201912/t20191202_1712936.html

Purchasing Managers' Index (PMI). (2019). *Investopedia*. Retrieved from: https://www.investopedia.com/terms/p/pmi.asp

Tsai, Y., Wang, H., & Yuan, C. (2015). Transformational Leadership and Job Performance. *The Case of SMEs in Taiwan.*, *4*(8), 57–71.

Wei, X. (2016). Error Orientation and Entrepreneurial Decision Making in Chinese Enterprises. *Opportunity Identification as Mediator*, *44*(4), 555–568.

Wu, B., & Deng, P. (2020). Internationalization of SMEs from emerging markets: An institutional escape perspective. *Journal of Business Research*, *108*, 337–350. Doi:10.1016/j.jbusres.2019.10.037

Yue, F., & Yu, H. A. N. (2008). Offshore Service Outsourcing: A SWOT Analysis of SMEs in Jiangsu Province. Academic Press.

Chapter 2
Challenges for Pakistani SMEs in Industry 4.0:
Applications of Disruptive Technologies

Qaisar Iqbal
https://orcid.org/0000-0002-6619-7243
Universiti Sains Malaysia, Malaysia

Noor Hazlina Ahmad
Universiti Sains Malaysia, Malaysia

ABSTRACT

Small and medium enterprises (SMEs) play a vital role in the development of any economy. The disruptive technologies of the fourth industrial revolution have ignited the flexibility and dynamic nature of the market. Industry 4.0 requires firms to deliver highly customized and high-quality products at low price and on time. However, the SMEs sector is not performing up to the standard, which is quite disturbing in the current economic situation of the country. This chapter has elaborated the application of advanced information and communication technologies of Industry 4.0 in the context of SMEs. Based on the requirements of Industry 4.0, this chapter has also explored the challenges faced by SMEs in Pakistan. The SMEs in Pakistan are presently coping the challenges such as limited access to finance, the undue compliance and excessive paperwork imposed by regulators, lacking mechanism of talent management, lacking skilled workforce, absence of networking and collaboration, mismanagement of raw material, and insufficient infrastructure.

DOI: 10.4018/978-1-7998-2577-7.ch002

INTRODUCTION

The fourth industrial revolution extensively fluctuates production in the manufacturing industry (Kagermann, Helbig, Hellinger, & Wahlster, 2013). Germany has taken the initiative of industry 4.0. A few countries from the U.S., Europe, and Asia are presently considering this framework (Ślusarczyk, 2018). Disruptive technologies of industry 4.0 drive the creation of innovation (Strandhagen, Alfnes, Strandhagen, & Vallandingham, 2017). Presently, most firms are adopting high technologies in the era of industry 4.0 (Oláh, Karmazin, Pető, & Popp, 2018). The firms in Pakistan so far could not achieve significant growth due to low technological improvements (Khan & Khan, 2010).

Pakistan is facing an extensive decline in its growth rate (Iqbal, Ahmad, & Ahmad, 2018). Pakistani exports are also consistently and massively declining for a long time. Because of this, a gross domestic product of Pakistan is only in 2019 (Pakistan Bureau of Statistics, 2016). Pakistan is lagging in the growth of gross domestic product (GDP) behind other countries such as Bangladesh, Vietnam, Cambodia, and Laos. Pakistani firms are lacking modern technologies and the market is highly volatile so its growth is lagging behind neighboring countries namely India, Malaysia, and China (Waseem-Ul-Hameed, Azeem, Aljumah, & Adeyemi, 2018). Disruptive technologies of industry 4.0 such as cyber-physical systems, smart factories, big data, and interoperability can tackle many issues through their applications.

SMEs play a vital role in the economic development of Pakistan. In Pakistan, SMEs comprise of a total of 90% enterprises. SMEs contribute to 40% of GDP and 30% in all exports. SMEs are located across the whole Pakistan such as 65.4% in Punjab, 18% in Sindh, 14.3% in Khyber Pakhtunkhwa, and 2.3% in Baluchistan (Zafar & Mustafa, 2017). SMEs in Pakistan employs 75 percent of the non-agriculture workers with 30 percent manufacturing output (Iqbal et al., 2018). Therefore, there is substantial significance to explore the potential challenges faced by SMEs in Pakistan. In the era of the fourth industrial revolution, there is also a pivotal need to elaborate on the application of its disruptive technologies in the domain of SMEs. According to Iqbal et al. (2018), there is also lacking research in SMEs in the context of industry 4.0. Therefore, the present chapter aims to explore the application of industry 4.0 technologies and challenges faced by Pakistani SMEs.

FOURTH INDUSTRIAL REVOLUTION INDUSTRY 4.0

Industry 4.0 undertakes the automation and data exchange in different manufacturing technologies. industry 4.0 consists of cognitive computing, cloud computing, internet of things, and cyber-physical systems which are generally known as the fourth industrial revolution (Stverkova & Pohludka, 2018). Currently, adaptable organizations are in a position to exploit numerous opportunities and deliver optimum performance (Rajnoha & Lesníková, 2016). Organizations have increased their productivity and profit by applying steam engine, power, and the transition from simple to computerized innovation.

Big Data

Big data is the sum of polluted and quality data or information (Iqbal & Nawaz, 2019; Iqbal, Yang, Nawaz, & Iqbal, 2019) where polluted information rises exponentially and quality information is increasing linearly. Big data is an umbrella term, refers to any technique that process a large volume of data or information-capture, transfer, storage, analysis curation, search, privacy, and visualization, includes both structured and unstructured data (Xu & Duan, 2019) (Xu and Duan, 2018). According to Hashem et al. (2015), big data refers to a rise in the volume of data that is hard to store and process. The big data requires substantial procedures to identify and translate the data into new insights. Big data constitutes three Vs; volume, velocity, and variety (Zhu, Yu, Wang, Ning, & Tang, 2018). Iqbal and Nawaz (2019) have claimed that big data is a new form of capital in today's market. In the presence of polluted information, practitioners are still unsuccessful to exploit the big data in terms of its advantages (Iqbal et al., 2019).

Cyber-Physical Systems (CPS)

a cyber-physical system is a system where humans interact with integrated computational and physical capabilities through numerous new models (Baheti & Gill, 2011). The human capability to interact and enlarge the abilities of the physical world with the help of computation and communication drive future technological developments.

Internet of Things (IoT)

Furthermore, the Internet of Things (IoT) concerns about the linkage of all devices to the internet as well as each other. The Internet of Things (IoT) consists of three components namely hardware, middleware, and presentation (Gubbi, Buyya, Marusic, & Palaniswami, 2013).

Interoperability

interoperability is in essence what occurs when we bring the above elements together. interoperability concerns the communication of humans, cyber-physical systems, smart factories, and human with each other through the Internet of Things (IoT). Through such a phenomenon, stakeholders could share quality information. Interoperability is a source of error-free transmission and translation.

SMALL AND MEDIUM ENTERPRISES (SMEs)

Different countries define the Small and Medium Enterprises (SMEs) in the context of their economy. SMEs are usually defined in terms of capital assets, or skill level of their labor or turnover level. The Bolton Committee (1971) has statistically and economically defined SMEs (Ali, 2013). Economically, SME is considered as an independent firm and managed by owners or partners themselves. Statistically, SME is defined by the size, its contribution to the GDP, export, and employment generation. According to Jordan, Lowe, and Taylor (1998), SMEs have many employees with less than 100 employees with a turnover of fewer than 15 million euros. The United Nations Industrial Development Organization-UNIDO (2002) has defined SMEs in terms of the number of employees from the perspective of developing and developed economies (Abor & Quartey, 2010).

The SMEs in developing economy are categorized as follows:

- Micro-firms have less than 5 employees.
- Small-firms have 5 to 19 employees.
- Medium-firms have 20 to 99 employees.

- Large-firms have 100 or more employees.

SMEs in developed countries are defined as follows:

- A small firm has equal to or less than 99 employees.
- Medium-firms have some employees in the range of 100 to 500.
- Large firms have 500 or more employees.

Nevertheless, SMEs are defined differently but are deemed as a potential source of job creation and contribute significantly to the economy. SMEs are also a vital source of poverty reduction, value-addition, and productivity growth.

SMEs Sector in Pakistan

State Bank of Pakistan has defined small and medium enterprises in terms of the number of employees and annual sales turnover. State Bank of Pakistan has also fixed the credit limit for small and medium enterprises. An enterprise that employees not more than 50 persons with sales turnover u to Rs. 150 million, is known as a small enterprise. Small enterprises can enjoy the credit limit up to Rs. 25 Million. The State Bank of Pakistan has provided different definitions of medium enterprises in the context of trading establishment and manufacturing and service establishments. In the case of trading establishments, the medium enterprise provides employment opportunities to the number of employees including contract workers in the range of 50 and 100. In the case of manufacturing and service establishments, this number lies in the range of 50 and 250. All medium enterprises are considered to have annual sales turnover in the range of Rs.150 Million and Rs. 800 Million. Commercial banks and credit firms can provide credit worth of Rs.25 million to Rs. 200 Million to medium enterprises.

Currently, the SME sector in Pakistan is deteriorating. As compared to SMEs, large-scale firms are operating in urban areas. Because of the operations of SMEs in rural areas, these provide employment opportunities to the poor rural workers. A well-developed SEMs sector in any open economy complements the export orientation. The strong network of SMEs in Pakistan is vital to establish robust industrialization. The government of Pakistan has announced SMEs as a vital driver of growth for its economy. SME sector in Pakistan comprises dairy, carpets, cotton weaving, jewelry, sports goods, fisheries, food and catering, and slaughtering, grain milling, and art silk.

SMEs enhanced the growth with low levels of income inequality in the Republic of Korea (Li & Luo, 2008). The SMEs in these economies have helped to reduce urban unemployment and absorb the surplus rural workers. But, The People's Republic of China has experienced a high level of growth with increased inequality. SMEs have significantly contributed to the employment generation and poverty reduction in African economies. SMEs sector is responsible for a total of 92% job creation in Ghana. SMEs sector contributes to 52-57% of the GDP and generates 61% of total jobs in South Africa (Abor & Quartey, 2010).

SMEs in Pakistan play a vital role in the growth of the economy. SMEs constitute approximately 90% of all enterprises in Pakistan. SMEs in Pakistan are responsible for a total of 80% job creation in the non-agriculture sector. Pakistani SMEs contribute to 40% of the annual GDP of the country. However, SMEs are facing financial and other constraints as compared to large manufacturing firms in Pakistan. Therefore, such a vital contribution of SMEs makes it imperative to develop a mechanism that would assist them in getting support from diverse functional units such as marketing, human resource training and development, and technology upgradation.

APPLICATION OF INDUSTRY 4.0 FOR SMES

SMEs in Pakistan comprises of jewelry, sports goods, slaughtering, grain milling cotton-weaving, etc. so it evolves around both the production and services domain. Production and service domains work together to meet the needs of customers. Efficient operation relies on the advanced technologies of industry 4.0. Industry 4.0 comprises artificial intelligence, big data analysis and augmented and virtual reality.

Disruptive technologies of industry 4.0 enable firms to identify the patterns in big data (Lycett, 2013). Big data assists firms to explore what is missing in the context. Big data is a very effective tool to attain efficiency in operations and increase profitability (Stoicescu, 2016). SMEs can access diverse information about the market and operational processes that may influence performance effectively. SMEs owners can use big data to extract meaning, trace hidden relationships, unforeseen patterns and startling connections among different industries (Stoicescu, 2016).

Application of cyber-physical systems (CPS) is the backbone of industry 4.0, that integrates the advanced information and communication technologies (Kagermann et al., 2013). The advanced communication technologies of industry 4.0 have influenced the communication between employees, stakeholders, between the firm and its clients which ultimately results in enhanced performance at the organizational level.

The smart factory is based on the cyber-physical systems (CPS) and the Internet of Things (IoT), which assists in collecting, sharing and accessing real-time information (Lucke, Constantinescu, & Westkämper, 2008). According to Radziwon, Bilberg, Bogers, and Madsen (2014), the smart factory provides a flexible and adaptive solution in the dynamic market of rapidly changing boundary conditions and complexity.

Industry 4.0 has to major attributes i.e. integration and interoperability. The interoperability process concerns the integrated operation of cyber-physical systems, the internet of things, big data, information communication technologies, and smart factories. The integrated and interoperability chrematistics of industry 4.0 ensures seamless operations across diverse units of the business (Ruggaber, 2006).

CHALLENGES FOR PAKISTANI SMEs TO OPERATE IN INDUSTRY 4.0 ERA

There are numerous issues with Pakistani SMEs, but its intensity varies across different sectors and regions. Some of the sectors have shown their progress in the shape of integrated value chains, trained personnel, advanced technology, and a long-term vision. Yet, the fundamental factors, hindering the growth of small and medium businesses are, more or less common across sectors and regions. Following are the major issues faced by SMEs in Pakistan;

- Limited access to finance
- The undue compliance and excessive paperwork imposed by the regulator
- Lacking mechanism of talent management
- Lacking skilled workforce
- Absence of networking and collaboration

- Mismanagement of raw material
- Insufficient infrastructure

Limited Access to Finance

SMEs always operate on a small capital base. All SMEs face hard to expand in terms of assets or sales turnover or augment the quality of products in the presence of limited financing availabilities. In Pakistan, commercial banks and leasing firms have insignificantly provided facilities to the SMEs. So far, SMEs in Pakistan has been experiencing a meager share of 16-17% with a declining trend. Even though, State Bank of Pakistan has emphasized banking sectors to expand their services to SMEs. As SMEs are deemed as difficult customers, presently very few credit firms feel comfortable dealing with small and medium companies. Under this scenario, SMEs in Pakistan are coping with issues which hinder their access to finance;

- Collateral as the prime security
- Higher interest rates
- Absence of suitable banking products aligned to SME needs
- Lack of awareness among SMEs
- Absence of credit enhancement procedures

The Undue Compliance and Excessive Paperwork Imposed by the Regulator

The Pakistani government has initiated reforms to deregulate and liberalize the economy. This process has abated the interface of SMEs with government agencies. Yet, SMEs in Pakistan still complain about the undue compliance requirements which result in excessive paperwork. Following is a brief description of problems in this regard.

The Pakistani government has initiated reforms to encourage documentation and expand the tax base. SMEs are only enjoying the exemption of sales tax registration for business with a turn over below Rs. 5 million. SMEs consider 16% sales tax high. The concessional income tax regime for SMEs could not attract a significant number of themselves because the required documentation and reporting outweigh the benefits such as easy access to credit. SMEs in Pakistan are also facing higher compliance costs, dealing with government regulations and tax authorities. SMEs in Pakistan have a tenuous relationship with tax authorities. Most of the SMEs contribute to the informal economy. Therefore, SMEs are more of a challenge than an opportunity.

Lacking Mechanism of Talent Management

There is a vital importance of the availability of a skilled and productive workforce at efficient prices, along with supportive standard operating procedures covering hiring, firing, inspections, and protection of employees as well as employer's rights for any economy. As the rigidity of employment index stands at 43 points so there is a scarcity of skilled employees in Pakistan. This rigidity of employment index has three inherent attributes such as the difficulty of hiring index-78 points, the rigidity of hours index- 20 points and difficulty of firing index at 30 points. SMEs in Pakistan hire informal workers paying them lower wages. So, there is a big problem for SMEs to survive with low skilled workers in the industry 4.0 era.

Absence of Networking and Collaboration

In the start, the structure of SMEs is seldom planned and organized. However, SMEs need to build networking with Government, educational institutes and large firms, besides spiraling with other SMEs through associations. Based on these lines, SMEs in Thailand, Korea, Malaysia, and Japan are substantially contributing to their economies. Pakistani SMEs are still lagging in these lines. Most of the Pakistani SMEs are working in isolation, without taking benefit of synergies and the potential leverage of horizontal cooperation. As there is no manifest urge to collaborate and build consortia for R & D, international trade, etc. so individual SMEs acknowledge the garnering resources to enjoy high business profits and expand their businesses. SMEs are also not making any effort to enhance their R & D through collaboration with educational institutes.

SMEs in Pakistan are not part of the value chain and contingent to the middleman for their sales and orders so loss large share of profit which is being gobbled up by the third party and they just receive the residual. To enhance the position of SMEs in Pakistan, there is a need to buttress these vendors through knitting them in the value chain through forging collaborations with the downstream industry. Furthermore, there is a need to create linkages with educational institutes to provide R & D support to SMEs.

Lacking Skilled Workers

Four M-Men, Machine, Money, and Materials play a vital role in the success of any business. SMEs need them to run the businesses as much as anybody else. Skilled labor refers to the quality of the human resource. Causal analysis in this context raises concern about the quality of training infrastructure available in the country such as the quality of trainer, curricula, and on-job training facilities, etc. SMEs in Pakistan is lacking skilled employees because most of the technical institutes in Pakistan focus on main sectoral-focused training namely Electrical, Chemical, and Mechanical. There is dire need to plan training programs for certain sectors such as Dairy, sports, Plastics, Hunting, Marble and granite, Gems and Jewelry in relations to the requirements of disruptive technologies in industry 4.0.

Despite the various initiatives taken by the Pakistani Government such as National Vocational and Technical Education Commission (NAVTEC), and Technology Upgradation and Skill Development Company (TUSDEC), There is still lacking skilled workers. SMEs own austere business ethic and down to earth business paradigm where labor is a cost, not an investment. So, there is dire need to identify and fill the skill gaps by undertaking detailed skills mapping in Pakistan.

Mismanagement of Raw Material

SMEs also deal with raw material constraints. They can not buy raw material in bulk. They also do not have the business acumen to go for forwarding transactions and future trading for hedging against international price fluctuations. There are practices to export raw material, which is used by the local industry. Neither the private sector, not Government have any policy to maintain a strategic management reserve in raw materials, otherwise to be imported at short notice. Ultimately, SMEs face with price fluctuations as well as shortages in the international markets.

Insufficient Infrastructure

SMEs usually operate either from the fringes of the city or dense areas in downtown, where they cope with restricted means of communication and transportation. Even though, the Pakistani government has tried to facilitate the SMEs by introducing dedicated industrial estates and industrial parks such as Sunder Industrial Estate. However, ordinary SMEs are lacking the strength and power to access such facilities.

REFERENCES

Abor, J., & Quartey, P. (2010). Issues in SME development in Ghana and South Africa. *International Research Journal of Finance and Economics*, *39*(6), 215–228.

Ali, S. (2013). The small and medium enterprises and poverty in Pakistan: An empirical analysis. *European Journal of Business and Economics*, *8*(2), 25–30. doi:10.12955/ejbe.v8i2.376

Baheti, R., & Gill, H. (2011). Cyber-physical systems. *The Impact of Control Technology*, *12*(1), 161–166.

Gubbi, J., Buyya, R., Marusic, S., & Palaniswami, M. (2013). Internet of Things (IoT): A vision, architectural elements, and future directions. *Future Generation Computer Systems*, *29*(7), 1645–1660. doi:10.1016/j.future.2013.01.010

Hashem, I. A. T., Yaqoob, I., Anuar, N. B., Mokhtar, S., Gani, A., & Khan, S. U. (2015). The rise of "big data" on cloud computing: Review and open research issues. *Information Systems*, *47*, 98–115. doi:10.1016/j.is.2014.07.006

Iqbal, Q., Ahmad, N. H., & Ahmad, B. (2018). Enhancing sustainable performance through job characteristics via workplace spirituality: A study on SMEs. Journal of Science and Technology Policy Management. doi:10.1108/JSTPM-02-2018-0022

Iqbal, Q., & Nawaz, R. (2019). Rife information pollution (infollution) and virtual organizations in industry 4.0: within reality causes and consequences. In *Big Data and Knowledge Sharing in Virtual Organizations* (pp. 117–135). IGI Global; doi:10.4018/978-1-5225-7519-1.ch005.

Iqbal, Q., Yang, S., Nawaz, R., & Iqbal, K. (2019). A multi-dimensional construct of perceived information pollution in the era of rife infollution. VINE Journal of Information and Knowledge Management Systems, 49(2), 162–180. doi:10.1108/VJIKMS-10-2018-0093

Jordan, J., Lowe, J., & Taylor, P. (1998). Strategy and financial policy in UK small firms. *Journal of Business Finance & Accounting*, *25*(1-2), 1–27. doi:10.1111/1468-5957.00176

Kagermann, H., Helbig, J., Hellinger, A., & Wahlster, W. (2013). *Recommendations for implementing the strategic initiative INDUSTRIE 4.0: Securing the future of the German manufacturing industry; final report of the Industrie 4.0 Working Group*. Forschungsunion.

Khan, A. A., & Khan, M. (2010). Pakistan textile industry facing new challenges. *Research Journal of International Studies*, *14*(14), 21–29.

Li, S., & Luo, C. (2008). Growth Pattern, Employment, and Income Inequality: What the Experience of the Republic of Korea and Taipei, China Reveals to the People's Republic of China. *Asian Development Review*, *25*(1/2), 100.

Lucke, D., Constantinescu, C., & Westkämper, E. (2008). A smart factory-a step towards the next generation of manufacturing. In *Manufacturing systems and technologies for the new frontier* (pp. 115–118). Springer; doi:10.1007/978-1-84800-267-8_23.

Lycett, M. (2013). 'Datafication': Making sense of (big) data in a complex world. *European Journal of Information Systems*, *22*(6), 381–386. doi:10.1057/ejis.2013.10

Oláh, J., Karmazin, G., Pető, K., & Popp, J. (2018). Information technology developments of logistics service providers in Hungary. *International Journal of Logistics Research and Applications*, *21*(3), 332–344. doi:10.1080/13675567.2017.1393506

Radziwon, A., Bilberg, A., Bogers, M., & Madsen, E. S. (2014). The smart factory: Exploring adaptive and flexible manufacturing solutions. *Procedia Engineering*, *69*, 1184–1190. doi:10.1016/j.proeng.2014.03.108

Rajnoha, R., & Lesníková, P. (2016). Strategic performance management system and corporate sustainability concept-specific parametres in Slovak Enterprises. *Journal of Competitiveness*, *8*(2), 107–124. doi:10.7441/joc.2016.03.07

Ruggaber, R. (2006). Athena-Advanced technologies for the Interoperability of heterogeneous enterprise networks and their applications. *Interoperability of Enterprise Software and Applications*, *1*, 459–460.

Ślusarczyk, B. (2018). Industry 4.0: Are we ready? *Polish Journal of Management Studies*, *17*(3), 232–248. doi:10.17512/pjms.2018.17.1.19

Stoicescu, C. (2016). Big Data, the perfect instrument to study today's consumer behavior. *Database Syst. J*, *6*, 28–42.

Strandhagen, J. W., Alfnes, E., Strandhagen, J. O., & Vallandingham, L. R. (2017). The fit of Industry 4.0 applications in manufacturing logistics: A multiple case study. Advances in Manufacturing, 5(4), 344–358. doi:10.1007/s40436-017-0200-y

Stverkova, H., & Pohludka, M. (2018). Business organizational structures of global companies: Use of the territorial model to ensure long-term growth. *Social Sciences*, *7*(6), 98. doi:10.3390/socsci7060098

Waseem-Ul-Hameed, S. N., Azeem, M., Aljumah, A. I., & Adeyemi, R. A. (2018). Determinants of e-logistic customer satisfaction: A mediating role of information and communication technology (ICT). Int. J Sup. Chain. *Mgt*, *7*(1), 105.

Xu, L. D., & Duan, L. (2019). Big data for cyber-physical systems in industry 4.0: A survey. *Enterprise Information Systems*, *13*(2), 148–169. doi:10.1080/17517575.2018.1442934

Zafar, A., & Mustafa, S. (2017). SMEs and its role in the economic and socio-economic development of Pakistan. International Journal of Academic Research in Accounting, Finance and Management Sciences, 6(4).

Zhu, L., Yu, F. R., Wang, Y., Ning, B., & Tang, T. (2018). Big data analytics in intelligent transportation systems: A survey. *IEEE Transactions on Intelligent Transportation Systems*, *20*(1), 383–398. doi:10.1109/TITS.2018.2815678

Chapter 3
The Effect of Artificial Intelligence on Management Process:
Challenges and Opportunities

Mustafa Sundu
https://orcid.org/0000-0003-4168-9273
Beykent University, Turkey

Sebnem Ozdemir
Istinye University, Turkey

ABSTRACT

Artificial intelligence has started to dominantly affect every sector in Industry 4.0. However, the adaptation of the concept to managerial processes are closely related to the concepts of data science and digital transformation. Because artificial intelligence applications being developed are within the scope of artificial narrow intelligence (ANI), that situation requires the company to have a digital transformation policy in order to use artificial intelligence in managerial processes. In addition, to avoid biased artificial intelligence applications, the learning set of artificial intelligence requires a highly rigorous design. This necessitates the establishment of a data science department within the company. In this chapter, digital transformation processes in managerial perspective and the surrounded effect of artificial narrow intelligence on management are discussed.

DOI: 10.4018/978-1-7998-2577-7.ch003

INTRODUCTION

Management and leadership practices have been observed since the existence of humanity on the planet. The essence of management activities is the effective and efficient execution of the works. Peter F. Drucker (1986, p. 36, 2018, p. 3) defined effectiveness as "doing the right thing" and efficiency as "doing things right" (Peter F.Drucker, 1986, p. 36). For example, in hunter-gathering and agricultural societies, those who know how to do things and manage resources efficiently can be the leaders of the group (Bracker, 2012, p. 219). Technical knowledge and management skills, in particular, are considered prerequisites for becoming a manager in ancient societies (Malinowski, 1960, p. 191). There is no point in assuming that managerial skills were not used to build the Egyptian pyramids or Machu Picchu in Peru thousands of years ago. MB.C. In 400, Socrates defined management as a skill separate from technical knowledge and experience. Plato also described management as a separate art and emphasized the necessity of the principles of expertise (Pindur, Rogers, & Kim, 2013, p. 59).

However, the concept of professional management emerged with the industrial revolution. After using the machines in the manufacturing process and gathering large groups of people in the workplace, certain levels of management were needed. When the production system in the form of handicrafts in small workshops turned into mass production with machines and people's cooperation, things became complicated. As a result, planning, organizing and influencing people came to the fore in these manufacturing factories (Pindur et al., 2013, p. 60).

The first applications of management science are called classical management movement and are divided into two main groups as scientific management and general administrative theory (Robbins & Coulter, 2002). While the scientific management focused on productivity, the General Administrative theory admitted the organization as a whole and focused on how to make this complex structure effective and efficient (Pindur et al., 2013, p. 60). In his speech to governors, Theodore Roosevelt, the president of the United States, emphasized that the issue of national productivity is more than a waste of natural resources. About this speech, Frederick Winslow Taylor, the founder of Scientific theory, argued that the greatest lack of national efficiency is due to the inefficient act of human which is an intangible asset of industry. Therefore, he argued that competition and prosperity would be ensured by the efficient working of the machine and the people together and he focused on finding the best way to achieve this (Taylor, 1913).

General management theory was an effort to develop a wider theory of management functions and is considered the pioneer of modern organizational theory. H.Fayol (1949) divided the activities of enterprises into six main groups: technical, commercial, financial, security, accounting, and management. He stated that the first five of these activities are well known in the industry but the management activity should be explained and discussed in detail. Eventually, he defined management functions as to forecast, to plan, to organize, to command, to co-ordinate and to control. Besides emphasizing efficiency and regulation of the works, he stated that it is one of the most important tasks of the management to determine the direction of the organization by predicting the future (Fayol, 1949).

The need for managers to be effective, that is, to predict the future to do the right job (Peter F.Drucker, 2018) is something that has existed since the beginning of managerial activities of the human being. Nowadays, the need for this ability has increased a lot. The artificial intelligence algorithms are expected to be the manager's number one assistant at this point. Current discussion topics, such as "how human beings will keep pace with technology?" or "how robots and people will work together efficiently?", are very similar to discussions like "how man and machine can be productive together?" in the scientific management time, which was led by Frederick Winslow Taylor. Continuous emphasis on productivity and a mechanical approach to production issues caused people to be ignored and many problems to have emerged. As a result of the studies of the human relations school (the 1920s and 1930s) which explained the effect of human behaviors in increasing productivity and efficiency, which are the main issues of managers, behavioral management movement emerged as a criticism of classical management theory (O'Connor, 1999).

During the Second World War, the use of mathematical models in the management of military operations and the efficient and effective use of national resources enabled the establishment of the quantitative management school. Quantitative management approaches are mainly planning and control activities; For instance, budgeting, queuing, scheduling, quality control, order cost, inventory, supply chain process, location selection, market-entry, and vehicle routing, and such. (Griffin, 2012; Robbins & Coulter, 2002). Perhaps the contribution of artificial intelligence applications that we discussed today to management processes will be the continuation of quantitative management. It is important to bear in mind that the scholar of the human relations movement discuses the rational decision-making processes which are ignoring human intervention (Lindblom, 1959).

The most important change in perspective emerged when managers focused on the environment as well as focusing on the organization. The system approach, which treats the organization as an open system and emphasizes adaptation to the environment, and contingency approach, which uses all approaches according to the different conditions in the environment, has formed the Modern Management Theory (Bolman, L. G., & Deal, 1984; Bracker, 2012; Certo, S. C., & Certo, 2006; Griffin, 2012; Koontz, 1961; Papanek, 2011; Pindur et al., 2013; Robbins & Coulter, 2002). Strategic management takes place in modern theories (Pindur et al., 2013). Strategic management is the use of resources for the organization to gain competitive advantage, adapt to the environment and exist in the long term. There are two main strategies for gaining a competitive advantage. Porter's (1986) very well known strategies for gaining competitive advantage are cost leadership and differentiation which AI applications can make a great contribution within the context of Industry 4.0. Moreover, strategic flexibility and effective decision-making process of SMEs are crucial for surviving in the volatile environment (Pal, Torstensson, & Mattila, 2014). To have such advantages both concepts Industry 4.0 and AI must be well-known and cultural transformation must be done.

Every technological and societal change brings some opportunities and challenges as discussed before mentioned. The last development in the computer and information technologies bring Industry 4.0 era. One of the fundamental concepts in Industry 4.0 is AI. It is obvious that the developments in the field of artificial intelligence, which affect every aspect of life and force states to take special measures (Cath, Wachter, Mittelstadt, Taddeo, & Floridi, 2018; Naudé & Dimitri, 2018). AI will contribute to the management processes at every level, and particularly to the strategic management processes. Predictive AI studies (artificial neural networks, machine learning, genetic algorithms, etc.), in which big data is analyzed, will support the environmental analysis of the strategic management process and enhance the strategic decision processes.

AI may be one of the biggest disruptive technologies since the invention of the computer. From this point of view, in this study, the opportunities of AI applications to SMEs management processes, and the challenges that may emerge in the Industry 4.0 era will be discussed depending on detailed literature research. For this purpose, firstly a broad SME, Industry 4.0 and AI definition and taxonomy will be given, followingly existing AI applications will be discussed from a historical perspective, followingly the recent developments in AI will be evaluated. In the last part of the study, the challenges that may arise from AI applications for SMEs in Industry 4.0 will be discussed.

SMALL MEDIUM ENTERPRISES

Each country and institution have its own Small Medium Enterprises (SMEs) definitions but all SME definitions are based on similar criteria such as the number of employees and the amount of annual turnover. (Durst & Edvardsson, 2012; European Commission, 2018, p. 13; Tsuruta, 2018; Valtakoski & Witell, 2018). EU Commission defines SMEs in three categories; micro, small and medium. Enterprises with employees less than 10 and with less than 2 million euro annual turnover is called micro, enterprise with employees less than 50 and with less than 10 million euro annual turnover is called small and enterprises with employees less than 250 and with less than 50 million annual turnover is called medium (European Commission, 2018). SMEs have an important role in the world economy. SMEs represent almost all business population and half of employment in the world. SMEs are accounted for %60 of employment and %99.7 of the business population in OECD countries (OECD, 2017). Due to surviving in a volatile environment, SMEs have to develop appropriate strategies to achieve competitive advantage in local and international markets (Hegge, 2010), create an innovative organizational climate, have an effective business network and be open to technological developments (Dabić, Lažnjak, Smallbone, & Švarc, 2018; Hervas-Oliver, Boronat-Moll, & Sempere-Ripoll, 2016; Lee, Park, Yoon, & Park, 2010; Love & Roper, 2015).

The management process and functions are similar regardless of the size of the organization and the level of management. However, the importance of each management function may be different, depending on the size of the organization. Opportunities and challenges an organization face may vary according to the size of the organization (Lee et al., 2010; Sullivan-Taylor & Branicki, 2011). SMEs are more vulnerable to environmental changes and unpredictable conditions. One of the enablers of SME resilience is the top management decision capability which ensures innovation and knowledge creation (Dabić et al., 2018; Durst & Edvardsson, 2012; Hervas-Oliver et al., 2016; Pal et al., 2014). The use of information and communication technologies is an important factor that will increase the competitive advantage of SMEs (Thong, 2015). However, it is necessary to have the appropriate human resources to use information technologies (Alshamaila, Papagiannidis, & Li, 2013). In many respects, SMEs have barriers to access the resources, but human resources and finance are the most difficult (Pal et al., 2014; Sullivan-Taylor & Branicki, 2011). Recruiting AI experts appears to be a major challenge for SMEs where big data in the shape of information pollution is getting bigger and bigger (Iqbal & Nawaz, 2019). Recent researches show that there is a shortage of business analytics expert and managers who know how to analyze big data to make an effective decision (H. Chen, Chiang, & Storey, 2018; Ellermann, Kreutter, & Messner, 2016).

If there is an advantage in any field, it is much easier to move forward in that field. (Thong, 2015; Thong, Yap, & Raman, 1994). The technological innovative approach of SMEs depends on many factors such as the characteristics of the organization, the competitive conditions in the environment, the level of technology and the executive characteristics. The most important of these factors is the technological experience of the SME, the innovative behaviors of the senior management and whether it has strategic human capital (Alshamaila et al., 2013; Dabić et al., 2018; Ghobakhloo, Aranda, D., & Amado, J., 2011; Irwin et al., 2018; Mendes & Lourenço, 2014; Thong, 2015).

Supplier support increases the effectiveness of information technologies more than consultancy support to SMEs (Thong et al., 1994). In particular, the support of the technology supplier makes a significant impact (Alshamaila et al., 2013). From this point of view, it can be said that companies' success in using AI applications requires making the right demands from the companies providing these technologies. Moreover, success in this area will be possible with executives who closely follow AI developments and can ask the right questions.

One of the most important elements of organizational culture that provides a competitive advantage is the ability to adapt new technologies to the organization (Dabić et al., 2018). Companies with the ability to adapt technological developments to the organization will benefit from AI applications. Therefore, they will perform better than the companies do not benefit from AI. Innovation and adaptation to the environment are as important as the efficiency of information management in SMEs' competitive advantage and survival. Deficiencies in human resources, finance and business network areas may adversely affect the stages of knowledge management which are knowledge identification, knowledge creation, knowledge storage/retention, knowledge transfer and knowledge utilization (Durst & Edvardsson, 2012). AI applications can make significant contributions to knowledge management processes.

THE CONCEPT OF ARTIFICIAL INTELLIGENCE (AI)

The artificial intelligence, which was firstly named by John McCarthy during the Dartmouth Conference in 1956, is one of the oldest dreams of human beings. The ancient philosopher Aristoteles (384-322 BC) referred to the automation side of artificial intelligence with the words "Imagine that every tool that we have, works either by our command or in our need" in his book (Nilsson, 2019).

Artificial intelligence, which was a curiosity point even in the philosophy of ancient times, continued its existence with the simple trials of developing mechanical tools, and questions of how to imitate human intelligence and how to design intelligent machines. For example, robotics, another research field of artificial intelligence, appeared for the first time with its very basic form in the play called "Rossum's Universal Robots", which was published by Czech playwright Karel Capec in 1920. In that play, robots that were produced without the function of thinking had taken on a role that fights for their rights. With that aspect, the play referred to the idea of building robots that have human elements.

The concept of intelligence is accepted as the ability of an individual to understand events, to be able to derive the cause and effect relationship and to develop action according to this relationship (Buchanan, 2005). According to Gartner, intelligence is the ability to adapt. The common point in both definitions is the perception of the environment and the development of action according to that perception. The main question in the process of perception and action development is how the machine can learn and think. In the Learning Machines Session, which held in 1955, the idea emerged that if the structures that can mimic the neuron cells in the brain can be constructed, learning can be realized in some way (Russell & Norvig, 2003). In the same session, the fundamental of computer-vision studies was started. Despite all the studies that would form the basis of artificial neural networks, "artificial intelligence" terminology was only introduced to the literature with a workshop held at Dartmouth College a year later. In that workshop, the issue of imitation of high levels of human thought has also gained an important place. In other words, not only how to construct the thinking process but also how to build a learning process for the machine constitutes the essence of artificial intelligence studies.

The year 1956 did not only include the developments in the mathematical and intellectual aspects of artificial intelligence. That year was also the year in which a new language, Fortran, was introduced in computer programming. However, all these developments were not sufficient for the advancement of artificial intelligence. Because, there was a need for a language, suitable for developing artificial intelligence applications on the machine. In 1958, John McCarthy developed the artificial intelligence programming language, called LISP, and so that need was partially met for that period (McCarthy, 1978). As a matter of fact, in 1961, Saint program, which was able to solve basic calculus problems, was built with LISP language (Newell, 1983). With the acceleration of artificial intelligence studies, the first chatbot, ELIZA, was developed. During that period, many public and private sector affiliates, especially DARPA, invested in artificial intelligence studies (Nilsson, 2019).

Because of the common emphasis in the reports, prepared in 1973, a brilliant period in artificial intelligence was ended and the period called "winter of artificial intelligence" was started. The common emphasis in reports was about the artificial intelligence being developed could not reach the targeted artificial intelligence, and impossibilities in imitating some of the human characteristics (Buchanan, 2005) (Nilsson, 2019). With the spread of that view, investments and supports in the field of artificial intelligence significantly decreased, and consequently, development studies came to a halt. That long winter of artificial intelligence began to gradually end with the spread of personal computers and the discovery of the Internet.

In 1997, Deep Blue, which was developed by IBM, defeated the world chess champion, Gary Kasparov, in the game of chess. Thus, that championship brought back the artificial intelligence excitement to mankind. With that excitement, artificial intelligence has gained incredible acceleration with new methods and new applications. 61 years after McCarthy's definition of artificial intelligence, Andrew Ng, the founder of Coursera and one of the important names in the field, said that artificial intelligence was the new electricity of humanity. By citing the transformation of mankind with the invention of electricity, Ng's definition refers that there will be a similar transformation based on artificial intelligence.

The Fundamental Issue in AI: Bias

Despite the exciting face of artificial intelligence, some new issues and questions arise with applications developed. The main source of that situation is related to the type of current artificial intelligence, also called artificial narrow intelligence.

Artificial narrow intelligence (ANI) is the artificial intelligence that cannot learn without sufficient amounts of correctly labeled data (Bostrom, 2019). Because of that, the design/creation phase of the data set is extremely important. Because every feature/event/state, which is not in that dataset, does not exist for artificial intelligence, so AI ignores them all. For example, when trying to teach artificial intelligence "what the beautiful person looks like", the features in the dataset created by the researchers will prevail. This group will never be considered a beautiful person for artificial intelligence unless people with dark skin are included in this dataset. This situation, which is called bias, may damage the trust in society, which is a vital bridge for artificial intelligence research.

Although bias is defined differently in many research areas, it is a concept that incorporates words such as mistake, fault, manipulation, backsliding, deviation, and prejudice (IBM, 2018). With the deviation side, meeting the target and how far away from the target is expressed. With the manipulation and unfair side, "bias" represent manipulation of the process by the developer, to serve the majority or a certain group, while being expected to be objective and fair in solving a problem. With the prejudice side, "bias" is defined that the culture and experiences of the individual constitute a strict, narrow, false perspective, and reflecting them into the artificial intelligence development process (Kozyrkov, 2019).

When the bias is formed in the process of developing an artificial intelligence application, it may affect not only the whole process but also the output (Manyika, 2019). That situation will cause the artificial intelligence application, which should be used for the benefit of humanity, to produce solutions for problems with an attitude that is racist, discriminatory, and interfering with rights and freedoms. The stages in which the bias can be formed in the process of developing an artificial intelligence application are as follows (Fulton, 2019) (Marr, 2019) (Villasenor, 2019):

- **Implementation Planning Phase:** Artificial intelligence applications are designed to solve problems in various fields. Therefore, even at the first stage where the problem is tried to be framed, bias can be formed according to the developer's culture, prejudices and the way of defining the purpose of his /her. That kind of bias, which is formed before the development of the AI application, can produce results that devastate the social values. Besides such biased applications can be accepted as a waste of investments. For example, suppose that a bank will apply a selection process to its customers to detect those who are worthy and those who do not. If the bank defines a framework that focuses just only on profit maximization, the developed artificial intelligence application accordingly will not be fair, it will produce discriminatory results. The fault here does not belong to artificial intelligence, it belongs to a company that determines profit maximization as the main objective. As a result, the main objective of artificial intelligence is to produce the appropriate output within the framework drawn by the human developer.
- **Data Collection:** As mentioned before, all artificial intelligence applications developed today are within the scope of artificial narrow intelligence. Therefore, the success of these applications depends on a sufficient amount of accurate data. For many problems, it is generally impossible to collect all data from the real world. To create a well-defined AI model, the developer may generate the sampling from the universe, which represents the real world. For example, it is not possible to collect data from all citizens to determine their voting tendency, before the political elections. To deal with such a problem, a smaller region/city containing the country's profile can be selected as the sample and data can be collected from this sample. The results obtained by the analysis of the sampling data can be interpreted by generalizing to the whole country. There may be a conflict based on results if the sampling does not reflect the universe. For example, suppose that the payment system in a restaurant is executed with an AI-based facial recognition application. The artificial intelligence in here needs to learn what the human face looks like. If the sampling used in that learning process consists only of people with fair skin and colored eyes, that application will inherently have a bias. The main source of the bias in artificial intelligence is the person who creates false sampling for the learning process and does not collect enough data to represent the universe.
- **Data Preparation:** The dataset learned by artificial intelligence should be designed to accommodate sufficient features for the problem that trying to be solved. For example, if the developer seeks to answer the question of what is the main source of "employee turnover" in a company, he/she should develop an artificial intelligence application that can predict reason and results. In this case, it is necessary to form a comprehensive sampling by compiling all the factors/attributes that cause this problem (burn-out, salary raising rates, job satisfaction, etc.). The lack of an important factor/attribute in that sampling will cause artificial intelligence to produce both false and biased

results. Especially in classical machine learning applications, bias can be occurred not only because of missing features but also adding more features. At this point, the developer needs to apply feature extraction methods objectively.

In artificial intelligence, bias can also be originated from the cognitive bias of the developer. Cognitive bias is one of the crucial obstacles to thinking objectively and free from prejudices and reviewing the events through an individual's filter. The source of cognitive bias can be one or more of the following:

- **Cliché, Stereotypes:** Prejudices, negative experiences and ideas, inherited from the culture that the developers are raised in, are the main sources of bias in the framing a problem (Dodou & de Winter, 2014).
- **Bandwagon Effect:** It is one of the cases defined within the scope of psychology. This phenomenon is defined as doing something by ignoring existing evidence or personal principles, because of others. The bandwagon effect is often observed in the issues, which has high entrainment potential, such as politics, consumer habits, and sports. The Bandwagon effect, the biggest obstacle to critical thinking, contributes to the formation of cognitive bias by creating the delusion of social pressure on the individuals. Similarly, public acclaim, decisions, and actions, taken to preserve existing comfort/position, are another aspect of the Bandwagon effect (Gearon, 2018) (Cherry, 2019).
- **Approval Bias:** That kind of bias means that the prejudice becomes more dominant/constant, because of the new knowledge acquired confirming an existing thought/prejudice. In this case, the individual continues to cling to his/her old bias even if he/she encounters any other information.

Many companies working in the field of artificial intelligence are trying to develop bias-free applications by learning from the negative experiences of the past years. According to IBM, one of the companies with the clearest policy in this regard, the number of artificial intelligence applications with bias will increase dramatically in 5 years. The main source of that situation is the learning process of artificial intelligence with biased, incorrectly collected data. In 2018, IBM announced that they could identify 180 different human-based bias, because of tests on artificial intelligence applications.

ARTIFICIAL INTELLIGENCE IN INDUSTRY 4.0

The dictionary meaning of industry is " *the companies and activities involved in the process of producing goods for sale, especially in a factory or special area*" ("Cambridge Dict.," 2019). The definition states collective production by machines in a factory for meeting human needs. But from the beginning of human civilization, meeting a human need by hunting and gathering or by handcrafted production has been ensured. The industrial revolution, which has been replaced human power by something non-human, was one of the biggest changes ever seen (Stearns, 2013). Therefore industry can be defined as "the production of material goods which are highly mechanized and automatized" (Lasi, H., Fettke, P., Kemper, H. G., Feld, T., & Hoffmann, 2014). Technological developments shaped and transformed the characteristics of machines, which has replaced human power. The improvement of technology generated four different industry revolution phases since the 18th century. The Industry 1.0 used water and steam power to mechanize production, the Industry 2.0 used electric power to generate mass production, and the Industry 3.0 used computers and information technology to automate production (Marcovitz, 2013; Popkova, Ragulina, & Bogoviz, 2019; Stearns, 2013). Currently, Industry 4.0 is developing based on mass digitalization, which is shaped by internet technologies. Symbols of the first two were a new source of power bigger than manpower, such as steam and electricity which was enabling mass production. The symbol of the third one was a computer, which enabled a perfect optimization and automation. The symbol of last one, Industry 4.0, was internet and digitalization, which is creating a network economy and integration of physical, digital and biological actors in the industry. Today, issues such as the Internet of Things (IoT), Digital Twins, Big Data Analytics, Cloud Computing/Technology, Blockchain, Cyber-Physical Systems, Artificial Intelligence come to fore and are shaping the future of the industry and natural society. Prominent technologies forming Industry 4.0 will be explained below;

- **Internet of Things (IoT):** Vermasen et al. (2011) describe IoT as "*an integrated part of internet and a dynamic global network infrastructure with self-configuring capabilities based on standard and interoperable communication protocols where physical and virtual "things" have identities, physical attributes, and virtual personalities and use intelligent interfaces, and are seamlessly integrated into the information network*". The things could be machines, robots, devices, or objects – such as Radio-Frequency Identification (RFID) tags, sensors, actuators, mobile phones, etc. (Atzori, Iera, & Morabito, 2010, p. 2787)
- **Digital Twins:** is a completely digital representation of every single product. This involves the real-life object's property, state, and action employing models and data (Haag & Anderl, 2018). The Digital Twin is the compound of digital productions containing engineering data, operation data, and behavior descriptions, combined in a simulation model. The Digital Twin simulation models are specific for their intended use and provide a solution for the problem to be solved (Hehenberger & Bradley, 2016).
- **Big Data Analytics:** The features of data is defined as the facts and statistics with the quantities, characters, or symbols, which may be stored and transmitted in the form of electrical signals and recorded on magnetic, optical, or mechanical recording media ("Oxford Dictionary," 2019). Such data can easily be analyzed by standard statistics and mathematical techniques. On the contrary big data refers to an enormous amount of data from various sources and types which are difficult to collect, manage, store and analyze when compared to traditional datasets (Addo-Tenkorang & Helo, 2016). The sources of big data could be Internet of things (IoT), mobile devices, online social networks, sensors, manufacturing process, supply chain interactions, etc. in structured, semi-structured, and unstructured formats with different attributes such as include text, audio, images, video, networks, and graphics (Mikalef, Pappas, Krogstie, & Giannakos, 2018; Nguyen, Zhou, Spiegler, Ieromonachou, & Lin, 2018; Philip Chen & Zhang, 2014). Big data is characterized by five dimensions which are volume, variety, velocity, veracity, and value (Russom, 2011; Wamba, S. F., Akter, S., Edwards, A., Chopin, G., & Gnanzou, 2015). Volume refers to the magnitude of data, variety refers to the fact that data can be generated from heterogeneous sources, velocity refers to the speed of data generation and delivery, veracity stresses the importance of data quality and level of trust due to the concern that many data sources inherently contain a certain degree of uncertainty and unreliability and value refers to the process of revealing underexploited values from big data to support decision-making (Nguyen et al., 2018). These five Vs substantially contribute to the polluted information as well (Iqbal & Nawaz, 2019; Iqbal, Yang, Nawaz, & Iqbal, 2019) . Big Data analytics techniques encompass many disciplines, including statis-

tics, data mining, machine learning, neural networks, social network analysis, signal processing, pattern recognition, optimization methods, and visualization approaches. A variety of specific techniques regarding these disciplines can be used together or separately (Philip Chen & Zhang, 2014). Industry 4.0 era definitely will generate big data from integrated industry applications such as smart factories, smart warehouses, smart cars, and smart cities, which has connections and interaction with each other, etc.

- **Cloud Computing/Technology:** Cloud computing technology enables ubiquitous, convenient, on-demand network access to configurable computing resources that can be rapidly provisioned and released with minimal effort or service provider interaction. Three service models and four deployment models compose any cloud computing model. Service models are Software as a Service (SaaS), Platform as a Service (PaaS) and Infrastructure as a Service (IaaS). Deployment models are private cloud, community cloud, public cloud, and hybrid cloud. A cloud computing model must have five features; on-demand self-service, broad network access, resource pooling, rapid elasticity and measured service (Mell & Grance, 2011). Cloud technology enables small-medium enterprises to reach cloud computing applications and analytics which is more affordable than a built-in system (Demirkan & Delen, 2013; Dinca, Dima, & Rozsa, 2019).
- **Blockchain:** is a decentralized trustless proof mechanism of all the transactions on the network. It is a system of the public ledger which allows disintermediation and decentralization of all transactions between parties all around the world at the same time (Swan, 2015). Every transaction in the public ledger is verified by all participants in the system in which information cannot be deleted (Crosby, Pattanayak, Verma, & Kalyanaraman, 2016; Swan, 2015). Blockchain will transform industry and commerce and trigger multiple applications in different fields such as supply chain, commercial financing, insurance industry, electronic medical records, registry, inventory and exchange of tangible and intangible assets (Nofer, Gomber, Hinz, & Schiereck, 2017; Swan, 2015; Underwood, 2016; Weber, 2018).
- **Cyber-Physical Systems (CPS):** are a combination of all technologies explained above and can be described as the systems which have data exchange capability and means to communicate with real-world and other systems. IoT is a version of CPS which uses internet connection to communicate with each other and with the real-world (Jazdi, 2014). CPS will be the most important factor to build smart cities, smart factories, smart industries, autonomous cars, etc. (Monostori, 2014).

ARTIFICIAL INTELLIGENCE FOR MANAGEMENT

Digitalization and the transformation it brings have an essential impact on the creation of a new and sustainable society. Every transaction that customers, employees, managers, suppliers, competitors or partners, perform in digital environments, generates large amounts of data. This creates a business analytics ecosystem that will radically change business methods and practices. This ecosystem is a threat to established and successful business models. In particular, it will fundamentally change decision-making, management practices, the formation of competitive strategies and value generation processes. (Loebbecke & Picot, 2015; Pappas, Mikalef, Giannakos, Krogstie, & Lekakos, 2018).

Today, the globalization of trade and the spread of e-commerce have become an opportunity for businesses, on the other hand, it has become a problem. For example, in any part of the world, the customer requests the delivery of a product purchased from the internet in a very short time. This example once again demonstrates the indispensability of the pull supply strategy which has been started to be applied since the early 1980s (Sarker & Fitzsimmons, 1989). This kind of transformation has forced businesses to be part of a supply chain that extends from the raw material to the customer (Mentzer, Keebler, Nix, Smith, & Zacharia, 2001). Supply chain management and optimization is a very difficult task and AI applications such as artificial neural networks, genetic algorithms, and agent systems are widely used in this field (Addo-Tenkorang & Helo, 2016; D. Q. Chen, Preston, & Swink, 2015; Govindan, Cheng, Mishra, & Shukla, 2018; Kaur & Singh, 2018; Liang & Huang, 2006; Min, 2010, 2010; Nguyen et al., 2018; Rohde, 2004; Tiwari, Wee, & Daryanto, 2018; Waller & Fawcett, 2013; Wang, Gunasekaran, Ngai, & Papadopoulos, 2016; Zhao, Liu, Zhang, & Huang, 2017; Zhong, Newman, Huang, & Lan, 2016).

The most important AI applications are business and big data analytics supporting the decision processes (Mikalef et al., 2018). These business analytics can support decisions regarding the changes in organizational culture, strategic sourcing, supply chain configuration, design and development of products or services, strategy development, operational efficiency, and financial performance. Moreover, business analytics can support the strategic management process to improve predictive insights into the strategy execution phase (Wang et al., 2016). Business analytics and big data analytics capability is also a very important sustainable competitive advantage. However, this capability must be based on three pillars. These are connectivity, compatibility, and modularity. Managers are responsible for the planning, budgeting, coordination, and control of this capability (Wamba et al., 2017).

Financial service is a sector with high digitalization and big data generation. For senior executives of this industry, predictive analytic methods help to make strategic decisions that create greater value by revealing the hidden information about trends, customers, and competitors. Similarly, there are many opportunities and applications in the health sector in terms of big data and data analytics. Special data on patients contribute to the sector in areas ranging from patient-specific treatment planning to new drug development. Moreover, in the field of manufacturing, real-time information collection and response to the problems by using big data analytics improve the quality of the manufacturing process. Monitoring of the products in operation with sensors contributes to the development of the product, transfers of the customer experience to the company, preventive maintenance of the product and perfect after-sales services (Zhong et al., 2016).

A multi-skilled team is needed to adapt AI applications to the organization. In this team, data analysts, databases, computer systems, distributed networks, sensors, designers, IT engineers, and employees who connect the management and decision processes of the organization are needed (Mayhew, Saleh, & Williams, 2016; Vidgen, Shaw, & Grant, 2017). The leadership of these teams will be a relatively advantageous information system managers who have long been involved in the organization and support the use of information in the production and management processes (Agarwal & Dhar, 2014). Therefore, companies that have already adapted management information systems to their processes and gained experience in this field will be advantageous, while those that are otherwise will be disadvantageous. In short, companies that have not completed the AI evolution will not benefit from the opportunities that AI offers.

Business analysis capability should be in the firm to create data-based value with AI applications. For business analytics capability, organization, technology, process, and human dimensions should be compatible with each other. First of all, the data of the company must be obtained following the needs of the company with the consent of the customers or related parties following the laws and ethical rules. The knowledge resulting from the analysis of the data should be used for both societal and commercial purposes. Sharing data with collaborating parties will increase the value of the data. Data should not always be considered a commercial commodity. For the organizational culture to become a data-driven understanding, it needs an organizational change and an understanding of innovation. The business analysis function should perform a deep understanding of the cause of the existence of the enterprise and develop an analysis strategy. Business analysis processes should be designed in such a way as to devote some capacity to exploit new opportunities while focusing on ethical rules, agility that can adapt to new software developments, and the solution of identified problems. Human resources should be capable of using related software, curious, working together or independently, and combining many elements (Vidgen et al., 2017). In terms of these four dimensions, SMEs have certain advantages and disadvantages. They must receive consultancy or supplier support on issues such as obtaining data following ethical rules and in alignment with the needs of the company and selecting proper technology. However, the most important disadvantage of SMEs is the lack of financial resources (Durst & Edvardsson, 2012; Pal et al., 2014; Sullivan-Taylor & Branicki, 2011) required to receive such a consultancy. On the other side some characteristics of SMEs such as flexibility, smallness and being less formal (Durst & Edvardsson, 2012; Klewes, Popp, & Rost-hein, 2017b), can be seen as an advantage for making the organizational culture data-oriented and innovative.

Digital transformation is a broader concept that includes artificial intelligence applications. Digital transformation has made drastic changes in the organization and business. But one of the most important changes occurred in the organizational communication style. This changes both interpersonal communication within the organization as well as communication with external elements such as customers and partners. For example, chatbots with artificial intelligence can communicate with the customer, and the organization can communicate with its products via "technology of the internet of things". These developments bring some advantages as well as disadvantages. AI and Big data analytics take place at the heart of this transformation and promises us big support to the decision making process and increases in performance, but it can bring some problems in our relationship with customers. Focusing on user-friendly technologies will probably become more important (Klewes, Popp, & Rost-hein, 2017a).

Moreover, there is also the need for digital leadership to achieve strategic and digital transformation within the scope of industry 4.0. (Ellermann et al., 2016). From this perspective, digital communication and digital transformation raise another issue concerning employees; e-leadership. E-leadership is a process of social interaction aimed at influencing the attitudes, behaviors, emotions, thoughts, and performance of individuals, groups, and organizations through information technologies and management information systems. E-leadership can occur at all hierarchical levels and may involve person-person, person-group or group-group interaction. (Avolio, Kahai, & Dodge, 2000). There are many theories about leadership and almost a new one is emerging every day (Dinh et al., 2014). Transformational and transactional leadership theories, which are considered to be one of the modern theories, appear as very important theories in the leadership theory taxonomy. Transactional leadership emphasizes a balanced relationship between the leader and the follower based on the exchange of benefits. The leader sets the standards and determines which prize will be awarded in return (Hartog, Muijen, & Koopman, 1997). In transformational leadership, there is an emotional unity between the leader and his followers, and a shared vision. Transformational leaders influence followers to disregard their interests for the sake of the group's interests (Bass, 1990; Yukl, 1999). Yukl (1999, p. 289) argued that; "*Transformational leadership includes individualized consideration, intellectual stimulation, idealized influence (charisma), and inspirational motivation*". Much research shows that the transformational leadership style is accepted better in terms of being satisfying and effective leaders according to colleagues, employees, and supervisors (Bass, 1990). E-leadership is not a new type of leadership, but a digital form of performing leadership activities. AI can make significant contributions to demonstrate e-leadership in a transformational style. In particular, it would be beneficial to identify employee profiles and communicate with them through individualized messages via digital means. However, AI bias effects should also be considered here. A bias-based communication failure can harm the entire leadership process and the leader-member exchange.

CONCLUSION

The implementation process of artificial intelligence is strongly related to the perception and conception of Industry 4.0 and data science. With the Industry 4.0 side, it refers to the well-defined internal processes of a company and the transformation of those processes as the digital assets. In other words, the digitally linked twin of a company should be created, which contains a high-level simulation from employees to physical assets, from managerial decision processes to customers, to suppliers based processes.

Industry 4.0 stipulates automation and integration of all actors by Cyber-Physical Systems (CPS) in any industry and ecosystem. Global supply chains, smart factories and smart cities without human intervention will be running on a global basis, because of technological improvements before mentioned. Blockchain technology, big data's predictive analysis, and cloud computing allow the automated operation of large areas of tasks through smart contracts (Mell & Grance, 2011; Swan, 2015) in the Industry 4.0 era. Blockchain technology is immutable, transparent and enables secure, fast, trustworthy transactions (Underwood, 2016). Thus blockchain can prevent market friction (Weber, 2018). Artificial intelligence could be a fostering tool for improving the capability and integrity of all actors in Industry 4.0. Industry revolution is a history of machines, which is taking over the role of a human in the industry. Artificial intelligence will enable machines to take over human roles requiring mental capacity.

Unfortunately, artificial intelligence applications in our age are within the scope of artificial narrow intelligence. For that reason, a company planning to make decisions based on artificial intelligence applications should firstly make accurate investments based on data. To make a decision, artificial narrow intelligence needs to the dataset for its learning process. The incorrect data compiling, pre-processing and analyzing are powerful enough to cause artificial intelligence to produce biased results. Because of that situation, the expectation of AI-based profit turns into a great loss or even loss of reputation. A well-built data science department in companies is very important in terms of preventing this negative situation. Besides, that department can also suggest data science solutions can have the same effect on making an administrative decision, instead of a costly artificial intelligence investment. Effective use of artificial intelligence and AI-based managerial decision making in internal processes are not only directed to profit and loss processes. Because such a change has the power to affect the internal culture deeply in the company.

Table 1. The old and new rules in the companies

Old Rules	New Rules
The career journey of the Employees must be defined by their managers/directors	The career journey of the individuals is related to their need in the team and their career goals
Career is related to ups and downs. If it is the downs there is no good career.	The career journey has multi-direction.
A company is the center of development and learning	A company creates the environment for development and supports for the learning experience
Managerial decisions are made in the light of experience, reports and short term forecasts.	Managerial decisions are made in the light of data directed experience, dynamic reports/dashboards, and not only short term forecasts but also long term forecasts are based on AI-based process.
The managerial board has the responsibility of producing the best decision	The managerial board has the responsibility of producing the best decision by using AI-based and/or data-based results.

When Table 1 is examined, the reflections of the artificial intelligence in the culture within the company and the radical change it creates are seen.

Consequently, artificial intelligence causes a critical and disruptive transformation in managerial processes. However, the success of such a transformation is closely related to the company's data policies and digital transformation skills/aspirations. Only just focusing on the concept of artificial intelligence as a technology-independent of these two concepts will lead to unsuccessful results. However, even if this trio is accurately constructed, a controlling loop is the vital key for the company to achieve an accurate and well-performed result with a set of bias-free applications.

REFERENCES

Addo-Tenkorang, R., & Helo, P. T. (2016). Big data applications in operations/supply-chain management: A literature review. *Computers & Industrial Engineering*, *101*, 528–543. doi:10.1016/j.cie.2016.09.023

Agarwal, R., & Dhar, V. (2014). Big data, data science, and analytics: The opportunity and challenge for IS research. *Information Systems Research*, *25*(3), 443–448. doi:10.1287/isre.2014.0546

Alshamaila, Y., Papagiannidis, S., & Li, F. (2013). Cloud computing adoption by SMEs in the northeast of England: A multi-perspective framework. *Journal of Enterprise Information Management*, *26*(3), 250–275. doi:10.1108/17410391311325225

Atzori, L., Iera, A., & Morabito, G. (2010). The Internet of Things: A survey. *Computer Networks*, *54*(15), 2787–2805. doi:10.1016/j.comnet.2010.05.010

Avolio, B. J., Kahai, S., & Dodge, G. E. (2000). E-Leadership: Implications For Theory, Research, and Practice. *The Leadership Quarterly*, *11*(4), 615–668. doi:10.1016/S1048-9843(00)00062-X

Bass, B. M. (1990). From transactional to transformational leadership: Learning to share the vision. Organi. *Organizational Dynamics*, *18*(3), 19–31. doi:10.1016/0090-2616(90)90061-S

Bolman, L. G., & Deal, T. E. (1984). *Modern approaches to understanding and managing organizations*. Jossey-Bass.

Bracker, J. (2012). Historical Development of Strategic Management Concept. *Management*, *5*(2), 219–224.

Cath, C., Wachter, S., Mittelstadt, B., Taddeo, M., & Floridi, L. (2018). Artificial Intelligence and the 'Good Society': The US, EU, and UK approach. *Science and Engineering Ethics*, *24*(2), 505–528. PubMed

Certo, S. C., & Certo, S. T. (2006). *Modern Management*. London: Pearson/Prentice Hall.

Chen, D. Q., Preston, D. S., & Swink, M. (2015). How the use of big data analytics affects value creation in supply chain management. *Journal of Management Information Systems*, *32*(4), 4–39. doi:10.1080/07421222.2015.1138364

Chen, H., Chiang, R. H. L., & Storey, V. C. (2018). Business Intelligence and Analytics: From Big Data to Big Impact. *Management Information Systems Quarterly*, *36*(4), 1165–1188. doi:10.2307/41703503

Crosby, M., Pattanayak, P., Verma, S., & Kalyanaraman, V. (2016). Blockchain technology: Beyond bitcoin. Applied Innovation Review, (2), 6–10.

Dabić, M., Lažnjak, J., Smallbone, D., & Švarc, J. (2018). Intellectual capital, organizational climate, innovation culture, and SME performance: Evidence from Croatia. *Journal of Small Business and Enterprise Development*. doi:10.1108/JSBED-04-2018-0117

Demirkan, H., & Delen, D. (2013). Leveraging the capabilities of service-oriented decision support systems: Putting analytics and big data in the cloud. *Decision Support Systems*, *55*(1), 412–421. doi:10.1016/j.dss.2012.05.048

Dictionary, C. (2019). Retrieved from Cambridge Dictionary website: https://dictionary.cambridge.org

Dictionary, O. (2019). Retrieved November 12, 2019, from Lexico Powered by Oxford website: https://www.lexico.com/en/definition/data

Dinca, V. M., Dima, A. M., & Rozsa, Z. (2019). Determinants of Cloud Computing Adoption by Romanian SMEs In The Digital Economy. *Journal of Business Economics and Management*, *20*(4), 798–820. doi:10.3846/jbem.2019.9856

Dinh, J. E., Lord, R. G., Gardner, W. L., Meuser, J. D., Liden, R. C., & Hu, J. (2014). Leadership theory and research in the new millennium: Current theoretical trends and changing perspectives. *The Leadership Quarterly*, *25*(1), 36–62. doi:10.1016/j.leaqua.2013.11.005

Drucker, P. F. (1986). *Management: Tasks, Responsibilities, Practices*. New York: Truman Talley Books/ E.P. Dutton.

Drucker, P. F. (2018). *The Effective Executive*. London: Taylor&Francis Group; doi:10.4324/9780080549354.

Durst, S., & Edvardsson, I. R. (2012). Knowledge management in SMEs: A literature review. *Journal of Knowledge Management*, *16*(6), 879–903. doi:10.1108/13673271211276173

Ellermann, H., Kreutter, P., & Messner, W. (2016). The Palgrave handbook of managing continuous business transformation. In *The Palgrave Handbook of Managing Continuous Business Transformation*. Academic Press.

European Commission. (2018). Annual Report on European SMEs 2017-2018. SMEs growing beyond borders.

Fayol, H. (1949). *General and Industrial Management*. London: Pitman&Sons Ltd.

Ghobakhloo, M., Aranda, D. A., & Amado, J. B. (2011). Adoption of e-commerce applications in SMEs. *Industrial Management & Data Systems*, *111*(8), 1238–1269. doi:10.1108/02635571111170785

Govindan, K., Cheng, T. C. E., Mishra, N., & Shukla, N. (2018). Big data analytics and application for logistics and supply chain management. *Transportation Research Part E, Logistics and Transportation Review*, *114*(May), 343–349. doi:10.1016/j.tre.2018.03.011

Griffin, R. W. (2012). *Management*. Mason, OH: Cancage Learning.

Haag, S., & Anderl, R. (2018). Digital twin – Proof of concept. Manufacturing Letters, 15, 64–66. doi:10.1016/j.mfglet.2018.02.006

Hartog, D. N., Muijen, J. J., & Koopman, P. L. (1997). Transactional versus transformational leadership: An analysis of the MLQ. *Journal of Occupational and Organizational Psychology*, *70*(1), 19–34. doi:10.1111/j.2044-8325.1997.tb00628.x

Hegge, B. (2010). *SMEs and European Integration*. London: Taylor&Francis Group.

Hehenberger, P., & Bradley, D. (2016). Digital twin—the simulation aspect. In *Mechatronic Futures* (pp. 59–74). Cham, Switzerland: Springer.

Hervas-Oliver, J. L., Boronat-Moll, C., & Sempere-Ripoll, F. (2016). On Process Innovation Capabilities in SMEs: A Taxonomy of Process-Oriented Innovative SMEs. *Journal of Small Business Management*, *54*, 113–134. doi:10.1111/jsbm.12293

Iqbal, Q., & Nawaz, R. (2019). Rife information pollution (infollution) and virtual organizations in industry 4.0: within reality causes and consequences. In *Big Data and Knowledge Sharing in Virtual Organizations* (pp. 117–135). IGI Global; doi:10.4018/978-1-5225-7519-1.ch005.

Iqbal, Q., Yang, S., Nawaz, R., & Iqbal, K. (2019). A multi-dimensional construct of perceived information pollution in the era of rife infollution. VINE Journal of Information and Knowledge Management Systems, 49(2), 162–180. doi:10.1108/VJIKMS-10-2018-0093

Irwin, K. C., Landay, K. M., Aaron, J. R., McDowell, W. C., Marino, L. D., & Geho, P. R. (2018). Entrepreneurial orientation (EO) and human resources outsourcing (HRO): A "HERO" combination for SME performance. *Journal of Business Research*, *90*(May), 134–140. doi:10.1016/j.jbusres.2018.05.016

Jazdi, N. (2014). Cyber-physical systems in the context of Industry 4.0. Proceedings of 2014 IEEE International Conference on Automation, Quality and Testing, Robotics, AQTR 2014, 1–4. doi:10.1109/AQTR.2014.6857843

Kaur, H., & Singh, S. P. (2018). Heuristic modeling for sustainable procurement and logistics in a supply chain using big data. *Computers & Operations Research*, *98*, 301–321. doi:10.1016/j.cor.2017.05.008

Klewes, J., Popp, D., & Rost-hein, M. (2017a). Digital Transformation and Communications: How Key Trends Will Transform the Way Companies Communicate. In Out-thinking Organizational Communications (pp. 7–31). doi:10.1007/978-3-319-41845-2

Klewes, J., Popp, D., & Rost-hein, M. (2017b). Digital Transformation and the Challenges for Organizational Communications: An Introduction. In Out-thinking Organizational Communications (pp. 1–6). doi:10.1007/978-3-319-41845-2

Koontz, H. (1961). Management Theory Jungle. *The Academy of Management Perspectives*, *4*(3), 174–188.

Lasi, H., Fettke, P., Kemper, H. G., Feld, T., & Hoffmann, M. (2014). Industry 4.0. *Business & Information Systems Engineering*, *6*(4), 239–242. doi:10.1007/s12599-014-0334-4

Lee, S., Park, G., Yoon, B., & Park, J. (2010). Open innovation in SMEs-An intermediated network model. *Research Policy*, *39*(2), 290–300. doi:10.1016/j.respol.2009.12.009

Liang, W. Y., & Huang, C. C. (2006). Agent-based demand forecast in the multi-echelon supply chain. *Decision Support Systems*, *42*(1), 390–407. doi:10.1016/j.dss.2005.01.009

Lindblom, C. E. (1959). The Science of " Muddling Through. *Public Administration Review*, *19*(2), 79–88. doi:10.2307/973677

Loebbecke, C., & Picot, A. (2015). Reflections on societal and business model transformation arising from digitization and big data analytics: A research agenda. *The Journal of Strategic Information Systems*, *24*(3), 149–157. doi:10.1016/j.jsis.2015.08.002

Love, J. H., & Roper, S. (2015). SME innovation, exporting and growth: A review of existing evidence. International Small Business Journal: Researching Entrepreneurship, 33(1), 28–48. doi:10.1177/0266242614550190

Malinowski, B. (1960). *A Scientific Theory of Culture* (2nd ed.). New York: Oxford University Press.

Marcovitz, H. (2013). *The Industrial Revolution*. San Diego, CA: ReferencePoint Press.

Mayhew, H., Saleh, T., & Williams, S. (2016). Making data analytics work for you- instead of the other way around. *The McKinsey Quarterly*, *4*(October), 1–15.

Mell, P., & Grance, T. (2011). The NIST-National Institute of Standards and Technology- Definition of Cloud Computing. NIST Special Publication 800-145.

Mendes, L., & Lourenço, L. (2014). Factors that hinder quality improvement programs' implementation in SME: Definition of a taxonomy. *Journal of Small Business and Enterprise Development*, *21*(4), 690–715. doi:10.1108/JSBED-03-2014-0054

Mentzer, J. T., Keebler, J. S., Nix, N. W., Smith, C. D., & Zacharia, Z. G. (2001). Journal of Business Logistics, Vol.22, No. 2, 2001 1. *The Journal of Business*, *22*(2), 1–25.

Mikalef, P., Pappas, I. O., Krogstie, J., & Giannakos, M. (2018). Big data analytics capabilities: A systematic literature review and research agenda. *Information Systems and e-Business Management*, *16*(3), 547–578. doi:10.1007/s10257-017-0362-y

Min, H. (2010). Artificial intelligence in supply chain management: Theory and applications. *International Journal of Logistics Research and Applications*, *13*(1), 13–39. doi:10.1080/13675560902736537

Monostori, L. (2014). Cyber-physical production systems: Roots, expectations, and R&D challenges. Procedia CIRP, 17, 9–13. doi:10.1016/j.procir.2014.03.115

Naudé, W., & Dimitri, N. (2018). The Race for an Artificial General Intelligence: Implications for Public Policy. SSRN Electronic Journal, (0123456789).

Nguyen, T., Zhou, L., Spiegler, V., Ieromonachou, P., & Lin, Y. (2018). Big data analytics in supply chain management: A state-of-the-art literature review. *Computers & Operations Research*, *98*, 254–264. doi:10.1016/j.cor.2017.07.004

Nofer, M., Gomber, P., Hinz, O., & Schiereck, D. (2017). GNRL_Blockchain. *Business & Information Systems Engineering*, *59*(3), 183–187. doi:10.1007/s12599-017-0467-3

O'Connor, E. (1999). The Politics of Management Thought: A Case Study of the Harvard Business Sc...: Discovery For the University of Southampton. *Academy of Management Review*, *24*(1), 117–131. doi:10.5465/amr.1999.1580444

OECD. (2017). *Small, Medium, Strong. Trends in SME Performance and Business Conditions*. Paris: OECD.

Pal, R., Torstensson, H., & Mattila, H. (2014). Antecedents of organizational resilience in economic crises - An empirical study of Swedish textile and clothing SMEs. International Journal of Production Economics, 147(Part B), 410–428. doi:10.1016/j.ijpe.2013.02.031

Papanek, M. L. (2011). Kurt Lewin and His Contributions to Modern Management Theory. Academy of Management Proceedings, 1973(1), 317–322. doi:10.5465/ambpp.1973.4981410

Pappas, I. O., Mikalef, P., Giannakos, M. N., Krogstie, J., & Lekakos, G. (2018). Big data and business analytics ecosystems: Paving the way towards digital transformation and sustainable societies. *Information Systems and e-Business Management, 16*(3), 479–491. doi:10.1007/s10257-018-0377-z

Philip Chen, C. L., & Zhang, C. Y. (2014). Data-intensive applications, challenges, techniques, and technologies: A survey on Big Data. *Information Sciences, 275*, 314–347. doi:10.1016/j.ins.2014.01.015

Pindur, W., Rogers, S. E., & Kim, P. S. (2013). The history of management: A global perspective. *Journal of Management History, 1*(1), 59–77. doi:10.1108/13552529510082831

Popkova, E. G., Ragulina, Y. V., & Bogoviz, A. V. (2019). Fundamental differences of transition to industry 4.0 from previous industrial revolutions. In Industry 4.0: Industrial Revolution of the 21st Century. Studies in Systems, Decision, and Control (Vol. 169, pp. 21–29). doi:10.1007/978-3-319-94310-7_3

Porter, M. E. (1986). Changing Patterns of International Competition. *California Management Review, 28*(2), 9–40. doi:10.2307/41165182

Robbins, S. P., & Coulter, M. (2002). *Management.* Upper Saddle River, NJ: Pearson Prentice Hall.

Rohde, J. (2004). Hierarchical supply chain planning using artificial neural networks to anticipate base-level outcomes. *OR-Spektrum, 26*(4), 471–492. doi:10.1007/s00291-004-0170-x

Russom, P. (2011). Big data analytics. Retrieved from https://vivomente.com/wp-content/uploads/2016/04/big-data-analytics-white-paper.pdf

Sarker, B. R., & Fitzsimmons, J. A. (1989). The performance of push and pull systems: A simulation and comparative study. *International Journal of Production Research, 27*(10), 1715–1731. doi:10.1080/00207548908942650

Stearns, P. N. (2013). *Industrial Revolution in World History*. Boulder, CO: Westview Press.

Sullivan-Taylor, B., & Branicki, L. (2011). Creating resilient SMEs: Why one size might not fit all. *International Journal of Production Research, 49*(18), 5565–5579. doi:10.1080/00207543.2011.563837

Swan, M. (2015). *Blockchain Blueprint for a New Economy* (T. McGovern, Ed.). Sebastopol, CA: O'Reilly.

Taylor, F. W. (1913). *The principles of scientific management*. New York: Harpers & Brothers Publisher.

Thong, J. Y. L. (2015). An Integrated Model of Information Systems Adoption in Small Businesses. *Journal of Management Information Systems, 15*(4), 187–214. doi:10.1080/07421222.1999.11518227

Thong, J. Y. L., Yap, C. S., & Raman, K. S. (1994). Engagement of external expertise in information systems implementation. *Journal of Management Information Systems, 11*(2), 209–231. doi:10.1080/07421222.1994.11518046

Tiwari, S., Wee, H. M., & Daryanto, Y. (2018). Big data analytics in supply chain management between 2010 and 2016: Insights to industries. *Computers & Industrial Engineering, 115*, 319–330. doi:10.1016/j.cie.2017.11.017

Tsuruta, D. (2018). SME policies as a barrier to the growth of SMEs. Small Business Economics. doi:10.1007/s11187-018-0119-0

Underwood, S. (2016). Blockchain beyond bitcoin. *Communications of the ACM*, *59*(11), 15–17. doi:10.1145/2994581

Valtakoski, A., & Witell, L. (2018). Service capabilities and serviced SME performance: Contingency on firm age. *International Journal of Operations & Production Management*, *38*(4), 1144–1164. doi:10.1108/IJOPM-06-2016-0328

Vermesan, O., Friess, P., Guillemin, P., Gusmeroli, S., Sundmaeker, H., Bassi, A., & Doody, P. (2011). Internet of Things Strategic Research Roadmap. In Internet of things-global technological and societal trends (Vol. 1, pp. 9–52). Retrieved from http://ec.europa.eu/information_society/policy/rfid/documents/in_cerp.pdf

Vidgen, R., Shaw, S., & Grant, D. B. (2017). Management challenges in creating value from business analytics. *European Journal of Operational Research*, *261*(2), 626–639. doi:10.1016/j.ejor.2017.02.023

Waller, M. A., & Fawcett, S. E. (2013). Data science, predictive analytics, and big data: A revolution that will transform supply chain design and management. *Journal of Business Logistics*, *34*(2), 77–84. doi:10.1111/jbl.12010

Wamba, S. F., Akter, S., Edwards, A., Chopin, G., & Gnanzou, D. (2015). How 'big data can make a big impact: Findings from a systematic review and a longitudinal case study. *International Journal of Production Economics*, *165*, 234–246. doi:10.1016/j.ijpe.2014.12.031

Wamba, S. F., Gunasekaran, A., Akter, S., Ren, S. J., Dubey, R., & Childe, S. J. (2017). Big data analytics and firm performance: Effects of dynamic capabilities. *Journal of Business Research*, *70*, 356–365. doi:10.1016/j.jbusres.2016.08.009

Wang, G., Gunasekaran, A., Ngai, E. W. T., & Papadopoulos, T. (2016). Big data analytics in logistics and supply chain management: Certain investigations for research and applications. *International Journal of Production Economics*, *176*, 98–110. doi:10.1016/j.ijpe.2016.03.014

Weber, R. M. (2018). An Advisor's Introduction to Blockchain. *Journal of Financial Service Professionals*, *72*(6), 49. Retrieved from http://search.ebscohost.com/login.aspx?direct=true&db=edb&AN=132685638&lang=de&site=eds-live&authtype=shib

Yukl, G. (1999). An evaluation of conceptual weaknesses in transformational and charismatic leadership theories. *The Leadership Quarterly*, *10*(2), 285–305. doi:10.1016/S1048-9843(99)00013-2

Zhao, R., Liu, Y., Zhang, N., & Huang, T. (2017). An optimization model for green supply chain management by using a big data analytic approach. *Journal of Cleaner Production*, *142*, 1085–1097. doi:10.1016/j.jclepro.2016.03.006

Zhong, R. Y., Newman, S. T., Huang, G. Q., & Lan, S. (2016). Big Data for supply chain management in the service and manufacturing sectors: Challenges, opportunities, and future perspectives. *Computers & Industrial Engineering*, *101*, 572–591. doi:10.1016/j.cie.2016.07.013

Section 2
Sustainability and SMEs in Industry 4.0

Chapter 4
Sustainability of SMEs and Health Sector in a Dynamic Capabilities Perspective

Bülent Akkaya
https://orcid.org/0000-0003-1252-9334
Manisa Celal Bayar University, Turkey

Sema Üstgörül
Manisa Celal Bayar University, Turkey

ABSTRACT

In Industry 4.0, enterprises have economic, social, and environmentally sustainable policies, and the implementation of these policies may lead to raising the national economy and society welfare. It can be achieved by firms' dynamic capabilities. Therefore, structuring of the activities of enterprises, especially SMEs and health sector organizations within the framework of sustainability and establishing standards by establishing control mechanisms, plays an important role in the development of the country. One of the most important responsibilities of managers in these sectors in implementing sustainable policies is to utilize the dynamic capabilities of the organization. In this context, it is necessary to have knowledge about what dynamic capabilities are and their relationship with sustainability. This study discusses the relationship between dynamic capabilities and sustainability of SMEs and the firms in health sector.

DOI: 10.4018/978-1-7998-2577-7.ch004

INTRODUCTION

Today, in industry 4.0 term, organizations operating in health institutions face some problems, especially in turbulence, complex and changeable environment. There are some compelling factors called PESTEL (Political, Environment, Social, Technology, Economical and Legal) force organizations to adapt that complex changeable environment. However, despite all these challenges, some organizations should adapt to a changeable environment and develop their strategies to deal with rapidly changing conditions to sustain growth in this critical industry 4.0. This, certainly, can be achieved with the help of using their dynamic capabilities which help them stay competitive in the long term and sustainability. The concept of sustainability, which is frequently used in many areas, is defined as a participatory process that creates a social perspective on the cautious use of social, cultural, scientific, and natural and human resources of the society (Iqbal, Ahmad, & Ahmad., 2018). Sustainability is perceived as the ability to sustain the functions, processes, and productivity of ecology and ecological systems in the future and the aim of it is to ensure permanent satisfaction and to improve the quality of life (WordNet, 2008). According to the definition of the International Council on Local Environmental Initiatives, sustainable development is the development that offers these services to everyone without threatening the existence of the natural, artificial and social systems to which the basic environment, economic and social services depend. In this context, this chapter discussed the relationship between dynamic capabilities and health organizations in industry 4.0.

SUSTAINABLE DEVELOPMENT

Sustainable development is often used interchangeably with sustainable growth, but sustainability and sustainable development are not synonymous (Reddy and Thomson 2015). The concept of sustainability was first used in the field of management of natural resources but then it has been used in different fields such as energy, tourism, agriculture, and health (Hallstedt, 2017). Sustainable development is defined as development that meets the needs of the present without compromising the ability of future generations to meet their own needs by the World Commission on Environment and Development in 1987(Harris., 2003). And it has been expanded over the years to include perspectives on human needs and well-being (including non-economic variables, such as health and education, clean water and air, and the protection of natural beauty (hdr.undp.org/human-development-report) (Iqbal, 2018). Sustainability is one of the most common concepts which find its place among all vital activities; it can be used together with many issues such as sustainable development, sustainable growth, sustainable economies, sustainable societies and sustainable agriculture (Moore et al., 2017; Iqbal & Hassan, 2018).

Starting with the industrial revolution and continuing until the 1970s, countries have used more natural resources to increase their economic growth by acting on the assumption that natural resources are unlimited in their development policies. Moreover, especially after the Second World War, the development of technology has increased production rapidly and the increase in the population has caused to increase the consumption. This situation, on the one hand, provided development. It caused environmental problems that have gradually increased from regionalism to a global dimension. The World Environment and Development Commission was established in 1983 by the United Nations (UN) and then the 1987 Brundtland Report was established, where the relationship between the environment and development was established. Reddy and Thomson (2015) the concept of sustainable development was getting important and the two fundamental elements of sustainable development, human centrism and the preservation of the resources of future generations, have brought up the issues of sustainability and sustainable development. It has many steps that were taken on international platforms. These steps are listed below:

- 1972 .... Stockholm Conference
- 1987 .... Our Common Future Report
- 1992 .... Rio Summit
- 1996 .... Habitat II Summit
- 1997 .... Rio+5 Summit
- 2002 .... Johannesburg Summit

The most important issue of sustainable development emerged from the Rio Summit, which was held in 1992, to a comprehensive and integrated development agenda, a concept of global product strategy, which was not been conceptualized and supported by economic, environmental and social strategies and action plans. With the increase in pressure on the environment, the healthy continuation of the ecosystem is threatened, the rapidly increasing production and consumption accelerated the pollution of the air, water, and soil, the natural resources have started to deteriorate and depleted, many plant and animal species have disappeared and the nature can renew itself power is damaged (Mackenbach, 2007). Therefore, sustainable development targets have been established in developing countries since 2000.

2030 Sustainable Development Goals

In 1987, The World Commission on Environment and Development report on our Common Future formulated the definition of sustainable development and put forward the issue that caused the conflict between environment and development (Harris, 2000; Toker and Çınar, 2017). The 2030 Sustainable Development Goals (SDG 2030), adopted by the signature of 193 member states at the United Nations' (UN) Sustainable Development Summit, consist of 17 main objectives and 169 objectives linked to them. This global agenda is up to 2030 for all human rights and the development of countries' development plans and policies.

Today, enterprises should not only create economic value but involve in activities that facilitate and improve living conditions as well (Caymaz, etc., 2014). There have been specific developments in areas such as the protection of nature and the fight against climate change, and prevention of discrimination based on gender, protection of nature and combating climate change; sustainable use of natural resources, combating poverty, increasing employment, ensuring the quality and accessibility of education and health services, increasing access to clean water, safe energy sources and food (https://sustainabledevelopment.un.org/content/documents/853turkey.pdf). They can achieve those activities by sustainability.

The Sustainable Development Goals 2030 (SDGs) is the UN's blueprint for a more sustainable future for all. Their adoption put environmental degradation, sustainability, climate change, and water security under the international spotlight. The global goals aim to leave no one behind and are vital to achieving CDP's vision for a thriving economy that works for people and the planet. Global targets set sustainability at the center of development, and the economic, environmental and social concerns are the common issue of all people living on earth. The aim of sustainable development is addressed not only through economic and environmental conflicts but also a holistic approach covering basic human needs, climate change, environmental protection, peace, democracy, fundamental rights and freedoms (https://www.cdp.net/en/policy-and-public-affairs/sustainable-development-goals).

The world aims to build the discourse of sustainable development through a Better World Vision in 2030. The goals of the global agenda are listed below:

1. End poverty in all its forms everywhere
2. End hunger, achieve food security and improved nutrition and promote sustainable agriculture
3. Ensure healthy lives and promote well-being for all at all ages
4. Ensure inclusive and equitable quality education and promote lifelong learning opportunities for all
5. Achieve gender equality and empower all women and girls
6. Ensure availability and sustainable management of water and sanitation for all
7. Ensure access to affordable, reliable, sustainable and modern energy for all
8. Promote sustained, inclusive and sustainable economic growth, full and productive employment and decent work for all
9. Build resilient infrastructure, promote inclusive and sustainable industrialization and foster innovation
10. Reduce inequality within and among countries
11. Make cities and human settlements inclusive, safe, resilient and sustainable
12. Ensure sustainable consumption and production patterns
13. Take urgent action to combat climate change and its impacts
14. Conserve and sustainably use the oceans, seas and marine resources for sustainable development
15. Protect, restore and promote sustainable use of terrestrial ecosystems, sustainably manage forests, combat desertification, and halt and reverse land degradation and halt biodiversity loss
16. Promote peaceful and inclusive societies for sustainable development, provide access to justice for all and build effective, accountable and inclusive institutions at all levels
17. Strengthen the means of implementation and revitalize the global partnership for sustainable development(https://www.cdp.net/en/policy-and-public-affairs/sustainable-development-goals/all-sustainable-development-goals)

Dimensions of Sustainability

Sustainability, as mentioned above, means that enterprises should create economic value and involve in activities that facilitate and improve living conditions. World Economic and Social Survey announced that the global challenges to sustainable development have been driven by changing demographic profiles, changing economic and social dynamics, advancements in technology and trends towards environmental deterioration (https://www.un.org; Kazamia&Kafaridou, 2018). In this context, sustainability is defined by three core dimensions which are called environmental management, social responsibilities and economic solutions(Reddy &Thomson, 2015; Cavagnaro & George, 2017; www.css.umich.edu).

Figure 1. The three spheres of sustainability
(Source: Aminuddin & Nawawi, 2013, p. 9.)

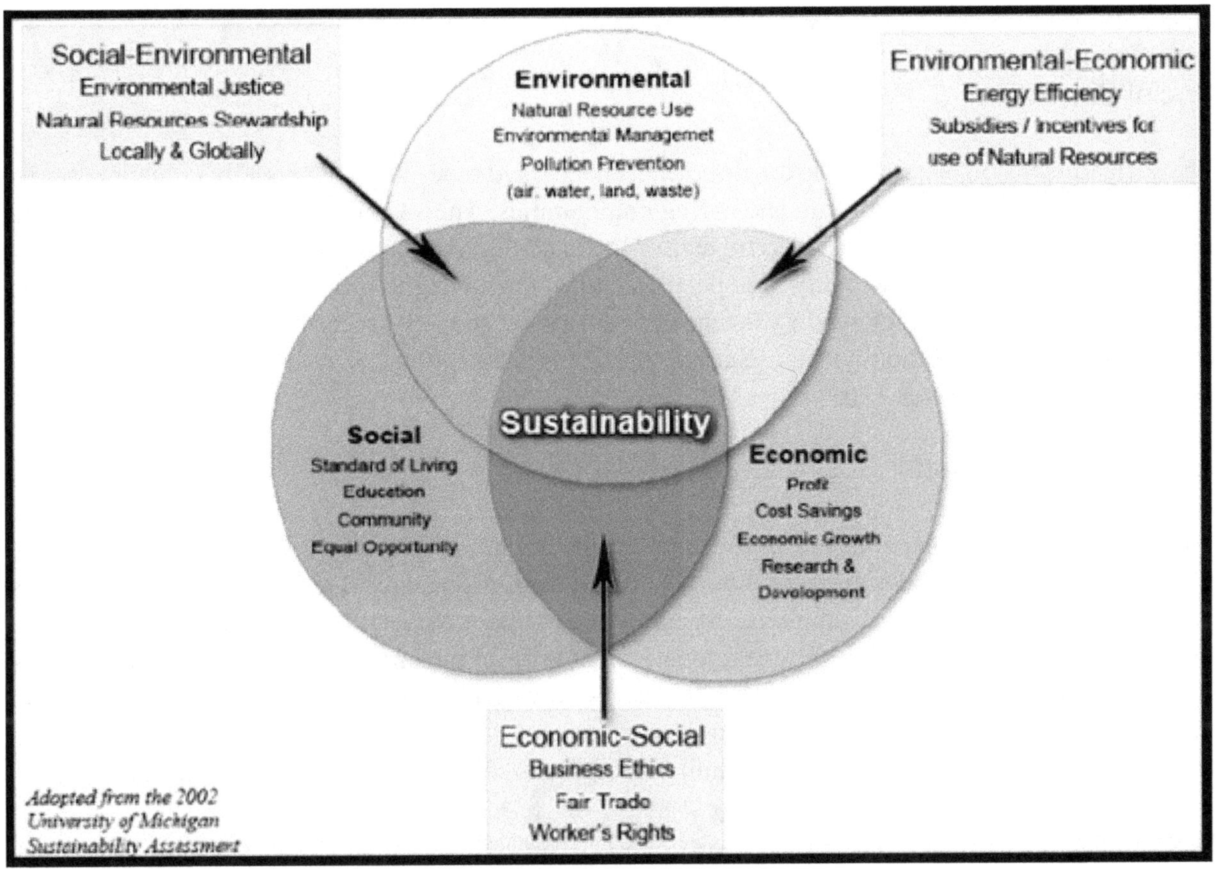

Environmental Dimension

The environmental dimension includes materials, water, waste, energy, biodiversity, emissions, effluents, products and services, and compliance. These are about the Earth system. The earth system has contained boundaries within which equilibrium is maintained. It can maintain its integrity or return to a state of equilibrium after a disturbance (Rockström et al., 2009). However, abrupt changes in the earth system can cause to lose this resilience and sustainability (Reddy & Thompson, 2015). Global warming, thinning of the ozone layer, reduction of animal and plant species diversity, observing the negative consequences of the spread of air, water, and soil pollution and the global dimension of these environmental problems cause the economic and environmental atmosphere to be affected. And, over 50% of our global population lives in cities. They are also responsible for around 70% of global energy-related emissions. They are on the frontline of both climate impacts and the transition to a sustainable future for all (www.cdp.net).

Critical and long-term climate changes in the climate system resulting from natural or human activities are among the most important indicators of environmental sustainability. These changes involve warming of the atmosphere and oceans, rising sea level, diminishing ice levels, increasing acidification of the oceans and increasing concentrations of greenhouse gases. Climate change has already begun to affect biodiversity. If species are not able to adjust to unfamiliar geographical distributions, their chances of survival will be reduced. It is predicted that, by the year 2080, about 20% of coastal wetlands could be lost due to sea-level rise (Reddy &Thompson, 2015).

Social Dimension

The social dimension of sustainable development is concerned especially with poverty reduction, social investment and the building of safe and caring communities. The social component also requires the provision of some objective and subjective data of life in addition to some political conditions in society (Orlitzky et al., 2011). In other words, the social component involves the survival of every member of the society following human dignity, the existence of democracy and legal security, housing, the existence of minimum living conditions, social security, education and health access, fair share and equality of opportunity (Dempsey et al., 2011).

Economic Dimension

The economic dimension of sustainability concerns the organization's effects on the economic conditions of its stakeholders, on economic systems at global, national, and local levels. Economic indicators include employees, customers, suppliers, the public sector and providers of capital (Choi & Ng, 2011).

Economic success and competitiveness for sustainable development, the economic viability of society, sustainability of production, social and human resources and the increase in these resources should be provided in terms of qualitative. The production and consumption of goods and services should be avoided as much as possible, and the consumption of goods should be fair (Esmaeilian et al., 2016).

Corporate Sustainability

Corporate sustainability is accepted as the equivalent of the sustainability approach at the enterprise level. According to this approach, it is equally important for enterprises to pursue corporate growth and profitability as well as social goals such as environmental protection, social equity, justice and economic development (Çalışkan, 2012). For a healthy sustainability application in companies, economic, social and environmental parameters, which are three sub-factors of sustainability, should include all basic, strategic and operational processes and decision-making mechanisms of companies (Turhan et al., 2018).

Kuşat (2012) stated that sustainable development contributes to corporate sustainability in two ways.

1. By demonstrating the need for businesses to focus on sustainable development,
2. By enabling businesses, government and civil society to form a common target for the realization of ecological, social and economic sustainability.

Corporate sustainability is considered as a micro-level implementation of sustainable development. Therefore, sustainable development is a matter not only at the national level but also at the level of the enterprises.

Figure 2 illustrates the link between sustainable development and corporate sustainability. Sustainable development when incorporated by the organization is called corporate sustainability and it contains, like sustainable development, all three pillars: economic, ecological and social (Baumgartner & Ebner, 2010).

Figure 2. Corporate sustainability strategies
(Source: Baumgartner & Ebner, 2010, p. 77)

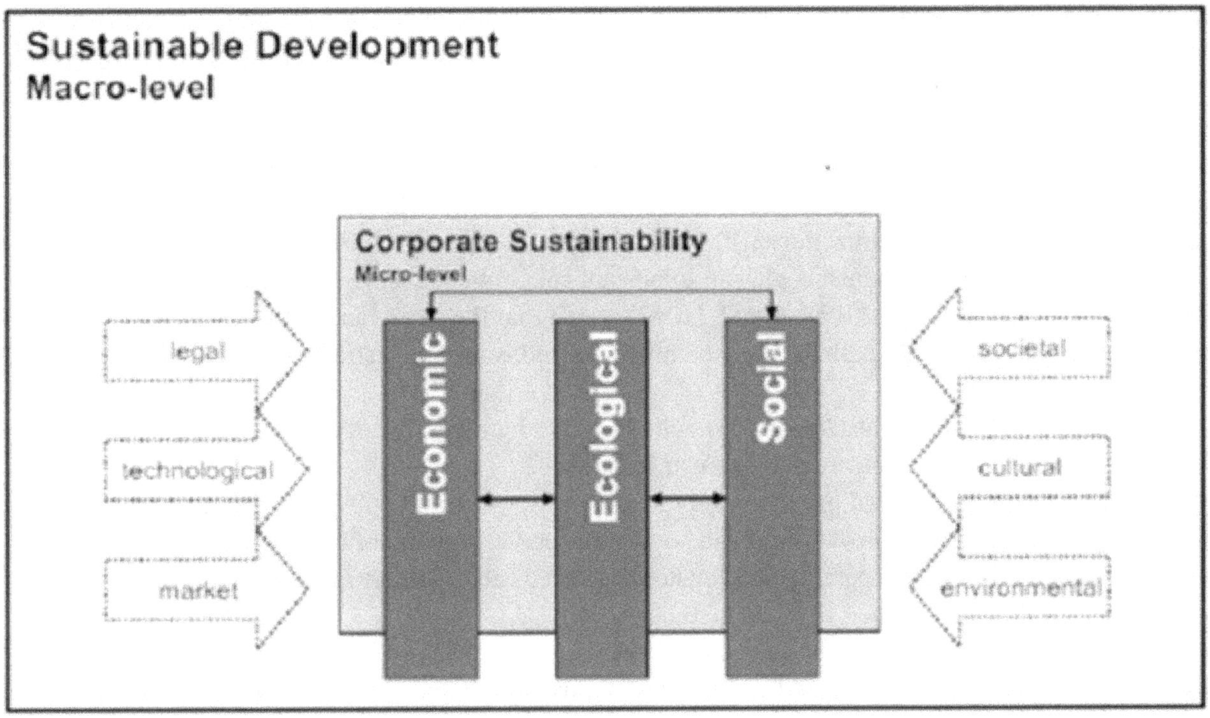

Environmental Integrity: Every business has an environmental impact, less or more. With reactive or proactive applications, businesses minimize environmental impact by minimizing the negative effects they create (Brown & Siri, 2012).

Social Equality: Businesses provide social equality through corporate social responsibility practices. Corporate social responsibility requires the adoption of economic, legal and ethical obligations not only of the financial stakeholders but also of all stakeholders. This creates equality in accessing resources by community members (Brown & Siri, 2012).

Economic Welfare: Businesses create value with the goods and services they produce. They enable value creation by increasing the effectiveness of goods and services (Brown & Siri, 2012). These are archived by some factors which are listed below.

Factors that corporate sustainability promotes businesses:

- Providing brand value, trust, and reputation,
- Increasing profitability by increasing cost,
- Ensuring the motivation of human resources,
- Provide consumer demands.

Health Systems Sustainability

Health is among the priority services for both societies and individuals (Resnik, 2007). Health services are one of the most important indicators of socioeconomic development levels of countries (Tutar & Kılınç, 2007). In this context, the health sector plays a critical role in the development of health economics all around the world. Being aware of this importance, the institutions operating in the health sector have economic, social and environmentally sustainable policies and the implementation of these policies may lead to the effects of raising the national economy and social welfare. Therefore, structuring of the activities of health sector organizations within the framework of sustainability and establishing standards by establishing control mechanisms play an important role in the development of the country (Tutar & Kılınç 2007; Toker & Çınar 2017). Akdağ (2011) stated that the main purpose of the health system is to improve and to raise the health level of society and listed some suggestions and advises to achieve it.

- All citizens should get health services, which should be accessible, equitable and quality.
- Health institutions should keep their sustainability.
- Health institutions should pay attention to human resources and public relations.
- They should follow environmental and social changes in contemporary technology.
- They should meet their patients' and customers' needs and expectations.
- They should improve their core competencies.
- They should keep their capabilities more dynamic.
- They should learn new care and treatment methods and integrate them into their institutions.

Apart from those suggestions, achieving sustainable development in the health sector should meet today's health needs and the needs of future generations. Because of that reason, the health expenditures of countries should be taken into consideration (Tamer, 2018). The provision of health services is unique and increases and diversifies health expenditures according to changing health needs. The amount of health expenditures in the total economy has been increasing more over the years than a gross domestic product (GDP) and there has been increasing interest in the relationship between health and economic growth over the last few years(Tamer, 2018). Therefore, health spending has been one of the main important subjects on which politicians and researchers have focused in recent years (OECD, 2018). The World Health Organisation (CMH, 2001) and the European Commission (European Commission, 2005) have produced extensive reports that have argued for greater spending on health as a means of promoting growth in GDP, for both developed and developing countries (www.ec.europa.eu).

According to OECD report in the 2002-2015 periods, per capita, health expenditures increased by 3.7 times in nominal terms and by 0.45 times in real terms. The average health expenditure per capita in OECD countries is SGP $ 3,621 (www.data.oecd.org).

Table 1 shows that health expenditures are getting increase year by year. This is probably because of health spending. Health spending measures the final consumption of health care goods and services (i.e. current health expenditure) including personal health care (rehabilitative care, curative care, long-term care, medical goods, and ancillary services) and collective services (prevention and public health services as well as health administration), but excluding spending on investments. Health care is financed through a mix of financing arrangements including government spending and compulsory health insurance ("Government/compulsory") as well as voluntary health insurance and private funds such as households' out-of-pocket payments, NGOs and private corporations ("Voluntary"). This indicator is presented as a

Table 1. Per Capita Health Expenditures, OECD Health Data

Year / Country	2010	2011	2012	2013	2014	2015	2016	2017	2018
	ΔV	ΔV	ΔV	ΔV	ΔV	ΔV	ΔV	ΔV	ΔV
Australia	42 812.2	44 419.3	43 879.3	47 761.2	47 638.7	47 351	50 262.6	51 996.2	**54 094.6**
Austria	42 006	44 452.7	46 457.3	47 922	48 802.3	49 877.7	51 655.5	53 879.3	**55 665.4**
Belgium	40 052	41 284.2	42 435.9	43 611.1	44 604.5	45 592.4	47 214.2	49 411.9	**50 470.4**
Canada	40 106.2	41 662.5	42 246.7	44 211.1	45 627.6	44 509.8	44 916.5	46 596.3	**48 261.8**
Denmark	42 999.6	44 403.4	44 804	46 726.9	47 901.4	49 058.5	50 694.2	54 356.4	**55 140.9**
Estonia	21 581.7	24 543.1	26 022.5	27 495.7	28 964.2	29 212.9	30 897.5	33 447.8	**35 497.4**
Finland	38 737.4	40 683.5	40 620.2	41 293.5	41 470.2	42 221	43 730	46 343.6	**48 274.5**
France	36 015.6	37 564.2	37 806.5	39 660.5	40 144	40 860.9	42 134.6	44 255.9	**45 383.8**
Germany	39 187.4	42 692.5	43 564.1	45 232.2	47 190.8	47 979.5	49 921.3	52 574.3	**53 823.2**
Greece	28 148.4	26 141.3	25 284.5	26 097.9	26 838.5	26 902.5	27 273.9	28 579.8	**29 555**
Italy	35 008.1	36 347.3	36 237.1	36 131.1	36 070.8	36 836.4	39 045.2	40 981.3	**41 594.2**
Japan	34 990.5	35 774.4	37 202	38 983.6	39 191.1	40 410.9	41 138.1	41 985.3	**42 913.4**
Netherlands	45 040.3	46 599	47 272.1	49 241.5	49 233.2	50 302.1	51 338.6	54 422	**56 444.1**
Norway	57 965.5	62 145	65 447.5	67 056.1	66 015.4	60 520	58 138.4	62 182.8	**65 830.6**
Sweden	41 632.7	43 808.5	44 774.4	45 722	46 572.5	48 437	49 084.1	51 404.8	**53 053.1**
Switzerland	53 067.7	56 183.8	57 849.6	60 108.5	61 902.2	63 939	64 215.9	66 299.6	**68 355.9**
Turkey	17 231.7	19 445.2	20 473.5	22 205	23 982.7	25 727.4	26 329.8	28 152.6	**28 413.4**
United Kingdom	36 012.7	36 820.4	37 911.3	39 505.3	40 874.3	42 051.1	42 966.7	44 896.3	**45 637**
United States	48 464.9	49 872.8	51 583.9	53 077.2	54 992.2	56 750.9	57 844.3	59 822.7	**62 502.6**

total and by type of financing ("Government/compulsory", "Out-of-pocket", "Voluntary") and is measured as a share of GDP, as a share of total health spending and in USD per capita (www.data.oecd.org).

If we look at the general situation of health expenditures in the world; for example, health expenditures in 2016, the USA is the country with the highest health expenditure in the world with17.2% based on the ratio to gross domestic product (GDP). Switzerland is followed by by12.4%. This figure is 4.3% for Turkey (OECD, 2018). Despite significant cross-country heterogeneity in health expenditure, all countries spend less than twenty percent of gross domestic product (GDP) on health care. Overall, as countries get richer, per capital expenditure on health care tends to increase).

In 2004, the WHO articulated health care as "an accessible, affordable, available, safe and comprehensive quality health service of the highest possible standard that is financially sound and founded on scientific principles to meet the present and future health needs of people, regardless of their ethnicity, geographic origin, gender or religious affiliation (WHO, 2009). In this context, the sustainability of health services depends on the provision of service inputs, the availability of consumer goods used in health services and the adequate financial resources related to them (www.who.int).

As mentioned above, the scope of health economics is stated in many ways in the literature. But Culyer (2005) is summarized as below.

- Health status and measurement
- Supply and demand for health services
- Cost-effectiveness and cost-benefit analysis
- Health insurance
- Health markets
- Financing of health services
- Treatment costs
- Workforce planning
- Medical procurement services
- Determinants of inequality in health care
- Hospital economics
- Budgeting in health services
- Regional resource allocation,
- Remuneration methods of medical personnel
- Health systems comparison

All of these elements represent the basic building blocks of a country's health care financing system. This kind of infrastructure has different dynamics that form financing strategies. Consequently, in the health market, this has a growing sector appearance, many factors that can be listed mainly as supply and demand causes health expenditures to increase. This has made health spending one of the areas where health economics has focused on the most in recent years (Tıraş & Hüseyin, 2018).

As a result, in parallel with the increasing world population, the increase in production and consumption processes brings with it many economic, social and environmental problems such as the rapid depletion of natural resources, unemployment, poverty, pollution, and disease. These problems force the public sector and the private sector to implement sustainable policies in the production of goods and services to leave a livable world for a present. The health sector is one of the most important sectors in the economic structure of countries. The health sector is one of the sectors with the highest share in the creation of a livable world due to its share in the national income and its contribution to the economic and social welfare of the country. Therefore, one of the most important responsibilities of health sector managers in implementing sustainable policies is to utilize the dynamic capabilities of the organization. In this context, it is necessary to know what dynamic capabilities mean. It is important to define the dynamic capabilities of the firms. As it is stated that companies bear to grow and die as living creatures (Kadrizade, 1986). Companies have some abilities such as adapting to a new situation and reaction to a new change as living creatures. It is called the capability of a company in literature. In this cycle, companies should survive by environmental changes and develop their capabilities in a competitive environment. Health institutions are also kind of company. So they also must cope with these environmental changes in that competitive environment. To survive and overcome the competition in this uncertain, unpredictable, dynamic and changeable environment, companies should make their capabilities more dynamic. Building these capabilities requires investment, taking many years but failure limits the future (Greaver, 1999). In this context, dynamic capability can be defined as companies' ability to change their capacity in changeable technology and environment. In particular, the dynamic capability refers to "the firm's ability to integrate, build and reconfigure both internal and external abilities to address rapidly changing environments" (Teece et.al., 1997).

DYNAMIC CAPABILITIES

Dynamic capability (DC) is defined as the ability to build and integrate new forms of competitive advantage (Teece et al., 1997; Eisenhardt & Martin, 2000) and explained as organizational-level capabilities system changes (Regner, 2008; Nieves and Haller, 2014). These are the abilities that are not imitated by others (Teece et al., 1997; Winter, 2003). Literature disagrees as to how many levels of DC exist (Ambrosini et al., 2009; Pavlou & El Sawy 2011). For this paper, we have selected Teece's framework of the three levels of dynamic capabilities which are prompting his 1997 article in the topic to become the most widely popular after that time.

Dynamic Capability is summarized by (Teece, 2007) as below:

- To sense opportunities and threats,
- To seize these opportunities and avoid these threats,
- To maintain competitiveness through enhancing and when necessary, reconfiguring the enterprises' intangible and tangible assets.

Sensing

Enterprises exist in a very fast-changing environment. Enterprises have to sense incoming and outcoming opportunities and threats created by the changing environment in a market place to be able to adapt these changes. This first dimension of DC is sensing. Sensing is the ability to recognize, understand these opportunities (Nieves & Haller, 2014).

For an enterprise to execute sensing, some activities and elements should be present:

- Managers or leaders should have correct decision-making capabilities requiring management abilities.
- The information should be distributed to employees by leaders or managers with an accurate perception of knowledge.
- Organizational knowledge should be correlated between managers and employees to improve dynamic capabilities.
- Measures should include familiarity with procedural knowledge (organizational tasks) (Nieves and Haller, 2014).
- Measures should be more declarative knowledge (Nieves and Haller, 2014).
- Measures should link to stakeholders (Teece, 2007).

Seizing

This dimension requires answering the central business model questions of when, where and how they create value (Teece, 2007). These decisions have been made to fulfill the goals of enterprises. In many manufacturing sectors, this is a critical key battleground with other firms. The adaptation to changeable technology is a difficult process, which is riddled with uncertainties due to dynamism and growth (Anand et al., 2009, p. 448).

Compatibility for sustainable business eco-systems and decision-making structure aims to ensure an opportunity has been discovered to be more effective and efficient in dynamic marketing (Kay, 2010). In this context, it explains the reason why some organizations are not being able to seize all opportunities. Thinking and seizing in a situation where the uncertainty is high is in the assessing of future resource distribution (Kahneman, 2011). These may be simply be combated with increased awareness about them, besides outside perspectives. It is also about enterprises' resource integrations. Eisenhardt and Martin identify resource integrations as product development (Nieves & Haller, 2014; Regner, 2008). This is a process that requires managing resources, ensuring continuous supply, and regulates them to the specific needs of the situation.

Reconfiguring

Sensing and seizing, two first dynamic capabilities, are used to identify opportunities in the environment. However, the last dynamic capability, called reconfiguration, is about adapting organizational assets when the opportunity changes (Ambrosini et al., 2009). Depending on the industry in a dynamic environment, changes may occur at different rates and times and therefore they require a different adjustment by the organization itself (Eisenhardt & Martin, 2000).

A dynamic capability is required for sensing and seizing by the way enterprises cope with the resistant to necessary change (Kay, 2010). Reconfiguration towards a new aim and opportunity as detected by the sensing capability takes agile leadership and management with a high level of knowledge. In other words, agile leadership and management capabilities are the organizational characteristics that should be created to develop the ability of the organization to respond to changeable situations rapidly. These features include four skills: flexibility, quickness, responsiveness, and competency. Leaders and managers need to adjust the systems, assets, and decision-making process to reach the strategic fit. They supervise the company from an internal perspective by four main functions: operation, strategy, policy, and regulation related decision-making (Kurzac & Heurich, 2015).

Reconfiguring directs incentives to avoid conflict based on changing goals. Knowledge management is an integral aspect of this dimension of DC (Nieves & Haller, 2014). This dimension involves the introduction of learning and feedback processes and intellectual property rights. In conclusion, organizations to maintain long-term alignment need to continuously examine and revise themselves. This means the organization has internally to examine if both assets and knowledge fit, and once the structures are sufficient.

CONTRIBUTION

In developed countries, most of the economic investments are allocated to public institutions (schools, hospitals, etc.). To increase the development of countries, the unemployment rate should be reduced, production (productivity) should be increased and social welfare should be kept at high levels. This creates the need for improvement and innovation in public services. Innovation is to solve existing problems with new methods, to produce and use new technologies and it is expressed as the key to ensuring sustainability in institutions (Gökçe, 2015). Sustainable development is a concept that includes countries and policies with sub-dimensions such as environmental, social and financial (Toker, 2017). The most important feature emphasized in this concept is the increase of the welfare level by meeting the needs of the present population to meet the needs of future generations, creating employment, ensuring satisfaction, and being sensitive to the environment and consumer health (Engin & Akgöz, 2013). Social responsibility and sustainability, which is one of the goals of the institutions, is undoubtedly related to the decisions of the executives and managers of that institution. In this context, to ensure the sustainability of the institutions, the executives and managers of the organization are required to realize the plans and projects designed for social benefit as well as profit in their activities using the dynamic abilities (Yıldırım & Uğuz, 2013). The dynamic capabilities that are stated as the capacity to respond quickly are the ability to use the internal and external competencies of the organization together (Teece, 2007). Dynamic capabilities have become increasingly important in the field of management and the importance of the relationship between strategic choices and environmental conditions has been emphasized (Gümüşlüoğlu, 2012; Lawson & Samson, 2001). They are necessary to adapt to the changing conditions of the enterprises. To adapt to a rapidly changing environment, enterprises must have dynamic capabilities and integrate them with management practices (Pavlov & El Sawy, 2011; Kozak & Doğantan, 2017). In today's world where globalization and competition are rapidly increasing, it is inevitable to adopt a dynamic and agile strategic perspective for sustainability in many sectors including the health sector and SMEs. It is also very important that managers in health institutions and SMEs use their dynamic skills to ensure the sustainability of their institutions. Tutar and Kılınç (2007) stated that the health sector is becoming an increasingly resourceful sector in the development of health economics. In this context, it is stated that the institutions operating in the health sector have economic, social and environmentally sustainable policies and implement these policies, which will have effects on increasing the national economy and the welfare of the society. Dynamic capabilities have been increasingly used to explain how companies gain a sustainable advantage (Parayitam & Guru-Gharana, 2010; Peteraf et al., 2013). Despite the variety of studies, this particular research considers the sustainability and structural nature of dynamic capabilities. In perspective, it is clear that these variables are founded on the importance of health institutions, SMEs routines, and managerial processes that combine to achieve adaptation to the environment. With this sense, the role of dynamic capabilities in the process is relevant because by designing and implementing a sustainable business model, it is possible to create value. This is even truer for small businesses. In this type of organization, due to the lack of resources, difficulties of social and economic factors in the external environment, and as a consequence of narrow internal scope and modest levels of diversification (Døving & Gooderham, 2008), dynamic capabilities are required to ensure survival for those enterprises mentioned above.

According to the results of the study mentioned above, it is seen that using the dynamic abilities of the managers working in health institutions and SMEs can positively affect the sustainability performance of the institution. This study emphasizes that these variables are related to each other. The link between health institutions, SMEs and dynamic capabilities has contributed to improving the understanding of the concept of dynamic capabilities and can also improve the knowledge about how the contemporary managerial process happens. The importance of dynamic capabilities for developing and sustaining SMEs is well-documented (Wang et al., 2015), however little is known about these capabilities are generated and appropriated within this context. In other words, the study addresses a gap in strategic management literature and practice, examining the interaction between health institutions, SMEs and dynamic capabilities in complex, fast-changing environments during industry 4.0. In this study, we present dynamic capabilities that facilitate innovative strategies in Small- and Medium-sized Enterprises and health institutions. Figure 3 shows the model of this research.

Figure 3. The Model that Dimensions of Dynamic Capabilities' Impact on Sustainability

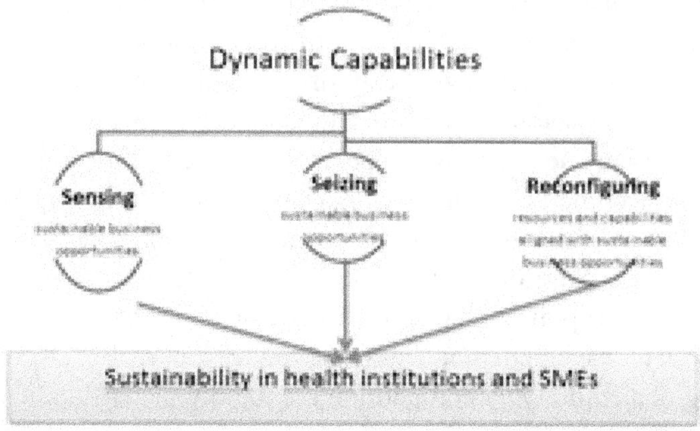

CONCLUSION

World health organization has recognized that health is as central to international development. Thus major efforts have been made to reduce morbidity and mortality either universally or through a focus on specific population subgroups (e.g. "women, elders and children "the poor"). In this context, to increase the level of development of the countries, health development should be ensured and sustainable (Buse & Hawkes, 2015). The dynamic capabilities allow organizations to adapt to the ever-changing market of assessing the abilities to sense and seize opportunities and reconfigure existing assets to meet both customer and environment new demands. In the health sector to achieve, enterprises should manage resources and the general flow of knowledge and can use their dynamic capabilities in the right place and at the right time (Akkaya & Tabak, 2017).

For many people, the main concern in their lives is their overall well-being and quality of life. In a poor economy and environment, people experience a poor quality of life. Sustainability encompasses many concepts that explain how decisions and actions can have an impact on the overall sustainability of our world. Sustainability must include a design that holistically accounts for and minimizes all aspects of economic, environmental and anthropogenic impacts. In general, sustainable components for new development would fall under the same categories as sustainability in its overall context.

To be sustainable, new development and infrastructure should complement the landscape and the area and new development should respect the natural laws of economics, the environment, and harmonize with societal values of users and residents. In other words, sustainability a set of policies, behaviors, and actions that serves to strike a balance between the rates at which we use resources and the rates at which those resources are replenished or replaced. Therefore, using of dynamic capabilities is at the heart of the sustainability ideology.

Besides, the dynamic capabilities that companies have to enable their sustainable management possible and solve social problems no longer remain in the business model for corporations alone. Not only state-run companies but also social enterprises are using their dynamic capabilities as a part of their management strategies to attain social values and achieve remarkable results (Kwon & Park, 2019). It is important to define core competencies and dynamic capabilities for public and private organizations.

They must survive by competing with economic, political, social and environmental changes to ensure sustainability (Akkaya & Tabak, 2017).

In literature, there are numerous researches on dynamic capabilities and a lot of on organizations' performance. For example, Malliari and Sirkeci (2017) studied on firms' performance of direct mail in building customer loyalty, Rozhkovet, et.al. (2017) researched the effect of workplace and performance. Odening et.al (2013) studied the dynamic efficiency under uncertainty. Attia (2016) studied the effect of quality management practices on the company's performance while Akkaya and Tabak (2017) studied the relationship between dynamic capabilities and firms' performance. However, there is a gap in the literature to explain the link between dynamic capabilities and sustainability in health institutions.

REFERENCES

Akdağ, R. (2011). *Kamu Hastanelerinin Genel Verimlik Değerlendirmesi*. Ankara: Araştırma Raporu, Sağlık Bakanlığı.

Akkaya, B., & Tabak, A. (2017). The impact of dynamic capabilities on firm perceived marketing performance of small and medium-sized enterprises. Transnational Marketing Journal, 5(2), 121–125. doi:10.33182/tmj.v5i2.383

Ambrosini, V., Bowman, C., & Collier, N. (2009). Dynamic capabilities: An exploration of how firms renew their resource base. *British Journal of Management*, *20*, 1–41. doi:10.1111/j.1467-8551.2008.00610.x

Aminuddin, A. S. A., & Nawawi, M. K. M. Investigation of the Philosophy Practised in Green and Lean Manufacturing Management International Journal of Customer Relationship Marketing and Management, 4(1), 1-12, January-March 2013. http://www.oecd.org/els/health-systems/health-data.htm

Anand, G., Ward, P., Tatikonda, M., & Schilling, D. (2009). Dynamic capabilities through continuous improvement infrastructure. *Journal of Operations Management*, *27*(6), 444–461. doi:10.1016/j.jom.2009.02.002

Attia, A. M. (2016). Effect of quality management on supply chain and organizational performance in the Egyptian textile industry. *International Journal of Business Performance Management*, *17*(2), 198–222. doi:10.1504/IJBPM.2016.075549

Baumgartner, R. J., & Ebner, D. (2010). Corporate sustainability strategies: Sustainability profiles and maturity levels. *Sustainable Development*, *18*(2), 76–89. doi:10.1002/sd.447

Bell, D. V., & Cheung, Y. K. A. (Eds.). (2009). *Introduction to Sustainable Development-Volume I*. EOLSS Publications.

Brown, K., & Siri, E. (2012). Sustainable adaptation to climate change: prioritizing social equity and environmental integrity. Routledge. doi:10.4324/9781849776912

Buse, K., & Howkes, S. (2015). Health in the sustainable development goals: Ready for a paradigm shift? *Globalization and Health*, *11*(1), 13. doi:10.1186/s12992-015-0098-8 PubMed

Çalışkan, A. Ö. (2012). Sürdürülebilirlik Raporlaması. Muhasebe ve Vergi Uygulamalari Dergisi (MUVU). *Journal of Accounting & Taxation Studies*, *5*(1).

Cavagnaro, E., & George, H. (2017). The three levels of sustainability. Routledge. doi:10.4324/9781351277969

Caymaz, E., Soran, S., & Erenel, F. (2014). The Relationship Between Corporate Sustainability And Corporate Social Responsibility In Business: Global Compact Turkey. *Journal of Management, Marketing, and Logistics.*, *1*(3), 208–217.

Çelik, Y. (2006). Sürdürülebilir kalkınma kavramı ve sağlık. *Hacettepe Sağlık İdaresi Dergisi*, *9*(1), 19–37.

Choi, S., & Ng, A. (2011). Environmental and economic dimensions of sustainability and price effects on consumer responses. *Journal of Business Ethics*, *104*(2), 269–282. doi:10.1007/s10551-011-0908-8

Culyer, A. J. (2005). Involving stakeholders in health care decisions: The experience of the National Institute for Health and Clinical Excellence (NICE) in England and Wales. *Healthcare Quarterly*, *8*(3), 56–60. doi:10.12927/hcq..17155 PubMed

Dempsey, N., Bramley, G., Power, S., & Brown, C. (2011). The Social Dimension of Sustainable Development: Defining Urban Social Sustainability. *Sustainable Development*, *19*(5), 289–300. doi:10.1002/sd.417

Doane, D. & MacGillivray, A. (2001). Economic Sustainability: The Business of Staying in Business. The SIGMA Project, R&D Report.

Døving, E., & Gooderham, P. N. (2008). Dynamic Capabilities As Antecedents Of The Scope Of Related Diversification: The Case Of Small Firm Accountancy Practices. *Strategic Management Journal*, *29*(8), 841–857. doi:10.1002/smj.683

Eisenhardt, K., & Martin, J. (2000). Dynamic Capabilities. What are they. *Strategic Management Journal*, *21*(10-11), 1105–1122. doi:10.1002/1097-0266(200010/11)21:10/11<1105::AID-SMJ133>3.0.CO;2-E

Engin, E., & Akgöz, B. E. (2013). Sürdürülebilir Kalkınma ve Kurumsal Sürdürülebilirlik Çerçevesinde Kurumsal Sosyal Sorumluluk Kavramının Değerlendirilmesi. *Selçuk Üniversitesi İletişim Fakültesi Akademik Dergisi*, *8*(1), 85–94.

Esmaeilian, B., Behdad, S., & Wang, B. (2016). The evolution and future of manufacturing: A review. *Journal of Manufacturing Systems*, *39*, 79–100. doi:10.1016/j.jmsy.2016.03.001

Gökçe, S. G. (2015). Kamuda İnovasyon ve Türkiye'deki Uygulamaları. *Journal of International Management and Social Researches*, *3*(1), 28–37.

Greaver, M. F. (1999). *Strategic outsourcing: a structured approach to outsourcing decisions and initiatives*. AMACOM Div American Mgmt Assn.

Gümüşlüoğlu, L. (2012). Dinamik Yeteneklerin Yeni Ürün Geliştirme Performansı Üzerine Etkileri. *Farklı İş Stratejileri İçin Sonuçlar, İktisat, İşletme ve Finans*, *27*(320), 61–90.

Hallstedt, S. I. (2017). Sustainability criteria and sustainability compliance index for decision support in product development. *Journal of Cleaner Production*, *140*, 251–266. doi:10.1016/j.jclepro.2015.06.068

Harris, J. M. (2003). Sustainability and Sustainable Development. Retrieved from https://www.researchgate.net/publication/23739820

Iqbal, Q. (2018). The era of environmental sustainability: Ensuring that sustainability stands on human resource management. *Global Business Review*, ▪▪▪, 0972150918778967.

Iqbal, Q., Ahmad, N. H., & Ahmad, B. (2018). Enhancing sustainable performance through job characteristics via workplace spirituality: A study on SMEs. Journal of Science and Technology Policy Management. https://doi.org/ doi:10.1108/JSTPM-02-2018-0022

Iqbal, Q., & Hassan, S. H. (2018). Green management matters: Green human resource management as blue ocean strategy. Firms' Strategic Decisions. Theoretical and Empirical Findings, 3, 214–236. doi:10.2174/9781681086255118030014

Kadrizade, R. (1986). *İşletmelerde Büyüme ve Türkiye'deki İşletmelerde Büyüme Büyüklük ve Karlılık İlişkileri*. İstanbul: Yüksek Lisans Tezi, İstanbul Üniversitesi, Sosyal Bilimler Enstitüsü.

Kahneman, D. (2011). *Thinking, fast and slow* (1st ed.). New York: Farrar, Straus and Giroux.

Kay, N. (2010). Dynamic capabilities as context: The role of decision, system, and structure. *Industrial and Corporate Change*, *19*(4), 1205–1223. doi:10.1093/icc/dtq028

Kazamia, K. I., & Kafaridou, M. (2018). An Interdisciplinary Approach to Three-Dımensional Sustainable Design. *The International Journal of the Arts in Society*, *11*(1), 35–43.

Kozak, A. M., & Doğantan, E. (2017). Dinamik Yeteneklerin Stratejik Planı Aracılığıyla Analizi: Bir Kamu Kurumu Örneği. *Turizm Akademik Dergisi*, *4*(1), 49–63.

Kurzac, K., & Heurich, C. (2015). *Connecting Project Interdependency Management to Dynamic Capabilities: Police Scotland's Transformation*. Academic Press.

Kuşat, N. (2012). Organizational Sustainability For Sustainable Corporations And Its Endogenous Determinants. *Afyon Kocatepe Üniversitesi, İİBF Dergisi*, *14*(2), 227–242.

Kwon, H. S., & Park, H. C. (2019). Creating Sustainable and Climate Shared Value in Public Institution: Lessons from a Case of Korea Army Cadet Military School. *Sustainability*, *11*(14), 37–96. doi:10.3390/su11143796

Lawson, B., & Samson, D. (2001). Developing Innovation Capability in Organisations: A Dynamic Capabilities Approach. *International Journal of Innovation Management*, *5*(3), 377–400. doi:10.1142/S1363919601000427

MacInerney-May, K. (2012). The Value of Dynamic Capabilities for Strategic Management (Doctoral dissertation). Universität zu Köln.

Mackenbach, J. P. (2007). Global environmental change and human health: A public health research agenda. *Journal of Epidemiology and Community Health*, *61*(2), 92–94. doi:10.1136/jech.2005.045211 PubMed

Malliari, L., & Sirkeci, I. (2017). Performance of direct mail in building customer loyalty in Greek automotive sector during the financial crisis. *International Journal of Business Performance Management*, *18*(1), 1–24. doi:10.1504/IJBPM.2017.080841

Moore, J. E., Mascarenhas, A., Bain, J., & Straus, S. E. (2017). Developing a comprehensive definition of sustainability. *Implementation Science; IS*, *12*(1), 110. doi:10.1186/s13012-017-0637-1 PubMed

Nieves, J., & Haller, S. (2014). Building dynamic capabilities through knowledge resources. *Tourism Management*, *40*, 224–232. doi:10.1016/j.tourman.2013.06.010

Odening, M., Wagner, C., Narayana, R., & Huettel, S. (2013). Measuring dynamic efficiency under uncertainty: an application to German dairy farms. In Agricultural & Applied Economics Associations AAEA & CAES Joint Annual Meeting, Washington, DC.

OECD, (2018). Health expenditure and financing: Health expenditure indicators. OECD 157 Health Statistics (database). doi:10.1787/data00349-en

Orlitzky, M., Siegel, D. S., & Waldman, D. A. (2011). Strategic corporate social responsibility and environmental sustainability. *Business & Society*, *50*(1), 6–27. doi:10.1177/0007650310394323

Parayitam, S., & Guru-Gharana, K. (2010). Economics Of Resource Based And Dynamic Capabilities View: A Contemporary Framework. *Academy of Strategic Management Journal*, *9*(1), 83–93.

Pavlou, P. A., & El Sawy, O. A. (2011). Understanding the elusive black box of dynamic capabilities. *Decision Sciences*, *42*(1), 239–273. doi:10.1111/j.1540-5915.2010.00287.x

Peteraf, M., Stefano, G., & Verona, G. (2013). The Elephant In The Room Of Dynamic Capabilities: Bringing Two Diverging Conversations Together. *Strategic Management Journal*, ▪▪▪, 34.

Reddy, L., & Thomson, J. (2015). Environmental. In *Social and Economic Sustainability: Implications for Actuarial Science, Actuaries Institute ASTIN, AFIR/ERM, and IACA Colloquia*. Institute of Actuaries of Australia.

Regnér, P. (2008). Strategy-as-practice and dynamic capabilities: Steps towards a dynamic view of strategy. *Human Relations*, *61*(4), 565–588. doi:10.1177/0018726708091020

Resnik, D. B. (2007). Responsibility for health: Personal, social, and environmental. *Journal of Medical Ethics*, *33*(8), 444–445.

Rozhkov, M., Cheung, B. C., & Tsui, E. (2017). Workplace context and its effect on individual competencies and performance in work teams. *International Journal of Business Performance Management*, *18*(1), 49–81. doi:10.1504/IJBPM.2017.080842

Tamer, G. (2018). Sağlık Kuruluşlarında Sürdürülebilirlik; Özel Sağlık Kuruluşlarında Bir Araştırma. Retrieved from gelisim.edu.tr/xmlui/bitstream/handle/11363/1284/17

Teece, D. (2007). Explicating dynamic capabilities: The nature and microfoundations of (sustainable) enterprise performance. *Strategic Management Journal*, *28*(13), 1319–1350. doi:10.1002/smj.640

Teece, D., Pisano, G., & Shuen, A. (1997). Dynamic Capabilities and Strategic Management. *Strategic Management Journal*, *18*(7), 509–533. doi:10.1002/(SICI)1097-0266(199708)18:7<509::AID-SMJ882>3.0.CO;2-Z

Tıraş, H. H., & Hüseyin, A. (2018). OECD Ülkelerinde Sağlık Harcamaları ve Ekonomik Büyüme İlişkisi: Panel Nedensellik Analizleri. Siyaset, Ekonomi ve Yönetim Araştırmaları Dergisi, 6(4).

Toker, K., & Çınar, F. (2017). Sağlık Sektöründe Kurumsal Sürdürülebilirlik Yönetimi ve İstanbul Avrupa Yakasında Faaliyette Bulunan Hastanelerde Bir Araştırma [Institutional Sustainability Management in the Health Sector and a Research on the Hospitals in European Side of İstanbul]. *International Conference on Eurasian Economies*.

Toker, K. (2017). *Tedarik Ağları, Sürdürülebilirlik ve Değer. İşletmelerde Sürdürülebilirlik Dinamikleri*. İstanbul: Beta.

Turhan, D. G., Özen, T., & Albayrak, R. S. (2018). Kurumsal Sürdürülebilirlik Kavramı, Stratejik Önemi ve Sürdürülebilirlik Performansı Ölçümü: Literatür Çalışması [Corporate Sustaınabılıty Concept, Strategıcal Importance and Measuring Sustaınability Performance: A Literature Review]. *Ege Stratejik Araştırmalar Dergisi*, *9*(1), 17–37.

Tutar, F., & Kılınç, N. (2007). Türkiye'nin Sağlık Sektöründeki Ekonomik Gelişmişlik Potansiyeli ve Farklı Ülke Örnekleriyle Mukayesesi. Afyon Kocatepe Üniversitesi İ.İ.B.F. *Dergisi*, *9*(1), 31–54.

Winter, S. (2003). Understanding Dynamic Capabilities. *Strategic Management Journal*, *24*(10), 991–995. doi:10.1002/smj.318

KEY TERMS AND DEFINITIONS

Corporate Sustainability: It is an approach aiming to create long-term stakeholder value through the implementation of a business strategy that focuses on the ethical, cultural, social, economic and environmental dimensions of doing business.

Dynamic Capabilities: It is the ability of a firm or organization to learn new methods occurred to produce and serve and to meet the needs of customers according to environmental and technological changes.

Economic Sustainability: The general definition of economic sustainability is the ability of an economy to support a defined level of economic production indefinitely.

Environmental Sustainability: It is concerned with whether environmental resources will be protected and maintained for future generations. Of the three pillars, the most important is environmental sustainability. If this is not solved, then no matter how hard we try the other pillars cannot be made strong because they are dependent on the greater system they live within, the environment.

Gross Domestic Product (GDP): It is the total monetary or market value of all the finished goods and services produced within a country's borders in a specific period. As a broad measure of overall domestic production, it functions as a comprehensive scorecard of the country's economic health. The top economic goal of most nations is growth. If a country's GDP goes flat, that's stagnation. If it falls for more than two quarters is an economic decline. No country has a GDP growth target of less than about 2%, except when recovering from a recession. Therefore, the de facto definition of economic sustainability is steady growth in total national GDP of a minimum of about 2% per year.

Social Sustainability: It is the ability of a social system, such as a country, family, or organization, to function at a defined level of social wellbeing and harmony indefinitely. Problems like poverty, war, widespread injustice, and low education rates are symptoms a system is socially unsustainable.

Sustainability: Meeting the needs of the present generation without compromising the ability of future generations to meet their own needs.

APPENDIX

Table 2. Core Competencies and Dynamic Capabilities Features

Core Competencies	Dynamic Capabilities	Core Competencies and Dynamic Capabilities
Static	Dynamic	Can not be marketed
Routine, protect firms abilities	Adapt abilities to change and time	Flexible
Learnt collectively	Learnt by new situation	Long-Short term
The main power company has	Company's main power correct usage	The information necessary for business goals
They use resources and assets in a specific strategy	They are used by rearranging the resources and assets according to the environment and technology	Take a basic role in the decision-making process
Can be duplicated, imitated, reproducible by competitors	Cannot be duplicated, imitated, reproducible by competitors	Customer benefits
Strategy to protect existing abilities	Strategy for improving existing capabilities	Provide a competitive advantage
Routines related to operational functions	Ability to change company routines	Goal to company sustainability
Mostly directed by Top Level Managers	It takes place in line with the ideas of R & D, Marketing, Production department together with Top Level Managers	Intent to increase the Business Performance
Resistance to changes	Adaptation to change	Sustain with change
Learned slowly and takes time	Learned quickly	Learn
Focus on basic production	Focus on agile production	Production maximization
Coordination	Learning	Integration

Source: Akkaya, B., & Tabak, A. (2017). The impact of dynamic capabilities on firm perceived marketing performance of small and medium-sized enterprises. Transnational Marketing Journal, 5(2), pp.121-125.

There have been many studies on the effect of dynamic capabilities on firm performance. While dynamic capabilities research has uncovered the characteristics of resources and capabilities and the market conditions that permit sustainable competitive advantage (e.g., Teece, Pisano and Shuen, 1997.), we have not met how the dimension of dynamic capabilities affects on firm marketing performance in literature. In this paper, we attempt to address this gap in dynamic capability literature by conceptually and analytically linking three dynamic dimensions (sensing, seizing, and configuration) with firm performance (Akkaya & Tabak, 2017).

The basic premise adopted in this paper is that dynamic capabilities are indirectly linked with firm marketing performance. While Teece (1997, 2007) states that the main reason a company to reach success or fail is to have dynamic capabilities or not, Eisenhardt and Martin (2000) states these capabilities provide competitive advantage by itself,(in other words, for being not imitated and transferred by competitors dynamic capabilities provide competitive advantage) but they can not survive competitive advantage because competitors can independently develop these in different ways and have similar dynamic abilities (Akkaya & Tabak, 2017).

In literature, there are many pieces of research on dynamic capabilities and numerous on company performance. However, there is a gap in the literature to explain the link between dynamic capabilities and firm perceived marketing performance (Akkaya & Tabak, 2017).

Chapter 5
Sustainable Performance of Tunisian SMEs in Industry 4.0

Abdullah Abdulaziz Alhumaidan
Universiti Sains Malaysia, Malaysia

Noor Hazlina Ahmad
Universiti Sains Malaysia, Malaysia

ABSTRACT

The research aims to know the impact of sustainability orientation on sustainable performance. The data has been collected through a survey and the probability-random sampling technique has been employed. The study sample is micro and small enterprises in Tunisia. The organizational level is the unit of analysis, which are the owners of these enterprises. It has been concluded that managers' orientations have an influence on environmental and social performance, but their orientations towards sustainability did not impact economic performance. The study has suggested that future research could investigate different organizations irrespective of their size and industry that would make it easy to generalize results.

DOI: 10.4018/978-1-7998-2577-7.ch005

INTRODUCTION

Enterprises have faced challenging circumstances to maintain their competitive positions in the business arena (Ubius, Alas, & Vanhala, 2009). Practitioners and academics have shown a noteworthy concern about environmental challenges (Iqbal, Ahmad, & Ahmad, 2018). Rules of games are changing over time, and enterprises have to cope with such a dynamic environment to keep their success. However, performing sustainably could illustrate an organization social legitimacy, and it improves clients' loyalty, which in turn improves the firm's market value (Luo & Bhattacharya, 2009; Fisman, Heal, & Nair, 2008). Moreover, sustainability contributes to the reduction of costs for daily bases operations; for instance, energy consumption (Maletic et al., 2015; Schaltegger & Burritt, 2010).

However, different variables can affect sustainable performance of firms such as sustainability awareness because it is viewed by many managers as a key driver of desirable achievement of organizations (Bos-Brouwers, 2010). But, the central concern is the commitment of the managers to ecology and social issues (Galpin, Whittington, & Bell, 2015). Several studies show that people backgrounds affect their choices and decisions consequently, hence, affect an enterprise outcome (Okoreley & Nkrumah, 2012; Kassel, 2012). As a result, it improves the economic value (Maletic et al., 2015). Nevertheless, desirable achievements may not be obtained without the social attitudes of enterprises leaders (Ciemleja & Lace, 2011; Ciasullo & Troisi, 2013).

Notably, the majority of background studies have investigated managers among larger corporations, and we know little about smaller firms' owners' orientations (Windolph, Schaltegger, & Herzig, 2014, Gao, 2017). Besides, these attempts are carried out in fragmented attempts such as only one aspect of sustainability (i.e. environment, social, economic) (Papagiannakis & Lioukas, 2012). This represents an obvious gap in the domain of sustainable performance in the context of SMEs wherein the owners-managers often are ones who are responsible for enterprises plans and decisions (du Plessis & Grobler, 2014; Baumgartner, 2014). Hence, despite those contributions, examining all sustainable dimensions in single research could enrich its field (Harik, El-Hachem, Medini, & Bernard, 2015).

Thus, the study aims to address previous literature gaps, mainly, to investigate the relationship between sustainable performance (economic, environmental and social) and sustainability orientation across smaller enterprises.

TUNISIAN'S SMES IN INDUSTRY 4.0

Disruptive technologies of industry 4.0 such as big data, robots, 3D printing, artificial intelligence, vertical and horizontal integration have made the market highly dynamic (Iqbal & Nawaz, 2019). Tunisian's small and medium enterprises face high challenging circumstances to cope with the dynamic- global environment (Harik et al., 2015). These enterprises mainly across the industry sector depend significantly on exporting to other countries (Franzoni, 2015). However, they should take into account factors such as revolution on the industry, and that they are in the era of the fourth industry radical evolution (Franzoni, 2015). Further, enterprises can take proactive steps to keep their market share and develop them (Alikaj et al., 2017). Otherwise, remaining on current inputs and operations could not lead to better performance or even protecting their positions in the market (Franzoni, 2015). Therefore, Tunisian's SMEs have to rethink their processes to meet customers' expectations, as a result, they will be satisfied and loyal.

However, Tunisian's SMEs should have tools to secure needed information, and they have to be flexible to adapt and change any process (OBG, 2016). Due to it, they depend widely on exportation, their speed to adapt and/or adopt new procedures and ideas are crucial to keep their clients satisfied (OBG, 2016). Further, many SMEs in Tunisia are dealing with other businesses (i.e. B2B) and they have to share knowledge. This sharing is based on using modern technologies; in other words, many of previous tools for contacting and exchanging knowledge with others may need to be developed or even changed (Chtourou & Triki, 2017). Thus, keeping a business effective and efficient, managers need to expand their knowledge and to take into consideration new developments in technology.

On the other hand, these types of enterprises face many challenges to cope with new technologies and accruing knowledge (El-Khasawneh, 2012). The main reason is a financial dilemma, owners believe that new techniques need more resources and they do not have enough budget to do so, which lead them to adopt changes incrementally rather than radically (Franzoni, 2015; Harik et al., 2015). Further, they argue that they need more employees for new technology and machines. In other words, the time for hiring and/or training workers can be seen to have more cost at least for the short-term (Chtourou & Triki, 2017). However, industry 4.0 can reduce cost for the long-run, but each manufacturer has its context; therefore, they should put forward a plan to overcome challenging issues (El-Khasawneh, 2012).

Even though many SMEs in Tunisia has taken further steps regarding industry 4.0, others are still depending on old strategies and technics (Franzoni, 2015). However, new technologies are not a choice anymore (Harik et al., 2015). In other words, competitors can take advantage of knowledge and technology, which lead to missing out on current or/and future customers since rivals are proactive (Alikaj et al., 2017). For example, larger organizations, who deal with smaller enterprises, select SMEs for different reasons, and a crucial reason is how selected enterprises are engaging in advanced technology. Thus, smaller firms have to reassure that they comply with new techniques regardless of their industrial sector.

Although many of medium manufacturers in Tunisia have renewed and developed some processes to cope with industry 4.0, smaller factories have yet to do so perfectly (Ben Salem & Zouaoui, 2017). Regardless of new small-sized manufacturers that have entered the market recently, many old ones still use old technologies and machines (Franzoni, 2015). However, it can be understood that medium enterprises have more knowledge and resources; smaller types should take industry 4.0 as an investment for long term vision rather than is just additional costs (Ben Salem & Zouaoui, 2017). In other words, the business arena is changing rapidly, and those firms have to keep their processes at low costs to be competitive in such a trade environment (Harik et al., 2015). Hence, SMEs in Tunisia need creative strategies to cope with rapid changes in the business domain.

SUSTAINABLE ORIENTATION AND SUSTAINABLE PERFORMANCE

The sustainable performance field has grown rapidly, and literature has highlighted its measures and advantages. However, studies have provided diverse views and motivations to explain its importance, and they have pointed out why sustainability should be a strategic objective.

Sustainable performance has been seen differently; for instance, Laitinen (2002) considered it as an enterprise ability to achieve its environmental and social objectives. Wood (1991) has focused on a firm practices and defined it as outcomes of an organization as a result of its social policies. Whereas McWilliams et al., (2006) have concentrated on societal benefits and observed it as an evaluation of the level and the degree that a corporation has achieved social benefits and that should go beyond financial profits. Elkington (2004) defined it as the firm's outcomes because of performing socially, environmentally and economically. Artiach, Lee, Nelson, and Walker (2010) see sustainable performance as a governance factor to determine the level of effectiveness of the organization's performance. According to Iqbal, Ahmad, et al. (2018), workplace spirituality mediate the association between job characteristics and sustainable performance.

Sustainable performance can provide numerous advantages for companies due to its ability to show enterprise planned goals whether financially or non-financially (Vincenza Ciasullo & Troisi, 2013). It provides a pure picture of enterprises' outcomes in different dimensions (i.e. economic, social, and environmental) with focusing on the requirements of efficiency and effectiveness in these factors (Dyllick & Hockerts, 2002). However, those components can show an organization social legitimacy, satisfaction, efficient consumption of resources, the loyalty of clients, brand equity, and consequently improve the enterprise's market share (Luo & Bhattacharya, 2009; Fisman, Heal, & Nair, 2008). Additionally, it contributes to costs and enhances energy consumption (Maletic et al., 2015), improves the financial outcome (Adams, 2002). Similarly, sustainable performance emerges out of the blue ocean strategy employed across organizations (Iqbal & Hassan, 2018). On the other side, Iqbal, Hassan, Akhtar, and Khan (2018) have concluded that employees' green behaviors such as working sustainably, conserving, avoiding harm, influencing others and taking the initiative to have a significant influence on sustainable performance in the manufacturing industry of Pakistan. Besides minimizing risks, enterprises might espouse a differentiation strategy since their products are different from their competitors (Schaltegger & Burritt, 2010).

However, sustainable performance factors have gained vary attention; for example, social sustainability receives less attention in the business field in comparison with economic and environmental performance (Seuring & Muller, 2008). McWilliams et al., (2006) have argued that social sustainability is beyond the financial profits of an enterprise. Further, Gadenne et al., (2012) pointed out that businesses' societal practices contribute to social performance since these activities have significant contributions to local community wellbeing and development. This engagement enhances a firm's image, also it improves interchangeable confidence with stakeholders (Mishra & Suar, 2013; Castaldo et al., 2009). Moreover, Iqbal and Hassan (2018) have emphasized the enhancement of green human resource practices on organizations as it is equivalent to the blue ocean strategy.

Ngai, Chau, Lo, & Lei, (2014) suggested that for scrutinizing sustainable performance, there is a need to understand enterprises owner's inspiration to be sustainable. For example, they argue that managers have different motivations to do so, and internal factors such as orientations are crucial since they have the main role in seniors' behavior regardless of tangible profits. Hence, examining sustainable performance without understanding owners' motivators could not lead to a clear picture (Ngai et al., 2014).

Horlings (2015) has argued that orientations can be realized as what an individual considers important in his/her life. Illies and Reiter-Palmon (2008) put forward these individuals during their lives to build up expectable behavior preferences, which reflect their priorities and system hierarchy. Chandrakumara (2011) has suggested that what people prioritize and how those preferences are central relatively to another, which may shape their orientations. Schwartz (1996) has claimed that different priorities of managers might influence their thoughts for social and environmental practices.

Priorities of orientations are changing over time and for different reasons (Chandrakumara, 2011). For instance, persons can choose acting in a way that is inconsistent alongside their sustainability orientation (Illies & Reiter-Palmon, 2008). On the other hand, literature illustrates that individuals' inner characteristics are never completely explained individual behavior or action, and in several cases values can be violated (Kennedy et al., 2009). Additionally, since individuals' features can be changed rapidly; social and environmental priorities will be affected (Vaske, Donnelly, Williams, & Jonker, 2001). Hence, orientations do not always decide the behavior, in other words, seniors may have some views on a certain issue, but they do rather else and sometimes might be recognized as contradictory (Collins et al., 2007).

According to Papagiannakis and Lioukas (2012), owners factors such as orientations affect the process of firms' strategic choices as Upper Echelon Theory (UET) suggested, in consequence, the organization's outcome. Hambrick and Mason (1984) have argued that strategic seniors address different issues based on their background such as experiences, values, orientations, ages and in many cases decisions have been taken based on them; thus, the enterprise performance is directly impacted. For these reasons, it has been proposed that understanding performance will be started by examining owners' traits (Hambrick & Mason, 1984). Therefore, UET could provide a clarification of the role of owners' decisions regarding social activities and the company's performance (Manner, 2010). Thus, the manager's background could strengthen or weaken the enterprise engaging in social activities, which can influence the outcome (Hambrick & Mason, 1984).

However, due to UET focuses on managers' antecedents, we need to take into account the differences across them, and how do these variations influence a firm's outcome (Mazutis, 2013). Finkelstein, Hambrick, and Cannella, (2009) have proposed that owners take the external circumstances over their orientations to limit the space of vision to affect the way of how they realize the dynamic changes in the business arena.

Hence, we need to know more about owners' sustainability orientation impact on sustainable performance because studies could not highlight them clearly (Waldman et al., 2006; Claudy et al., 2016; Sung & Park, 2018). Therefore, the research proposed the following hypotheses:

H1: There is an impact of sustainability orientation on economic performance.
H2: There is an impact of sustainability orientation on social performance.
H3: There is an impact of sustainability orientation on environmentally performance.

METHODOLOGY

Population and Sample

The population for the study is micro and small manufacturers in Tunisia. National Register Enterprises (NRE) has classified them in Tunisia as a firm that employs less than 50 workers (INS, 2017). The sector contributes about 76% of the state total export (Mattoussi & Ayadi, 2017; OBG, 2016; INS, 2017). Moreover, those enterprises contribute significantly to the industrial sector across the globe, particularly, in underdeveloped areas, for instance, innovation, employment, production, etc. (Sajan et al., 2017). Further, these enterprises diffuse across rural areas and have a significant role in their economy and development. However, due to every element of the population has an equivalent chance to be a unit of the sample, probability-random sampling technique is chosen to achieve research goals.

Research Design

A quantitative method has been adopted to examine the relationship between owners' sustainability orientation and enterprises' sustainable performance. The study conducted across-sectional approach that is dependent and independent variables were measured simultaneously, to collect needed data, a survey has been conducted to achieve the objective.

Measurement

The study investigated two variables, sustainability orientation, and that can be seen as owners views in integrating social and ecological considerations in the manufacturer's plans, and (Kuckertz & Wagner, 2010) scale has been adopted. The second factor is sustainable performance, which can be defined as a factory's ability to perform socially, environmentally, and economically (Iqbal et al., 2018; Pierto, 2012). It has been assessed through environmental, social, and economic sustainable performance over the last three years (Golini et al., 2014), and it has adopted (Iqbal, Ahmad, et al. 2018; Pierto, 2012) scales. The same measurement scale has been employed by Iqbal (2018) and Iqbal, Ahmad, et al. (2018) in their studies which were conducted across SMEs. Iqbal (2018) has measured sustainable performance as a second-order construct. But this study has investigated sustainable performance as the first-order construct. The research has used Statistical Package for Social Science (SPSS) for analyzing the collected data.

RESULTS

Following table 1, descriptive analysis shows variables means and standard deviations. The highest value is for managers' sustainability orientation, which is (3.69). On the other hand, the lowest scores were economic sustainable performance (2.27) and social sustainable performance (2.87).

Table 1. Descriptive Statistics

Variable	N	Mean	Std. Deviation
Sustainability Orientation	87	3.69	.510
Economic Sustainable Performance	87	2.27	.606
Social Sustainable Performance	87	2.87	.616
Environmental Sustainable Performance	87	2.92	.560

Source: Authors' Own

In table 2 a correlation matrix has been provided to identify the nature of the association across those variables. The correlation between sustainability orientation and economic sustainable performance is weak because of R^2 is .001 and R is .036. However, sustainability orientation and social, environmental sustainable performance values were medium since R values are .312 and .310 respectively.

Table 2. Correlation Matrix

Independent Variable Dependent Variable R R^2
Sustainability Orientation Economic Sustainable Performance.036.001
Sustainability Orientation Social Sustainable Performance.312.097
Sustainability Orientation Environmental Sustainable Performance.310.096

Source: Authors' Own

The following table has illustrated the role of owners' sustainability orientation on sustainable performance. For instance, table 3 shows that enterprises managers' orientation does not affect economic sustainable performance since the t-test value is -.328 and P-value is .744. Hence, the first hypothesis has been rejected **due to** is not significant.

Table 3. Regression Coefficients

Independent Variable Unstandardized Coefficients Standardized Coefficients t-value P-value
B Beta
(Constant) 2.431
Sustainability Orientation -.042 -.036 -.328.744

Source: Authors' Own
Note: Dependent Variable: Economic Sustainable Performance
* Significant at 0.05 level

Moreover, social sustainable performance is found to be influenced by enterprise owners' orientation toward sustainability. Table 4 depicts the analysis of data that the t-value was 3.025 and is significant since P-value is .003. Additionally, the beta of this association is more than 31%. Therefore, the second hypothesis was accepted, in which owners' sustainability orientation has an impact on small manufacturers' social sustainable performance.

Table 4. Regression Coefficients

Independent Variable Unstandardized Coefficients Standardized Coefficients t-value P-value
B Beta
(Constant) 1.485
Sustainability Orientation .376 .312 3.025 .003*

Source: Authors' Own
Note: Dependent Variable: Social Sustainable Performance
* Significant at 0.05 level

Table 5. Regression Coefficients

Independent Variable	Unstandardized Coefficients	Standardized Coefficients	t-value	P-value
	B	Beta		
(Constant)	1.667			
Sustainability Orientation	.340	.310	3.007	.003*

Source: Authors' Own
Note: Dependent Variable: Environmental Sustainable Performance
* Significant at 0.05 level

Table 5 provides the influence of managers' sustainability orientation on environmental sustainable performance. This hypothesis has been proved since the t-value is 3.007 and is significant due to P-value is .003; besides, the beta of this relationship was .310. Hence, micro and small manufacturers owners' orientations toward sustainability have affected environmental and social sustainable performance. In general, social and ecological sustainable performances are influenced by micro and small enterprise owners' orientations. On the other hand, those views towards sustainability do not affect economic sustainable performance.

CONCLUSIONS

The research has investigated the role of sustainability orientation on sustainable performance, and UET has been applied. It has been found that owners' orientations towards sustainability concerns have a key role in enterprises social and environmentally sustainable performance such as literature suggested (e.g. Jamali et al., 2008; Nejati et al., 2016). On the other hand, it concluded that economic sustainable performance is not influenced by those orientations, which could be seen as paradoxical results compared with several studies. It might be justified that external circumstances have interfered with such a relationship. For instance, Tunisian's government added extra financial load against trade enterprises; consequently, economic performance has not been improved. Furthermore, the investment climate is not very steady, which can affect those types of firms because micro and small firms are sensitive in any change in the business arena in comparison with larger and medium enterprises. Therefore, these manufacturers should be aware of external factors and the government should take into account the influences of its plans on the private sector, particularly smaller enterprises.

Implications

The study has provided further arguments on the role of owners' sustainability orientation on sustainable performance. Those concepts are debatable for the last decade, and still on-going. These findings could be seen as an index of how seniors' backgrounds are crucial for determining an enterprise's outcomes. The study has applied UET due to its promises for better organizations' achievement once owners have a positive thought towards social challenges. The research also adds to the knowledge that these views can determine a firm's plans, in consequence, performance. Besides, it contributes to knowledge by shedding light on how UET can explain the impacts of individuals' features on performance and could obtain a better result.

Regarding the practical implications, small and micro manufacturers should not disregard the external business' area. In other words, even though ethical beliefs are significant for enterprises, owners have to be aware of around circumstances such as medium and larger companies do. Moreover, leaders need to believe that sustainability and its issues are an opportunity to avoid penalties and fines, mainly across manufacturers due to they consume more raw materials and generate emissions. Further, those firms need to rethink whether their thoughts towards environmental and social issues completely fit their contexts since each society differs from others. Besides, policymakers need to have better relationships with those organizations when they put forward new taxes and/or changing the existing economic policy.

Limitation and Future Research

The study has several limitations; firstly, it has examined a single independent variable, which is sustainability orientation, future research could add other factors; for example, moral perceptions and their role on enterprises strategies to understand their influences comprehensively. Secondly, they also might add a moderator or mediator variables such as the company's culture and activities since they could strengthen or weaken and explain such associations. As Iqbal, Ahmad, et al. (2018) have emphasized a positive relationship of job characteristics with a sustainable performance so further research is suggested to investigate the present framework concerning perceived job characteristics. Thirdly, the study has investigated the manufacturing sector, so other segments may be examined because they have other contexts, in consequence, it would improve our knowledge about them. Laslty, the study is cross-sectional; future research can carry out a longitudinal approach to provide further understanding. Hence, although the study has few limitations, it provides some insights about small and micro manufacturers owners' orientations and sustainable performance.

REFERENCES

Adams, A. (2002). Internal organizational factors influencing corporate social and ethical reporting: Beyond current theorizing. *Accounting, Auditing & Accountability Journal, 15*(2), 223–250. doi:10.1108/09513570210418905

Alikaj, A., Nguyen, C. N., & Medina, E. (2017). Differentiating the impact of CSR strengths and concerns on firm performance. *Journal of Management Development, 36*(3), 401–409. doi:10.1108/JMD-04-2016-0058

Artech, T., Lee, D., Nelson, D., & Walker, J. (2010). The determinants of corporate sustainability performance. *Accounting and Finance, 50*(1), 31–51. doi:10.1111/j.1467-629X.2009.00315.x

Asah, F., Fatoki, O. O., & Rungani, E. (2015). The impact of motivations, personal values, and management skills on the performance of SMEs in South Africa. *African Journal of Economic and Management Studies, 6*(3), 308–322. doi:10.1108/AJEMS-01-2013-0009

Baumgartner, R. (2014). Managing corporate sustainability and CSR: A conceptual framework combining values, strategies, and instruments contributing to sustainable development. *Corporate Social Responsibility and Environmental Management, 21*(5), 258–271. doi:10.1002/csr.1336

Ben Salem, C., & Zouaoui, M. (2017). A Taxonomic Approach for the Study of Manufacturing Tunisian SME. *Journal of Organizational Management Studies, 2017*, 1–11. doi:10.5171/2017.189595

Bos-Brouwers, H. (2010). Corporate sustainability and innovation in SMEs: Evidence of themes and activities in practices. *Business Strategy and the Environment, 19*(7), 417–453.

Chandrakumara, A. (2011). Value of values for practicing managers and leaders. *Problems and Perspectives in Management, 9*(2), 80–88.

Chtourou, H., & Triki, M. (2017). Commitment to corporate social responsibility and financial performance: A study in the Tunisian context. Social Responsibility Journal, 13(2), 370–389. doi:10.1108/SRJ-05-2016-0079

Claudy, M. C., Peterson, M., & Pagell, M. (2016). The Roles of Sustainability Orientation and Market Knowledge Competence in New Product Development Success. *Journal of Product Innovation Management, 33*, 72–85. doi:10.1111/jpim.12343

du Plessis, N., & Grobler, A. F. (2014). Achieving sustainability through strategically driven CSR in the South\nAfrican retail sector. *Public Relations Review, 40*(2), 267–277. doi:10.1016/j.pubrev.2013.11.009

Dyllick, T., & Hockerts, K. (2002). Beyond the business case for corporate sustainability. *Business Strategy and the Environment, 11*, 130–141.

Galpin, T., Whittington, L., & Bell, G. (2015). Is your sustainability strategy sustainable? Creating a culture of sustainability. *Corporate Governance, 15*(1), 1–17. doi:10.1108/CG-01-2013-0004

Gao, Y. (2017). Business leaders' values, organizational culture, and market orientation. *Journal of Strategic Marketing, 25*(1), 49–64. doi:10.1080/0965254X.2015.1076879

Hambrick, D., & Mason, P. (1984). Upper Echelons: The organization as a reflection of its top managers. *Academy of Management Review*, *9*(2), 193–206. doi:10.5465/amr.1984.4277628

Harik, R., El Hachem, W., Medini, K., & Bernard, A. (2015). Towards a holistic sustainability index for measuring the sustainability of manufacturing companies. *International Journal of Production Research*, *53*(13), 4117–4139. doi:10.1080/00207543.2014.993773

Horlings, L. (2015). Value in place; A value-oriented approach toward sustainable place-shaping. Regional Studies. *Regional Science*, *2*(1), 257–274.

Iqbal, Q. (2018). The era of environmental sustainability: Ensuring that sustainability stands on human resource management. *Global Business Review*.

Iqbal, Q., Ahmad, N. H., & Ahmad, B. (2018). Enhancing sustainable performance through job characteristics via workplace spirituality: A study on SMEs. Journal of Science and Technology Policy Management. https://doi.org/" doi:10.1108/JSTPM-02-2018-0022

Iqbal, Q., & Hassan, S. H. (2018). Green management matters: Green human resource management as a blue ocean strategy. Firms' Strategic Decisions. Theoretical and Empirical Findings, 3, 214–236. doi :10.2174/9781681086255118030014

Iqbal, Q., Hassan, S. H., Akhtar, S., & Khan, S. (2018). Employee's green behavior for environmental sustainability: A case of the banking sector in Pakistan. World Journal of Science. *Technology and Sustainable Development*, *15*(2), 118–130.

Iqbal, Q., & Nawaz, R. (2019). Rife information pollution (infollution) and virtual organizations in industry 4.0: within reality causes and consequences. In *Big Data and Knowledge Sharing in Virtual Organizations* (pp. 117–135). IGI Global; doi:10.4018/978-1-5225-7519-1.ch005.

Kassel, K. (2012). The circle of inclusion: Sustainability, CSR and the values that drive them. *Journal of Human Values*, *18*(2), 133–146. doi:10.1177/0971685812454482

Kennedy, E. H., Beckley, T. M., McFarlane, B. L., & Nadeau, S. (2009). Why we don't 'walk the talk': Understanding the environmental values/behavior gap in Canada. *Human Ecology Review*, *16*(2), 151–160.

Kuckertz, A., & Wagner, M. (2010). The influence of sustainability orientation on entrepreneurial intentions-investing the role of business experience. *Journal of Business Venturing*, *25*(5), 524–539. doi:10.1016/j.jbusvent.2009.09.001

Luo, X., & Bhattacharya, C. B. (2009). The debate over doing good: Corporate social performance, strategic marketing levers, and firm idiosyncratic risk. *Journal of Marketing*, *73*(6), 198–213. doi:10.1509/jmkg.73.6.198

Maletic, M., Maletic, D., Dahlgaard, J., Dahlgaard-Park, S. M., & Gomišcek, B. (2015). Do corporate sustainability practices enhance organizational economic performance? *International Journal of Quality and Service Sciences*, *7*(2/3), 184–200. doi:10.1108/IJQSS-02-2015-0025

Manner, M. H. (2010). The Impact of CEO Characteristics on Corporate Social Performance. *Journal of Business Ethics*, *93*(S1), 53–72. doi:10.1007/s10551-010-0626-7

Mattoussi, W., & Ayadi, M. (2017). The dynamics of exporting and innovation: Evidence from the Tunisian manufacturing sector. *Journal of African Economies*, *26*(1), 52–66. doi:10.1093/jae/ejw025

Mazutis, D. D. (2013). The CEO Effect: A Longitudinal, Multilevel Analysis of the Relationship Between Executive Orientation and Corporate Social Strategy. *Business & Society*, *52*(4), 631–648. doi:10.1177/0007650313490510

McWilliams, A., Siegel, D. S., & Wright, P. M. (2006). Corporate social responsibility: Strategic implications. *Journal of Management Studies*, *43*(1), 1–18. doi:10.1111/j.1467-6486.2006.00580.x

Mishra, S., & Suar, D. (2013). Salience and corporate responsibility towards the natural environment and financial performance of Indian manufacturing firms. *Journal of Global Responsibility*, *4*(1), 44–61. doi:10.1108/20412561311324069

Ngai, E. W. T., Chau, D. C. K., Lo, C. W. H., & Lei, C. F. (2014). Design and development of a corporate sustainability index platform for corporate sustainability performance analysis. *Journal of Engineering and Technology Management*, *34*, 63–77.

Papagiannakis, G., & Lioukas, S. (2012). Values, attitudes and perceptions of managers as predictors of corporate environmental responsiveness. *Journal of Environmental Management*, *100*, 41–51. doi:10.1016/j.jenvman.2012.01.023 PubMed

Pierto, D. (2012). Does internal and external environmental management contribute to the triple bottom line? *International Journal of Operations & Production Management*, *32*(3), 265–290. doi:10.1108/01443571211212574

Sajan, M., Shalij, P., Ramesh, A., & Biju Augustine, P. (2017). Lean manufacturing practices in Indian manufacturing SMEs and their effect on sustainability performance. *Journal of Manufacturing Technology Management*, *28*(6), 772–793. doi:10.1108/JMTM-12-2016-0188

Sami El-Khasawneh, B. (2012). Challenges and remedies of manufacturing enterprises in developing countries. *Journal of Manufacturing Technology Management*, *23*(3), 328–350. doi:10.1108/17410381211217407

Schwartz, S. (1996). Value priorities and behavior: applying a theory of integrated value systems. The Psychology of Values: The Ontario Symposium, 8, 1-24.

Seuring, S., & Muller, M. (2008). Core issues in sustainable chain management- a Delphi study. *Business Strategy and the Environment*, *17*(8), 455–466. doi:10.1002/bse.607

Ubius, U., Alas, R., & Vanhala, S. (2009). Innovation and corporate social responsibility in Estonian organizations. *Problems and Perspectives in Management*, *7*(1), 135–145.

Vincenza Ciasullo, M., & Troisi, O. (2013). Sustainable value creation in SMEs: A case study. *The TQM Journal*, *25*(1), 44–61. doi:10.1108/17542731311286423

Vincenza Ciasullo, M., & Troisi, O. (2013). Sustainable value creation in SMEs: A case study. *The TQM Journal*, *25*(1), 44–61. doi:10.1108/17542731311286423

Windolph, S., Schaltegger, S., & Herzig, C. (2014). Implementing corporate sustainability what drives the application of sustainability management tools in Germany? Sustainability Accounting Management and Policy Journal, 5(4), 378–404. doi:10.1108/SAMPJ-01-2014-0002

Zhu, Q., Sarkis, J., & Lai, K. (2008). Confirmation of a measurement model for green supply chain management practices implementation. *International Journal of Production Economics*, *111*(2), 261–273. doi:10.1016/j.ijpe.2006.11.029

Section 3

Resources and SMEs in Industry 4.0

Chapter 6
Innovation Capability for SME Biomass Industry Performance:
Perspectives of HRM, OC, KMC in Industry 4.0

Teoh Ming Fang
https://orcid.org/0000-0002-5987-8809
Universiti Sains Malaysia, Malaysia

Lee Heng Wei
https://orcid.org/0000-0002-9914-1916
UOW Malaysia KDU Penang University, Malaysia

Rajendran Muthuveloo
Universiti Sains Malaysia, Malaysia

ABSTRACT

Industry 4.0 exerts great pressure on the organization today to innovate its business model in order to stay competitive. This study examines the positive and indirect effect of human resource management, organizational culture, knowledge management capabilities on organizational performance, with the mediating effect of organizational innovation capability among small and medium-sized enterprise (SME) in biomass industry in Malaysia. In addition, this study integrates resource-based view (RBV) and dynamic capabilities theories to investigate how the organization utilize its resources and capabilities to enhance organizational performance. Data were collected using survey questionnaire from biomass SMEs located in Malaysia. Structural equation modelling (Smart PLS 3.0) was used to test and analyze the data. The findings reveal that knowledge management capability and organizational culture exert a positive influence on organizational innovation capabilities. Similarly, organizational innovation capabilities also found to positively affect organizational performance.

DOI: 10.4018/978-1-7998-2577-7.ch006

INTRODUCTION

SMEs Biomass Industry (Malaysia) in Industry 4.0

In 2018, Malaysia's small and medium enterprises (SMEs) contributed to gross domestic product (GDP) at 38.3% (RM521.7 billion) and total exports at 17.3% (RM171.9 billion) (Department of Statistics Malaysia, 2019). It shows that SMEs play a significant role in the economic growth of Malaysia. To prosper and survive in Industry 4.0, SMEs in the biomass industry require new paradigms to improve its internal resources, capabilities and organizational performance. Table 1 depicts the definition of SME in Malaysia (SME Corporation Malaysia, 2019).

Table 1. Description of Small and medium enterprise (SME)

Sector	Annual Sales Turnover	Full-time Employees
Manufacturing	≤ RM50 million	≤ 200
Service	≤ RM20 million	≤ 75

Source: SME Corporation Malaysia, 2019

Unlike other countries, Malaysia has abundant of sustainable and accessible biomass resources, such as empty fruit bunches, palm kernel shell, rice straw, wood biomass, municipal solid waste, manure, oil palm trunks and able to produce biomass output such as biopolymers, bio-energy, bio-fertilizer, bio-composites, bio-chemical (Malaysia Industry-Government Group for High Technology (MIGHT), 2013). Biomass is a carbon-neutral fuel that can assist Malaysia to reduce carbon emission intensity per unit of GDP at 45% in 2030 (World Energy Council, 2018). The renewable energy from biomass can generate electricity, reduce the dependency on 90.5% of imported coal (Hamzah, Tokimatsu, & Yoshikawa, 2019), replace fossil fuel, diesel and diminish greenhouse gas emissions in Malaysia (Mekhilef, Barimani, Safari, & Salam, 2014).

Japan, Korea, and China are the leading importer of biomass pellets (Malaysia Industry-Government Group for High Technology (MIGHT), 2013). In the year 2020, the European Union plan to consume more than 50% of biomass energy and South Korea will import up to 80% of pellets into their country (Malaysian Industry-Government Group for High Technology (MIGHT), 2014). To fulfill the global demand, Malaysian SMEs in the biomass industry should improve organizational innovation capability and performance by using digital technologies (Ministry of International Trade and Industry (MITI), 2017).As industry 4.0 comprises of cyber-physical system (CPS), internet of things (IoT), cloud computing (Iqbal & Nawaz, 2019) so SMEs in the biomass industry should incorporate these technologies to digitize the manufacturing and organizational processes. CPS is the integration of physical components, algorithms, communication and control systems that help the biomass manufacturing SMEs to have autonomous production processes and real-time control on the machines (Moeuf, Pellerin, Lamouri, Tamayo-Giraldo, & Barbaray, 2018; Vaidya, Ambad, & Bhosle, 2018; L. Da Xu, Xu, & Li, 2018). IoT technology refers to real-time communication using physical component, for instance, radio-frequency identification (RFID), mobile devices and global positioning system (GPS), in which these devices can connect with cellular network, Wi-Fi to assist managers in biomass SMEs to make decentralize decision, trace any error and changes earlier, and support improvement initiatives on operation processes (Moeuf et al., 2018; L. Da Xu et al., 2018). Cloud computing allows biomass SMEs to communicate, share information, collaborate with stakeholders globally (Moeuf et al., 2018). This can strengthen the relationship with customers, suppliers and business partners, seeking new customers worldwide and aid in penetration into a new market. Digital twins is a simulation modeling that supports new product development process, indicate precise productivity and maintenance projection based on the valid data (Rodič, 2017). Long term value creation and capture by biomass SMEs supersede the substantial capital on the investment of digital technologies. This will improve productivity and streamline the production processes to maximize the utilization of production capacity.

However, biomass SMEs faced many challenges in this Industry 4.0 era. The challenges include a lack of adequate ICT infrastructure and software, protection on confidential information, and integration process with producers, suppliers, and customers (L. Da Xu et al., 2018). Moeuf et al., (2018) conducted systematic bibliographical research on 23 case studies, found that SMEs not actively exploit digital technologies in Industry 4.0, only a few SMEs using cloud computing and RFID technology. Qualitative research by Müller, Maier, Veile, & Voigt (2017) posit that challenges of the cooperation among SMEs to purchase technology include lack of trust and coordination efforts among SMEs partners, reluctant to share the confidential information and prefer autonomy in making a purchase decision. In Malaysia context, SMEs in biomass industry has low entry barriers, in which new entrants can quickly enter biomass industry and compete with existing organizations, high dependency on imported and patented technology (not able to reproduce the required technology in Malaysia), fluctuate pricing of biomass resources and needs to follow the technical, quality, sustainability standards in foreign countries (Malaysia Industry-Government Group for High Technology (MIGHT), 2013). Another challenge includes an inconsistent supply of biomass due to different maturities of the oil palm trunks (Agensi Inovasi Malaysia, 2013). Most biomass SMEs in Malaysia is not able to produce higher-value biomass product because they are lack of expertise, engineering and technical know-how on product design, advanced technology, differentiation strategy and branding (Malaysia Industry-Government Group for High Technology (MIGHT), 2013).

In the organizational trajectory, traditional management practice is not effective in Industry 4.0. Biomass SMEs can improve their internal resources and capabilities to seize ample opportunities, response to external threats and achieve more significant market share before competitors using similar ways. Even though biomass SMEs have limited resources yet facing many challenges, Moeuf et al., (2018) advocate that SMEs have high flexibility to improve their innovation capability as compared to a large organization with rigid and centralize structure. In the contemplation to improve organizational innovation capability required effective human resource management, organizational culture, and knowledge management capabilities, which can lead to superb organizational performance.

Key Terms

1. **Human resource management:** Human resource management is the effective management of human resources in an organization to achieve organizational goals (Sabiu, Ringim, Tang, & Joarder, 2019).
2. **Organizational culture:** Organizational culture is the shared norm, values, beliefs that guide employee's behavior (Chang, Liao, & Wu, 2017) and provides an identity, coherence to an organization (Liao, Hu, Chen, & Lin, 2015).

3. **Knowledge management capabilities:** Knowledge management capabilities refer to the organization's capability to acquire, share, store, improve existing knowledge and create new knowledge that enhances organizational innovation capability (Kuo, 2011).
4. **Organizational innovation capability:** Organizational innovation capability refers to the ability of an organization to perform product, process, managerial and strategy innovation (Liao et al., 2015).
5. **Organizational performance:** Organizational performance reflects the ability of the managers and employees to achieve their business objectives and goals by using the organization's resources to perform business activities in effective and efficient ways (Jiang, Jiang, & Nakamura, 2019).
6. **Resource-based View:** Resource-based view delineates the internal resources and capabilities that possesses by an organization with the attributes which are a rarity, valuable, difficult to imitate and replace can assist the organization to respond positively to the external opportunities and threats in the long term (Barney, 1991; Sabiu et al., 2019).
7. **Dynamic Capabilities:** Dynamic capabilities theory extend the resource-based view theory, and it explains that organization needs to review, update, rearrange its existing resources and capabilities to apply new competencies in this rapidly changing environment (Miles, 2012).

LITERATURE REVIEW

Resource-Based View

The resource-based view (RBV) is the dominant theory applied in this study. Barney (1991) delineates the essential resources and capabilities possesses by an organization with the attributes such as rarity, valuable, difficult to imitate, and replace to assist the organization to respond positively to the external opportunities and threats in the long term.

RBV theory is frequently used to measure the influence of human resource management on organizational performance (Tan & Nasurdin, 2011). Sabiu, Ringim, Tang, & Joarder (2019) argue that internal resources, for instance, human resource management is intangible and valuable resources that can lead to competitive advantage, enhance an organization's competitiveness in the dynamic environment. Based on the RBV perspective, Farouk, Abu Elanain, Obeidat, & Al-Nahyan (2016) posit that effective human resource management can develop human capital and ensure the organization's survival and sustainability.

Even though intangible resources, such as, efficient business practice, organizational culture, goodwill, intellectual capital, can only be developed in long term, but it has a more significant impact than tangible resources, which can be obtained easily by rivalries (Barney, 2001). Therefore, SMEs in the biomass industry could outperform rivalries by developing its intangible resources. Fu (2015) and Yousif Al-Hakim & Hassan (2013) point out that knowledge management capability and organizational innovation capability are the strategic resources and capabilities that can lead to the successful performance of an organization. Knowledge management capabilities can contribute to business growth in the long term (Aboelmaged, 2014). An organization with strong innovation capability has a higher competitive advantage because this capability is difficult to imitate by the competing organization (Dhewanto et al., 2012).

Every organization has idiosyncratic resources and capabilities; nevertheless, RBV theory does not explain the most efficient methods to utilize these resources to achieve competitive advantage in the long run (Miles, 2012). Precisely, this theory does not imply which type of resources has the most substantial effect on organizational performance. To bridge this gap, this study will investigate how human resource management, organizational culture, knowledge management capabilities can influence biomass SME's performance in Industry 4.0, with the mediator role of organizational innovation capability.

Dynamic Capabilities Theory

Dynamic capabilities theory is known as a dynamic perspective on RBV (Araújo, Pedron, & Bitencourt, 2018) and extends the RBV theory. It indicates that the organization needs to review, update, rearrange its existing resources and capabilities to apply new capabilities in this rapidly changing environment (Miles, 2012). Dynamic capabilities refer to the organization make changes in business routines and practices with the purpose to respond promptly to external changes (Amui, Jabbour, de Sousa Jabbour, & Kannan, 2017). It shows that organizations with stronger dynamic capabilities can achieve better performance than competing organizations. Pavlou and Sawy (2011) point out that an organization can explore the internal strengths and external opportunities, reconfigure particular types of internal resources and capabilities, and subsequently apply the new competences in the dynamic marketplace.

Organizational innovation capability and knowledge management capability are dynamic capabilities than enable the organization to make changes to the existing product range, produce new products to fulfill the needs and wants of targeted customers (Araújo et al., 2018; Sáenz, Aramburu, & Rivera, 2009). The innovation capability of an organization is the dynamic capabilities that support business growth strategies and compete intensely with competitors to better financial performance (Breznik & Hisrich, 2014). An organization can formulate short-term strategies to get financial benefits instead of rearranging its existing capabilities, which is costly and time-consuming (Miles, 2012).

However, this theory has been criticized that not necessary that organization possesses dynamic capabilities can have successful performance; an organization with poor performance and remain its status quo in management system own dynamic capabilities too (Miles, 2012). This theory does not explain why some organizations with dynamic capabilities not able to achieve better organizational performance. Pavlou & Sawy (2011) remarks that there is a lack of precise and appropriate measurement to evaluate the dynamic capabilities of an organization. To fill this gap, this study will examine the influence of biomass SME's resources and capabilities on organizational performance.

Organizational Performance

Organizational performance (OP) reflects the ability of the managers and employees to achieve their business objectives and goals by using the organization's resources to perform business activities in effective and efficient ways (Jiang et al., 2019). It has been suggested that organizational performance can illustrate how well an organization achieving its predetermined goals (Terry Kim, Lee, Paek, & Lee, 2013). High performing organization has innovative, future-oriented strategies and higher competitive advantage as compared with the underperforming organization. Performance of Mexico SMEs is influenced by an organization's ability to perform product, process, and marketing innovation to achieve a higher financial growth rate (Maldonado-Guzmán, Garza-Reyes, Pinzón-Castro, & Kumar, 2019).

Organizational performance can exert a significant influence on an organization's survival and competitiveness. Excellent OP means an organization can launch new products faster than its rivalries, efficient business practice, on-time delivery and lower defect rate in the manufacturing processes (Terziovski, 2010). Prior studies using similar or slightly different dimensions to measure OP. The tangible and financial measures include profit margin, return on sales, return on assets and return on equity (Y. Wang, Bhanugopan, & Lockhart, 2015). Donkor, Donkor, Kankam-Kwarteng, and Aidoo (2018) conducted quantitative research on Ghana SMEs using sales revenue, the growth rate in sales, profitability, market share, return on sales and return on investment to measure the financial performance of an organization.

Saunila (2014) measures OP based on its operational (quality, customer satisfaction, productivity) and financial performance (profit, market share). According to the study on SMEs of the ICT industry in Malaysia, Salim & Sulaiman (2011) utilize to market and financial performance to measure OP. Market performance on profit ratio, satisfaction level of customers, market share meanwhile financial performance on return on investment, profit and growth rate of sales revenues. Due to the difficulty to collect the confidential, objective and latest data, Lu, Zhu, and Bao (2015) used subjective measurement to evaluate OP, such as competitive position, perception on sales growth and market share of an organization. Another study on Taiwan technology organizations conducted by Kuo (2011), indicated that product/ service innovation, employee retention, ability to attract recruits, customer satisfaction, the relationship between management and employees can be used to measure OP.

A large and growing body of literature has investigated the importance of OP. Research models to evaluate organizational performance have evolved from determinants that can directly influence OP to the limited studies on the indirect relationship between latent variables, mediator and OP.

Human Resource Management

Human resource management involves the effective management of human resources in an organization as a means to achieve organizational goals (Sabiu et al., 2019). Human resource management is a pivotal element that can influence organizational innovation capabilities positively (Aryanto, Fontana, & Afiff, 2015; Farouk et al., 2016; Fu, Flood, Bosak, Morris, & O'Regan, 2015; Lu et al., 2015). Effective human resource management can motivate and raise the competency level of human resources to engage in innovation activities, which in turn improves innovation capability of biomass SMEs in industry 4.0. Bos-Nehles, Renkema, & Janssen (2017) argue that training and development, constructive feedback, reward and compensation, autonomy can raise the capability of the organization to generate and execute innovative ideas. They further postulate that training and development allow employees to progress beyond their existing capabilities and using new knowledge, skills, and abilities to transform the innovative idea into a physical product. Constructive feedback is essential for those employees eagerly seeking ways to improve their innovative work behavior (Bos-Nehles et al., 2017).

HR executives in biomass SMEs can review and reconfigure HR policy to ensure it is compatible with industry 4.0. They can revise the required job description and qualification for the recruits, motivate employees to explore new methods to accomplish the projects, identify training needs for existing employees, discussion with the labor union to get their support to raise innovation capability of the organization (Bamber, Bartram, & Stanton, 2017). They further delineate that line manager can cooperate with HR for the interest of encouraging employees to take a risk, not penalize them for minor mistake when they make a risky yet innovative decision, involve employees in the decision-making process, reward employees that can create the differentiated products (Bamber et al., 2017). Indeed, experienced and senior employees are familiar with the operation, policies and working processes of an organization, and thus, they are fundamental to detect the current problem and generate blue ocean strategies. When managers trust and value their recommendations, this can further motivate them to engage themselves to improve an organization's innovation capability.

Kuo (2011) found that human resource management (effective recruitment, performance appraisal, workforce participation, compensation, training, and development) enhance the innovation capability of an organization. Likewise, both high-tech and non-high-tech industries in China, (Wang & Chen, 2013) holds the same view and further highlight that teamwork is equally important because it allows employees to discuss and finalize simplify, innovative, user-friendly operation processes to produce new products. Human capital is the organization's critical assets and resources, when HR executives hire the recruits with required attitudes/personality, for instance, adaptive to changes and innovation will help the organization respond innovatively to the rapid changes in the marketplace. Performance appraisal can measure to what extent employees achieve the preset targets and determine training needs to foster the innovation capability of an organization. Meanwhile, workforce participation in the strategy formulation aid the organization to extend the maturity stage of the product life cycle with innovative extension strategies. Compensation encourages employees to reciprocate with the organization's expected behavior. Alarmingly, without the training on the cyber-physical system (CPS), smart factory, internet of things (IoT), big data and artificial intelligence (AI), managers and employees lack comprehensive knowledge in these areas can impede their capability to produce unique and innovative ideas in industry 4.0.

Hypothesis Development

Hypothesis One: Human resource management has a positive relationship with organizational innovation capability.

Organizational Culture

Organizational culture is the shared norm, values, beliefs that guide employees' behavior (Chang et al., 2017) and provides an identity, coherence to an organization (Liao et al., 2015). Uzkurt, Kumar, Kimzan, & Eminoğlu (2013) point out that organizational culture deliberates management practice, structure, and policy. The ideology, values, rituals have an influential impact on employee attitude as compared with the formal rules and regulations (Wu, Huang, Huang, & Du, 2019). The shared values, assumptions, and philosophies embedded in the organization can influence employees' behavior to perform the task, the way they communicate in the organization and with external stakeholders; it has powerful forces on organizational innovation capability (Chang et al., 2017). According to Duong & Swierczek (2019), the data from 15 top banks in Vietnam concludes that organizational culture can improve the capability of the banks to undertake process innovation and product/service innovation.

There are different types of culture in this business world. Based on Demircan & Ert's (2010) study of Turkey SMEs, organizational culture with uncertainty avoidance has a negative relationship with organizational innovation capability. SMEs with a high level of uncertainty avoidance has a formal and rigid structure, in which employees tend to compliance with the rules and policy, reluctant to take risk and initiative to think innovatively. Conversely, a low level of uncertainty avoidance encourages employees to take the risk, incorporate new technology and software to perform tasks, seeking new opportunities and solutions to improve the innovation capability of an organization in Industry 4.0.

Another study by Sánchez-Báez, Fernández-Serrano, & Romero (2019) on 194 small organizations in Paraguay, they applied Competing Values Framework (CVF) in their study. They found that adhocracy, follow by market culture, has a direct and positive connection with the organization's capability to implement product innovation. Besides that, adhocracy culture can influence organizational, marketing, and process innovation positively; a surprisingly hierarchical culture which is an internal focus and control-oriented has a positive effect on process innovation (Sánchez-Báez et al., 2019). They further assert that adhocracy and market culture are the external focus, in which adhocracy culture prioritizes creativity, risk-taking, flexible response to the external environment, and market culture dwell on competitiveness, stability, and productivity. The hierarchical culture that practices by small organizations in developing countries is crucial as it can imitate or learn from established firms about efficient process innovation at effective cost and apply it in their organizations (Sánchez-Báez et al., 2019). In Spanish organizations, adhocracy culture can support the innovation strategies while hierarchical culture with formal rules, coordination can foster imitation initiatives and hurts the organization capability to perform product innovation (Naranjo-Valencia, Jiménez-Jiménez, & Sanz-Valle, 2011; Naranjo Valencia, Sanz Valle, & Jiménez Jiménez, 2010). In sum, this shows that not all of the four cultures in CVF (Cameron & Quinn, 2011) has a significant influence on organizational innovation capability.

Chang et al. (2017) delineate that innovative and collaborative culture has a profound influence on the organization's innovation capability. Innovative culture can raise the competency and capability of an organization to respond to a dynamic marketplace, and collaborative culture can motivate team members to exchange their knowledge and perspectives to support the innovative strategies of the organization (Chang et al., 2017). On the other hand, weak innovative and collaborative culture can restrain an organization to execute an innovation initiative and changes. Wang, Guidice, Tansky, & Wang (2010) supported Chang et al. (2017) perspectives and further depict that organizational culture with a team and innovation-oriented have utilized R&D funds effectively to enhance the organization's capability in process innovation.

Based on the154 responses collected from the top 10 innovative banks located in Turkey, Uzkurt et al. (2013) remark that innovative culture can inspire managers and employees to generate a creative solution to solve the complex problems. Also, the data from 17 SMEs in Taiwan show that an innovative culture and flexible operation strategy can influence the process innovation capability of an organization (Wu et al., 2019).

Liao et al. (2015) conducted a study on 10 Taiwan semiconductor organization, found that supportive culture, followed by innovative culture and bureaucratic culture can affect organization's innovation capability significantly, in which supportive culture has the highest impact on the improvement of innovation capability meanwhile bureaucratic culture can inhibit it. According to Liao et al. (2015) and Wallach (1983), supportive culture pertinent to working environment surrounded with trust, security, fair practice, social cohesion, encouragement, and collaboration; innovation culture refers to an organization that emphasizes on risk-taking, creativity, ability to cope with challenges and exploit new opportunities. Bureaucratic culture refers to an organization with a hierarchical structure that indicates the chain of command, responsibilities, and authority of each management level, along with systematic, organized working procedure, policy and regulation (Liao et al., 2015; Wallach, 1983).

The Organizational culture assessment instrument (OCAI) based on the Competing Values Framework was initially developed from the organizational effectiveness research (Cameron & Quinn, 2011). Hence, it may have a vague relationship between CVF and organizational innovation capability. The dimension of organizational cultures proposed by Liao et al. (2015) is adapted in this study because they emphasize the differentiation in managerial practices on organizational innovation capability.

Hypothesis Development

Hypothesis Two: Organizational culture has a positive relationship with organizational innovation capability.

Knowledge Management Capabilities

Knowledge management capabilities are the catalyst to stimulate organizational innovation capabilities of biomass SMEs in Industry 4.0. Knowledge management capabilities refer to the organization's capability to acquire, share, store, improve existing knowledge and create new knowledge that enhances organizational innovation capability (Kuo, 2011).

Knowledge management capabilities pertinent to the capability of an organization to add new knowledge into the organization with the purpose to update and replace existing knowledge, organize the knowledge accumulated from the prior experiences, store the knowledge in written form or electronic database (Nawab, Nazir, Zahid, & Fawad, 2015). They further highlighted that cultural diversity, lack of open-minded, trust, a discussion will influence the knowledge sharing effectiveness and inhibit the innovation capability of the banking industry. Managers and employees can apply the new knowledge to create innovative strategies and business plans, evaluate existing operation activities and revise it when necessary (Nawab et al., 2015).

The study on Jordan SMEs indicates that knowledge management capability has a statistically significant and direct relationship with the organization's capability to implement product and process innovation (Alshanty, Emeagwali, Ibrahim, & Alrwashdeh, 2019). The knowledge collected from external stakeholders can facilitate innovation strategies in an unpredictable environment. By sharing and combining the relevant knowledge within teams can accelerate the innovation process and create new ideas (Hussein, Singh, Farouk, & Sohal, 2016). The capability of an organization to share and transfer the knowledge among employee raise organizational innovation capability, and this is because an employee can apply and practice the new knowledge in their daily tasks and support the innovation activities (Ologbo & Nor, 2015).

According to the investigation of Xu (2015) on the top ten Chinese industrial businesses, knowledge management capabilities has a profound effect on new product development. Knowledge assets can raise the propensity of employees to perform innovation activities. When employees acquire and explore new knowledge about customer preference, the latest market trend and market knowledge, they possess the relevant knowledge to support the new product development process. In the context of Industry 4.0, an organization can use cloud computing that aid real-time management. The organization can establish a good relationship with the customer, supplier, producers to get feedback, suggestions on product improvement and competitor information (Xu, 2015). Effective communication channel in the organization allows employees to share and exchange knowledge about sophisticated production processes and technologies that can raise the productivity level efficiently and reduce defect rate. Knowledge can be share, circulate via formal, casual discussion, brainstorming session, regular meeting, and then apply it effectively at the workplace.

Interestingly, knowledge sharing can contribute to new knowledge creation that eventually improves organizational innovation capability. To do so, an organization can discard existing knowledge; take advantage of the technology revolution to produce a completely new product (Xu, 2015). Since knowledge assets are the heart of an organization, an organization can pay attention to cybersecurity, develop policy and the system to store the intellectual assets, confidential information to avoid anyone misuse it or hack by unauthorized parties.

Ultimately, prior literature indicates that there is a connection between knowledge management capabilities and innovation capability of an organization (Alshanty et al., 2019; Nawab et al., 2015; Xu, 2015; Aboelmaged, 2014; Noruzy, Dalfard, Azhdari, Nazari-Shirkouhi, & Rezazadeh, 2013).

Hypothesis Development

Hypothesis Three: Knowledge management capabilities have a positive relationship with organizational innovation capability.

Organizational Innovation Capability

Organizational innovation capability is the strategic resource of an organization. It refers to ability of an organization to produce brand new products with unique features that demanded by targeted customers, new management practice and strategies, modify and update existing machinery, using digital technologies to perform process innovation, exploit new opportunities, enter new market successfully to support growth and achieve superior organizational performance (Liao et al., 2015). Organizational innovation capability can distinguish an organization with its direct rivalries. Kuo's (2011) findings indicate that the capability of an organization to implement technological and administrative related innovation can positively influence organizational performance.

Study on 320 SMEs in Malaysia indicate that organizational innovation capability on production processes, produce distinctive products with attractive packaging, innovative marketing mix, management-related innovation, for instance, cost reduction in each functional department, changes on business practice, improve employee satisfaction, productivity resulting in better organizational performance (Salim & Sulaiman, 2011). They further explain that innovation capability is vital for both SMEs and large organizations in Malaysia. Based on the study on 308 SMEs in Mexico, Maldonado-Guzmán, Garza-Reyes, Pinzón-Castro, & Kumar (2019) support Salim and Sulaiman (2011) point of view and propose that innovation capability of an organization can enhance the competitiveness of SMEs and achieve competitive advantage.

According to Donkor, Donkor, Kankam-Kwarteng, and Aidoo (2018), a high level of innovation capability can lead to high organization's financial performance of 340 SMEs located in Ghana. In the context of Industry 4.0, IoT, together with RFID technology, can be used to manage inventory, utilize digital technology to integrate with suppliers, customer globally at a faster and cheaper way. Furthermore, using digital technologies to execute mass production and innovative production process can improve flexibility, efficiency; achieve economies of scale and lower defect rate. Digital technologies, for instance, autonomous robotics can perform the task accurately, reduce measurement error, improve product quality, and optimize production. Any mistakes and error can be traced faster before the small error ruin the whole production line. Consequently, this can be resulting in lower average costs and allow an organization to earn a higher profit.

Another study by Saunila (2014) found that organizational innovation capability has the most significant influence on an organization's financial performance compared with the operational performance of SMEs in Finland. Terziovski (2010) found that Australian SME's performance can be influenced by their ability to undertake managerial and strategy innovation, in which SMEs can benchmark these innovation initiatives implemented by established and large organizations.

Hypothesis Development

Hypothesis Four: Organizational innovation capability has a positive relationship with organizational performance.

On the other hand, human resource management, organizational culture, knowledge management capability are closely associated with organizational innovation capability, which in turn affects organizational performance indirectly.

Organizational innovation capability has a mediating effect in the relationship between human resource management and organizational performance in China service industry (Lu et al., 2015). They further explain that improvement of human resource management in recruitment, training, performance appraisal, employee motivation, and welfare can promote effective implementation of innovation strategies, resulting in superb organizational performance. According to Farouk et al. (2016), the data collected from 168 managers in UAE banks, organizational innovation capability play the full mediating roles in the relationship between human resource management and organizational performance. In the context of Industry 4.0, even though digital technologies such as AI, robotics, can imitate human work, but they are fixed with a specific algorithm, data, and setting, not flexible like a human. Indeed, not all-human capital can be replaced with digital technologies. For instance, AI not able to detect, respond proactively with any unexpected or the brand new problem that never happens before. Thus, organizations need human resources to manage, control, and incorporate digital technology to generate innovation strategies, as a means to sustain and survive in a dynamic environment. When HR executives recruit the employee with expected attitude and behaviors, for instance, recruits who can adapt to any significant changes in the workplace, prefer challenging tasks and support the organization's innovation activities, this can raise organizational innovation capability and organizational performance. Training on new technology can improve the competency level of employees, organizational innovation capability and Spanish organizational performance (Diaz-Fernandez, Bornay-Barrachina, & Lopez-Cabrales, 2015). They further point out that the most innovative organizations have a creative value-added process that can compete intensely with their rivalries.

There are inadequate studies on the indirect relationship between organizational culture and organizational performance, in which innovational organizational capability serves as the mediating variable. According to the study on 10 top banks in Turkey, Uzkurt et al. (2013) suggest that innovative organizational culture drives the capability of an organization to produce a new range of products/ services that have not offered by their competitor and create a distinctive solution. The products/services that can satisfy customer needs and wants allow the organization to earn higher market share and profit in the long term; meanwhile the distinctive strategy promote sustainability and competitive edge (Uzkurt et al., 2013). An influential culture means employees in the organization practice similar ways to accomplish their tasks, achieve the business objective and communicate with both internal, external stakeholders. This is extremely important to heighten the performance of an organization in the fast-changing environment and carry out any innovative changes in Industry 4.0. Conversely, weak culture means employees confuse with the organization's values, norms, and beliefs, resulting in poor future direction and failure to achieve organizational goals.

Organizational innovation capability mediates the relationship between knowledge management capabilities and organizational performance (Nawab et al., 2015). They further posit that the ability of the organization to disseminate, organize, apply the knowledge pertinent to Industry 4.0 and digital technologies stimulate organizational innovation capability in the banking industry and contributing to excellent bank performance. Banks can revise and revamp their existing practice to enhance efficiency and customer satisfaction. Knowledge on how to cope with internal and external changes, implement the innovation activities, and response to issues promptly can support organizational innovation capability, for instance, methods to use new technologies to produce new product and improve production planning leads to higher organizational performance. Aboelmaged (2014) delineates that when functional managers can improve knowledge management capabilities, this can boost the capability of an organization to implement management and technical innovation with the purpose to raise its performance. Besides, the relationship between knowledge management capabilities and organizational performance is partially mediated by organizational innovation capability, according to Yousif Al-Hakim & Hassan (2013).

Hypotheses Development

Hypothesis Five: Organizational innovation capability mediates the relationship between human resource management and organizational performance.
Hypothesis Six: Organizational innovation capability mediates the relationship between organizational culture and organizational performance.
Hypothesis Seven: Organizational innovation capability mediates the relationship between knowledge management capabilities and organizational performance.

RESEARCH MODEL

This study proposes a research model (Figure 1.) to investigate the mediation effect of organizational innovation capability between human resource management, organizational culture, knowledge management capabilities and organizational performance.

Figure 1. Research model

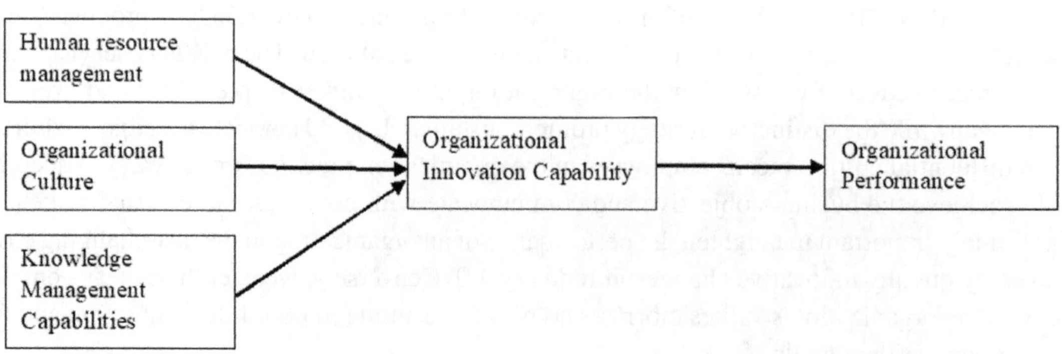

METHODOLOGY

Data Collection Method

The research population in this study refers to the organizations of the biomass industry in Malaysia. According to Matrade (2018), there are a total of 228 SMEs in the biomass industry, Malaysia. With the sampling frame provided, this study used a census sampling method to collect the data. The data collection process started with an email sent to the Chief Executive Officer (CEO) of the biomass company to ask for their permission to conduct the questionnaire survey. After the permission was granted, the researcher visited the company and delivered the questionnaire form. A power analysis was conducted to estimate the required sample size (Chin & Newstead, 1999). The output from G*Power 3.1.9.2 showed that the minimum sample required in this study was 77. A total of 130 responses were collected and used in the data analysis indicating the adequacy of the sample size. The data is subsequently analyzed using SmartPLS 3.2.8.

Measurement of Variables

A total of 35 questions were asked in the questionnaire form on demographic profiles and to measure the constructs. A five-point Likert scale was employed to measure the items. All the questions used in the questionnaire form were adapted from the literature.

Organizational Performance (OP)

The items of this construct from Terry Kim, Lee, Paek, & Lee (2013) were used in this study to evaluate biomass SMEs' performance in industry 4.0 because it includes both financial and non-financial measures and recorded Cronbach's alpha at 0.92. Their study was conducted in five-star hotels in Korea, and therefore, the authors rephrase 'our hotel' to 'our organization', which is appropriate and relevant to this study.

Human Resource Management (HRM)

The human resource management dimensions proposed by Kuo (2011) and D. Wang & Chen (2013) were widely used by prior researchers to measure human resource management, and hence, it was adapted in this study. Effective recruitment, performance appraisal, workforce participation, compensation, training and development proposed by Kuo (2011) and D. Wang & Chen (2013) was used to measure HRM. The authors do changes on the item of 'Your organization values individual training as well as team training' Kuo (2011) that consists of double-barrel issues, changed to 'Our organization invests in various kinds of training programs' (D. Wang & Chen, 2013).

Organizational Culture (OC)

The dimension of organizational cultures proposed by Liao et al. (2015) and Wallach (1983) are adapted in this study because they highlight the differentiation in managerial practices on organizational innovation capability, which is appropriate to apply in biomass SMEs in Industry 4.0. The composite reliability is more significant than 0.7 (Liao et al., 2015). The authors rephrase 'In your firm' to 'in our organization' to standardize the questionnaires.

Knowledge Management Capabilities (KMC)

This study adapted the items developed by Kuo (2011) to measure knowledge management capabilities. The authors made minor changes, which is from 'Your organization' changed to 'Our organization' as a means to standardize all of the survey questions. The composite reliability for this construct is more significant than 0.8 (Kuo, 2011).

Organizational Innovation Capability (OIC)

Process, product/service, strategy, management-related innovation adapted from Liao et al. (2015) was used to measure organizational innovation capability. The wording was changed from 'In your firm' to 'in our organization' to standardize the sentence structure of the items.

DATA ANALYSIS AND FINDINGS

Assessment of Measurement Model

Internal consistency reliability in this study was assessed using composite reliability. According to Hair, Hult, Ringle, and Sarstedt (2017), internal consistency is achieved if the composite reliability is higher than 0.7. On the other hand, the Average Variance Extracted (AVE) was used to assess convergent validity. Convergent validity is obtained when items measuring the same construct are highly correlated (Sekaran & Bougie, 2016). Hair et al. (2017) stated that convergent validity is achieved when AVE is higher than 0.5. Besides, discriminant validity is established when items that are not supposed to be correlated theoretically are observed, to be not correlated (Sekaran & Bougie, 2016). As such, the discriminant validity of this study was assessed using the heterotrait-monotrait (HTMT) ratio of correlations approach as proposed by (Henseler, Ringle, & Sarstedt, 2015). The HTMT ratio of the correlations approach offers two ways to assess the discriminant validity, which are the criterion test and also the statistical test. Firstly, in the criterion test, the HTMT value should not greater than HTMT0.9 (Gold, Malhotra, & Segars, 2001) to indicate discriminant validity. Secondly, in the statistical test, the confidence interval of HTMT values for the structural paths should not contain the value of 1 to indicate discriminant validity (Henseler et al., 2015). Table 2 demonstrates the measurement model analysis results. Table 3 illustrates the HTMT analysis.

Assessment of Structural Model

Coefficient of Determination, R2

A total of 62.5% of the variance in organizational innovation capability can be explained using human resource management, organizational culture, and knowledge management capability ($R2 = 0.625$). Moreover, 31.6% of the variance in organizational performance can be explained using organizational

Table 2. Measurement model analysis results

Construct	Items	Loadings	AVE	CR
Human Resource Management	HRM2	0.738	0.653	0.849
	HRM4	0.862		
	HRM5	0.819		
Organisational Culture	OC2	0.724	0.661	0.921
	OC3	0.833		
	OC4	0.759		
	OC5	0.817		
	OC6	0.864		
Knowledge Management Capability	KMC1	0.793	0.641	0.899
	KMC3	0.773		
	KMC4	0.886		
	KMC5	0.795		
	KMC6	0.851		
	KMC7	0.773		
Organizational Innovation Capability	OIC1	0.734	0.654	0.904
	OIC3	0.863		
	OIC4	0.806		
	OIC5	0.834		
	OIC6	0.802		
Organizational Performance	OP1	0.802	0.664	0.908
	OP2	0.867		
	OP3	0.715		
	OP4	0.865		
	OP5	0.817		

Note: AVE = Average Variance Extracted, CR= Composite Reliability. HRM1, HRM3, OC1, KMC2, and OIC2 were dropped due to their loadings below 0.7.

Table 3. HTMT analysis

	1	2	3	4	5
1. Human Resource Management					
2. Organizational Culture	0.457 CI.90 [0.329;0.539]				
3. Knowledge Management Capability	0.615 CI.90 [0.465;0.742]	0.895 CI.90 [0.834;0.947]			
4. Organizational Innovation Capability	0.479 CI.90 [0.307;0.614]	0.763 CI.90 [0.680;0.832]	0.875 CI.90 [0.821;0.918]		
5. Organizational Performance	0.536 CI.90 [0.429;0.627]	0.789 CI.90 [0.731;0.836]	0.764 CI.90 [0.693;0.819]	0.632 CI.90 [0.539;0.713]	

innovation capability (R2 = 0.316). According to Cohen (1988), this model indicated a substantial level of predictive accuracy (R2 > 0.26).

Level of Path Coefficients

Assessment of path coefficients was performed using a bootstrapping function. 5000 samples were bootstrapped with the number he number of cases equals the exact number of observations in the original sample. The result of the assessment showed that organization culture (β=0.183, t=2.405), knowledge management capability (β=0.639, t=8.438) are positively related to organizational innovation capability. However, human resource management (β=0.002, t=0.035) has found to have no relationship with organization innovation capability since the relationship is not significant at 0.05 nor 0.01 significant level. Also, organization innovation capability (β=0.565, t=12.553) is positively related to organizational performance. As a result, H2, H3, and H4 were accepted while H1 was rejected. Table 4 and Figure 2 presents the results of the structural equation model estimation.

Table 4. Hypothesis testing

No	Relationship	Std. Beta	Std. Error	t-value	p-value	Confidence Interval (BC)		Decision
						LL	UL	
Hypothesis One	Human resource management-> Organizational innovation capability	0.002	0.050	0.035	0.485	-0.080	0.074	Rejected
Hypothesis Two	Organizational culture -> Organizational innovation capability	0.183	0.076	2.405***	0.000	0.068	0.315	Accepted
Hypothesis Three	Knowledge management capability -> Organizational innovation capability	0.639	0.076	8.438***	0.006	0.513	0.75	Accepted
Hypothesis Four	Organizational innovation capability -> Organizational performance	0.565	0.045	12.553***	0.000	0.489	0.637	Accepted

***p<0.01, **p<0.05

Figure 2. Measurement Model

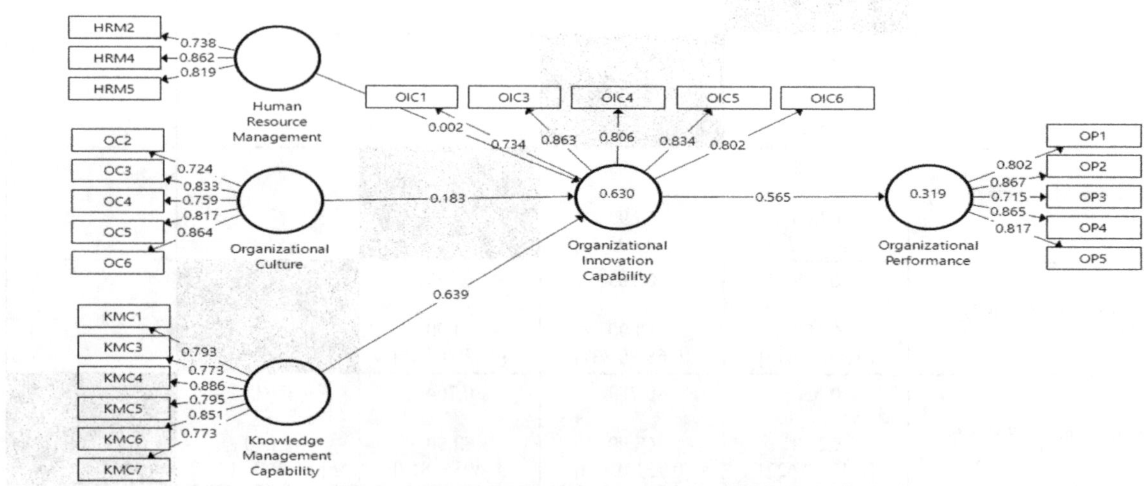

Assessment of Mediation Effect

Bootstrapping the indirect effect method, as proposed by Preacher and Hayes (2004;2008) was used to assess the mediation effect in this study. The bootstrapping analysis showed that only two indirect effects, OC -> OIC -> OP (β=0.103, t=2.335) and KMC -> OIC -> OP (β=0.361, t=6.297) were significant and the 95% Boot CI Bias Corrected: [LL = 0.027, UL = 0.462], [LL = 0.261, UL = 0.462] do not straddle a 0 in between indicating that there was a mediation effect (Preacher and Hayes, 2004;2008). The indirect effect, HRM -> OIC -> OP (β=0.001, t=0.035) was not significant and the 95% Boot CI Bias Corrected: [LL = -0.050, UL = 0.062] straddle a 0 in between indicating that there was no mediation effect. Hence, H5 was rejected, and H6 and H7 were accepted. Table 5 summarized the hypothesis testing on the mediation effect.

Table 5. Hypothesis testing on mediation effect

No	Relationship	Std. Beta	Std. Error	t-value	p-value	Confidence Interval (BC)		Decision
						LL	UL	
Hypothesis Five	Human resource management -> Organizational innovation capability -> Organizational performance	0.001	0.029	0.036	0.486	-0.050	0.062	Rejected
Hypothesis Six	Organizational culture -> Organizational innovation capability -> Organizational performance	0.103	0.052	2.335**	0.000	0.027	0.462	Accepted
Hypothesis Seven	Knowledge management capabilities -> Organizational innovation capability -> Organizational performance	0.361	0.044	6.297***	0.009	0.261	0.462	Accepted

***p<0.01, **p<0.05

DISCUSSION

Findings in the present study suggested that knowledge management capability plays the most significant role in influencing organizational innovation capability. Knowledge management capability has positive and significant effects on organizational innovation capability. These findings highlight the critical roles of knowledge management capability, which enable the value creation process via a strategic flow of relevant knowledge throughout the organization. Development of Industry 4.0 requires an innovative mechanism to manage the way of knowledge acquisitions, conversion and applications. Within the Industry 4.0 framework, big data are collected various automate electronic devices such as sensors and stored in a cloud-based database which eventually analyzed by much artificial intelligent system to provide real-time monitoring and control. Knowledge management capability of an organization becomes crucial for the company to achieve a competitive advantage through highly effective data processing and analyzing the process. Organizational innovation capability relying heavily on the organization's capability to crystallize and connect process, which includes knowledge development, discovery, and capture.

This study presented that organizational culture demonstrated a positive relationship with organizational innovation capability. These findings are consistent with Khan and Mir (2019) where organizational capabilities to innovate and change are deeply rooted in an organization's ability to build on its traditions and past and to learn and be able to drive innovation streams. An influential organizational culture that includes the norms and values with support the generation of creative ideas that contribute to sustaining innovation in a company. A standard set of shared belief and understanding is vital in developing an organizational culture that promotes organizational innovation capability. Safe innovative environments that allow collaboration across various organizational boundaries; sharing and teaching among and across business units and alliances can be effective ways of promoting collaborative innovation.

Contrary to expectations, this study did not find a significant relationship between human resource management and organizational innovation. An explanation for this could be related to the reduction of human interaction in the Industry 4.0 framework. Many data collection and analyzing processes have done using artificial intelligence. Data are collected, processed and interpreted by computer software which required very minimal human interaction. Most of the research explained that human resource management practices such as sourcing, deployment, and upgrading of human capital would influence organizational innovation performance level. However, within Industry 4.0 framework has disrupted the traditional human resource management. Many of the HR processes will be automated using new technologies such as Internet-of-Things, Big Data, and artificial intelligence. As a result, this could affect the established relationship between human resource management practices and organizational innovation capability.

These findings suggest that organizational innovation capability will positively influence organizational performance. The findings showed a consensus result with the literature (Donkor, Donkor, Kankam-Kwarteng, & Aidoo, 2018; Saunila 2014). Organizational innovation involves the invariable implementation of new organizational practices that improve process efficiency and effectiveness. Within the Industry 4.0 framework, reconfiguration of the business model is required based on a different degree of innovation to embrace the challenges posed by the digitalization of the business process. Ibarra, Ganzarain, and Igartua (2018) emphasized that disruptive innovation that provides the change of almost all the elements of the business model is needed for the organization to compete in the Industry 4.0 environment. To improve organizational performance from a traditional business model, incremental innovation of both value creation and value delivery is essential. Radical innovation on the actual business model is needed through reconfiguration and diversification of value network ecosystem focusing on product innovation, service innovation, and customer innovation.

This study proved that organizational innovation capability mediates the relationship between organizational culture and organizational performance. In order words, the positive effect of organizational culture occurs because of culture fosters innovation capability among the employees, which eventually improves the organization's performance as innovation is a process of transforming business ideas into something practical and profitable. Therefore, encouragement to supply ideas needs to be substantial to channel the creative ability of the employees to convert ideas into innovations. Positive organizational culture promotes creativity, risk-taking attitude, freedom, and flexibility, which is an excellent recipe for organizational innovation. Only when the culture is in favor of innovation, employees will be worry-free to express their ideas and encouraged to challenge the existing way of doing things. Organizational culture is influencing organizational performance indirectly in such a way that it provides a positive environment to encourage innovation, and subsequently, organization performance improves with improvement achieve in any business deliveries.

This research has investigated and concluded that the positive relationship between knowledge management capability and organizational performance is mediated by organizational innovation capability. The findings explained that excellent knowledge management capability would heighten organization innovation capability and subsequently improve organization performance. Knowledge management capability has been considered as a strategic resource for an organization to sustain a competitive advantage. Knowledge management capability ensures effective dissemination of knowledge throughout the firm and contributes to organizational perform via the enhanced capability to respond to new and unusual situations. As a result, knowledge management capability allows knowledge gaps to be identified, complex data to be organized into useful information, and stimulating creative thinking skills that lead to innovation. Organizational innovation capability helps the organization to reshapes the competitive landscape and creates new market opportunities. All this will not happen without a proper knowledge management system to serve as the backbone to manage the abundance of big data in the Industry 4.0 environment. As such, an excellent knowledge management capability will influence organization innovation capability and ultimately improve organizational performance.

CONCLUSION

There has been relatively little literature on the organizational performance of Malaysian SMEs in the biomass industry, especially with the mediating role of organizational innovation capabilities. This study provides theoretical contributions and bridges the gaps of prior literature by providing insights on the positive and indirect effect of human resource management, organizational culture, knowledge management capabilities on organizational performance, with the mediating effect of organizational innovation capability. The present study integrates RBV and dynamic capabilities theories to enrich further understanding associated with the dominant influence of organizations' resources and capabilities on organizational performance. The empirical result reflected that organizational culture, knowledge management capabilities are significantly influencing organizational innovation capability and in the end, impact on organization performance.

Due to the turbulent business environment in Industry 4.0, the practical contribution of this study revealed the salient information that can be applied by business managers in SMEs biomass industry, who are struggling to achieve higher organizational performance. The business managers should strive to remove the cultural barrier that inhibits innovation capability. A good strategy on knowledge management should be in place to ensure organizational innovation capability can be promoted. A precise knowledge management strategy should provide a clear communicable plan about the knowledge management process in the organization by indicating where we are now, where we want to go, and how to get there. Top management support is paramount in making this a success. Future research could focus on delineating and decomposing the knowledge management capability and organizational culture and examine how possible of each dimension of the variable could influence organization innovation capability.

REFERENCES

Aboelmaged, M. G. (2014). Linking operations performance to knowledge management capability: The mediating role of innovation performance. *Production Planning and Control*, *25*(1), 44–58. doi:10.1080/09537287.2012.655802

Agensi Inovasi Malaysia. (2013). National Biomass Strategy 2020: New wealth creation for Malaysia's biomass industry. Cyberjaya. Retrieved from https://docs.wixstatic.com/ugd/43b4fe_00564483596c43d5a1619e82131f1832.pdf

Alshanty, A. M., Emeagwali, O. L., Ibrahim, B., & Alrwashdeh, M. (2019). The effect of market-sensing capability on the knowledge creation process and innovation evidence from SMEs in Jordan. Management Science Letters, 9(5), 727–736. doi:10.5267/j.msl.2019.1.016

Amui, L. B. L., Jabbour, C. J. C., de Sousa Jabbour, A. B. L., & Kannan, D. (2017). Sustainability as a dynamic organizational capability: A systematic review and a future agenda toward a sustainable transition. *Journal of Cleaner Production*, *142*, 308–322. doi:10.1016/j.jclepro.2016.07.103

Aryanto, R., Fontana, A., & Afiff, A. Z. (2015). Strategic Human Resource Management, Innovation Capability, and Performance: An Empirical Study in Indonesia Software Industry. *Procedia: Social and Behavioral Sciences*, *211*(September), 874–879. doi:10.1016/j.sbspro.2015.11.115

Bamber, G. J., Bartram, T., & Stanton, P. (2017). HRM and workplace innovations: Formulating research questions. *Personnel Review*, *46*(7), 1216–1227. doi:10.1108/PR-10-2017-0292

Barney, J. B. (1991). Firm Resources and Sustained Competitive. *Journal of Management*, *17*(1), 99–120. doi:10.1177/014920639101700108

Barney, J. B. (2001). Resource-based theories of competitive advantage: A ten-year retrospective on the resource-based view. *Journal of Management*, *27*(6), 643–650. doi:10.1177/014920630102700602

Bos-Nehles, A., Renkema, M., & Janssen, M. (2017). HRM and innovative work behavior: A systematic literature review. *Personnel Review*, *46*(7), 1228–1253. doi:10.1108/PR-09-2016-0257

Breznik, L., & Hisrich, R. D. (2014). Dynamic capabilities vs. innovation capability: Are they related? *Journal of Small Business and Enterprise Development*, *21*(3), 368–384. doi:10.1108/JSBED-02-2014-0018

Cameron, K. S., & Quinn, R. E. (2011). *Diagnosing and Changing Organizational Culture: Based on the Competing Values Framework*. San Francisco, CA: Jossey-Bass.

Chang, W. J., Liao, S. H., & Te Wu, T. (2017). Relationships among organizational culture, knowledge sharing, and innovation capability: A case of the automobile industry in Taiwan. *Knowledge Management Research and Practice*, *15*(3), 471–490. doi:10.1057/s41275-016-0042-6

Chin, W. W., & Newstead, P. (1999). Structural Equation Modelling Analysis with Small Samples Using Partial Least Squares. In *Statistical Strategies for Small Sample Research* (pp. 307–341). Thousand Oaks, CA: Sage Publications.

Cohen, J. (1988). *Statistical power analysis for the behavioral sciences* (2nd ed.). Hillsdale, NJ: Lawrence Erlbaum Associates.

Da Xu, L., Xu, E. L., & Li, L. (2018). Industry 4.0: State of the art and future trends. *International Journal of Production Research, 56*(8), 2941–2962. doi:10.1080/00207543.2018.1444806

de Araújo, C. C. S., Pedron, C. D., & Bitencourt, C. (2018). Identifying and assessing the scales of dynamic capabilities: A systematic literature review. Revista de Gestão, 25(4), 390–412. doi:10.1108/REGE-12-2017-0021

Demircan, N., & Ert, A. (2010). Comparing Innovation Capability of Small and Medium-Sized Enterprises : Examining the Effects of Organizational Culture and Empowerment. *Journal of Small Business Management*, *48*(3), 325–359. doi:10.1111/j.1540-627X.2010.00297.x

Department of Statistics Malaysia. (2019). Small and Medium Enterprises (SMEs) Performance 2018. Retrieved from https://www.dosm.gov.my/v1/index.php?r=column/cthemeByCat&cat=159&bul_id=R0Vka2RpeVJ0cUlpR3BqdjhudDZhdz09&menu_id=TE5CRUZCblh4ZTZMODZIbmk2aWRRQT09

Dhewanto, W., Prasetio, E. A., Ratnaningtyas, S., Herliana, S., Chaerudin, R., Aina, Q., … Rachmawaty, E. (2012). Moderating Effect of Cluster on Firm's Innovation Capability and Business Performance: A Conceptual Framework. Procedia - Social and Behavioral Sciences, 65(ICIBSoS), 867–872. doi:10.1016/j.sbspro.2012.11.212

Diaz-Fernandez, M., Bornay-Barrachina, M., & Lopez-Cabrales, A. (2015). Innovation and firm performance: The role of human resource management practices. Evidence-Based HRM, 3(1), 64–80. doi:10.1108/EBHRM-10-2012-0012

Donkor, J., Donkor, G. N. A., Kankam-Kwarteng, C., & Aidoo, E. (2018). Innovative capability, strategic goals and financial performance of SMEs in Ghana. Asia Pacific Journal of Innovation and Entrepreneurship, 12(2), 238–254. doi:10.1108/APJIE-10-2017-0033

Duong, D. H., & Swierczek, F. W. (2019). The Impact of Top Management Team and Organizational Culture on Product/Service and Process Innovation in Vietnamese Banks. *Applied Finance and Banking*, *9*(2), 55–68.

Farouk, S., Abu Elanain, H. M., Obeidat, S. M., & Al-Nahyan, M. (2016). HRM practices and organizational performance in the UAE banking sector: The mediating role of organizational innovation. *International Journal of Productivity and Performance Management*, *65*(6), 773–791. doi:10.1108/IJPPM-01-2016-0010

Fu, N. (2015). The role of relational resources in the knowledge management capability and innovation of professional service firms1. *Human Relations*, *68*(5), 731–764. doi:10.1177/0018726714543479

Fu, N., Flood, P. C., Bosak, J., Morris, T., & O'Regan, P. (2015). How do high-performance work systems influence organizational innovation in professional service firms? *Employee Relations*, *37*(2), 209–231. doi:10.1108/ER-10-2013-0155

Gold, A. H., Malhotra, A., & Segars, A. H. (2001). Knowledge Management: An Organizational Capabilities Perspective. *Journal of Management Information Systems*, *18*(1), 185–214. doi:10.1080/07421222.2001.11045669

Hair, J. F., Hult, T. M., Ringle, C. M., & Sarstedt, M. (2017). *A Primer on Partial Least Square Structural Equation Modeling (PLS-SEM)*. Sage Publications.

Hamzah, N., Tokimatsu, K., & Yoshikawa, K. (2019). Solid fuel from oil palm biomass residues and municipal solid waste by hydrothermal treatment for electrical power generation in Malaysia: A review. *Sustainability*, *11*(1060), 1–23. doi:10.3390u11041060

Henseler, J., Ringle, C. M., & Sarstedt, M. (2015). A new criterion for assessing discriminant validity in variance-based structural equation modeling. *Journal of the Academy of Marketing Science*, *43*(1), 115–135. doi:10.1007/s11747-014-0403-8

Hussein, A. S. T. T., Singh, S. K., Farouk, S., & Sohal, A. S. (2016). Knowledge sharing enablers, processes, and firm innovation capability. *Journal of Workplace Learning*, *28*(8), 484–495. doi:10.1108/JWL-05-2016-0041

Ibarra, D., Ganzarain, J., & Igartua, J. I. (2018). Business model innovation through Industry 4.0: A review. Procedia Manufacturing, 22, 4–10. doi:10.1016/j.promfg.2018.03.002

Iqbal, Q., & Nawaz, R. (2019). Rife information pollution (infollution) and virtual organizations in industry 4.0: within reality causes and consequences. In *Big Data and Knowledge Sharing in Virtual Organizations* (pp. 117–135). IGI Global; doi:10.4018/978-1-5225-7519-1.ch005.

Jiang, Y., Jiang, Y., & Nakamura, W. (2019). Human capital and organizational performance based on organizational innovation: Empirical study on China. *Revista de Cercetare si Interventie Sociala*, *64*, 156–166. doi:10.33788/rcis.64.13

Khan, S. J., & Mir, A. A. (2019). Ambidextrous culture, contextual ambidexterity, and new product innovations: The role of organizational slack and environmental factors. *Business Strategy and the Environment*, *28*(4), 652–663. doi:10.1002/bse.2287

Kuo, T. H. (2011). How to improve organizational performance through learning and knowledge? *International Journal of Manpower*, *32*(5), 581–603. doi:10.1108/01437721111158215

Liao, S. H., Hu, D. C., Chen, C. C., & Lin, Y. L. (2015). Comparison of competing models and multi-group analysis of organizational culture, knowledge transfer, and innovation capability: An empirical study of the Taiwan semiconductor industry. *Knowledge Management Research and Practice*, *13*(3), 248–260. doi:10.1057/kmrp.2013.46

Lu, K., Zhu, J., & Bao, H. (2015). High-performance human resource management and firm performance: The mediating role of innovation in China. *Industrial Management & Data Systems*, *115*(2), 553–582. doi:10.1108/IMDS-10-2014-0317

Malaysia Industry-Government Group for High Technology (MIGHT). (2013). Malaysian Biomass Industry Action Plan 2020: Driving SMEs towards a sustainable future. Retrieved from http://www.biomass.org.my/files/editor_files/files/Msia Biomass Industry Action Plan 2020.pdf

Malaysian Industry-Government Group for High Technology (MIGHT). (2014). *Biomass Benchmarking Study: Potential Value Creation for Commercial Utilization of Biomass in Malaysia*. Author.

Maldonado-Guzmán, G., Garza-Reyes, J. A., Pinzón-Castro, S. Y., & Kumar, V. (2019). Innovation capabilities and performance: Are they truly linked in SMEs? *International Journal of Innovation Science, 11*(1), 48–62. doi:10.1108/IJIS-12-2017-0139

Mekhilef, S., Barimani, M., Safari, A., & Salam, Z. (2014). Malaysia's renewable energy policies and programs with green aspects. *Renewable & Sustainable Energy Reviews, 40*, 497–504. doi:10.1016/j.rser.2014.07.095

Miles, J. A. (2012). *Management and Organization Theory. A Jossey-Bass Reader*. John Wiley & Sons.

Ministry of International Trade and Industry (MITI). (2017). International Biomass Conference Malaysia 2017: Biomass Industry Revolution 4.0. Retrieved from https://www.miti.gov.my/index.php/pages/view/4349

Moeuf, A., Pellerin, R., Lamouri, S., Tamayo-Giraldo, S., & Barbaray, R. (2018). The industrial management of SMEs in the era of Industry 4.0. *International Journal of Production Research, 56*(3), 1118–1136. doi:10.1080/00207543.2017.1372647

Müller, J. M., Maier, L., Veile, J., & Voigt, K.-I. (2017). Cooperation strategies among SMEs for implementing Industry 4.0. *Proceedings of the Hamburg International Conference of Logistics (HICL)*, 301–318. 10.15480/882.1462

Naranjo Valencia, J., Sanz Valle, R., & Jiménez Jiménez, D. (2010). Organizational culture as a determinant of product innovation. *European Journal of Innovation Management, 13*(4), 466–480. doi:10.1108/14601061011086294

Naranjo-Valencia, J. C., Jiménez-Jiménez, D., & Sanz-Valle, R. (2011). Innovation or imitation? The role of organizational culture. *Management Decision, 49*(1), 55–72. doi:10.1108/00251741111094437

Nawab, S., Nazir, T., Zahid, M. M., & Fawad, S. M. (2015). Knowledge Management, Innovation, and Organizational Performance. *International Journal of Knowledge Engineering-IACSIT, 1*(1), 43–48. doi:10.7763/IJKE.2015.V1.7

Noruzy, A., Dalfard, V. M., Azhdari, B., Nazari-Shirkouhi, S., & Rezazadeh, A. (2013). Relations between transformational leadership, organizational learning, knowledge management, organizational innovation, and organizational performance: An empirical investigation of manufacturing firms. *International Journal of Advanced Manufacturing Technology, 64*(5–8), 1073–1085. doi:10.1007/s00170-012-4038-y

Ologbo, A. C., & Nor, K. M. (2015). Knowledge management processes and firm innovation capability: A theoretical model. *Asian Social Science, 11*(18), 10–17. doi:10.5539/ass.v11n18p10

Pavlou, P. a, & Sawy, O. a El. (. (2011). Understanding the Black Box. Decision Sciences, 42(1), 239–273. doi:10.1111/j.1540-5915.2010.00287.x

Preacher, K. J., & Hayes, A. F. (2004). SPSS and SAS procedures for estimating indirect effects in simple mediation models. *Behavior Research Methods, Instruments, & Computers, 36*(4), 717–731. doi:10.3758/BF03206553 PubMed

Preacher, K. J., & Hayes, A. F. (2008). Asymptotic and resampling strategies for assessing and comparing indirect effects in multiple mediator models. *Behavior Research Methods*, *40*(3), 879–891. doi:10.3758/BRM.40.3.879 PubMed

Rodič, B. (2017). Industry 4.0 and the New Simulation Modelling Paradigm. Organizacija, 50(3), 193–207. doi:10.1515/orga-2017-0017

Sabiu, M. S., Ringim, K. J., Tang, S. M., & Joarder, M. H. R. (2019). Relationship between human resource management practices, ethical climates and organizational performance, the missing link. PSU Research Review, PRR-12-2016-0022. doi:10.1108/PRR-12-2016-0022

Sáenz, J., Aramburu, N., & Rivera, O. (2009). Knowledge sharing and innovation performance: A comparison between high-tech and low-tech companies. *Journal of Intellectual Capital*, *10*(1), 22–36. doi:10.1108/14691930910922879

Salim, I. M., & Sulaiman, M. (2011). Organizational Learning, Innovation and Performance: A Study of Malaysian Small and Medium-Sized Enterprises. *International Journal of Business and Management*, *6*(12), 118–125. doi:10.5539/ijbm.v6n12p118

Sánchez-Báez, E. A., Fernández-Serrano, J., & Romero, I. (2019). Organizational culture and innovation in small businesses in Paraguay. Regional Science Policy and Practice, 1–15. doi:10.1111/rsp3.12203

Saunila, M. (2014). Innovation capability for SME success: Perspectives of financial and operational performance. *Journal of Advances in Management Research*, *11*(2), 163–175. doi:10.1108/JAMR-11-2013-0063

Sekaran, U., & Bougie, R. (2016). *Research Methods For Business: A Skill Building Approach*. Wiley.

SME Corporation Malaysia. (2019). SME Definitions. Retrieved from http://www.smecorp.gov.my/index.php/en/policies/2015-12-21-09-09-49/sme-definition

Tan, C., & Nasurdin, A. (2011). Human resource management practices and organizational innovation: Assessing the mediating role of knowledge management effectiveness. *Electronic Journal of Knowledge Management*, *9*(2), 155–167.

Terry Kim, T., Lee, G., Paek, S., & Lee, S. (2013). Social capital, knowledge sharing, and organizational performance: What structural relationship do they have in hotels? *International Journal of Contemporary Hospitality Management*, *25*(5), 683–704. doi:10.1108/IJCHM-Jan-2012-0010

Terziovski, M. (2010). Research notes and commentaries innovation practice and its performance implications in small and medium enterprises (SMEs) in the manufacturing sector: A resource-based view. *Strategic Management Journal*, *31*(8), 892–902. doi:10.1002mj.841

Uzkurt, C., Kumar, R., Kimzan, H. S., & Eminoğlu, G. (2013). Role of innovation in the relationship between organizational culture and firm performance: A study of the banking sector in Turkey. *European Journal of Innovation Management*, *16*(1), 92–117. doi:10.1108/14601061311292878

Vaidya, S., Ambad, P., & Bhosle, S. (2018). Industry 4.0 - A Glimpse. Procedia Manufacturing, 20, 233–238. doi:10.1016/j.promfg.2018.02.034

Wallach, E. J. (1983). Individuals and organizations: The cultural match. *Training and Development Journal*, *37*(2), 28–35.

Wang, D., & Chen, S. (2013). Does intellectual capital matter? High-performance work systems and bilateral innovative capabilities. *International Journal of Manpower*, *34*(8), 861–879. doi:10.1108/IJM-07-2013-0167

Wang, S., Guidice, R. M., Tansky, J. W., & Wang, Z.-M. (2010). When R&D spending is not enough: The critical role of culture when you want to innovate. *Human Resource Management*, *49*(4), 767–792. doi:10.1002/hrm.20365

Wang, Y., Bhanugopan, R., & Lockhart, P. (2015). Examining the quantitative determinants of organizational performance: Evidence from China. *Measuring Business Excellence*, *19*(2), 23–41. doi:10.1108/MBE-05-2014-0014

World Energy Council. (2018). World energy issues monitor 2018: Perspectives on the grand energy transition. Retrieved from http://www.im.worldenergy.org/

Wu, L. F., Huang, I. C., Huang, W. C., & Du, P. L. (2019). Aligning organizational culture and operations strategy to improve innovation outcomes: An integrated perspective in organizational management. *Journal of Organizational Change Management*, *32*(2), 224–250. doi:10.1108/JOCM-03-2018-0073

Xu, S. (2015). A study on knowledge management capabilities towards new product innovation type and development performance of Chinese businesses. *Acta Oeconomica*, *65*(s2), 145–157. doi:10.1556/032.65.2015.S2.11

Yousif Al-Hakim, L. A., & Hassan, S. (2013). Knowledge management strategies, innovation, and organizational performance: An empirical study of the Iraqi MTS. *Journal of Advances in Management Research*, *10*(1), 58–71. doi:10.1108/09727981311327767

Chapter 7
Health 4.0:
Learning, Innovation, and Collaboration of Small and Medium Private Hospitals in India

Sahrish Ahmad
Universiti Sains Malaysia, Malaysia

Hasliza Abdul Halim
Universiti Sains Malaysia, Malaysia

Mohammad Jamal Khan
Saudi Electronic University, Saudi Arabia

Noor Hazlina Ahmad
Universiti Sains Malaysia, Malaysia

ABSTRACT

In the new era of Industry 4.0 and on the basis of current knowledge about innovation in Industry 4.0, it has become a pretty clear that Industry 4.0 had a major impact on the manufacturing sector. At its origin, this industry is evolving from manufacturing to service providers. This chapter explains how innovation of new digital services such as Industry 4.0 integrates towards the healthcare system such as Health 4.0 in India. Although innovation is significant among the manufacturing sector, the practice of this concept is still lacking among the service sector such as hospitals. This study will investigate the impact of organizational learning on horizontal technology collaboration and vertical technology collaboration. The study is designed as a quantitative study and the non-probability purposive sampling technique was used. The data was collected from the doctors of small and medium private hospitals. The findings of data analysis reveal that organizational learning has significant positive impact on horizontal technology collaboration and vertical technology collaboration.

DOI: 10.4018/978-1-7998-2577-7.ch007

INTRODUCTION

The 4th Industrial Revolution or "Industry 4.0" integrate smart technologies and cyber-physical systems in the manufacturing process. In healthcare, this revolution has brought in various technologies that aim to improve the quality and efficiency of patient care (Dinh, 2017). The revolution is integrating data directly into electronic medical records or using Artificial Intelligence to increase diagnosis accuracy, both globally and in India. Over the next few years, this revolution is likely to change the healthcare delivery system. This revolution is called Health 4.0.

The healthcare system in India comprises five segments such as hospitals, pharmaceuticals, medical equipment and supplies, medical insurance and diagnostics (India Brand Equity Foundation, 2017). From these five segments hospital is the largest segment. Hospitals contribute 71% of the industry revenue, pharmaceuticals contribute 13%, medical equipment and supplies contribute 9%, medical insurance contributes 4%, and diagnostics contributes 3%. As the hospital segment constitutes more than 70% of the Indian healthcare market and is among the fastest-growing segments in the healthcare spectrum, therefore, this paper focuses on the hospital sector of India.

The healthcare system in India has been transformed by three forces such as an increase in healthcare demand, technological acceptance, and a rise in patient awareness. First, the Indian health care system lacks sufficient infrastructure to meet the health care demands of the country. As per India Brand Equity Foundation (IBEF) the compound annual growth rate of hospitalized cases from 2008 till 2018 for cardiac diseases (18%), oncology (16%) and diabetes (19%). These factors, along with a rising population, are all leading to rising demand for specialized health care in India. However, an increasing need for specialized care is expected to increase and challenges related to the infrastructure of health care are expected to intensify soon. Due to the lack of sufficient health care infrastructure, there is an imbalance of supply-demand of the health care facilities and a decline in the performance of the hospitals. Second, as per the report of the Ministry and IT in 2018, India holds the second spot globally (after China) on various dimensions of digital adoption, which shows that it is one of the fastest adopters of technology. This brings into play that the adoption of technology is affecting the health care system of India. Third, people are becoming increasingly curious and are spending more time on search engines and social media apps to understand health-related topics. There is a visible shift from reactive to proactive care with rising health consciousness. Therefore, to overcome this problem healthcare practitioners are advised to focus more on collaboration, coherence, and convergence to make the healthcare system more predictive and personalized.

LITERATURE REVIEW

Health 4.0 Small and Medium Private Hospitals India

Industry 4.0 which started in Germany and is being adopted by several countries around the globe. USA, France, and Japan were the first to adopt this fourth revolution in manufacturing as well as service sectors (Global Skill Summit, 2019). Several countries are moving towards the fourth industrial revolution in terms of the smart healthcare sector, from which India is one of them.

India is moving towards a smart country with smart cities and with smart healthcare. Though India is moving towards the fourth healthcare revolution, still it's hard to access quality healthcare services in smaller cities, towns, and villages where the majority of the population resides (Govil, 2017). Therefore, small and medium private hospitals playing crucial roles in providing healthcare services to small cities, towns, and villages. Health 4.0 has been adopted by small and medium private hospitals in terms of IoT devices, smart beds, and digital technologies (Shrinivasan, 2018). IoT devices are used for monitoring patient's blood sugar, blood pressure, oxygen levels, etc and this has made the work easier for both patients and doctors. Smart beds are used to detect the occupancy and leaving of a patient. It also ensures the appropriate pressure and support applies to the patient. Digital technologies are used to improve the quality, affordability, and accessibility of health care solutions

Small and medium private hospitals are making their place in the fourth industrial revolution and providing services to the majority of the people in India. Still, there is a long road ahead for small and medium private hospitals to become healthcare smart (Govil, 2017). Therefore, to explore more in the health 4.0 innovation and collaboration would lead them to achieve their goal of providing more and more healthcare service to the people of India (Shrinivasan, 2018).

Organizational Learning

In the academic and business worlds, organizational learning accomplishes growth (Chiva & Alegre, 2005). Organizational learning is all about acquiring and transferring knowledge to the organization so that it can be more innovative. The literature pointed out that organizational learning has four steps process which is acquisition, dissemination, interpretation, and development (Tippins & Sohi, 2003). Organizational learning and innovation play a key role in increasing a firm's competitive advantage (Jiménez-Jiménez & Sanz-Valle, 2011).

However, organizational learning can also be defined as a cognitive and social process of knowledge in organizations (Gomes & Wojahn, 2017). In the cognitive perspective, organizational learning is based on psychology and individual learning, whereas, from a social perspective, it is based on sociology and social learning (Chiva & Alegre, 2005). In a competitive business environment, knowledge is an important factor for organizations. Organizations that maintain this learning process can survive and improve performance in difficult situations (McGill & Slocum, 1993).

Learning helps organizations to create, transfer and integrate knowledge and experience. In organizations, an organizational learning process is an essential tool for the improvement of performance. This research study considers the dimensions of learning such as knowledge acquisition, knowledge distribution, knowledge interpretation, and organizational memory (Jiménez-Jiménez & Sanz-Valle, 2011). Studies (Darroch & McNaughton, 2003; Jiménez-Jiménez & Sanz-Valle, 2011; Tippins & Sohi, 2003) analyzed the process of organizational learning on innovation and the improved performance of firms.

1. *Knowledge Acquisition*: The first is knowledge acquisition. The organization uses this for obtaining new information and knowledge. In terms of improvement in performance, organizations should acquire and gather valuable information (Kohli & Jaworski, 1990). Valuable information can be collected from direct experiences, knowledge of others, and the organization system (Slater & Narver, 1995). Firstly, information can be acquired from both internal and external sources. Secondly, information can be acquired from the knowledge of others, i.e., customers (Kohli & Jaworski, 1990). Thirdly, it can be acquired from the system of organizations, as it acts as a warehouse or storeroom where all previously acquired information is there (Sinkula, 1994). Organizational memory plays an important role while acquiring and interpreting information from the market (Moorman & Miner,

1997). This acquired information will develop knowledge, and that acquired knowledge is useful to the organization in the improvement of performance.

2. *Knowledge Distribution*: Second is knowledge distribution. In this, the acquired knowledge is distributed among organizational members. The knowledge which employees acquire from different sources, i.e. internal or external will be distributed within the organizations so that everyone can gain new information. Once the market information is acquired, it must be distributed among the employees in the organization. Slater and Narver (1995) said that the distribution of knowledge is the expansion of information which is obtained by the organization and it should be shared within the organization through formal and informal channels. Distribution of information provides an advantage to the organization, as each employee acts and shares their thoughts regarding innovation and performance.
3. *Knowledge Interpretation*: Third is knowledge interpretation. In this step, the acquired and distributed information will transform into new common knowledge. The employees in the organization will give new meaning and reconstruct the information into new knowledge (Jiménez-Jiménez & Sanz-Valle, 2011). Regarding new meaning to information, each member of the organization should contribute and maintain unity. As the information is distributed throughout the organization, it will be the responsibility of employees to maintain harmony in transforming the information among them. Maintaining cooperation will help in understanding what the information is about and how that information will lead the organization in the future. Interpretation of knowledge plays an important part in the acquisition and analysis of future information (Slater & Narver, 1995). New interpreted information will lead the organization to innovation.
4. *Organizational Memory*: After the information is interpreted, the last step in the process is organizational memory. In this step, the information which is leftover or of no use after the interpretation then that information will be stored in the organizational memory for future use. Organizational memory is considered a warehouse of information for the organization (Sinkula, 1994). Furthermore, memory in organizations refers to the storage of information and knowledge in different aspects of organizations (Moorman & Miner, 1997). In organizational learning, process memory plays two crucial roles. First, it provides and supports a change in generative learning processes. Second, it has a powerful impact on the learning process, and it can determine the information and analyze it (Slater & Narver, 1995). Organizational memory can be characterized as declarative and procedural. In declarative memory facts and events are considered for knowledge, while in procedural memory all procedures, routines, and processes are considered for knowledge.

Open Innovation

In the manufacturing and service sector, innovation is essential for improved performance (McDermott & Prajogo, 2012). Over the past several years, innovation was applied in the manufacturing sector and has now made its way into the service sector as well. In the service sector, innovation represents a new idea, new or improved product or service, new ways of marketing, new or improved technology, or new methods (Verbano & Crema, 2016). It can also be defined as creating or introducing new ideas to the organization. It is a continuous process of exploring, searching and learning. The outcome of this continuous process is the introduction of new products or services, new markets, and new technologies and techniques (Marques, 2014).

Many studies on open innovation found that firms which collaborate with competitors, suppliers, and customers found it to be an effective performance enhancer (Bianchi, Campodall'Orto, Frattini, & Vercesi, 2010; Laursen & Salter, 2006; Spithoven, Vanhaverbeke, & Roijakkers, 2013; Van de Vrande, De Jong, Vanhaverbeke, & De Rochemont, 2009; Weng & Huang, 2017). Collaboration is achieved when firms allow access to external knowledge and technology into the organization's innovation system. Collaboration with competitors and customers increases firm performance (Parida, Westerberg, & Frishammar, 2012). Large firms are collaborating in the context of open innovation successfully in their strategies. Small firms are less attracted to internal and external collaboration with customers, suppliers, and competitors, which is due to the organization's characteristics, culture and strategy. Researchers found that smaller firms are a source of future growth (Colombo, Piva, & Rossi-Lamastra, 2014). Small firms can benefit from open innovation as they have less bureaucracy, can take risks, and can easily adopt a volatile environment. According to (Gassmann, Enkel, & Chesbrough, 2010), open innovation is useful for both large and small firms. Open innovation is a useful tool for small and medium firms, and compared to large firms, small firms can overcome their challenges faster and increase performance. Open innovation is a model in which the boundaries between the firm and its environment become flexible allowing for a two-way flow of knowledge from inside the firm out (outbound) and from outside in (inbound) (Hochleitner, Arbussà, & Coenders, 2017).

Studies in the context of open innovation have collaborated in terms of technology such as horizontal technology collaboration (HTC) and vertical technology collaboration (VTC) and examined their impact on innovation performance (Chesbrough, Vanhaverbeke, & West, 2006; Lichtenthaler, 2008; Parida et al., 2012; Van de Grande et al., 2009). Parida et al. (2012) identified two significant external resources of knowledge for supporting innovation performance as horizontal technology collaboration and vertical technology collaboration. This study will focus on two specific open innovation activities, namely horizontal technology collaboration and vertical technology collaboration.

Horizontal Technology Collaboration

According to Wang, Chang, and Shen (2015), horizontal technology collaboration (HTC) refers to "a firm's ability to collaborate and connect with external partners and competitors, from which the firm can acquire new knowledge and technologies to generate its innovation efforts". According to Parida et al. (2012), HTC refers to "collaborating with partners that are not part of the value chain of an SME. These linkages could include partners from similar or other industries, such as competitors or noncompetitors, and they can be large firms or other SMEs". Organizations that are unable to develop their technology, idea or knowledge can receive help from external actors like competitors and suppliers. These external actors act as sources for new ideas and knowledge (Chesbrough, 2003b). For internal innovation development, these new ideas and knowledge from external actors are valuable to the firm (Chesbrough, 2003a; Laursen & Salter, 2006). Therefore, collaboration with different competitors helps organizations in the innovation process and solution to problems.

The literature regards horizontal technology collaboration as playing an important role for firms as a contributor to innovation, which results in further innovative performance (Hagedoorn, Roijakkers, & Kranenburg, 2006; Hamel, Doz, & Prahalad, 1989; Parida et al., 2012). Studies show that organizations must follow a proper collaboration system (HTC) so that they can acquire the right technology and knowledge from external partners that result develop the innovation process and improve performance (Gnyawali & Park, 2009; Hagedoorn et al., 2006; Parida et al., 2012; Tether, 2002). Therefore, to obtain longer-term profits and better performance, firms should be more stable at the time of acquiring ideas and technology. Firms that perform horizontal technology collaboration have great potential to achieve competitive advantage and improved performance (Belderbos, Carree, & Lokshin, 2004; Fey & Birkinshaw, 2005; Laursen & Salter, 2006; Parida et al., 2012). Hence, organizations collaborating with competitors and suppliers are more up to date about innovation which results in improved performance.

Vertical Technology Collaboration

In an open innovation context, researchers claim that collaboration between organizations and customers is essential for improved performance and innovation processes (Brockhoff, 2003; Gassmann, 2006; Hauser, Tellis, & Griffin, 2006). Collaboration with customers means organizations consider their feedback regarding innovation in new or improved technology and knowledge. The collaboration of organizations in terms of technology and knowledge with customers is termed vertical technology collaboration. According to Wang et al. (2015), "a collaborative relationship with customers that allows organizations to capture technologies and knowledge of market development trends in an appropriate manner" is termed vertical technology collaboration.

From the viewpoint of customers, innovation is crucial for every organization (Durst, Mention, & Poutanen, 2015; Hauser et al., 2006). Most organizations take feedback from customers about their innovative products or service. The collaboration of organizations with their customers helps them to improve their services and innovation performance. This could happen when customers suggest innovative or new ideas related to technology, learning, service or product. The literature has determined several benefits of collaborating with customers such that organizations can know about the market trends, technological development, advancement in the existing services (Chesbrough et al., 2006; Hauser et al., 2006; Shaw, 1995). These benefits help organizations to know about the present conditions of the market.

In organizations, the customers' viewpoint is essential because their views allow organizations to immediately interpret their customers' needs (Verma & Jayasimha, 2014), and gain feedback on the initial experience of using products and services of an organization (O'Cass & Sok, 2013). In this manner, the customer can add or suggest creative or innovative ideas to the process of innovation of the organization and the learning of the organization for improved performance (Calantone, Cavusgil, & Zhao, 2002; Verma & Jayasimha, 2014). In summary, customers are a primary source for the organization for sharing relevant information, suggestions, and feedback about innovation for improved firm performance.

Theoretical Framework

Figure 1. Theoretical framework

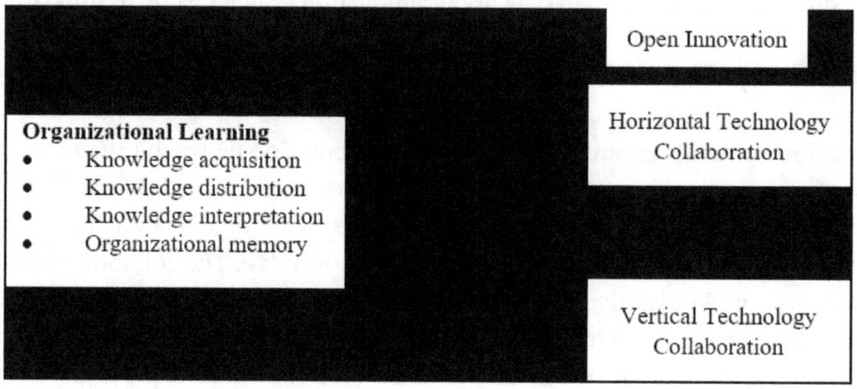

HYPOTHESIS DEVELOPMENT

Relationship between Organizational Learning and Horizontal Technology Collaboration

This chapter will analyze the relationship of organizational learning on horizontal technology collaboration. Previous studies suggest that organizations should collaborate with their competitors and customers so they can learn from external actors and use that learning into the internal innovation process and upgrade innovation (Hurley & Hult, 1998; Narula, 2004; Pisano & Verganti, 2008). Several studies have analyzed the relationship between organizational learning and innovation, and it has a significant relationship with each other (W. M. Cohen & Levinthal, 1990; Hall & Andriani, 2003; Nonaka, 2002; Sørensen & Stuart, 2000). This indicates that organizational learning has a positive relationship with innovation.

Jiménez-Jiménez and Sanz-Valle (2011) argue that for innovation in an organization, an organization must share the acquired knowledge with its members. The knowledge should be acquired, distributed, interpreted to improve the innovation process. The knowledge can be acquired from outside as well as inside the organization depending on the ability of the organization (W. M. Cohen & Levinthal, 1990). Open innovation requires the exploitation of existing knowledge. Therefore, it indicates that organizational learning allows the development, acquisition, transformation, and exploitation of new knowledge which enhances organizational innovation. The results of the study show that organizational learning is positively related to horizontal technology collaboration. Therefore, it can be hypothesized that:

H1: Organizational Learning has a significant positive influence on Horizontal Technology Collaboration

Relationship between Organizational Learning and Vertical Technology Collaboration

Organizations that collaborate with competitors in terms of acquiring knowledge can help organizations to develop and increase their performance. Acquired knowledge from external sources must fit in the innovation process, and that knowledge must meet the needs (Wang et al., 2015). Therefore, the results show that external knowledge will help in the internal innovation process which leads to improving performance (Parida et al., 2012).

Keskin (2006) analyzed the relationship between organizational learning and innovation. He examined the relationship among market orientation, learning orientation and innovativeness in SMEs in Turkey. Many studies are conducted on large firms rather than small and medium firms in terms of organizational learning and innovation. Organizational learning in small and medium firms is sensitive, firm-specific, and work-based by nature and can produce operational efficiency in the short-run (Chaston, Badger, Mangles, & Sadler-Smith, 2001). However, the exploitation of knowledge within or outside the boundaries of the firms can help employees in developing the innovation and employees can improve their ways of thinking (Hurley & Hult, 1998). Therefore, organizational learning will positively lead to vertical technology collaboration in small and medium firms. Therefore, it can be hypothesized that:

H2: Organizational Learning has a significant positive influence on Vertical Technology Collaboration

METHODOLOGY

Data Collection Procedure and Sampling

Data were collected from a small and medium private hospital from three states in India i.e., Delhi, Uttar Pradesh, and Uttarakhand. The primary respondents for the study were doctors. Purposive sampling technique was used, and respondents were invited to deliberately participate in the survey. According to Sekaran (2003), 'purposive sampling is confined to specific types of people who can provide the desired information, either because they are the only ones who have it or conform to some criteria set by the researcher'.

The data was collected from 173 doctors of small and medium private hospitals. To ensure there is no common method bias in the questionnaire survey, Harman's single factor test was performed. The first factors explained 44.60% of the total variance and found below the given threshold of 50% of the total variance.

Researcher identifies that in determining the sample size (Chin, 2010) have indicated the sample size should be equal to the larger of 10 times the largest number of structural paths directed at a construct in the structural model. The previous study identified that the minimum sample size of 100 is adequate for PLS-SEM (Bosco, Reinartz, & Müller, 2009). Hence, the sample size of this study is adequate for PLS analysis.

Measurements

In this study, the instrument was developed by adapting the items from previous studies that use well-established scales (Jiménez-Jiménez & Sanz-Valle, 2011; Wang et al., 2015). The items were measured on a seven-point Likert scale that ranged from (1) strongly disagree to (7) strongly agree. The variable organizational learning has three items each adapted from (Jiménez-Jiménez & Sanz-Valle, 2011), horizontal technology collaboration has three items adapted from (Wang et al., 2015) and three items for vertical technology collaboration adapted from (Wang et al., 2015)

DATA ANALYSIS AND RESULTS

All the 173 respondents of the survey were doctors of Small and Medium private hospitals. The majority of the respondents were male (57.2%) and female (42.8%). Most of the respondents fall under the age group of 25-35 which is 41.6% and a majority of the hospitals were individually owned by the doctors (67.6%). Table 1 shows the profile of respondents.

Table 1. Socio-demographic Profile of Respondents (N = 173)

Variable	Category	Frequency	Percent
Gender	Male	99	57.2
	Female	74	42.8
Age Group	25-35	72	41.6
	36-45	55	31.8
	46-55	33	19.1
	56-65	13	7.5
Ownership	Individually Owned	117	67.6
	Partnership	56	32.4
Years of Establishment	Median	11	
Years of Current Position	Median	8	

The study followed the guidelines of Henseler, Christian and Ringle (2015) to report the PLS-SEM approach. Since PLS-SEM is a nonparametric approach, it does not require the data to be normally distributed. However, it is important to verify that the data are not too far from normal distribution as extreme non-normal data could cause problems in assessing the significance of parameters (J. F. J. Hair Jr, Sarstedt, Hopkins, & G. Kuppelwieser, 2014). Subsequently, skewness and kurtosis were used before data analysis to evaluate the extent to which a variable's distribution is symmetrical (Joseph F Hair, Hult, Ringle, & Sarstedt, 2014). The skewness and kurtosis values of all items were well below 2.828 and 12 respectively as suggested for extreme non-normal data by (Kock, 2014).

Assessment of Measurement Model

The study used a structural equation model (SEM) with the PLS approach and applied the smart PLS 3.2.8 data analysis tool for model estimation and multivariate analysis. PLS-SEM is a multivariate analysis approach used to estimate path models with latent variables. First, the convergent validity of the model was analyzed which included indicator loading, average variance extracted (AVE), and composite reliability (CR). Table 2 presents the indicator loadings of all the items that exceeded the recommended value of 0.708 as suggested by J. F. Hair Jr, Hult, Ringle, and Sarstedt (2014). Item KA1with factor loading 0.656 was retained as the AVEs of the latent variables of this item were 0.658. Three items (KA3, KD1, and KI2) were deleted due to low factor loadings. The AVE of all the variables was in the range of 0.563 to 0.906, which exceeds the recommended value of 0.50, and CR ranged from 0.788 to 0.950, which exceeds the recommended value of 0.70 given by J. F. Hair Jr et al. (2014).

Table 2. Assessment of Measurement Model (Convergent Validity and Reliability)

First Order Construct	Second-Order Construct	Items	Factor Loading	CR	AVE
Knowledge Acquisition (KA)		KA1	0.656	0.788	0.658
		KA2	0.941		
Knowledge Distribution (KD)		KD2	0.866		
		KD3	0.794		
Knowledge Interpretation (KI)		KI1	0.894	0.892	0.806
		KI3	0.901		
Organizational Memory (OM)		OM1	0.937	0.933	0.823
		OM2	0.916		
		OM3	0.867		
Horizontal Technology Collaboration (HTC)		HTC1	0.870	0.916	0.785
		HTC2	0.889		
		HTC3	0.899		
Vertical Technology Collaboration (VTC)		VTC2	0.947	0.950	0.906
		VTC3	0.956		
	Organizational Learning	*KA*	*0.818*	*0.837*	*0.563*
		KD	*0.759*		
		KI	*0.708*		
		OM	*0.711*		

The discriminant validity of the model was tested by the Heterotrait-Monotrait (HTMT) ratio. Henseler, Ringle, and Sarstedt (2015) explained that the HTMT ratio is a superior criterion compared to other methods such as the Fornell-Larcker criterion. They suggested two different cut-off values of 0.85 and 0.90 for the HTMT criterion to establish discriminant validity. This study used a more conservation level of 0.85 (i.e., $HTMT_{.85}$) to establish the discriminant validity of the model. The discriminant validity of the model was established since all the results of the $HTMT_{.85}$ criterion were below the critical value of 0.85 (refer to Table 3). In total, the measurement model demonstrated adequate convergent validity and discriminant validity. Figure 2 details the assessment of the measurement model.

Table 3. Discriminant Validity ($HTMT_{.85}$ Criteria)

		1	2	3	4	5	6
1	HTC						
2	KA	0.444					
3	KD	0.259	0.67				
4	KI	0.284	0.813	0.212			
5	OM	0.518	0.402	0.39	0.484		
6	VTC	0.733	0.587	0.111	0.329	0.106	

Figure 2. Output of measurement model

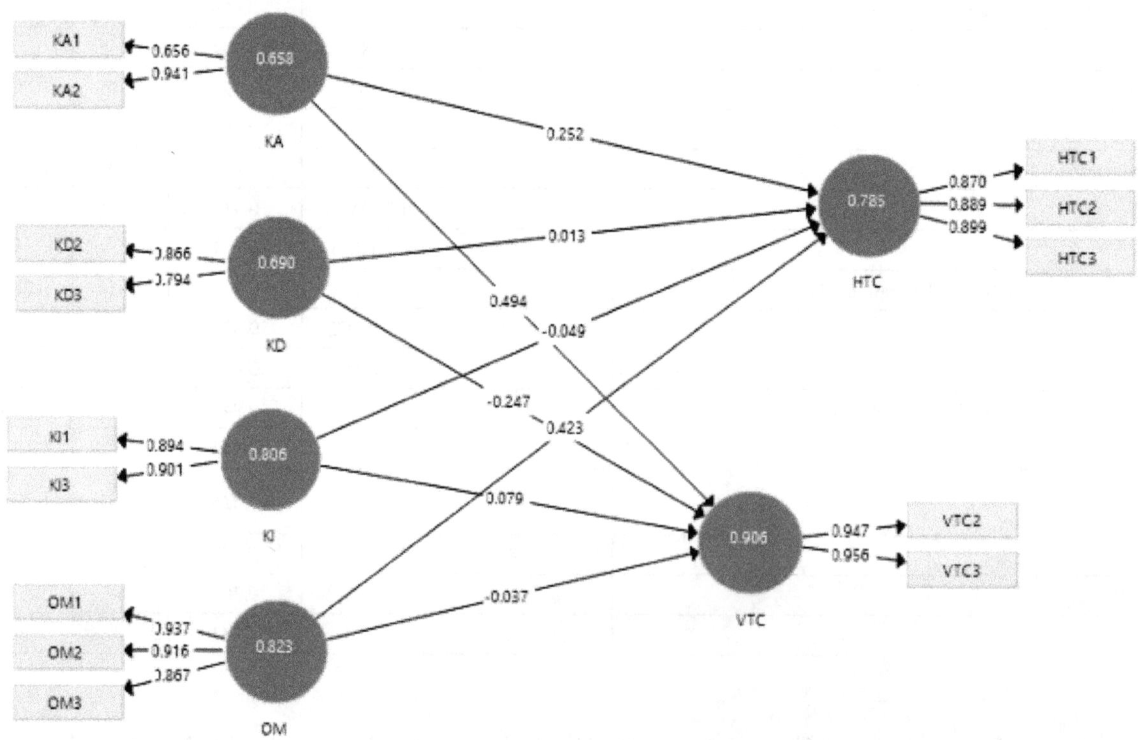

Assessment of Structural Model

In PLS, the main evaluation criterion for the goodness of the structural model is that the R^2 measures the coefficient of determination and the level of significance of the path coefficient (beta value) (Joe F Hair, Ringle, & Sarstedt, 2011). The recommended value (J. Cohen, 1988) for R^2 is between 0.02 and 0.12 for weak, 0.13 and 0.25 for moderate, and 0.26 and above substantial. However, Joe F Hair et al. (2011) qualified these figures and suggested that high R^2 is dependent on specific research contexts. The R^2 value for horizontal technology collaboration (HTC) and vertical technology collaboration (VTC) were 0.288 and 0.247 respectively suggests that 28.8% of the variance of HTC and 24.7% of the variance of VTC can be explained by Knowledge Acquisition, Knowledge Distribution, Knowledge Interpretation, and Organisational Memory.

The path coefficient in the structural model represents the hypothesized relationship between variables (J. F. Hair Jr et al., 2014). In the study, the path coefficients of the structural model were measured, and bootstrap analysis (re-sampling = 1000) was performed to assess the statistical significance of the path coefficient. The results revealed that organizational learning had a significant positive relationship with HTC (β= 0.452, $p < 0.01$). Therefore, hypothesis H1 was supported. OL also has a significant positive relationship with VTC β= 0.343 and significant at $p < 0.01$. Thus, hypothesis H2 was also supported. Table 4 details the results of the assessment of the structural model.

Table 4. Assessment of the Structural Model

Hypothesis	Relationship	Beta	SE	T-Value	P-Value	Result	f^2	VIP	Q^2
H1	OL ® HTC	0.452	0.043	10.48	0.000	Supported	0.257	1.000	0.138
H2	OL ® VTC	0.343	0.059	5.853	0.000	Supported	0.134	1.000	0.094

Figure 3. Output of the structural model

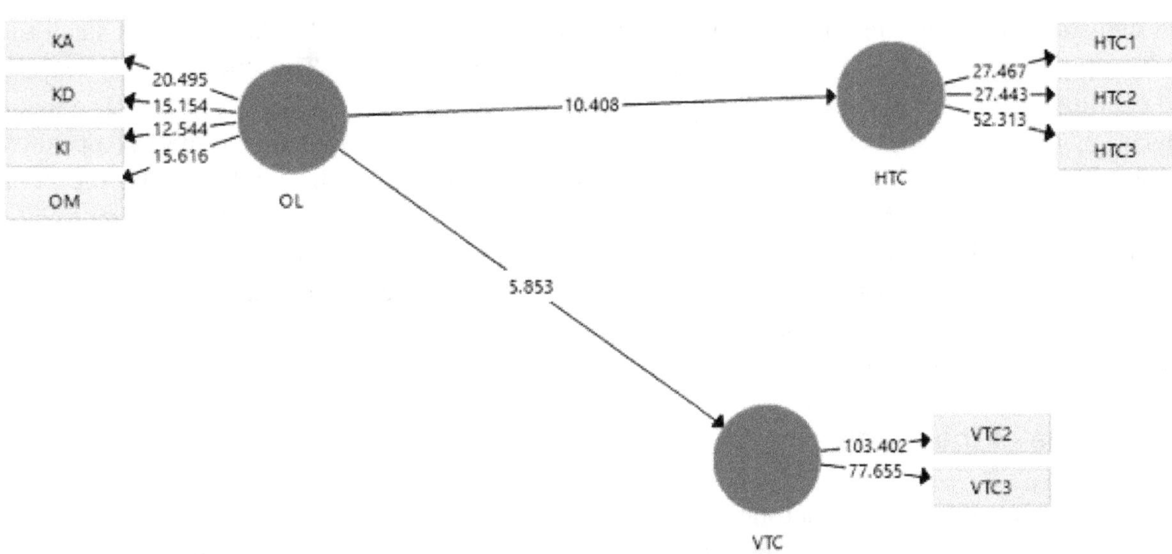

DISCUSSION

The study aims to analyze the relationship between organizational learning and open innovation (horizontal technology collaboration and vertical technology collaboration) of small and medium private hospitals. In the context of small and medium private hospitals, there is a lack of literature that investigates the relationship between organizational learning and horizontal technology collaboration, and organizational learning and vertical technology collaboration. Therefore, the study seeks to bridge the research gap by implementing the relationship between factors important in small and medium private hospitals. Previous literature has investigated the relationship between HTC and VTC with performance (Parida et al., 2012; Wang et al., 2015). But there is a lack of literature that shows the relationship between organizational learning, horizontal technology collaboration and vertical technology collaboration in small and medium private hospitals. A thorough literature review revealed that 80% of the population receive healthcare services from small and medium private hospitals but the literature is scarce which shows that how small and medium private hospitals functions and India is still waiting to receive the due importance by researchers in small and medium private hospitals.

The results of the study revealed that H1 organizational learning has a positive relationship with horizontal technology collaboration ($\beta = 0.452$, *p-value* $= 0.000$). These results are consistent with findings of previous studies (Chang & Cho, 2008; Yli-Renko, Autio, & Sapienza, 2001) in which they hypothesized that organizational learning factors lead to innovation and define that the use of external information and the utilization of methods for retaining knowledge will enhance innovation.

The study also finds that H2 organizational learning has a positive relationship with vertical technology collaboration ($\beta = 0.343$, *p-value* $= 0.000$). The findings are consistent with findings of (Parida et al., 2012), which define external knowledge resources are a crucial source for supporting performance. This impact is due to the ability of the organization in terms of collaboration and connect with external partners and competitors, which helps organizations in acquiring new knowledge and technology to achieve, enhance or improve its performance.

Implications of the Study

The study provides interesting findings and outcomes which can be helpful for the doctors of small and medium private hospitals to improve or enhance their working practices. The study has implications and contributions made by the academic study should be practical and free from complexity so that it can be implemented easily. The findings of the study show that organizational learning has a positive relationship with both technology collaboration (horizontal and vertical). This implicates that the learning process improves collaboration with supplier, competitor and external partners by developing better knowledge and understanding. It can easily acquire and store new knowledge from within and outside the organization. The positive finding also indicates that hospitals are sharing the best practice among employees of different departments, using teamwork, and employees are capable of accepting suggestions internally and externally.

Limitations of the Study

Although the research study has substantial implications, the study also has some limitations. The first limitation is that the study was performed on small and medium private hospitals in three states in North

India, i.e., Delhi, Uttar Pradesh, and Uttarakhand. The second limitation is that the study is restricted to a specific country, industry and organizational size (small and medium hospitals). The last limitation is the sample size of the study, as it does not represent the view of all small and medium private hospitals of India.

CONCLUSION

India is a population of 1.34 billion people and its resources are developed, to say the least. However, the findings reveal that small and medium private hospitals in these three states (Delhi, Uttar Pradesh, and Uttarakhand) have to rework the way it has historically dealt with issues, the healthcare facilities around the world are changing. The health 4.0 is on its way to occupy the world and likely provides large opportunities. By adopting Heath 4.0 small and medium private hospitals will profit most and have a major competitive advantage over global competitors in the healthcare sector.

In conclusion, the findings from the study expand the information on open innovation dimensions such as horizontal technology collaboration and vertical technology collaboration. It contributes to the existing literature on the subject. Though the concept of open innovation in small and medium private hospitals is not so easy to understand through this, the organization will be aware of the innovation concept. This study will help them to understand the importance of the variables organizational learning towards the open innovation (horizontal technology collaboration and vertical technology collaboration). Also, this study tries to educate both policymakers and doctors on the importance of organizational learning and its relationship to horizontal technology collaboration and vertical technology collaboration. The study paves the way for further studies into the understanding of organizational learning towards open innovation in small and medium private hospitals in the era of health 4.0.

REFERENCES

Belderbos, R., Carree, M., & Lokshin, B. (2004). Cooperative R&D and firm performance. *Research Policy, 33*(10), 1477–1492. doi:10.1016/j.respol.2004.07.003

Bianchi, M., Campodall'Orto, S., Frattini, F., & Vercesi, P. (2010). Enabling open innovation in small and medium-sized enterprises: How to find alternative applications for your technologies. *Research Management, 40*(4), 414–431.

Bosco, A., Reinartz, B., & Müller, S. (2009). *Differential Reynolds stress model and grid adaptation for hypersonic double wedge simulations.* Paper presented at the ICHMT Digital Library Online. 10.1615/ICHMT.2009.TurbulHeatMassTransf.650

Brockhoff, K. (2003). Customers' perspectives on involvement in new product development. *International Journal of Technology Management, 26*(5-6), 464–481. doi:10.1504/IJTM.2003.003418

Calantone, R. J., Cavusgil, S. T., & Zhao, Y. (2002). Learning orientation, firm innovation capability, and firm performance. *Industrial Marketing Management, 31*(6), 515–524. doi:10.1016/S0019-8501(01)00203-6

Chang, D. R., & Cho, H. (2008). Organizational memory influences new product success. *Journal of Business Research, 61*(1), 13–23. doi:10.1016/j.jbusres.2006.05.005

Chaston, I., Badger, B., Mangles, T., & Sadler-Smith, E. (2001). Organizational learning style, competencies, and learning systems in small, UK manufacturing firms. *International Journal of Operations & Production Management, 21*(11), 1417–1432. doi:10.1108/EUM0000000006224

Chesbrough, H. (2003a). *Open innovation.* Boston: Harvard Business School Press.

Chesbrough, H. (2003b). Open Innovation: The New Imperative for Creating and Profiting from Technology. Harvard Business School Publishing Corporation.

Chesbrough, H., Vanhaverbeke, W., & West, J. (2006). *Open innovation: Researching a new paradigm.* Oxford University.

Chin, W. W. (2010). How to write up and report PLS analyses. Handbook of partial least squares, 655-690.

Chiva, R., & Alegre, J. (2005). Organizational learning and organizational knowledge: Towards the integration of two approaches. *Management Learning, 36*(1), 49–68. doi:10.1177/1350507605049906

Cohen, J. (1988). *Statistical power analysis.* Academic Press.

Cohen, W. M., & Levinthal, D. A. (1990). Absorptive capacity: A new perspective on learning and innovation. *Administrative Science Quarterly, 35*(1), 128–152. doi:10.2307/2393553

Colombo, M. G., Piva, E., & Rossi-Lamastra, C. (2014). Open innovation and within-industry diversification in small and medium enterprises: The case of open source software firms. *Research Policy, 43*(5), 891–902. doi:10.1016/j.respol.2013.08.015

Darroch, J., & McNaughton, R. (2003). Beyond market orientation: Knowledge management and the innovativeness of New Zealand firms. *European Journal of Marketing*, *37*(3/4), 572–593. doi:10.1108/03090560310459096

Dinh, D. N. (2017). *Medschool 4.0: how to succeed in the smart revolution of healthcare*. Retrieved 26/7/2019 https://europeansting.com/2017/03/18/medschool-4-0-how-to-succeed-in-the-smart-revolution-of-healthcare/

Durst, S., Mention, A.-L., & Poutanen, P. (2015). Service innovation and its impact: What do we know about? *Investigaciones Europeas de Dirección y Economía de la Empresa*, *21*(2), 65–72. doi:10.1016/j.iedee.2014.07.003

Fey, C. F., & Birkinshaw, J. (2005). External sources of knowledge, governance mode, and R&D performance. *Journal of Management*, *31*(4), 597–621. doi:10.1177/0149206304272346

Gassmann, O. (2006). Opening up the innovation process: Towards an agenda. *Research Management*, *36*(3), 223–228.

Gassmann, O., Enkel, E., & Chesbrough, H. (2010). The future of open innovation. *Research Management*, *40*(3), 213–221.

Global Skill Summit. (2019). *Skill Development for Industry 4.0*. Retrieved 27/11/2019 http://www.globalskillsummit.com/Whitepaper-Summary.pdf

Gnyawali, D. R., & Park, B. J. R. (2009). Co-opetition and technological innovation in small and medium-sized enterprises: A multilevel conceptual model. *Journal of Small Business Management*, *47*(3), 308–330. doi:10.1111/j.1540-627X.2009.00273.x

Gomes, G., & Wojahn, R. M. (2017). Organizational learning capability, innovation, and performance: A study in small and medium-sized enterprises (SMEs). *Revista de Administração (São Paulo)*, *52*(2), 163–175. doi:10.1016/j.rausp.2016.12.003

Govil, N. (2017). *Smart Healthcare for Smart India || IoT in Healthcare*. Retrieved 27/11/2019 https://iotdunia.com/smart-healthcare-for-smart-india/

Hagedoorn, J., Roijakkers, N., & Kranenburg, H. (2006). Inter-firm R&D networks: The importance of strategic network capabilities for high-tech partnership formation. *British Journal of Management*, *17*(1), 39–53. doi:10.1111/j.1467-8551.2005.00474.x

Hair, J. F., Hult, G. T. M., Ringle, C., & Sarstedt, M. (2014). *A Primer on Partial Least Squares Structural Equation Modeling*. PLS-SEM.

Hair, J. F. Jr, Hult, G. T. M., Ringle, C., & Sarstedt, M. (2014). *A primer on partial least squares structural equation modeling (PLS-SEM)*. Sage Publications.

Hair, J. F., Ringle, C. M., & Sarstedt, M. (2011). PLS-SEM: Indeed a silver bullet. *Journal of Marketing Theory and Practice*, *19*(2), 139–152. doi:10.2753/MTP1069-6679190202

Hair, J. F. J. Jr, Sarstedt, M., Hopkins, L., & Kuppelwieser, V. (2014). Partial least squares structural equation modeling (PLS-SEM) An emerging tool in business research. *European Business Review*, *26*(2), 106–121. doi:10.1108/EBR-10-2013-0128

Hall, R., & Andriani, P. (2003). Managing knowledge associated with innovation. *Journal of Business Research*, *56*(2), 145–152. doi:10.1016/S0148-2963(01)00287-9

Hamel, G., Doz, Y. L., & Prahalad, C. K. (1989). Collaborate with your competitors and win. *Harvard Business Review*, *67*(1), 133–139.

Hauser, J., Tellis, G. J., & Griffin, A. (2006). Research on innovation: A review and agenda for marketing science. *Marketing Science*, *25*(6), 687–717. doi:10.1287/mksc.1050.0144

Henseler, J., Ringle, C. M., & Sarstedt, M. (2015). Testing measurement invariance of composites using partial least squares. *International Marketing Review*.

Hochleitner, F. P., Arbussà, A., & Coenders, G. (2017). Inbound open innovation in SMEs: Indicators, non-financial outcomes, and entry-timing. *Technology Analysis and Strategic Management*, *29*(2), 204–218. doi:10.1080/09537325.2016.1211264

Hurley, R. F., & Hult, G. T. M. (1998). Innovation, market orientation, and organizational learning: An integration and empirical examination. *Journal of Marketing*, *62*(3), 42–54. doi:10.1177/002224299806200303

India Brand Equity Foundation. (2017). *Healthcare Industry in India*. Author.

Jiménez-Jiménez, D., & Sanz-Valle, R. (2011). Innovation, organizational learning, and performance. *Journal of Business Research*, *64*(4), 408–417. doi:10.1016/j.jbusres.2010.09.010

Keskin, H. (2006). Market orientation, learning orientation, and innovation capabilities in SMEs: An extended model. *European Journal of Innovation Management*, *9*(4), 396–417. doi:10.1108/14601060610707849

Kock, N. (2014). Advanced mediating effects tests, multi-group analyses, and measurement model assessments in PLS-based SEM. *International Journal of e-Collaboration*, *10*(1), 1–13. doi:10.4018/ijec.2014010101

Kohli, A. K., & Jaworski, B. J. (1990). Market orientation: The construct, research propositions, and managerial implications. *Journal of Marketing*, *54*(2), 1–18. doi:10.1177/002224299005400201

Laursen, K., & Salter, A. (2006). Open for innovation: The role of openness in explaining innovation performance among UK manufacturing firms. *Strategic Management Journal*, *27*(2), 131–150. doi:10.1002mj.507

Lichtenthaler, U. (2008). Open innovation in practice: An analysis of strategic approaches to technology transactions. *IEEE Transactions on Engineering Management*, *55*(1), 148–157. doi:10.1109/TEM.2007.912932

Marques, J. P. (2014). Closed versus open innovation: Evolution or combination? *International Journal of Business and Management*, *9*(3), 196. doi:10.5539/ijbm.v9n3p196

McDermott, C. M., & Prajogo, D. I. (2012). Service innovation and performance in SMEs. *International Journal of Operations & Production Management*, *32*(2), 216–237. doi:10.1108/01443571211208632

McGill, M. E., & Slocum, J. W. Jr. (1993). Unlearning the organization. *Organizational Dynamics*, *22*(2), 67–79. doi:10.1016/0090-2616(93)90054-5

Moorman, C., & Miner, A. S. (1997). The impact of organizational memory on new product performance and creativity. *JMR, Journal of Marketing Research*, *34*(1), 91–106. doi:10.1177/002224379703400108

Narula, R. (2004). R&D collaboration by SMEs: New opportunities and limitations in the face of globalization. *Technovation*, *24*(2), 153–161. doi:10.1016/S0166-4972(02)00045-7

Nonaka, I. (2002). A dynamic theory of organizational knowledge creation. *The strategic management of intellectual capital and organizational knowledge*, 437-462.

O'Cass, A., & Sok, P. (2013). Exploring innovation-driven value creation in B2B service firms: The roles of the manager, employees, and customers in value creation. *Journal of Business Research*, *66*(8), 1074–1084. doi:10.1016/j.jbusres.2012.03.004

Parida, V., Westerberg, M., & Frishammar, J. (2012). Inbound open innovation activities in high-tech SMEs: The impact on innovation performance. *Journal of Small Business Management*, *50*(2), 283–309. doi:10.1111/j.1540-627X.2012.00354.x

Pisano, G. P., & Verganti, R. (2008). Which kind of collaboration is right for you. *Harvard Business Review*, *86*(12), 78–86.

Sekaran, U. (2003). *Research Method For Business, a skill-building approach.* Wiley India.

Shaw, B. (1995). *User/supplier links and innovation. In The handbook of industrial innovation.* Edward Elgar Publishing.

Shrinivasan, S. (2018). *Life Sciences 4.0: transforming health care in India.* Retrieved 27/11/2019, from https://www.ey.com/Publication/vwLUAssets/ey-transforming-health-care-in-india/$File/ey-transforming-health-care-in-india.pdf

Sinkula, J. M. (1994). Market information processing and organizational learning. *Journal of Marketing*, *58*(1), 35–45. doi:10.1177/002224299405800103

Slater, S. F., & Narver, J. C. (1995). Market orientation and the learning organization. *Journal of Marketing*, *59*(3), 63–74. doi:10.1177/002224299505900306

Sørensen, J. B., & Stuart, T. E. (2000). Aging, obsolescence, and organizational innovation. *Administrative Science Quarterly*, *45*(1), 81–112. doi:10.2307/2666980

Spithoven, A., Vanhaverbeke, W., & Roijakkers, N. (2013). Open innovation practices in SMEs and large enterprises. *Small Business Economics*, *41*(3), 537–562. doi:10.100711187-012-9453-9

Tether, B. S. (2002). Who co-operates for innovation, and why: An empirical analysis. *Research Policy*, *31*(6), 947–967. doi:10.1016/S0048-7333(01)00172-X

Tippins, M. J., & Sohi, R. S. (2003). IT competency and firm performance: Is organizational learning a missing link? *Strategic Management Journal*, *24*(8), 745–761. doi:10.1002mj.337

Van de Vrande, V., De Jong, J. P., Vanhaverbeke, W., & De Rochemont, M. (2009). Open innovation in SMEs: Trends, motives and management challenges. *Technovation*, *29*(6), 423–437. doi:10.1016/j.technovation.2008.10.001

Verbano, C., & Crema, M. (2016). Linking technology innovation strategy, intellectual capital and technology innovation performance in manufacturing SMEs. *Technology Analysis and Strategic Management*, *28*(5), 524–540. doi:10.1080/09537325.2015.1117066

Verma, R., & Jayasimha, K. (2014). Service delivery innovation architecture: An empirical study of antecedents and outcomes. *IIMB Management Review*, *26*(2), 105–121. doi:10.1016/j.iimb.2014.03.002

Wang, C.-H., Chang, C.-H., & Shen, G. C. (2015). The effect of inbound open innovation on firm performance: Evidence from the high-tech industry. *Technological Forecasting and Social Change*, *99*, 222–230. doi:10.1016/j.techfore.2015.07.006

Weng, R.-H., & Huang, C.-Y. (2017). The impact of exploration and exploitation learning on organizational innovativeness among hospitals: An open innovation view. *Technology Analysis and Strategic Management*, *29*(2), 119–132. doi:10.1080/09537325.2016.1210120

Yli-Renko, H., Autio, E., & Sapienza, H. J. (2001). Social capital, knowledge acquisition, and knowledge exploitation in young technology-based firms. *Strategic Management Journal*, *22*(6-7), 587–613. doi:10.1002mj.183

Chapter 8
The Labour, Machine, and Material as Sources of Value-Addition for SMEs:
An Empirical Evidence From India

Mokhalles Mohammad Mehdi
Tezpur University, India

Tridib Ranjan Sarma
Tezpur University, India

ABSTRACT

Value addition is a process of changing (converting) input into output with an investment of optimum resources. The present study aims to identify the variables of value addition among MSMEs and its performance in an economy. The study is based on a review of literature from various published sources and analyses to uncover the required variables. Past reviews highlighted that SME performance can be categorized into financial and non-financial characteristics. The previous studies have identified that SME performance depends on the financial factors, marketing factors, production factors, operation activities, and human resources of the enterprises. A survey was conducted among four MSMEs in district industries and commerce centre (DIC), Jorhat (Assam), India using a structured questionnaire constructed from the variables found in past studies. The survey findings highlighted the growth indicators and the challenges that MSMEs faced.

DOI: 10.4018/978-1-7998-2577-7.ch008

INTRODUCTION

Constant technological changes and increasing competition in the market demanded smaller companies to focus on the value delivery in their products. Value addition (VA) is changing the inputs into a product or service with the increased value of outputs compared to the sum of the value of inputs (Adam, Jr. and Ebert, 2007). Value addition is an alternative to measure the productive value of firms. It is the difference between the value of output and the value of intermediate input.

The value-added process or manufacturing is nothing but modifications to the existing products. Bishop (1990) defined value-added as "adding those manufacturing or service steps to a commodity product, which the customer perceives as increasing its value". Customers are ready to pay for a value-added product if they believe that the product offers value. VA is influenced by flexibility, quality, and production process. Flexibility is how a firm can react and quickly changes that according to the market requirement. Quality is an important parameter in the value addition process at a lower cost and it is expected by the customer. Production methods and processes contribute to improving value-addition (Benetto et al., 2009).

Value-added product at lower costs improves the performance of a firm. The VA of a product in a manufacturing unit could be achieved by reducing activity time, cost of methods and procedures processes, recognizing bottlenecks, and so on. This will improve and develop the production process and provide value-addition to the products (Mehta, 2009). The VA can be successful with the close collaboration and support of different functional departments of organizations such as Purchasing, Quality, Production, Engineering, Marketing, and Finance (Shukla and Misra, 2013).

So, the present study focused on Small and Medium Enterprises (SMEs) and planned to understand the value addition of MSMEs. The SME sector has a significant contribution to the economic development and social development of an economy. The definition of SMEs is varied from country to country in the manufacturing and services sector both. Each country possesses diverse businesses in the category of micro, small and medium-size industries. There is no uniformity in the definition of MSMEs/ SMEs in the world economy and industry. Similar industries in different countries have defined MSMEs/SMEs in different ways. However, across the world economy, MSMEs or SMEs are defined using the criterion either the number of employees or amount of capital investment or maybe both (Ghose, 2001). However, the SMEs are categorized into small-sized businesses employing less than 50 workers; medium-sized businesses employing between 50 and 199 workers; and larger sized businesses employing 200 employees and above by the World Bank (1984), the United Nations Industrial Development Organization (1985) and the Asian Development Bank (1990) (Jamil & Mohamed, 2011).

Value addition is frequently used as an important dimension to assess micro, small and medium enterprises (MSMEs') strength, competence in changing inputs to outputs, and possibilities. Therefore, the present study attempted to identify factors that influence value addition among the MSMEs.

REVIEW OF LITERATURE

Past relevant studies were reviewed to uncover the variables that influence the value addition of an enterprise. The reviews were categorized into several parameters to understand the influence of variables in the value addition of MSMEs and its performance.

Value Addition Process and Productivity

The production and operation department of an organization generates the output: physical product or service. The output is a common phenomenon across diverse organizations. Manufacturing organization produces the physical good (product)[1] through a process of conversion. The elements of operation were common across the institution. The key elements of the operating system are input, conversion process, output, and feedback (Adam, Jr. and Ebert, 2007). The inputs are the land, labor, capital (in the form of building, equipment, and merchandise) and management resources applied and modified through the conversion process (a change process) to generate the output either the physical product or service. Post generation of output, the actual product is compared with the desired level to understand the variation in the output and to examine the required level of modification (if any). The variation or random fluctuations in the product happened due to the unplanned changes in the external environment or internal forces (human error, material, and equipment deficiencies). However, the conversion process ensures the smooth production of a value-addition[2] in the output eliminating the level of deficiencies' and the product is converted into cash to procure adequate resources to continue the conversion process. The operation or conversion process aims to offer a value-added output to the customers instead of summing all input material making the product worthy.

The value addition of physical product through a transformation process can be measured by the assessment of output versus input to understand the performance of an organization. The overall achievement of the organization in terms of its input and output is possible to calculate through efficiency and productivity analysis. The productivity (efficiency) can be referred to as a ratio of outputs to inputs (Chary, 2012; Panneerselvam, 2015; Bedi, 2015; Adam, Jr. and Ebert, 2007).

Arthur (1994) in his study on the Effects of Human Resource Systems on Manufacturing Performance and Turnover evaluated 30 United States strip mills to measure the impact on labor efficiency and scrap rate. He revealed enterprises with a high commitment to human resource strategy had considerably higher levels of productivity and quality. Youndt et al. (1996) identified that the human resource system dedicated to human assets management was directly related to multiple dimensions of operational performance such as employee productivity, machine efficiency, and customer alignment. Ichniowski and shaw (1999) conducted a comparative study among the 41 steel production lines of the United States and Japan to evaluate the effects human resource management practices on worker productivity and revealed that the Japanese lines are considerably more fruitful than the U.S. lines.

Shah et al. (2014) in their study conducted at the central Gujarat region, India and specified that productivity is vital for the growth in reducing the loss of project or increased profit. They recommended low payment, poor construction methods, use of technology, delays in material delivery were the most important factors affected productivity. Khaled and Remon (2014) in their study indicated about 30 productivity factors and categorized them into three classifications as Human/labor, Industrial and Management. They identified five most important factors such as Labour experience and skills, Incentive programs, Availability of the material and ease of handling, Leadership, and competency, and Competency of labor supervision in construction labor productivity in Egypt.

Further, Saravanan and Surendar (2016) in their study determined eleven factors namely, time, quality, safety, managerial factors, the experience of labor, type of project, misunderstanding, external factors, motivation, material/tools, and natural factors influenced the labor productivity. Attar et al. (2012) in their study recognized factors affecting labor productivity for small, medium and large companies in Sangli, Kolhapur and Pune districts of India. They revealed that factors such as supervision, material, execution plan, and design are highly effective and equipment factors are in large companies. On the other hand, owner/consultant factors require superior attention in small and medium companies.

Past research highlighted that productivity can be stated either on a total factor or a partial factor basis. The total factor basis productivity (TFP) (Chary, 2012; Panneerselvam, 2015; Bedi, 2015; Adam, Jr. and Ebert, 2007).

Total Factor Productivity (TFP) = Outputs / (Labour + Capital + Materials + Energy)

On the other hand, outputs relative to the individual input such as labor, capital, materials or energy are known as partial factor basis productivity (PFT) (Chary, 2012; Panneerselvam, 2015; Bedi, 2015; Adam, Jr. and Ebert, 2007). PFT can be calculated for each input separately,

§ Capital productivity = Output / Capital input
§ Labour productivity = Output / Labour input
§ Material productivity = Output / Material input
§ Machine productivity= Output/ Machine input
§ Energy productivity= Output/ Energy input

Moreover, previous researches in Indian MSMEs indicated that the growth and productivity of MSMEs were calculated with certain specific parameters namely, total number of MSMEs unit, fixed investment (Rupees in crore) by the MSMEs, production of MSMEs (rupees in crore at current prices), total person employed by the MSMEs (in lakh), and total exports from MSMEs (Rupees in crore) in a given financial year (Bala Subrahmanya, 2004; Bargal et al., 2009; Dixit & Pandey, 2011; Singh et al., 2012; Goel & Prakash, 2014; Rajpal, 2015; Meganathan et al., 2015; Sankaraiah & Mohan, 2016; Das, 2017; Khanna & Singh, 2018).

Determinants of Performance

To evaluate the success of MSMEs, it is important to measure the profitability of a business. Edmister (1970) among other researchers have suggested that small firms need to concentrate on profitability. Ross et al. (1999) suggested methods such as profit margin or return on sales, return on assets, and return on equity are important to measure the profitability of a business.

The success of MSMEs depends on few characteristics identified by the previous researchers in their study. The characteristics were such as commitment to change (Smallbone et al., 1995); duration of business operation (age) (Woldie et al., 2008; Kristiansen et al., 2003); size of enterprise (Woldie et al., 2008; McMahon, 2001); legal status (Woldie et al., 2008); sector of business operation (Woldie et al., 2008); style of operation (Hudson et al., 2001); influence of personal and family factors in decision making (Smallbone et al., 1995); same owners and managers (Pansiri and Temtime, 2008); competence and level of expertise of managers (Anggadwita and Mustafid, 2014; Kinyua, 2014; Pansiri and Temtime, 2008;); managers age, managers education level, the specialty and risk-averse effect of manager (Islam et al., 2011); dependency upon external finance (McMahon, 2001); and financial flexibility (Kristiansen et al., 2003) had a positive effect on the growth of SMES.

Past researchers also identified some influencing variables such as market access (Swierczek & Ha, 2003; Mead & Liedholm, 1998); identification and respond towards the new market opportunities

(Smallbone et al., 1995); market stability (Kristiansen et al., 2003); market orientation for creation of behavior for making and providing superior value to customers (Verhees & Meulenberg, 2004); technological changes (Gundry et al., 2003) and its adoption were determined the performance of MSMEs. Some other variables such as access to information (Swierczek & Ha, 2003; Gundry et al., 2003; Duh, 2003; Kristiansen, 2002; Mead & Liedholm, 1998); networking (Kristiansen, 2004; Gundry et al., 2003; Aldrich & Zimmer, 1986); adequate marketing strategy; advancement of the firms technology; wider access to the capital; support from government agencies, universities and other entities (Indarti and Langenberg, 2004) are the essential element for the success of MSMEs.

Also, some other factors such as ðnance and customer (Wang et al., 2015); internal business, work satisfaction, pay and beneðts, innovation and technology, etc., determine the organizational performance (Tasliyan et al., 2018; Wang et al., 2015).

The scarcity of resource personnel, managerial time, financial stability, and security (Singh et al., 2008); obsolete technology and lack of tools & equipment (Swierczek & Ha, 2003; Hashim, 2000); shortage of skilled workers, shortage of raw materials, insufficient infrastructure, lack of human resource expertise (managerial, marketing and technical) were the main problems of SMEs (Hashim, 2000). Moreover, lack of access to capital and credit schemes (Meier & Pilgrim, 1994; Steel, 1994; Marsden, 1992); lack of support from bank and financial institutions and high-interest rate in loan (Robinson, 1993); and informal way of control, and coordination activity (Davila, 2000) are the limitations for SMEs growth. Hence, in this backdrop, the present research aims to uncover the variables of value addition among MSMEs.

OBJECTIVE

The key objective of the study is to identify the variables of value addition among MSMEs and its performance.

METHODOLOGY

The study adopted relevant secondary information to build the foundation of the paper. Secondary data of relevant published research papers from journals, online articles, and news reports were collected.

The study aimed to identify the factors of value addition among the select MSMEs. A survey was conducted using a structured questionnaire with entrepreneurs (owners) or the managers of four MSMEs situated at the district industries and commerce center (DICC), Jorhat district, Assam (India). The questionnaire constructed from the few selected variables found in the literature reviewed. The questionnaire designed with a 5-point liker-t scale to record the response. A list of variables and measurement criteria identified from the past studies were highlighted in Table 1. The variables such as profitability, SMEs characteristics, Managerial characteristics, internal factors to the MSMEs, financial support, and marketing factors to the MSMEs considered to identify and evaluate the importance of factors.

The liker-t scale parameters were assigned weight value of 5 to 1 from positive towards negative parameters to calculate the total value and weighted value of each statement highlighted in the questionnaire. The data were synthesized and presented simply to fulfill the objectives.

Table 1. List of variables and its measurement criteria's

Variables	Measurement criteria
Economic indicator	Estimated number of units Total employment Employment per unit Fixed investment
Productivity	Labor productivity Capital productivity Material productivity Machine productivity
Profitability	Return on sales Return on assets Return on equity
SMEs characteristics	Duration of business operation (age) Size of enterprise Legal status The sector of business operation Style of operation Dependency upon external finance Financial flexibility
Managerial characteristics	Commitment to change Influence of personal and family factors in decision making Same owners and managers Competence and level of expertise of managers Managers age, managers education level, specialty, and risk-taking
Internal factors	Top management support and entrepreneurial orientation Short term business planning Method of doing business and collaboration, firm's resources and finance The informal way of control, and coordination activity Internal business, work satisfaction, pay and beneðts Shortage of skilled workers and lack of human resources expertise of SMEs Shortage of raw materials Access to information Networking Technological changes Innovation and technology Suppliers
Financial support	Wider access to the capital Support from government agencies, universities and other entities Lack of support from the bank and financial institutions; high-interest rate in loan
Marketing factors	Adequate marketing strategy Market access Identification and respond towards the new market opportunities Market stability Market orientation for superior value to customers Customers Competitors, banks and investment environment

Source: Compiled from past literature, 2019

CONCEPTUAL FRAMEWORK

The conceptual framework derived from the past studies reviewed. It consists of input (independent) and output (dependent) variables (see figure 1). The independent variables impacted on value addition process leading to the firm's performance. SME's performance was measured in terms of profitability and productivity. The details of variables that affect the organizations' value addition and its performance were mentioned in Table 1. The input variables such as labor, machine, and material allow the organization to create a significant change in the output in terms of the value-added output. The list of variables is vital for all the input variables of the conceptual model and significant in determining the SMEs' performance.

Figure 1. Conceptual model of value addition
Source: Author, 2019

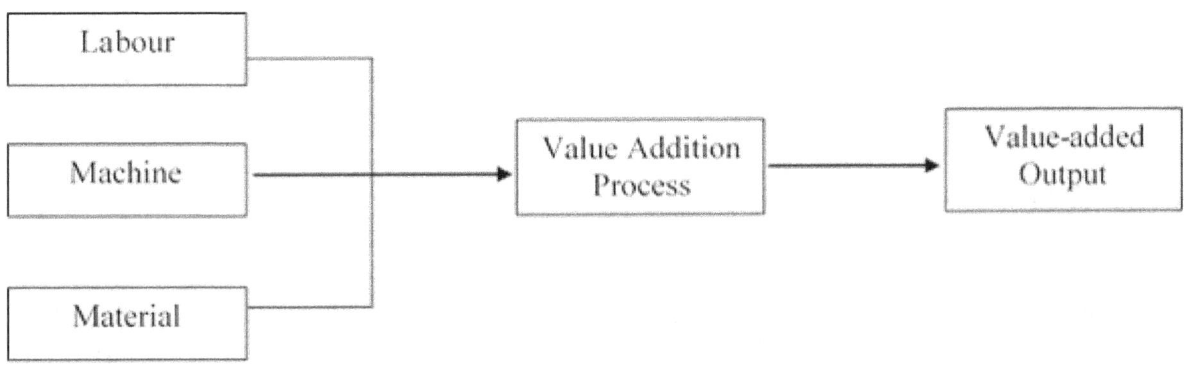

DATA ANALYSIS AND FINDINGS

The findings are divided into three key areas: firms demographics, growth drivers of MSMEs, and problem areas of MSMEs.

Firm's Demographic Profile

The findings of the survey highlighted the profile of four MSMEs located at Jorhat district of Assam, India. The MSMEs were into the Manufacturing/ Processing/ Assembling type of business operations. The survey revealed that the owner is the key decision-maker in those MSMEs. Out of four MSMEs, three MSMEs are more than 10 years old, and one falls in the age bracket of 4 to 6 years. The total number of employees working in the MSMEs were categorized and highlighted in Table 2. Similarly, annual turnover (in million India rupees) of these MSMEs were highlighted in Table 3.

Furthermore, a survey focused on the growth drivers or performance indicators' of MSMEs and the problems faced by those MSMEs in operating their businesses. A list of statements related to MSMEs activities was applied to understand and analyze the situation. The responses of MSMEs owners and or managers are considered on a 5 point liker-t scale for each of those states.

Table 2. Number of employees

Number of employees working in the firm	Frequency	Percent
5 to 10	1	25
11 to 20	2	50
21 to 50	1	25
Total	4	100

Source: Primary survey conducted by the author, 2018

Table 3. Annual turnover of the firm

Annual turnover of the firm (in Indian rupees)	Frequency	Percent
1.5 million to less than 2.5 million	1	25
2.5 million to less than 5 million	1	25
5 million to 10 million	1	25
More than 1o million	1	25
Total	4	100

Source: Primary survey conducted by the author, 2018

Growth Drivers

To assess the growth drivers of MSMEs, 5-point liker-t scale with the parameters Extremely Relevant (ER), Relevant (R), Neutral (N), Irrelevant (I), Extremely Irrelevant (EI), Don't Know/ Can't say (DK/ CS) were applied and assigned a weight of 5, 4, 3, 2, and 1 respectively for each of these options. Subsequently, calculated the total weight,

Total weightage= Sum of weight = Weight of ER + Weight of R + Weight of N + Weight of I + Weight of EI = 5+4+3+2+1 = 15

Total value (TV) calculated on total response for statement,

TV (Long term business planning) = Weight * response = 5*4 + 4*0 + 3*0 + 2*0 + 1*0 = 20

Weighted value (WV) for Long term business planning = TV/Sum of Weights = 20/15 = 1.33

Similarly, calculated the total value and weighted value for each of these states of growth drivers and highlighted in table 4. However, the calculation not considered the values of Don't Know/ Can't say (DK/CS) in the Weighted average calculation.

Table 4. Drivers /Performance indicators of SMEs

	ER	R	N	I	EI	DK/ CS	Total	TV	WV
The weight assigned on the options	5	4	3	2	1		15		
Long term business planning	4	-	-	-	-	-	4	20	1.33
Owners provided support for the business growth	4	-	-	-	-	-	4	20	1.33
Providing superior or quality value (product) delivery to customers	3	1	-	-	-	-	4	19	1.27
Enterprises focus on the customer requirement	3	1	-	-	-	-	4	19	1.27
Wider access to capital	2	2	-	-	-	-	4	18	1.20
Provided training to the employees and technicians	2	2	-	-	-	-	4	18	1.20
Employees stability within the organization	2	2	-	-	-	-	4	18	1.20
Sufficient information technology environment for business operation	1	3	-	-	-	-	4	17	1.13
Adopted new technology for product development	-	4	-	-	-	-	4	16	1.07
Received support from government agencies	2	-	2	-	-	-	4	16	1.07
Adequate performance measurement system for business growth	2	-	2	-	-	-	4	16	1.07
Wider access to business and technical information	1	1	2	-	-	-	4	15	1.00
Improved the firm's new technology for value addition	1	1	2				4	15	1.00
Identification of market opportunities	2	1	-	-	-	1	4	14	0.93
Encourage innovation in business operation and product development	2	1	-	-	-	1	4	14	0.93
Adequate performance measurement system for employees	-	2	2	-	-	-	4	14	0.93
Wider business network	1	2	-	-	-	1	4	13	0.87
Devised an adequate marketing strategy	1	2	-	-	-	1	4	13	0.87
Proper employee promotional benefits available	1	-	1	2		-	4	12	0.80
Dependent on external financial support for business operation	1	-	-	2	1	-	4	10	0.67
Responding towards market opportunities	1	1	-	-	-	2	4	9	0.60
Senior management provided support for the business growth	1			2		1	4	9	0.60
Enterprise has collaborated with others for business operation	-	1	-	2	1	-	4	9	0.60
Have short term business planning	-	-	-	2	2	-	4	6	0.40

Source: Calculated by the author, Primary survey 2018; Note: Excluded the response of DK/CS in the WV calculation

The result of higher weighted values indicates that those parameters are more important for the growth and success of MSMEs as compared to lower weighted value. The growth parameters of MSMEs are ranked higher weighted value to lower weighted value namely, Long term business planning; Owners provided support for the business growth; Providing superior or quality value (product) delivery to customers; Enterprises focus towards the customer requirement; Wider access to capital; Provided training to the employees and technicians; Employees stability within the organization; Sufficient information technology environment for business operation; Adopted new technology for product development; Received support from government agencies; Adequate performance measurement system for business growth; Wider access to business and technical information; Improved the firms new technology for value addition; Identification of market opportunities; Encourage innovation in business operation and product development; Adequate performance measurement system for employees; Wider business network; Devised adequate marketing strategy; Proper employee promotional benefits available; Dependent on external financial support for business operation; Responding towards market opportunities; Senior management provided support for the business growth; Enterprise has collaborated with others for business operation, and Have short term business planning. The owners and or managers of MSMEs focus are on the higher weighted value parameters for the growth and performance of their units.

Problems of MSMEs

On the other hand, problems of MSMEs were assessed considering the 5-point liker-t scale mentioning the parameters Strongly Agree (SA), Agree (A), Neutral (N), Disagree (D), Strongly Disagree (SD), Don't Know/ Can't say (DK/CS) and assigned a weight of 5, 4, 3, 2, and 1 respectively for each of these options. Subsequently, calculated the total weight,

Total weightage= Sum of weight = Weight of SA + Weight of A + Weight of N + Weight of D + Weight of SD = 5+4+3+2+1 = 15

Total value (TV) calculated on total response for statement,

TV (Shortage of skilled workers) = Weight * response = 5*2 + 4*0 + 3*2 + 2*0 + 1*0 = 16

The weighted average (WA) for Shortage of skilled workers = TV/Sum of Weights =16/15 = 1.07

Similarly, calculate the total value and weighted average value for each of the statements related to problem areas of MSMEs and highlighted in table 5. However, the calculation not considered the values of Don't Know/ Can't say (DK/CS) in the Weighted average calculation.

Table 5. Problems faced by MSME's

Problems faced by MSMEs	SA	A	N	D	DA	DK/CS	Total	TV	WA
The weight assigned on the options	5	4	3	2	1		15		
Shortage of skilled workers	2	-	2	-	-	-	4	16	1.07
Shortage of skilled technicians	2	-	2	-	-	-	4	16	1.07
Shortage of raw materials	1	-		3	-	-	4	11	0.73
Lack of access to capital and credit schemes	1	-	2	-	-	1	4	11	0.73
Control and coordination among the department	-	-	3	1	-	-	4	11	0.73
Lack of support from the bank and financial institutions	1	-	-	2	-	1	4	9	0.60
High interest in a loan	1	-	-	2	-	1	4	9	0.60

Source: Calculated by the author, Primary survey 2018; Note: Excluded the response of DK/CS in the WV calculation

The result of higher weighted values indicates that those parameters with high values were the key concern area. The major challenges faced by MSMEs are listed from their higher weighted value to lower value such as Shortage of skilled workers; Shortage of skilled technicians; Shortage of raw materials; Lack of access to capital and credit schemes; Control and coordination among the department; Lack of support from bank and financial institutions; and High interest in loan. Hence, owners and managers of MSMEs need to overcome these challenges for the growth and performance of their units.

Demographic Profile of Respondent

Table 6 highlighted the demographic profile of the respondent (owner and or manager of the MSMEs). The findings indicated that all the respondents were male and the majority of the respondents were the owner of MSMEs and they are graduates.

Table 6. Demographic Profile of Respondent

Gender of respondent	Frequency	Percent
Male	4	100
Respondent designation in the firm		
Owner	3	75
Manager	1	25
Total	4	100
The age group of respondent		
31 to 40 years	1	25
51 to 60 years	2	50
Above 60 years	1	25
Total	4	100
Level of education of the respondent		
10th standard pass	1	25
Graduate	3	75
Total	4	100

Source: Primary survey conducted by the author, 2018

CONCLUSION AND FUTURE RESEARCH

SMEs play a vital role in the growth and development of developing and developed economies. SMEs play an essential role in the growth and development of business, entrepreneurship, economy, generation of employment, and output growth in India. Gamage (2003) indicated that a small investment SMEs contributed to the growth of the socio-economic benefits of the nation. Some of the challenges for SMEs are inefficient management, lack of technical know-how, improper marketing strategy, little focus on R&D and up-to-date modern technology (Grimsholm & Pobelete, 2010) and lack of finance (Hussain et al., 2012). Some other shortcomings were short term business planning and not focused on long term business planning (Hudson et al., 2001).

The key variables namely, strategy, leadership, structure, quality, innovation and development, information technology, performance measurement, employees, corporate governance, external environment (Gavrea et al., 2011), top management support and entrepreneurial orientation (Lo et al, 2016); method of doing business and collaboration, firm's resources and finance (Chittithaworn et al., 2011) have an impact in the growth of SMEs. Further, some of the internal factors are: SME's characteristics (Indarti & Langenberg, 2005); managerial characteristics (Kemayel, 2015); and ways (methods) of doing business (Islam et al. 2008; Kemayel, 2015) and the external factors such as customers, suppliers (Kemayel, 2015; Chittithaworn et al., 2011; Islam et al., 2008); competitors, banks and investment environment (Kemayel, 2015) were also affects the performance.

Past literature has indicated about the variables of MSMEs' performance. SMEs have a key role in the development of an economy and there was no relevant study available in the attempted area of value addition on MSMEs. Hence, a conceptual framework was developed including the input (raw material, machine, manpower, and energy) and output to understand the relationship between the MSMEs' input and output. The conceptual framework of the present study will be useful to assess the value addition among SMEs of various locations.

The survey findings highlighted variables namely, identification of market opportunity and responding, providing superior value to customers, the use of new technology for product development, business network, marketing strategy, access to capital, and government agencies support drives the success of MSMEs. The survey revealed few growth indicators of MSMEs such as long term business planning, encourage innovation, and a sufficient information technology environment for business operation. Last, MSMEs faced some of the key challenges namely, shortage of skilled workers and the shortage of skilled technicians.

The present study is limited to the productivity and value addition process of SMEs. The study attempted to uncover the variables that drive the growth and concern for SMEs were highlighted. Hence, the future assessment on the variables of value addition of MSMEs must consider aforesaid limitations to cover and focus on the other areas of organizational parameters. However, future researchers can aim in other organizational variables not considered in the study.

ACKNOWLEDGMENT

The present paper is a part of ongoing Ph.D. research work in the Department of Business Administration, Tezpur University, Assam carried by the author.

REFERENCES

Adam, E. E., Jr., & Ebert, R. J. (2007). Production and Operations Management Concepts, Models, and Behaviour (5th ed.). New Delhi, India: Prentice-Hall of India Private Limited.

Aldrich, H., & Zimmer, C. (1986). Entrepreneurship through a social network. In D. L. Sexton & R. W. Smilor (Eds.), *The Art and Science of Entrepreneurship* (pp. 3–25). Cambridge, UK: Ballinger Publishing.

Anggadwita, G., & Mustafid, Q. Y. (2014). Identification of factors influencing the performance of small-medium enterprises (SMEs). *Procedia: Social and Behavioral Sciences, 115*, 415–423. doi:10.1016/j.sbspro.2014.02.448

Arthur, J. B. (1994). Effects of Human Resource Systems on Manufacturing Performance and Turnover. *Academy of Management Journal, 37*, 670–687.

Attar, A. A., Gupta, A. K., & Desai, D. B. (2012). A Study of Various Factors Affecting Labour Productivity and Methods to Improve It. *IOSR Journal of Mechanical and Civil Engineering,* 11-14. Online available at http://www.iosrjournals.org/iosr-jmce/papers/sicete(civil)-volume1/3.pdf

Bala Subrahmanya, M. H. (2004). Small Industry and Globalization: Implications, Performance, and Prospects. *Economic and Political Weekly, 39*(18), 1826–1834.

Bargal, H., Dashmishra, M., & Sharma, A. (2009). Performance Analysis of Small Scale Industries - A Study of Pre-liberalization and Post-liberalization period. *International Journal of Business and Management, 1*(2), 17–26.

Bedi, K. (2015). *Production and Operations Management* (3rd ed.). New Delhi, India: Oxford University Press.

Benetto, E., Becker, M., & Welfring, J. (2009). Life Cycle Assessment of Oriented Strand Boards (OSB): From Process Innovation to Ecodesign. *Environmental Science & Technology, 43*(15), 6003–6009. doi:10.1021/es900707u PMID:19731710

Bishop, J. (1990). In value-added manufacturing, customer calls the shots. *Forest Industries, 1990*, 29–31.

Chary, S. N. (2012). *Production and Operations Management* (5th ed.). New Delhi, India: Tata McGraw Hill Education Private Limited.

Chittithaworn, C., Islam, M. A., Keawchana, T., & Yusuf, D. H. M. (2011). Factors Affecting Business Success of Small & Medium Enterprises (SMEs) in Thailand. *Asian Social Science, 7*(5), 180–190. doi:10.5539/ass.v7n5p180

Das, P. (2017). Micro, Small and Medium Enterprises (MSME) in India: Opportunities, Issues & Challenges. *Great Lakes Herald, 11*(1), 77–88.

Davila, T. (2000). An empirical study on the drivers of MCS: Design in new product development. *Accounting, Organizations and Society, 25*(4-5), 383–409. doi:10.1016/S0361-3682(99)00034-3

Dixit, A., & Pandey, A. K. (2011). SMEs and Economic Growth in India: Cointegration Analysis. *The IUP Journal of Financial Economics, 9*(2), 41–59.

Duh, M. (2003). Family enterprises as an important factor in economic development: The case of Slovenia. *Journal of Enterprising Culture, 11*(2), 111–130. doi:10.1142/S021849580300007X

Edmister, R. O. (1970). *Financial ratios as discriminant predictors of small business failure* (Doctoral dissertation). The Ohio State University, Columbus, OH.

ENDNOTES

Gamage, A. (2003). *Small and Medium Enterprises in Sri Lanka: A Review.* Retrieved from http://202.11.2.113/SEBM/ronso/no3_4/aruna.pdf

Gavrea, C., Ilieş, L., & Stegerean, R. (2011). Determinants of Organizational Performance: The Case of Romania. *Management & Marketing Challenges for the Knowledge Society, 6*(2), 285–300.

Ghose, A. K. (2001). SMEs and environment protection. *Productivity, 42*(2), 101–117.

Goel, M. M., & Prakash (2014). Micro Enterprises in Haryana: An Analysis. *Voice of Research, 3*(1). Retrieved from http://www.voiceofresearch.org/doc/Jun-2014/Jun-2014_15.pdf

Grimsholm, E., & Poblete, L. (2010). *Internal and External Factors Hampering SMEs growth: A qualitative case study of SMEs in Thailand.* Retrieved from http://hgo.diva-portal.org/smash/get/diva2:323837/FULLTEXT01

Gundry, L., Kickul, J., Welsch, H. P., & Posig, M. (2003). Technological innovation in women-owned firms: Influence of entrepreneurial motivation and strategic intention. *The International Journal of Entrepreneurship and Innovation, 4*(1), 265–274. doi:10.5367/000000003129574324

Hashim, M. K. (2000). SMEs in Malaysia: Past, Present, and Future. *Malaysian Management Review, 35*(2), 22–30.

Hudson, M., Smart, A., & Bourne, M. (2001). Theory and practice in SME performance measurement system. *International Journal of Operations & Production Management, 21*(8), 1096–1115. doi:10.1108/EUM0000000005587

Hussain, I., Farooq, Z., & Akhtar, W. (2012). SME Development and Failure Avoidance in Developing Countries through Public-Private Partnership. *African Journal of Business Management, 6*(4), 1581–1589.

Ichniowski, C., & Shaw, K. (1999). The Effects of Human Resource Management Systems on Economic Performance: An International Comparison of U.S. and Japanese Plants. *Management Science, 45*(5), 704–721. doi:10.1287/mnsc.45.5.704

Indarti, N., & Langenberg, M. (2004). Factors affecting business success among SMEs: empirical evidence from Indonesia. *Proceedings of the (19) 20 & 21 September 2004 Second Bi-Annual European Summer University* (pp. 1-14). University of Twente.

Indarti, N., & Langenberg, M. (2005). A Study of Factors Affecting Business Success among SMEs: Empirical Evidences from Indonesia. *Asian Social Science, 7*(5), 67–86.

Islam, M. A., Khan, M. A., Obaidullah, A. Z. M., & Alam, M. S. (2011). Effect of Entrepreneur and Firm Characteristics on the Business Success of Small and Medium Enterprises (SMEs) in Bangladesh. *International Journal of Business and Management, 6*(3), 289–299.

Islam, M. A., Mian, E., & Ali, M. H. (2008). Determinants of Business Success of Small and Medium Enterprises (SMEs) in Bangladesh. *Business Review (Federal Reserve Bank of Philadelphia)*, *4*(2), 45–57.

Jamil, C. M., & Mohamed, R. (2011). Performance Measurement System (PMS) In Small Medium Enterprises (SMEs): A Practical Modified Framework. *World Journal of Social Sciences*, *1*(3), 200–212.

Kemayel, L. (2015). Success Factors of Lebanese SMEs: An Empirical Study. *Procedia: Social and Behavioral Sciences*, *195*, 1123–1128. doi:10.1016/j.sbspro.2015.06.158

Khaled, M. E., & Remon, F. A. (2014). Factors Influencing Construction Labor Productivity in Egypt. *Journal of Management Engineering*, *30*(1), 1–9. doi:10.1061/(ASCE)ME.1943-5479.0000168

Khanna, R., & Singh, S. P. (2018). Status of MSMEs in India: A Detailed Study. *Journal of Applied Management-Jidnyasa*, *10*(2), 1–14.

Kinyua, A. N. (2014). Factors Affecting the Performance of Small and Medium Enterprises in the Jua Kali Sector In Nakuru Town, Kenya. *IOSR Journal of Business and Management*, *16*(1), 80-93.

Krishnan, V., & Ulrich, K. T. (2001). Product Development Decisions: A Review of the Literature. *Management Science*, *47*(1), 1–21. doi:10.1287/mnsc.47.1.1.10668

Kristiansen, S. (2002). Competition and Knowledge in Javanese Rural Business. *Singapore Journal of Tropical Geography*, *23*(1), 52–70. doi:10.1111/1467-9493.00118

Kristiansen, S. (2004). Social network and business success: The role of sub-cultures in an African context. *American Journal of Economics and Sociology*, *63*(5), 1149–1171. doi:10.1111/j.1536-7150.2004.00339.x

Kristiansen, S., Furuholt, B., & Wahid, F. (2003). Internet cafe entrepreneurs: Pioneers in information dissemination in Indonesia. *The International Journal of Entrepreneurship and Innovation*, *4*(4), 251–263. doi:10.5367/000000003129574315

Lo, M. C., Wang, Y. C., Wah, C. R. J., & Ramayah, T. (2016). The critical success factors for the organizational performance of SMEs in Malaysia: A partial least squares approach. *Revista Brasileira de Gestão de Negócios*, *18*(61), 370–391. doi:10.7819/rbgn.v18i61.3058

Marsden, K. (1992). African Entrepreneurs - Pioneers of Development. *Small Enterprise Development*, *3*(2), 15–25. doi:10.3362/0957-1329.1992.015

McMahon, R. G. P. (2001). Growth and performance of manufacturing SMEs: The influence of financial management characteristics. *International Small Business Journal*, *19*(3), 10–28. doi:10.1177/0266242601193001

Mead, D. C., & Liedholm, C. (1998). The dynamics of micro and small enterprises in developing countries. *World Development*, *26*(1), 61–74. doi:10.1016/S0305-750X(97)10010-9

Meganathan, M., Kumar, P. B., & Saravanan, R. (2015). Sustainable Trends of MSME in India: An Empirical Study. *International Journal of Research in Management. Economics & Commerce*, *5*(2), 42–51.

Mehta, M. (2009). A + E = LEAN. *Industrial Engineering (American Institute of Industrial Engineers)*, *41*, 28.

Meier, R., & Pilgrim, M. (1994). Policy-Induced Constraints on Small Enterprise Development in Asian Developing Countries. *Small Enterprise Development*, *5*(2), 66–78. doi:10.3362/0957-1329.1994.017

Panneerselvam, R. (2015). *Production and Operations Management* (3rd ed.). Delhi, India: PHI Learning Private Limited.

Pansiri, J., & Temtime, Z. T. (2008). Assessing managerial skills in SMEs for capacity building. *Journal of Management Development*, *27*(2), 251–260. doi:10.1108/02621710810849362

Rajpal, N. K. (2015). Micro, Small and Medium Enterprises in North East India: Performance and Prospects. *The IUP Journal of Entrepreneurship Development*, *11*(3), 7–21.

Robinson, M. S. (1993). Beberapa strategi yang berhasil untuk mengembangkan Bank Pedesaan: Pengalaman dengan Bank Rakyat Indonesia 1970-1990. In S. Sugianto, Purnomo & M. S. Robinson (Eds.), Bunga Rampai Pembiyaan Pertanian Pedesaan (pp. 31-224). Jakarta: Institut Bankir Indonesia.

Ross, S. A., Westerfield, R. W., & Jaffe, J. (1999). Corporate Finance (5th ed.). Boston, MA: Irwin and McGraw-Hill.

Sankaraiah, M., & Mohan, B. (2016). Growth and Development of MSMEs – An Analytical View. *International Journal of Research and Development - A Management Review*, *5*(4), 48-56.

Saravanan, M., & Surendar, G. (2016). Analysis of Various Factors Influencing Labour Productivity in Construction Project. *International Journal of Emerging Technology in Computer Science & Electronics*, *22*(2), 179–181.

Shah, M. P., Pitroda, J. R., & Bhavsar, J. J. (2014). Analysis of Factors Influencing Productivity: Survey of Construction Projects in Central Gujarat Region of India. *International Journal of Engineering Sciences & Research Technology*, *3*(4), 3082–3087.

Shukla, O. J., & Misra, A. K. (2013). Easily & Economically Feasible Value Analysis &Value Engineering Concepts for Manufacturing Industry. *Engineering Management Reviews*, *2*(3), 81–85.

Singh, R., Verma, O. P., & Anjum, B. (2012). Small Scale Industry: An Engine of Growth. *Zenith International Journal of Business Economics & Management Research*, *2*(5), 210–221.

Singh, R. K., Garg, S. K., & Deshmukh, S. G. (2008). Strategy development by SMEs for competitiveness: A review. *Benchmarking: An International Journal*, *15*(5), 525–547. doi:10.1108/14635770810903132

Smallbone, D., Leig, R., & North, D. (1995). The characteristics and strategies of high growth SMEs. *International Journal of Entrepreneurial Behaviour & Research*, *1*(3), 44–62. doi:10.1108/13552559510100657

Steel, W. F. (1994). Changing the Institutional and Policy Environment for Small Enterprise Development in Africa. *Small Enterprise Development*, *5*(2), 4–9. doi:10.3362/0957-1329.1994.013

Swierczek, F. W., & Ha, T. T. (2003). Entrepreneurial orientation, uncertainty avoidance and firm performance: An analysis of Thai and Vietnamese SMEs. *International Journal of Entrepreneurship and Innovation*, *4*(1), 46–58. doi:10.5367/000000003101299393

Taşlıyan, M., Eren, A. S., & Yücel, D. K. (2018). Defining the Determinants of Organizational Performance in Turkish Manufacturing Sees. *IOSR Journal of Business and Management, 20*(5), 26-35.

Verhees, F. J. H. M., & Meulenberg, M. T. G. (2004). Market Orientation, Innovativeness, Product Innovation, and Performance in Small Firms. *Journal of Small Business Management*, *42*(2), 134–154. doi:10.1111/j.1540-627X.2004.00102.x

Wang, Y., Bhanugopan, R., & Lockhart, P. (2015). Examining the quantitative determinants of organizational performance: Evidence from China. *Measuring Business Excellence*, *19*(2), 23–41. doi:10.1108/MBE-05-2014-0014

Woldie, A., Leighton, P., & Adesua, A. (2008). Factors influencing small and medium enterprises (SMEs): An exploratory study of owner/manager and firm characteristics. *Banks and Bank Systems*, *3*(3), 5–13.

Youndt, M. A., Snell, S. A., Dean, J. W. Jr, & Lepak, D. P. (1996). Human resource management, manufacturing strategy, and firm performance. *Academy of Management Review*, *39*(4), 836–866.

1 Product development is a process of converting the market opportunity and a set of speculation about product technology into a product available for sale (Krishnan and Ulrich, 2001). The key areas of a company view product development process in different ways: a bundle of attributes (marketing), an artifact resulting from an organizational process (organizations), a complex assembly of interacting components (engineering design) and a sequence of development and/ or production process steps (operations management) (Krishnan and Ulrich, 2001).

2 Value-added defined as mixing of inputs into a physical product or service with an augmented value of outputs equated to the total sum of the values of inputs (Adam, Jr. and Ebert, 2007).

Chapter 9
Employer's Role Performance Towards Employees' Satisfaction:
A Study of SME Industry 4.0 in Malaysia

Siti Noorjannah Abd Halim
Universiti Sains Malaysia, Malaysia

Siti Noorhaslina Abd Halim
Universiti Teknologi MARA, Malaysia

ABSTRACT

The wave of the Fourth Industrial Revolution (IR4.0) is a phenomenon in which one or more technologies are replaced by another technology in a short amount of time. In small and medium-sized enterprises (SMEs), some internal and external problem are occurring that suggest change from classical to technological approach. Thus, this chapter aims to establish the relationship between the employees' satisfaction toward their employer's role performance. Based on the power-dependence and agency theories, this study contributes to the SMEs industry in Malaysia and will involve IR4.0 by offering a much more comprehensive theoretical perspective to aid understanding and prepare for the revolution internally. The sample of this study comprises of employees who are working in various sectors of the SMEs industry. G-power technique was employed to find the minimum sample size in this study. Meanwhile, the SPSS and PLS will be used to analyse the data. The practical implication of this research concerns the factors that can enhance employee satisfaction if their company jumps into the IR4.0. Thus, the employer should play the right role to make sure the employees are ready and well prepared for the revolution despite there being environmental uncertainty happening in the process.

DOI: 10.4018/978-1-7998-2577-7.ch009

1.0 INTRODUCTION

The movement towards the Fourth Industrial Revolution (IR4.0) is rapidly changing in which one or more technologies are replaced by another technology in a certain period of time. The term of "Industry 4.0" is originating from a project in the high-tech strategy which promotes digitalization of manufacturing by the German government (Kowang et al., 2019). This concept applies the current trend of automation and data exchange including cyber-physical systems, the Internet of things, cloud and cognitive computing in manufacturing technologies (Hermann, Pentek, & Otto, 2015). Thus, this on-going technology development requires organization change to keep up with the competition in industry.

There would be a problem with Small and Medium-Sized Enterprises (SMEs) to move from classical to technological approach for the changes would bring an impact on the employees whereby they might lose their job because of the digitalisation application in company (Kleindienst & Ramsauer, 2012). Some of these researchers argue with losing job when applying this revolution because by having digitalisation approach, this may help employment rates go up and more advanced (Zambon, Cecchini, Egidi, Saporito, & Colantoni, 2019). The top management should apply the change models when they want to move for IR4.0 in their manufacturing companies.

The term industrial 4.0 itself is a well-known revolution phenomenon in today's business strategy(Ghaz, 2017). This phenomenon will give direct and indirect impact to the labour market in SMEs industry. The labour market here means a place for workers and employees (to) interact with each other(Shanock & Eisenberger, 2006). For instance, employers compete to hire the best employees for their organization, while workers compete for the best satisfying job as they can. Thus, the role performance from employers is very important and become the main role in order to gain satisfaction from employees.

The dispersal of IR4.0 within companies or organization depends on their size. For instance, the large companies which are having more resources, processes and more structured tend to deploy IR4.0 technologies more advance as compared to SMEs companies (Woon, Kei, May, Yi, & Mei, 2019). However, SMEs also should be catching up with this revolution from becoming victims of large companies which are having more resources and skills compare to them (Saleh & Ndubisi, 2006). Thus, the employer of SMEs companies should play their role and guide the employees to be prepared for this revolution in terms of competition with the large companies out there.

The role performance from the employer becomes important to organization especially to deal with employees. In SMEs, (the) employer really depends on employees in terms of production and services of their companies. Some of the employees cannot understand why their companies have to apply this IR4.0 and keep changing from time to time (Safar, Sopko, Bednar, & Poklemba, 2018). To emphasize, the employer has to explain clearly and show a good behaviour in the way to change into this new revolution (Griffin & Parker, 2007). Thus, the IR4.0 in this study refers to the environmental uncertainty which is known as a moderator in this study.

In a way the employer shows a good performance to their employee, the revolution might disrupt the satisfaction from the employees (Luco, Mestre, Henry, Tamayo, & Fontane, 2018). Some of the changes will make the employees feel not satisfied and unease with that. Likewise, adopting a new technology in companies, may take some times for employees to be suit with it especially in SMEs industries. With limited numbers of resources and employees, the employer should strengthen their role to encourage their employees in these changes (Fauziah, Yusoff, Jia, Azizan, & Ramin, 2013). Thus, environmental uncertainty might strengthen or weaken the relationship between role performance or employer and employees' satisfaction in this IR4.0.

2.0 BACKGROUND OF THE STUDY

This study will look at the challenges and strategies for SMEs towards the IR4.0. In manufacturing companies, changes are most of the time happening drastically both in internal and external environment. This new revolution is characterized by an unknown level of talent and skill mobility, then the employees need to wide their potential to make sure their talent align with current revolution (Harrison, Kelly, Harrison, & Kelly, 2010). This trend makes a major transformation that involved almost every aspect of the business (Ostdick, 2017). The transformation would motivate the SMEs to make a move and keep competitive advantages in their industry field. For instance, employees should play their roles very well in order to help their company toward to IR4.0.

There are two organizational change models that dominated the literature, that of planned and emergent change (Kidwell, Nygaard, & Silkoset, 2007). The planned model is applied when the operation of an organization is in stable and predictable environment where changes are driven by the top-down approach (Nkundabanyanga, Balunywa, Tauringana, Ntayi, & Stephen, 2014). This model assumes that structures, processes, technology and human skills, capabilities and knowledge can be changed due to successful organization. On the other hand, the emergent change model is applied when the organization operates in an unpredictable and complex environment that driven by a bottom-up approach (Louis, 1986). The IR4.0 is not a joke of SMEs especially in technology savvy that they must get in it. The era of globalization where opportunities are abundance creates chances for firms to apply the new technology (Schröder, 2017). SMEs are required to aggressively venture into their backyard and accept the IR4.0 challenges. This opportunity will remain them in the industry and still competitive among others.

SMEs need to put their efforts to strategize their capabilities to accept the IR4.0 to respond to the global competition and business chances (Radanliev et al., 2017). As SMEs accept and apply new technology, their employees also have to be ready physically and mentally. For the SMEs, their firms operating and engaging in international business especially have no choice and have to accept IR4.0 by keep sustainable competitive advantages (Umrani & Johl, 2018). SME's employee plays an important role in order to get successful in IR4.0. In the time, a firm decided for IR4.0, the employees must follow and try to make it happen (Saleh & Ndubisi, 2006). However, it is important to note that development and growth of SMEs arena have substantially contributed to the economic benefits. Thus, IR4.0 can be good or not is depending on the firm to handle it.

3.0 SMEs IN MALAYSIA

The history of SMEs in Malaysia can be traced back to the late 1990s with playing an important role in Malaysian economy. During the 1990s, SMEs were more viable compared with large enterprises. However, Malaysia has recognized the importance of SMEs development since early in 1960s. In the mid-1990s, the functions of SMEs in the development of the Malaysian economy became more significant. For instance, SMEs have been at the core of Malaysia's economic transformation since the 1990s to an upper-middle income nation and is an important driver of employment and growth (Saleh & Ndubisi, 2006). Thus, SMEs industries are significant besides they become the backbone of Malaysia's economy until now.

In line with Malaysia vigour to become a high-income nation by 2020, the country has given a special focus on SMEs industry in Malaysia. By 2020, Malaysia aims to push SMEs' contribution to GDP to 41% and the share of the country exports from SMEs to 23%. In fact, the government of Malaysia is aware of the SMEs' potential for a way to move for IR4.0. There are many different sectors involved in SMEs activity such as agriculture, mining and quarrying, manufacturing, construction and services. Currently, the main contribution in SMEs activity are services and manufacturing with combined share of 82.4% in 2018. Hence, SMEs activities in Malaysia still relevant especially in Malaysian economic growth.

3.1 Malaysia's SMEs Performance

In Malaysia, SMEs become one of the established business activities that contribute to nation economy growth. Consequently, Malaysia has attracted much attention internationally by recoding an extraordinary economic performance. Malaysia's 2012-2020 SMEs Masterplan seeks to advance SMEs development and increase their contributions to the economy. The key element of Malaysia Masterplan is to focus on innovation and technology adaptation. It is aligning with the new industry revolution 4.0 that require SMEs to enhance their innovation especially in technology adaptation. Overall performance of SMEs still on track to achieve the target of 41% to GDP by 2020 as envisaged under the Dasar Keusahawanan Nasional 2030 (DKN 2030) recently. In addition, based on the Department of Statistics Malaysia (DOSM), Malaysia's SMEs recorded a higher contribution of 38.3& to GDP in 2018 amounting to RM521.7 billion as compared to 37.8 % amounting to RM491.2 billion in 2017. Thus, it shows that SMEs in Malaysia (are) still relevant and competitive advantage to Malaysia's economy growth.

4.0 PROBLEM STATEMENT

There are conflicting ideas about SMEs in IR4.0 between the employer and employees in their organization. This revolution disrupts structures of labour markets such as low-skilled and mid-skilled jobs may become vulnerable due to mechanisation of process, systems and people-oriented work (Safar et al., 2018). Role performance from employers is very important **via** it influences the behaviour of employees towards them (Raemy et al., 2018). For instance, when this revolution makes a change especially from human workforce to technology adaptive, it can be frustrated for employees. Since the early years, Malaysian government has put an attention and gave priority to develop the capabilities of SMEs to be more competitive in IR4.0. To energize SMEs towards IR4.0, they need to recognize the on-going technology transformation and rise on challenge of having the capability and willing to change it (Zambon et al., 2019).

SMEs can get competitive advantage by offering high quality products at low price in the industry 4.0 era (Schröder, 2017). Thus, some employers do not play their role very well especially to achieve employees' satisfaction. In fact, an early challenge to SMEs to changes from previous revolution to current revolution is lack of comprehensive strategy (Szamosi, 2002). It is because most of the business does not give their attention on digitalisation journey (Woon et al., 2019). Hence, it is limited to SMEs to adapt to current revolution and for routine application.

Employees in SMEs industry are worry beucase of negative impact of automation on their job where most of them will lose their job in company (Ristuccia, 2019). It will occur as the technology such as arising out of machinery used as major systems in organization. For instance, if the company wants to change from human workforce to machine oriented, the employer should play their role by advising the employees properly (Kleindienst & Ramsauer, 2012). Thus, when SME industry makes major changes in the highest technology level, it will give priority to the cyber-physical systems to make decision on their own without the need for the human. The reality is that, majority of Malaysian SME has been in the comfort zone for too long and is not ready to compete locally and internationally. In fact, if the IR4.0 arises, they feel that they cannot accept the challenges and not ready for a change especially for those who are already many years in this industry (Woon et al., 2019).

5.0 PURPOSE OF THE STUDY

The purpose of the study is to review the literature and subsequently propose a model linking role performance and satisfaction with moderating effect of environmental uncertainty among SME industry employees in Malaysia. From the academic perspective is to review current literature which evaluates whether the role performance can build satisfaction by having the environmental uncertainty of the business. In addition, this study provides useful information about IR4.0 and how employers play their role to satisfy their employees during this industrial revolution changes. Employer should be interested to know the employees' satisfaction with their role performance has significant relations payback (Yin & Qin, 2019). For instance, before turn to IR4.0, employer can consider back on that technology by taking consideration of their employees.

5.1 Research Questions

The research questions of this study are as below:

Does role performance positively and significantly affect satisfaction?

Does the impact of role performance on satisfaction is higher with lower levels of environmental uncertainty than with higher levels of environmental uncertainty?

6.0 LITERATURE REVIEW

6.1 Power Dependency Theory

It is a simple theory of power relations that had developed to resolve some ambiguities surrounding "power", "authority", "legitimacy", and power "structures" that bring them together in a coherent scheme (Emerson, 2014). This theory analysed about the dependency on the power between two parties or partnerships and the resources that brings into the relationship (Berthon, Pitt, Ewing, & Bakkeland, 2003).

This theory also stated that one party will depend on the other party based on that party has power and doing well (Davis & Cobb, 2010). Whenever the employees believe on their employer, they will depend on their employer especially in business strategy. At the same time, effective role performance influences the satisfaction very well. Thus, employees need to make sure that the quality is following the standard given.

Dependency Theory can be defined to explain the development of economic in terms of external influences such as political, economic and cultural. There are some characteristics as the dependency theory which characterize on the international system that described the dominant and dependent. According to the Pfeffer (1993), there are some advantages for the members given that there is some expertise, easy to excess the resources, and the legitimacy.

6.2 Agency Theory

Agency theory is a principle that used to describe and resolve issues especially in relationship between business principals and agents (Lafontaine, 1992). According to Kidwell, Nygaard, and Silkoset (2007), most commonly the relationship involved in stakeholders are the shareholder as a principal and company executive as an agent. Thus, the principal refers to employers and agent would be employees.

Traditionally, Agency Theory has developed along two streams which are positivist and principle-agent (Jensen & Jensen, 1983) both streams share a common unit of analysis (principle and agent). Both positivists and principle-agent stream also share common assumptions about people, organizations, and information. However, they differ from their mathematical rigor, dependent variable, and style. Table 1.0 shows the Agency theory overview of a variety of settings.

Table 1. Agency theory overview in variety of settings

Terms	Explanations
Key idea	Principal-agent relationship should reflect efficient organization of information and risk-bearing costs.
Unit of analysis	Contract between principal and agent
Human assumptions	Self-interest Bounded rationally Risk aversion
Organizational assumptions	Partial goal conflict among participants Efficiency as the effectiveness criterion Information asymmetry between principal and agent
Information assumption	Information as a purchasable commodity
Contracting problems	Agency (moral hazard and adverse selection) Risk sharing
Problem domain	Relationships in which the principal and agent have partly differing goals and risk preferences (e.g., compensation, regulation, leadership, impression management, whistle-blowing, vertical integration, transfer pricing)

Sources: Eisenhardt (1985)

There are two agency problems that arise from this context which is horizontal and vertical problems (Combs, Michael, & Castrogiovanni, 2004). The horizontal agency problem concerns about the brand and quality of the organization but for vertical agency problems more towards on employees' satisfaction. The employer consistently has to deal with employees with varying degrees of risk tolerance. Thus, employers should play their role as employees amazingly.

6.3 Role Performance

The role of performance consists of the performing tasks which is related to the formal requirement and include the behaviours that are formally required by the company (Buil, Martínez, & Matute, 2018). To measure the role performance needs to include the factor analyses self-report. As an employer, the role that they play towards the employees is very important especially to maintain a good relationship between them (Raemy et al., 2018). In SMEs, the employer has to deal with the employees due to limited numbers of employees. Thus, every person in organization has to play their role in order to maintain the success of the business.

According to Harmon & Griffiths (2008), the role performance is described such as "the total set of performance responsibilities played by the right person for the right position". It is difficult to describe a specific role in organization due to each organization may split or divide the role according to their needs (Ouedraogo & Ouakouak, 2018). For instance, there are individual task behaviour, team member behaviours and organization member behaviour. Thus, employer in SME might have different role compare to the employer at large companies.

6.4 Satisfaction

Satisfaction has been investigated as a positive affective behaviour resulting from the expectation being met (Dickey, Harrison McKnight, & George, 2008). The concept of satisfaction is referred to as "an overall affective orientation on the part of individuals regarding their work roles that they have currently" (Valaei & Rezaei, 2016). In SME business relationships, satisfaction is considered as a guiding philosophy that is an important factor of the success of the business (Altinay, Brookes, Yeung, & Aktas, 2014). The level of employees' satisfaction is based on the partnership period and experience in their employers. Thus, in SME sector, employees satisfaction is defined as the positive perception from the employers based on good economic return and psychological expectation in captive the IR4.0.

Employee will satisfy if they can achieve firm's requirement especially on their work performance. Despite they need to learn new things and change their mind-set for IR4.0, they still do it well as good as they can. In this IR4.0 situation, they do not have any choice for that. Researchers commonly find that satisfaction is a strong predictor of behavioral outcomes, such as loyalty (Ravald and Gro¨nroos, 1996; Wang et al., 2006; Kassim and Abdullah, 2010). Employees with higher levels of satisfaction are more likely to remain in the firm and contribute more to the relationship (Robinson, 1997).

Clark and Oswald (1995), describes satisfaction as a "self-reported positive emotional state resulting from the appraisal of one's job or from job experiences". Based on his review of empirical studies on satisfaction, Locke determined that seven work issues are typically associated with job satisfaction including mentally challenging work, personal interest in the specific job, work that is not too physically tiring, perceived equitable rewards, appropriate working conditions, employee self-esteem, management assistance in managing the workplace by minimizing conflict and ensuring that work is interesting and good pay or promotions are available.

6.5 Environmental Uncertainty

Environmental uncertainty mean changes in the business environment that influence the development of company by having unexpected issues (H. Zhang & Lv, 2015). It arises out of contingencies that describe the context of economic exchange become difficult to predict and cannot be specified in the contract (Geyskens & Steenkamp, 2006). More importantly, this environmental uncertainty is about how well the companies adapt to external environmental changes in their internal relationship especially for SMEs system (Michael, Harrison, & Joey, 2007).

Previous study indicated that environmental uncertainty influences the development of company by having unexpected issues (K. Z. K. Zhang et al., 2015). Usually, environmental uncertainty has a negative effect on the allocation of decision rights to employees due to the employer exercises more control over decisions (Mumdziev & Windsperger, 2013). Therefore, the present study presents an extended employees' satisfaction from the role performance shown by their employer towards the IR4.0.

Environmental uncertainty refers to the firm external environment in terms of technology, consumer tastes and preferences and competitors' actions; it is characterized by an absence of patterns, unpredictability, and unexpected change (Wang, Chueh, Lee, Wang, & Lee, 2013). Such environmental uncertainty required both parties to develop the capability to understand and adapt to environment. Thus, employees as a part of the business need to adapt and face any of the changes either it will give profit of not for their business due to revolution changes (Didonet et al., 2012).

6.6 Research Framework

Figure 1. Research Framework

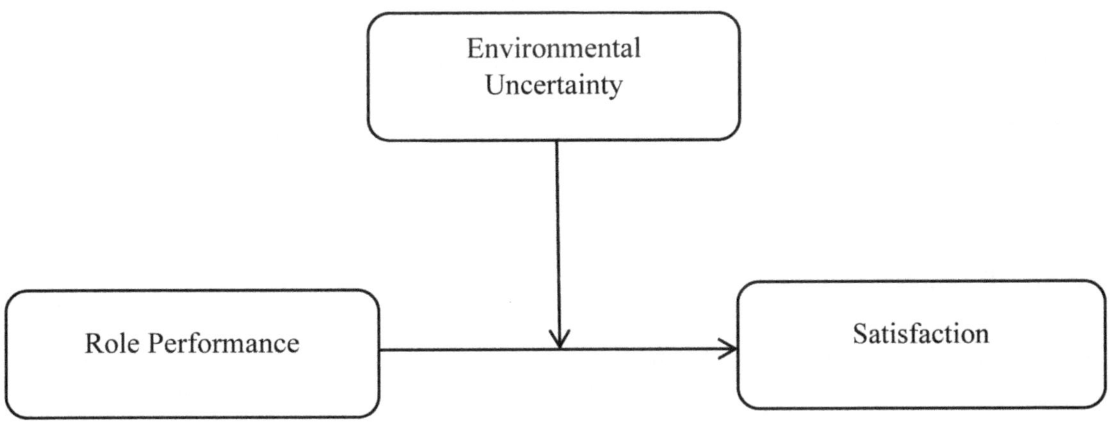

7.0 PROPOSITIONS DEVELOPMENT

7.1 Relationship between Role Performance and Satisfaction

Related to the challenges for SME in IR4.0, employers should consider their employees for future planning (Umrani & Johl, 2018). This could be happening once employers change the human workforce to the technology savvy in their business. According to (Szamosi, 2002) one of the common issues existed in the relationship between employers and employees once the SME applied the industrial 4.0 in their company. The past study stated that employers should know employees' needs and desire before involving in the revolution (Luco et al., 2018). However, the company also have to look on their company sustainability and grow because it is important to remain competitive in the industry.

It is important to build the role of employers due to increasing the employees' satisfaction level (Harmon & Griffiths, 2008). This role performance consists of the performing tasks which related to the formal requirement and include the behaviours that are formally required by the company (Kowang et al., 2019). In fact, the IR4.0, employees need a very specific attention and guidance from the employer to make it happen. Thus, role performance from the employer is very important to make sure the employees are satisfied with guidance from the employer.

Proposition 1: There is a significant and positive relationship between role performance and satisfaction.

7.2 Environmental Uncertainty as a Moderator between Role Performance and Satisfaction

Employer plays an important role in their SME business especially their relationship with employees (Davies, Lassar, Manolis, Prince, & Winsor, 2011). Based on organizational set-up, the changes in external environment also need to be considered. (Hence), when the company decided on applying IR4.0, the employer and employees will have to work together and make sure to get competitive advantage in the market (Zambon et al., 2019). Thus, both parties have to be alert to changes in the business environment that will affect them. The effectiveness of cooperative strategy of the partners depends on the environmental uncertainty (Stehouwer, 2014). Therefore, the employers will be alert to the threat to their business at the same time will give more attention to their employees.

Proposition 2: The impact of role performance on satisfaction is higher with lower levels of environmental uncertainty than with higher levels of environmental uncertainty.

8.0 RESEARCH METHODOLOGY

This section will discuss the methods and procedures used in this research. The research approach in this study is quantitative research that attempts to collect facts and data to examine the relationship between independent and dependent variables and analysed it by using statistical method (Zikmund, 2010).

8.1 Research Design

This is a cross-sectional study, with all variables and data gathered over a set period of time in order to answer the research questions. Data collection will be collected from SME's employees in Malaysia. In this study, all variables will be measured at an individual level. The data will be collected by using survey questionnaire (quantitative study) and the respondents belonged to the SME industry in Malaysia.

8.2 Population and Sampling

The population of this study is individual SME's employees in Malaysia with focusing on Selangor, Kuala Lumpur, Perak and Penang. The chosen states based on the most SME landed in Malaysia. The reliability test will be run to know the internal reliability of items in the questionnaires based on Cronbach's Alpha value (values). Then, correlation coefficient and regression analysis will be used to check relationship between variables. The present research will utilise non-probability sampling to obtain information about those who are most readily (from selected location) available. Purposive sampling is used due to the SME's employees are the only ones who can respond to the survey, or they can conform to some criteria set by the researcher.

8.3 Data Collection Method

This study will adopt the primary data collection method by using survey questionnaire to respondent in SME industry in Malaysia. This method is pre formulated written sets of questions to which respondents record their answers and generally designed to collect large numbers of quantitative data (Sekaran & Bougie, 2016). The questionnaire will be collected from the respondents by personally administered questionnaires through drop off and collect method. For the personally administered questionnaires, the researcher will drop-off the questionnaires to the respondents and collect it after two weeks.

8.4 Measurement Scales

This section consists of all variables that are discussed on the items and scales of measurement in detail. There are independent, dependent and moderator variables' items.

8.4.1 Role Performance

Role performance instrument is developed by(Shanock & Eisenberger, 2006) and Lynch et al. (1999) and consists of 11-items. This instrument is scored using a 5-Likert scale (Likert, 1932) ranging from 1=strongly disagree, 2=disagree, 3=neutral, 4=agree and 5=strongly agree. The purpose of this instrument is to investigate role performance measured the in-role performance and extra role performance obtained by the employees from their employer.

8.4.2 Satisfaction

A scale developed by Andaleeb (1995) and (Dwyer, 1987) having 6 items was adopted and adapted to measure satisfaction construct. The 5-Likert scale (Likert, 1932), used as an instrument to score this satisfaction construct ranging from 1=strongly disagree, 2=disagree, 3=neutral, 4=agree and 5=strongly agree. The purpose of this instrument is to investigate satisfaction from employees' perspective towards their employer. The factor loading for these items are statically significant ($p < 0.05$) and the Cronbach's alpha for this constructs; satisfaction by Andaleeb, $\alpha = 0.71$ and for Dwyer and Oh, $\alpha=0.779$.

8.4.3 Environmental Uncertainty

Environment Uncertainty instrument is developed by Duncan (1972) and (Bourgeois, Daniel, & Terence, 1978) and consists of 5-items and is scored using a 5-Likert scale (Likert, 1932) ranging from 1= never predictable, 2= unpredictable, 3= neutral, 4= predictable, and 5= always predictable. The purpose of this instrument as a moderator for role performance and satisfaction is to strengthen the relationship between these two variables. The factor loading for these items are statically significant ($p < 0.05$) and the Cronbach's alpha for this constructs; satisfaction by Duncan, $\alpha = 0.70$ and for Bourgeois et al., $\alpha=0.88$.

9.0 CONTRIBUTIONS OF THIS STUDY

Based on the preceding review of the literature and consistent effect of employers role performance and employees satisfaction with environmental uncertainty as moderator, a model has been developed as depicted in Figure 2.1. Role performance is viewed as an independent variable that has a direct effect on satisfaction. Besides, environmental uncertainty would be (a) moderator in this model.

In terms of theoretical contributions, the current study contributed critically to the theoretical framework related to role performance and satisfaction with the environmental uncertainty as a moderator in SMEs' activities. In addition, this study also contributes to the extending traditional theory of Power Dependency and Agency Theory. For instance, Power Dependency Theory is to resolve some doubts happen that related to the power of authority in SMEs business. On other hand, the Agency Theory also used in this study to describe and resolve issues regarding unexpected issues arises out of this industry. Moreover, this unexpected problem will affect the role performance of the employees in SMEs industry.

The present study hopes to cover a number of key relationship business issues concerning the important of environmental uncertainty of SMEs' business to several practitioners. In addition, this study will bring ideas holistically to the firms on how environmental uncertainty will strength or weaken the relationship of role performance and satisfaction of SMEs' employee in their work field. Furthermore, this research will motivate them to enhance their performance while having any unexpected issues or problems in future. Thus, this study will benefit the SMEs to develop in future and get ready with any problem arise.

10.0 CONCLUSIONS

There are a rising number of researches in IR4.0. However, most of the study focused on the process of how to be in IR4.0 and the impact on SMEs companies. In addition, there is lack of study that go through the relationship between employer and employee in SME on how they will deal with this revolution if their company decided to do so. Thus, there is a crucial need for future research to study further about employees' satisfaction with their employers' role performance when come to deal on IR4.0.

This paper contributes to the on-going discussion about the challenges and difficulties for employer in SME industry to maintain their role performance towards their employees. There is role performance acts as independent variable in this study which is chosen based on the behaviour that requires form an employer to employees if they want to apply this revolution in their company. This is also supported by the previous research conducted by Safar et al., (2018), even though there is limited empirical research on the issues, it is possible to study and can contribute for future researches in the same field.

Industrial revolution 4.0 is changing in terms of technology and it moves very fast. According to (Conti & Passarella, 2018), SME also should change into technology savvy and make sure that there is still competition in the industry. By addressing environmental uncertainty as the moderator in this study, the employer also has to look on it and make sure employees also understand why company needs for a change. Thus, employer with a good role performance towards their employees can help the company move forward and gain more profit in future.

11.0 FUTURE TRENDS

Specifically, this study provides new features and benefits to the SMEs Industry 4.0, which this section presents a research plan according to an overarching goal to ensure that the strategic plan for future revolution period (goes well). In future, other new industrial revolution needs to be caught up and SMEs companies also should be ready on that time. Although, most research states that the IR4.0 suits with large companies due to their advanced resources and processes, but as SME companies also should be on that position and ready for changes (Woon et al., 2019). It is important especially to maintain in this global business where everything based on technology savvy used.

REFERENCES

Altinay, L., Brookes, M., Yeung, R., & Aktas, G. (2014). Franchisees' perceptions of relationship development in franchise partnerships. *Journal of Services Marketing*, *28*(6), 509–519. doi:10.1108/JSM-09-2013-0240

Bourgeois, D. W., & Terence, R. (1978). *The effects of different organizational environments upon decisions about organizational structure*. Academic Press.

Buil, I., Martínez, E., & Matute, J. (2018). The role of identi fi cation, engagement and proactive personality. *International Journal of Hospitality Management Transformational Leadership and Employee Performance*.

Combs, J. G., Michael, S. C., & Castrogiovanni, G. J. (2004). *Franchising: A Review and Avenues to Greater Theoretical Diversity*. Academic Press.

Conti, M., & Passarella, A. (2018). *The Internet of People : A human and data-centric paradigm for the Next Generation Internet*. Academic Press.

Davies, M. A. P., Lassar, W., Manolis, C., Prince, M., & Winsor, R. D. (2011). A model of trust and compliance in franchise relationships. *Journal of Business Venturing*, *26*(3), 321–323. doi:10.1016/j.jbusvent.2009.09.005

Davis, G. F., & Cobb, J. A. (2010). *Resource Dependence Theory : Past and future*. Academic Press.

Dickey, M. H., Harrison McKnight, D., & George, J. F. (2008). The role of trust in franchise organizations. *The International Journal of Organizational Analysis*, *15*(3), 251–282. doi:10.1108/19348830710880938

Didonet, S., Simmons, G., Villavicencio, G. D., Palmer, M., Didonet, S., & Simmons, G. (2012). The relationship between small business market orientation and environmental uncertainty. *Marketing Intelligence & Planning*, *30*(7), 757–779. doi:10.1108/02634501211273841

Dwyer, O. (1987). *Output Sector Munificence Effects on the Internal Political Economy of Marketing Channels*. Academic Press.

Elbanna, S., & Gherib, J. (2012). Miller' s environmental uncertainty scale : An extension to the Arab world. *International Journal of Commerce and Management*, *22*(1), 7–25. doi:10.1108/10569211211204483

Emerson, R. W. (2014). Assessing Awuah v. Coverall North America, Inc.: The Franchisee as a Dependent Contractor. *Stanford Journal of Law, Business & Finance, 19*(2), 203–235.

Fauziah, W., Yusoff, W., Jia, L. C., Azizan, A. Z., & Ramin, A. K. (2013). *Business Strategy of Small Medium Enterprises (SMEs): A Case Study among selected Chinese SMEs in Malaysia*. Academic Press.

Geyskens, I., & Steenkamp, J. E. M. (2006). *Make, buy, or ally: A transaction cost theory meta- analysis Make, Buy, or Ally : A Transaction Cost Theory*. Academic Press.

Ghaz. (2017). *Industry 4.0: Are Malaysian SMEs Ready?* Academic Press.

Griffin, M. A., & Parker, S. K. (2007). A New Model Of Work Role Performance. *Positive Behavior In Uncertain And Interdependent Contexts The University of Queensland*, *50*(2), 327–347.

Harmon, T. R., & Griffiths, M. A. (2008). Franchisee perceived relationship value. *Journal of Business and Industrial Marketing*, *23*(4), 256–263. doi:10.1108/08858620810865834

Harrison, J. L., Kelly, S. J., Harrison, J. L., & Kelly, S. J. (2010). Perceived environmental uncertainty ' s effect on commitment in business-to-business channels. *Marketing Intelligence & Planning*, *28*(6), 792–803. doi:10.1108/02634501011078165

Idris, R. (2019). *Industrial Revolution 4.0: An Overview of Readiness and Potential Economic Effects in Malaysia from Millennial's Perspective*. Academic Press.

Jensen, M. C., & Jensen, M. C. (1983). *Organization Theory and Methodology*. Academic Press.

Kidwell, R. E., Nygaard, A., & Silkoset, R. (2007). *Antecedents and effects of free riding in the franchisor-franchisee relationship*. Academic Press.

Kleindienst, B. M., & Ramsauer, C. (2012). *SMEs and Industry 4 . 0 – Introducing a KPI based Procedure Model to identify Focus Areas in Manufacturing Industry*. Academic Press.

Kowang, T. O., Ying, Y. C., Yew, L. K., Hee, O. C., Fei, G. C., Long, C. S., … Saiful, M. (2019). *Industry 4.0 Competencies for Production Equipment Manufacturers in Malaysia*. Academic Press.

Lafontaine, F. (1992). Agency Theory and Franchising: Some Empirical Results. *The Rand Journal of Economics*, *23*(2), 263–283. doi:10.2307/2555988

Louis, W. (1986). *Interorganizational relations in marketing channels*. Academic Press.

Luco, J., Mestre, S., Henry, L., Tamayo, S., & Fontane, F. (2018). *Industry 4.0 in SMEs : a sectorial analysis*. Academic Press.

Michael, H., Harrison, D., & Joey, F. (2007). *The role of trust in franchise organizations*. Academic Press.

Mumdziev, N., & Windsperger, J. (2013). An Extended Transaction Cost Model of Decision Rights Allocation in Franchising. *The Moderating Role of Trust*, *182*(February), 170–182.

Nkundabanyanga, S. K., Balunywa, W., Tauringana, V., Ntayi, J. M., & Stephen, K. (2014). *Board role performance in service organisations : the importance of human capital in the context of a developing country*. Academic Press.

Ouedraogo, N., & Ouakouak, M. L. (2018). Impacts of personal trust, communication, and affective Commitment on Change Success. *Journal of Organizational Change*, *31*(3), 676–696. doi:10.1108/JOCM-09-2016-0175

Radanliev, P., Roure, D. C. De, Nurse, J. R. C., Burnap, P., Anthi, E., Ani, U., … Montalvo, R. M. (2017). *Design principles for cyber risk impact assessment from Internet of Things (IoT)*. Academic Press.

Raemy, P., Beck, D., Hellmueller, L., Raemy, P., Beck, D., & Hellmueller, L. (2018). Swiss Journalists ' Role Performance: The relationship between conceptualized, narrated, and practiced roles. *Journalism Studies*, *0*(0), 1–18.

Ristuccia, C. (2019). *Industry 4.0: SMEs Challenges and Opportunities in the Era of Digitalization*. Academic Press.

Robinson, M. (1997). *1997_Morrison and Robinson_a model of how psychological contract violation develops.pdf*. Academic Press.

Safar, L., Sopko, J., Bednar, S., & Poklemba, R. (2018). *Concept of SME Business Model for Industry 4.0 Environment*. Academic Press.

Saleh, A. S., & Ndubisi, N. O. (2006). *An Evaluation of SME Development in Malaysia*. Academic Press.

Schröder, C. (2017). *The Challenges of Industry 4 . 0 for Small and Medium-sized Enterprises*. Academic Press.

Shafer, W. E., & Wang, Z. (2010). *Effects of ethical context on conflict and commitment among Chinese accountants*. Academic Press.

Shanock, L. R., & Eisenberger, R. (2006). When Supervisors Feel Supported : Relationships With Subordinates. *Perceived Supervisor Support, Perceived Organizational Support, and Performance*, *91*(3), 689–695.

Stehouwer, K. (2014, Dec.). Northwood University Pioneers Undergraduate Major in Franchising Management. *Olive Software*.

Szamosi, L. T. (2002). *Just what are tomorrow's SME employees looking for?* Academic Press.

Umrani, A. I., & Johl, S. K. (2018). *How Different Ownership Structures Perform in Industry 4.0: A Case of Malaysian Manufacturing SMEs*. Academic Press.

Umrani, A. I., & Johl, S. K. (2020). *How Different Ownership Structures Perform in Industry 4.0: A Case of Malaysian Manufacturing SMEs*. Academic Press.

Valaei, N., & Rezaei, S. (2016). Job satisfaction and organizational commitment. *Management Research Review*, *39*(12), 1663–1694. doi:10.1108/MRR-09-2015-0216

Wang, E. T. G., Chueh, N., Lee, A., Wang, E. T. G., & Lee, N. C. (2013). Using power regimes to explore perceived environmental uncertainty. *Industrial Management & Data Systems*, *113*(7), 950–966. doi:10.1108/IMDS-02-2013-0072

Woon, B. C., Kei, C. W., May, L. S., Yi, T. Y., & Mei, T. J. (2019). *Reasons Against Audit Exemption Among Sme*. Academic Press.

Yin, Y., & Qin, S.-F. (2019). A smart performance measurement approach for collaborative design. *Advances in Mechanical Engineering*, *11*(1), 1–15. doi:10.1177/1687814018822570

Zambon, I., Cecchini, M., Egidi, G., Saporito, M. G., & Colantoni, A. (2019). *Development for SMEs*. Academic Press.

Zhang, H., & Lv, S. (2015). Effect of HR practice on NPD performance The moderating role of environmental. *Nankai Business Review International*, *6*(3), 256–280. doi:10.1108/NBRI-03-2015-0008

Zhang, K. Z. K., Benyoucef, M., & Zhao, S. J. (2015). Computers in Human Behavior Consumer participation and gender differences on companies ' microblogs : A brand attachment process perspective. *Computers in Human Behavior*, *44*, 357–368. doi:10.1016/j.chb.2014.11.068

Chapter 10
Cultural Elements in Spanish SME Websites and Social Media:
From Localization to Transcreation?

Celia Castillo Rodríguez
https://orcid.org/0000-0002-4367-9354
University of Granada, Spain

María Dolores Olvera-Lobo
https://orcid.org/0000-0002-0489-7674
University of Granada, Spain

Elena Moya-Molina
University of Granada, Spain

ABSTRACT

The establishment of a professional online corporate presence is an indispensable step for most companies. However, this online presence must consider linguistic, cultural, and technical differences, as well as variations in user expectations across markets. The language industry has responded to these needs by offering two services, namely localization and transcreation, which may act as valuable tools for the adaptation of corporate communications and whose benefits may be particularly advantageous for smaller companies. This study analyzes the application of localization and transcreation processes and strategies in the corporate context, with a focus on Spanish SMEs and English-speaking markets. Results suggest that the signs of the application of these activities in the corporate online field are still scarce. Furthermore, the online presence of both Spanish SMEs and large US corporations show numerous deficiencies, such as partial translations, typos, a non-updated use of social media, and little adaptation to the addressed markets.

DOI: 10.4018/978-1-7998-2577-7.ch010

INTRODUCTION

In recent decades, the Internet has evolved into a communicative phenomenon that has transformed both interpersonal and commercial relationships. Not only has this medium become a driving force for information dissemination and marketing processes in most economic sectors, but it also has made it possible for companies to perform economic transactions beyond geographical barriers. Given its text-based nature, in the beginnings of the Internet, there appeared to exist indications that this medium would be dominated by the languages of a select group of economically and technologically advanced countries. However, improvements in technology, together with the creativity of millions of users who act as recipients and transmitters of content, have turned the Internet into a fundamentally multilingual place (Seeba, 2016).

Hence, it is unquestionable that the Internet has transformed how companies and markets come into contact. Therefore, the establishment of a professional online presence is an essential step for the majority of companies. For this purpose, corporate websites and social media platforms are two basic tools that offer a broad range of advantages, including an increased business visibility and competitiveness, the removal of geographical restrictions, the access to contact information and customer preferences, and the possibility of real-time transactions (Marín Dueñas & Lasso de la Vega, 2017; Mbatha, 2013). Despite these advantages, company online presence should still take into consideration language and cultural differences, relative to the expectations of users from different markets. The language industry currently offers two tools: localization and transcreation, whose multi-dimensional adaptation of communications between companies and the public may constitute a valuable way of facing up to these new challenges.

OBJECTIVES

The objective of the present study has been to examine three main dimensions of online presence and adaptation in the Spanish corporate context: a) Spanish SME processes of information dissemination and interaction with users on social media through web translation and localization; b) Spanish SME adaptation of cultural elements incorporate websites; c) the first signs of application of transcreation strategies in websites belonging to large companies.

The analysis of the results denotes that there is still a scarce application of these services, and there has even been an appreciation of several deficiencies in the quality of company online presence, both in the case of small and medium-sized enterprises (hereinafter SMEs) and in the case of many world-leading companies.

LITERATURE REVIEW

In recent times, companies belonging to nearly all industries and sectors have acknowledged the importance of having a professional online presence. Even when there is no intention of carrying out online transactions, the so-called practice of webrooming has driven the large majority of physical enterprises to realize the necessity of publishing information on their products and services on the Internet. Webrooming consists in searching for information on a product online and purchasing it in a physical store to reduce uncertainty and increase the level of trust with which the decision to purchase is made (Flavián et al., 2016). Webrooming is becoming ever more frequent. 35% and 48% of European consumers of electronics, clothing, and footwear, respectively, get their information on products from the Internet before purchasing them in a physical establishment (Google Consumer Barometer, 2015). In this sense, IAB Spain (2018) indicates that 57% of Spanish users employ the Internet, and specifically social media platforms, to inform themselves on products and services, 4% up on the previous year.

The previously mentioned benefits of having a professional online corporate presence are multiplied if such presence is subjected to a website localization process. Localization is a relatively new field of activity in the language industry which consists in taking a product and making it linguistically, culturally and technically appropriate for a local, that is, the target country and the language in which said product will be used and sold (LISA, 2003, Gutiérrez-Artacho & Olvera-Lobo, 2017a). Despite the term localization appearing mainly associated with the software, videogames, and apps, recent years have witnessed the unprecedented growth of website localization. The transformations that can be introduced into a website to adapt it to a new market are extremely varied. Examples of these actions include placing a link column on the right instead of the left so that it is more easily accessible in the context of right-to-left script languages, employing colors with appropriate connotations for the target culture, carrying out modifications on icon usage, performing currency and measurement conversions, and adapting time formats, amongst others.

Out of the three, previously referenced dimensions of localization (linguistic, cultural, technical), the adaptation of cultural elements is particularly relevant in the field of website localization as it can contribute greatly to the fulfillment of the purpose of a website. Specifically, several authors have employed an anthropological perspective based on Hofstede's cultural dimensions theory (1980, 1991) to demonstrate how the reflection of culture in the user interface of websites can improve usability (Ahmed, Mouratidis, & Preston, 2009; Barber & Badre, 1998; De Troyer et al., 2006; Dormann & Chisalita, 2002; Singh, Zhao, & Hu, 2003). Following Hofstede (1980, 1991), cultural differences are based on deep-rooted values in the population that can be categorized into five fundamental dimensions: power distance, collectivism versus individualism, masculinity versus femininity, uncertainty avoidance, and long-term orientation versus short-term orientation. Thus, in their application of this theoretical framework to the area of cultural elements in websites, Marcus and Gould (2000) point out that in a website for a university in Malaysia, a country with a high power distance index (degree to which members of an organization accept the fact that there are other members with more power), plenty of images of the official university seal and prominent figures within the organization were found, whereas pictures in a Dutch university website focused particularly on the students. For their part, Barber and Badre (1998) analyzed a wide sample of websites from which they identified a series of cultural indicators specific to each country or world region, with special emphasis on design features. They identified, for example, the extensive use of the color green as a cultural indicator specific to Middle Eastern websites. Besides, they coined the term *culturability* to refer to this relationship between culture and usability in web design.

From this usability viewpoint, not adapting carefully the cultural elements present on a website imposes a barrier for users from regions and cultures different from the original. As already stated, the localization of a website does not merely consist in translating its text, despite this task being by no means insignificant. Amongst other aspects mentioned above, the localization process should take into account preferences relating to the design of the interface for the target public and the local perception of usability. An illustrative example is that of Nestlé's websites, with their simple and clear lines for the American public (www.nestleusa.com) and the disjointed, multi-image and column version localized for the Japanese public (www.nestle.jp). The absence of a careful adaptation of the cultural elements present on a website imposes a barrier for users from regions and cultures different to the original resulting, for example, in the need for a greater cognitive effort to access the information they need (Luna et al., 2002; Nantel and Glaser, 2008).

Sun (2001) argues that the identification and introduction of cultural indicators incorporate websites that permit a reduction of localization costs (which can be particularly beneficial for SMEs) and increases web usability. However, using cultural indicators in isolation to reflect cultural sensitivity could result in an accidental stereotyping of other cultures. To this end, an in-depth study of the market at which the web product is aimed should always be performed. Ideally, this process is an integral part of the localizing activity.

Given that the success of a corporate website can have a crucial repercussion on the development of a specific business, website localization can be a particularly beneficial tool for websites belonging to SMEs considering the numerous benefits that it offers in exchange for a relatively small cost. Although there is no standard international definition, according to European Commission recommendation 2003/361/EC (European Commission, 2003), SMEs are considered to be all companies employing fewer than 250 people and which have an annual turnover not exceeding 50 million euros, or which have a general annual balance not exceeding 43 million euros. In Spain, SMEs make up 99.8% of the Spanish business sector (General Secretariat of Industry and SMEs, 2018), a similar percentage to that for Europe as a whole (Papadopoulos et al., 2019). Due to their decisive contribution to the world economic sector, it is essential to drive the potential of SMEs, even more so in recent years, marked by an economic slowdown in a large number of countries. Notwithstanding, due to the inherent limitations of this type of company, which include limited access to capital, human and technological resources (Davis & Vladica, 2006), SMEs are disproportionately affected by barriers and inefficiencies in the area of enterprise. In specific countries, small businesses are still fighting against the prolonged impact of the 2007-2008 global crisis, which widened the gap between SMEs and large companies in terms of productivity growth (OECD, 2017a, 2017b). Spain is a clear reflection of this situation, being a country in which even in 2017 SMEs had recovered less than half of the employment lost during the crisis (INE, 2019).

However, in spite of the benefits that a multilingual, market-adapted online corporate presence offers, many Spanish SMEs do not have a corporate website and, if they do, it is often localized in an unprofessional way. According to Ureña, Ballestero, and Prieto (2017), although 77.5% of SMEs with 10 or more workers have their website, this percentage drops to 31.5% in the case of those with fewer than 10 employees. As regards website localization, according to the analysis of a sample of medium-sized companies performed by Gutiérrez-Artacho and Olvera-Lobo (2017b), it can be stated that Spanish SME websites present an acceptable quality from their technical aspect and the information they provide. However, they are left wanting in terms of the quality of the service they offer (a dimension including aspects such as interactivity, empathy, aesthetic attractiveness of the site, and capacity for maintaining users' attention). In terms of electronic commerce, only 18% of SMEs with 10-49 employees and 28% of SMEs with 50-240 employees, respectively, had e-commerce sales in 2016, compared to 41% of enterprises with 250 employees or more (INE, 2019). Likewise, although there is very limited research in the field of SME website localization, some studies suggest that the contents of SME websites from neighboring European countries such as Portugal similarly display serious deficiencies (Lopes & Melão, 2016).

Concerning the level of social media adoption amongst Spanish companies, according to a report by Telefónica & Red.es (2014), social media management is usually done by non-specialized internal staff and content publication tends to lack planning and strategy. One of the few research studies dealing with Spanish SMEs and social media is that of Sixto García, Aguado Domínguez and Riveiro Castro (2017), who focused on Galician SMEs and concluded that the use of social media by these companies lacked engagement and user interaction. Furthermore, Spanish SME social media use and activity do not seem to match that of the rest of the population. According to IAB Spain (2018), social media penetration reaches 85% of Spanish Internet users between 16 and 65 years of age (over 19 million users). Facebook is the most used social media service (87% of respondents use it) followed by WhatsApp (87%), YouTube (69%) and Instagram (49%). In the era of disruptive information and communication technologies, users face perpetually increasing polluted information (Iqbal, Hassan, & Ahmad, 2018).

Several authors have begun to use the term Industry 4.0 to refer to the wide application of new technological advancements such as artificial intelligence, the Internet of Things or Big Data, along with breakthroughs in nanotechnology, biotechnology, new materials, 3D printing, and robotization. According to Iqbal and Nawaz (2019), big data comprises of polluted and quality information where information pollution appears as a big dilemma for practitioners and academicians to deal with. From a global viewpoint, these developments are causing profound transformations in social and economic spheres, and it is expected that over 5 million jobs will be lost between 2015-2020 due to numerous factors including the automation of a high number of tasks (World Economic Forum, 2016).

In Spain, Kuzmenko and Roienko (2017) assert that the Fourth Industrial Revolution will increase social inequities in the medium and long term. This tendency will particularly affect SMEs due to their limited resources. Thus, changes need to be introduced if such a tendency is to be changed (Kuzmenko & Roienko, 2017).

According to Observatorio Vodafone's report on the state of Spanish companies and public administrations (Observatorio Vodafone, 2019), SMEs are aware that the use of ICTs can improve their internal operations and allow them to save both time and economic resources. However, only 14% of SMEs have a specific digitalization plan, whereas the rest address their digital needs as they arise. One of the aspects that hinders Spanish SME digital transformation is the lack of qualified staff, which forces SMEs to hire external resources. Additionally, almost half of SMEs (47%) are not undertaking actions to promote their products and services online, which shows a deficient perception of the current global market and its recent changes.

The Digital Economy and Society Index (DESI) report (European Commision, 2019) summarizes several indicators of Europe's digital performance and tracks the evolution of European Union member states in digital competitiveness. In 2019's DESI report, Spain held the 11th position out of 28 European Union member states (European Commision, 2019), one position lower concerning 2017. The report highlights Spain's level of digitalization of public services and points out good progression in the integration of digital technology. This is a consequence of the fact that ever more Spanish companies are making use of the advantages offered by e-commerce, as shown by the fact that 19% Spanish SMEs sell goods on the Internet, compared with an average of 17% for the EU as a whole.

ADEI (2017) affirm that an appropriate immersion of Spain in the digital economy could result in a growth of the Spanish gross domestic product of almost 40% and the creation of 2 million jobs by 2030. They also point out that Spain shows numerous strengths that may contribute to its digital transformation, such as a generalized use of mobile phones and the Internet, young people's high level of education and a considerable number of dynamic companies with a global presence. However, Ballestero and Pérez (2017) indicate the lack of a general political strategy in Spain that aims to address the economic changes brought about by these recent transformations. The lack of such a strategy may prevent Spain from properly addressing the challenges posed by the Industry 4.0.

In recent years, the language industry has also witnessed the surge of a new activity closely linked to translation and cultural adaptation known as transcreation. Transcreation, according to Gaballo (2012), is a reinterpretation of a text to adapt it to the readers of a target language taking into account conceptual, linguistic and cultural differences. This process takes into account numerous aspects that go well beyond a translation or cultural adaptation, since it also considers the expectations of the target audience or the need to maintain the company's brand voice across markets in the case of corporate texts, among other elements. The final objective of such an adaptation is to elicit in the target readers the same effect (e.g. an emotional and persuasive effect in the case of advertising or corporative texts) as the original does in the source audience.

The origin of transcreation, as a process linked to interlinguistic communication, can be situated in the first translations of sacred texts in Sanskrit, for which a greater degree of freedom and creativity was granted to translators to make its content more accessible to readers (Di Giovanni 2008: 34). Nevertheless, from these uses initially linked solely to literary translation, this concept began to extend to the linguistic industry to refer to the adaptation of texts and other products in the field of marketing and publicity that, due to their characteristics, require a deeper level of adaptation than that offered by translation. Thus, this activity is based on the evidence that word-for-word translations perform particularly badly with sensitive and culturally-bound material such as marketing and advertising texts as pointed out by Roturier (2015), whereas translation tries to reuse at least certain specific elements of the source text (words, phrases, information structure), in the context of transcreation, all possible modifications can be made to the original text as long as the final text or product fulfills the desired objective – e.g., convincing readers to make use of a given service or make a purchase.

Currently, the transcreation service is now offered by a considerable number of companies in the language sector, with Google searches for the term *transcreation* obtaining 461,000 results as of October 2019, and even the ISO 17100 2015 (AENOR 2015: 26) standard has recognized transcreation as a value-added service within the language services industry. Therefore, it involves a reality the deserves to be analyzed, especially if what is sought is to encourage its application not just in the context of large enterprises, but also SMEs. Also, despite the growing popularity of transcreation activity in the industry and the academic sphere, to date, there have been no studies investigating the degree of application of transcreation in the communication processes of companies with potential online users and clients. This is particularly noteworthy if it is taken into account that the combined application of the linguistic, technical and cultural adaptation aspects involved in localization (Gutiérrez-Artacho & Olvera-Lobo, 2017a) together with transcreation is relevant and even recommendable in the field of corporate websites due to the double information and publicity function of these products (Morón & Calvo, 2018; Rike, 2013).

Regarding the differences between the localization and transcreation processes, one of the most standout points is that the former only gives rise to a product that is completely different to the original on specific occasions, whereas for the latter what is habitual is the reinterpretation and creation of a new text or product (Gaballo 2012: 100). Furthermore, as Dam, Brøgger, and Zethsen (2019: 3) point out, the characteristics that until recently did little to distinguish translation localization (adaptation to the user, intensive use of technology or multimodality) form part of the majority of translation tasks today. This would justify the need for a new concept that would enable the design of a group of tools for the deep reinterpretation and transformation of texts and products in terms of form and content. In short, despite any adaptation task applied to a digital product until recently being linked to localization, it is important to take into consideration that the application of transcreation processes and strategies gives rise to partially or new products, which means going a step beyond the linguistic, cultural and technical adaptation specific to localization activity (Olvera-Lobo, Gutiérrez-Artacho & Díaz-Millón 2019: 5). Authors including Fernández Rodríguez (2019: 241) also indicate a marked absence of studies in the sphere of Translation that focuses not as much on the cultural adaptation component as the adaptation of the communicative purposes of the source text. As a result, it is imperative to begin to adopt a wider approach that takes into consideration the importance of the communicative perspective in a field as related to the spheres of marketing and advertising as that of corporate websites.

HYPOTHESIS DEVELOPMENT

This study starts with three initial hypotheses, namely:

Hypothesis One: website and social media localization is a tool that is still seldom used in the sphere of Spanish SMEs;

As it has been pointed out previously, websites and social media are still being scarcely used in the field of SMEs. Therefore, when used, they may not be subjected to an appropriate adaptation to different markets.

Hypothesis Two: cultural elements present in Spanish SME websites are not being appropriately adapted;

Previous studies have shown that cultural elements are often not subjected to thorough treatment in the sphere of corporate websites. Therefore, given the limitations that SMEs face, more particularly in countries affected by recent economic recessions, it may well be expected that cultural elements in websites are not adapted to the corresponding target locales, in spite of the many benefits that such a treatment would bring to the interaction between SMEs and audiences in the field of corporate websites.

Hypothesis Three: companies with greater infrastructures and economic resources are more prone to apply transcreation processes and strategies from which SMEs and translation professionals can learn.

Transcreation is an activity of relatively recent apparition in the language industry and it is regarded as an added-value service (AENOR, 2015). Hence, it tends to have a higher cost than services such as translation or even localization (Translator's Studio, 2019). Therefore, it is expected that this service will be first applied in the context of larger corporations. The results of such an application and the experience accumulated could then be leveraged by smaller companies.

RESEARCH METHODOLOGY

To carry out the study three groups of samples were used. In the two initial analyses, the authors started from the selection made by the London Stock Exchange Group (2017, 2018) concerning the 1000 European companies with the best future outlook. Thus, the first analysis was carried out on the websites of 70 Spanish SMEs. The second analysis considered the 25 Spanish SME websites translated into English and French. For its part, the sample for the third analysis was taken from the Fortune Global 500 list

(Fortune, 2018), an annual classification of the 500 top companies in the world according to income. In this example, the 26 websites belonging to American companies adapted to the Spanish market were taken into account.

Further details on the methodology applied are provided below in each section of the analysis. Data collection periods spanned from January 2018 to May 2019.

RESULTS

First Evaluation: SME Information Dissemination and User Interaction through Web Translation/Localization and Social Media

For this initial part of the study, focused on analyzing the processes of information dissemination and user action via translation, web localization and social networks, a sample of 70 Spanish companies was taken, extracted from the *1000 Companies to Inspire Europe 2017* report (London Stock Exchange Group, 2017). The examination of the online presence of the Spanish SMEs and their corresponding adaptation to other markets was carried out through the application of a series of criteria based on the works of Gutiérrez-Artacho and Olvera-Lobo (2017a), Michelidou, Siamagka and Christodoulides (2011), Nobre and Silva (2014), and Yamazaki (2011). The applied criteria are shown in Table 1.

Table 1. Evaluation criteria applied to the first analysis

Websites	**Translation/localization languages: identification and number**	**Number and variety of translation/ localization languages**
		Degree of translation/localization
Social media	SME social media presence	
	Amount of profiles on social media platforms	
	Amount of followers	
	Update frequency	
	Location of links to social media on corporate websites	
	Visibility of social media presence on corporate websites	

Websites

According to the results obtained in the analysis of the sample websites, nearly three-quarters of sample SMEs (74%) have had their websites translated into at least one language. As Figure 1 shows, 26% (18 SMEs) offer their contents in one single language whereas the biggest group is comprised of SMEs that offer their websites in two languages. In the 8% of websites that can be accessed in 6 or more languages, the most remarkable case is that of a site translated into 18 languages, the highest number found in the sample.

Figure 1. Sample SME websites grouped by the number of target languages

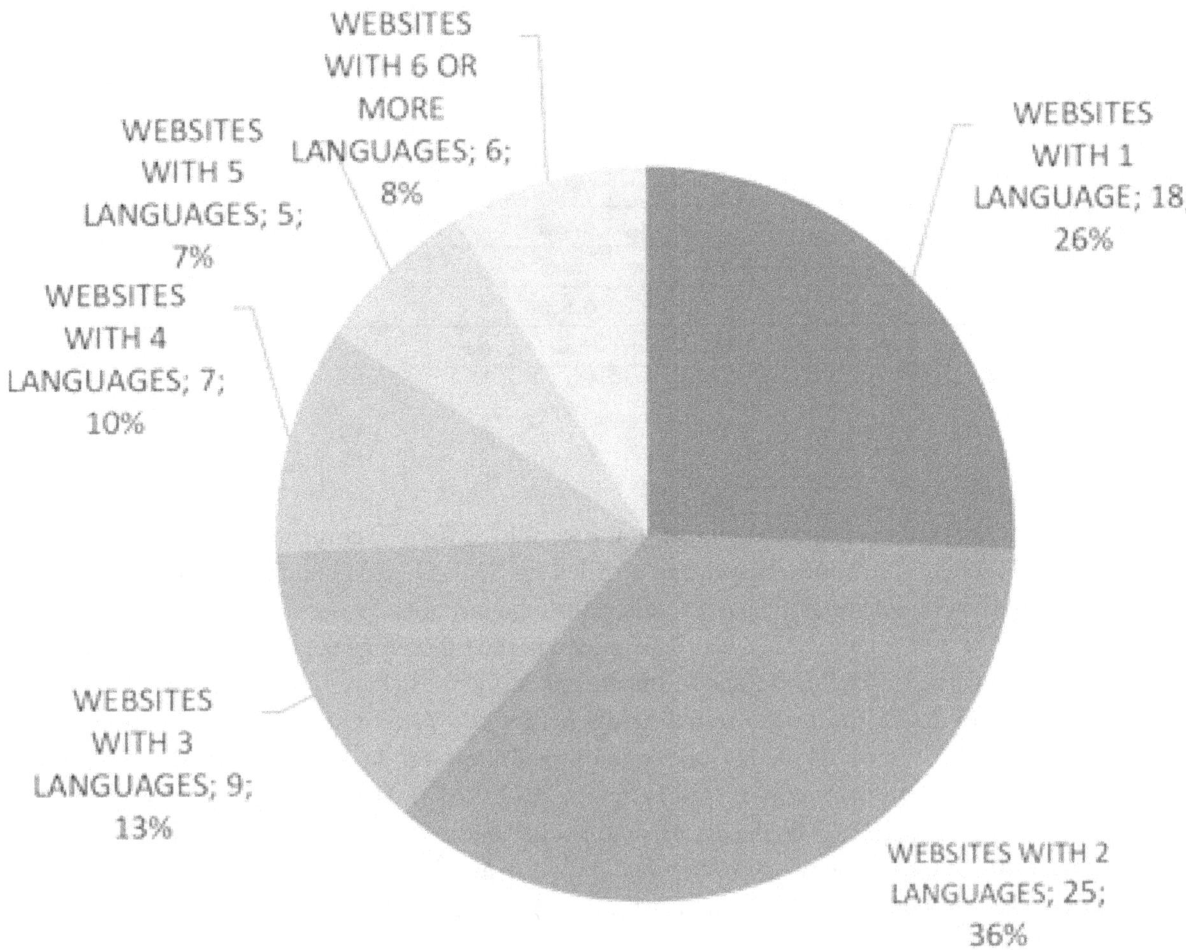

Attention has also been paid to the variety of languages offered on the sample corporate websites as well as the degree to which the websites have been translated. As can be seen in Table 1, it is interesting to note that 96% of the sample websites offer their contents in Spanish, which means that 4% (3 SMEs) only provide their texts in a different language, specifically English. This decision may indicate that these companies have given priority to users from anywhere in the world being able to access their information. English is also the most frequent target language followed by French, Portuguese and German. Likewise, there is a considerable presence of languages spoken by a relatively low number of speakers, an indication that companies do not only seek to communicate with the largest possible number of users, but they are also taking into account the languages of their target markets.

To assess the degree of translation of the sample websites, the authors have considered as cases of partial translation to be every website in which at least one source-language sentence could be found in its localized versions. According to this criterion, 36% of sample websites had all their text translated, 38% were only partially translated and 26% had not been translated at all. Broken links or links that redirect to pages in the original language constituted another frequent error on localized websites.

Table 2. Target languages in sample corporate websites

Language	% (#)	Language	% (#)
Spanish	96% (67)	Chinese	7% (5)
English	74% (52)	Japanese	6% (4)
French	24% (17)	Polish	6% (4)
Portuguese	17% (12)	Dutch	6% (4)
German	17% (12)	Basque	3% (2)
Italian	11% (8)	Arabic	3% (2)
Catalan	10% (7)	Galician	1% (1)
Russian	7% (5)	Other languages	7% (5)

Social Media

Concerning the analysis of social media presence, the sample SMEs (70 companies) have a total of 261 profiles on social media. The average number of profiles per SME is 3.73 (standard deviation of 2.219). Only 8 sample SMEs (11.4%) do not have a single profile on any social media platform.

The online presence of sample SMEs was determined in the following social media platforms: Facebook, Twitter, YouTube, LinkedIn, Google+, Instagram, Vimeo, Flickr, and Pinterest. As it is shown in Figure 2, Facebook is the most used social media platform – 74% of sample SMEs have a profile on it. The second most used social media service is LinkedIn, even though this platform is the seventh most used social media platform in Spain (IAB Spain, 2017, 2018). However, its heavy use could be justified considering that this is a business-oriented social media platform. Twitter's third position is striking considering that it is one of the social media platforms with the biggest loss of users in recent years. According to the studies by IAB Spain (2017, 2018), only half of respondents were Twitter users.

Figure 2. Percentage of sample SMEs with profiles on each social media platform

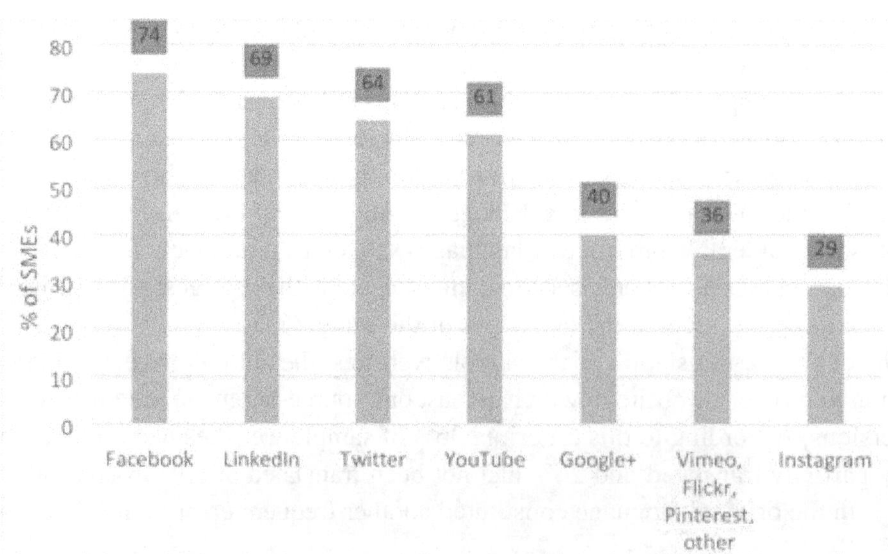

The three social media platforms that accumulate the highest number of followers are Facebook, Twitter, and Instagram. The high number of followers on Instagram is consistent with the increase in the number of users that this platform has experienced in recent years in Spain (IAB Spain, 2018). By contrast, YouTube holds the fifth position despite having been the third most used platform in 2018 (IAB Spain, 2018) and the fourth with the highest number of sample SME profiles. One of the factors that would explain the lack of followers on YouTube could be the infrequent updates since, as will be discussed later, only 21% of companies with a profile on this media platform updated their profiles during the data collection period. The low number of followers on Google+, one of the platforms worst rated by users (IAB Spain, 2017), is not striking considering that this platform disappeared shortly after the data collection period, precisely in April of 2019 (Google, 2019).

To determine the degree of activity of corporate profiles on social media, profiles where at least one post had been published during the data collection period were registered. Although only 29% of SMEs are registered on Instagram, it is noteworthy that 85% of them updated their profiles at some point throughout the data collection month (as shown in Figure 3). Twitter profiles were also updated more often than other social media profiles. Both microblogging social media platforms prioritize audiovisual content and feature short posts with minimum text, thus facilitating quick dissemination of information to a large number of users. The third most updated social media platform is Facebook, which is the most widely used social platform in Spain (IAB Spain, 2018) and its use may, therefore, contribute to the wider dissemination of online content. For the rest of the social media sites, less than 50% of profiles were updated.

Figure 3. Percentage of SME social media profiles which were updated at some point during the data collection period

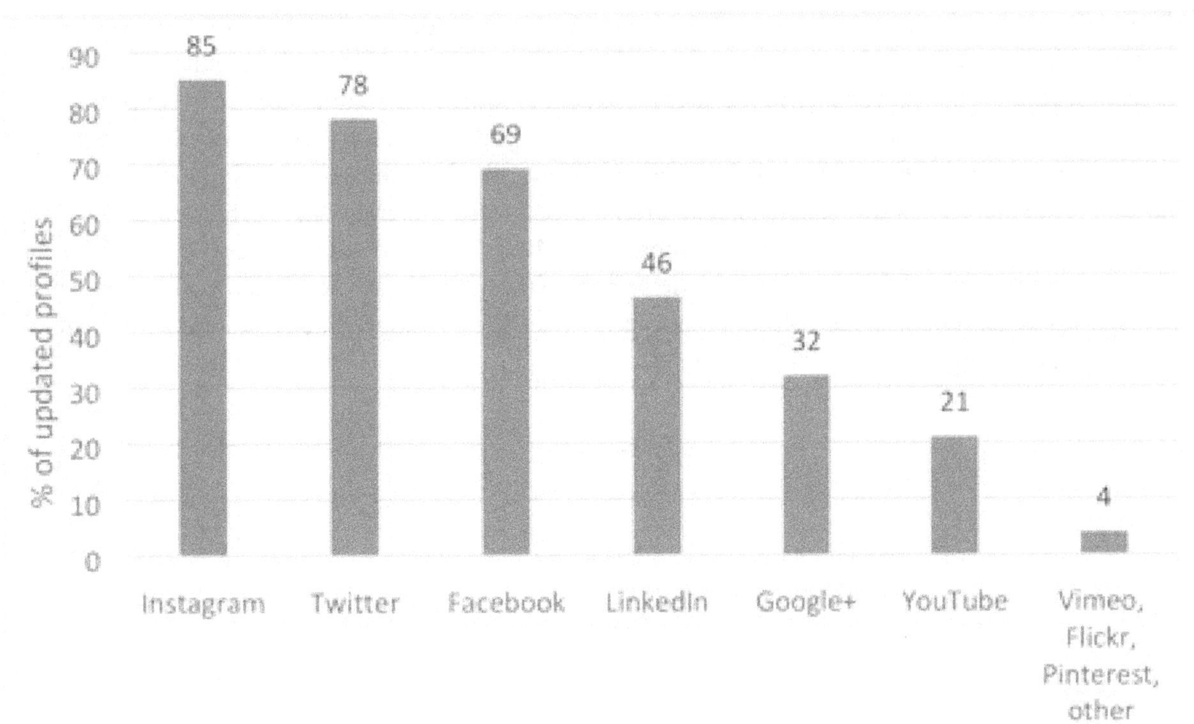

Second Evaluation: Adaptation of Cultural Elements in SME Corporate Websites

The second part of the study aimed to assess the level of adaptation of the cultural elements present on Spanish SME multilingual corporate websites. With this aim, a series of website localization assessment indicators based on Gutiérrez-Artacho and Olvera-Lobo (2017b) was applied to a sample of 25 Spanish SMEs drawn from the *1000 Companies to Inspire* report (London Stock Exchange Group, 2018) that had been translated into English and French. The indicators proposed by Gutiérrez-Artacho & Olvera-Lobo comprise three subsets of criteria for the assessment of the adaptation of linguistic, cultural, and technical elements in website localization. For this study, only the second set of indicators was applied. These were divided into two subgroups: a) indicators to assess the adaptation of cultural elements in website localization and b) indicators to assess the frequency of errors in the localization of cultural elements. For the first set, the following rating scale was used: *a)* "not present" (in other words, the element subject to evaluation is not found on the website analyzed), *b)* "no/insufficient" (the element is not localized whatsoever or appears insufficiently adapted on the website) and *c)* "yes/sufficient" (the element is totally localized or has been sufficiently adapted on the website). For the second set, a frequency scale with the following items was used: never, 1-2 occasions, 3-4 occasions, 5-6 occasions, and +6 occasions.

Assessment of the Adaptation of Cultural Elements

One of the main difficulties encountered in this section of the study is that many of the indicators proposed by Olvera-Lobo and Gutiérrez-Artacho (2017) could not be applied as they were not present in the analyzed websites. As Table 2 shows, this was the case for indicators 2, 4, 5, 6, 7 and 10 (news specific to the target country, localized games, and competitions, only products available in the target country are offered, links to websites in the target language, correct currency and localized graphics). Thus, as regards indicator 6 (links to websites in the target language), 40% of the sample fail to offer this resource, whereas 56% of those corporate websites offering it shows links to web pages in the source language, which indicates that these elements have not been localized. Likewise, in the case of indicator 7 (adapted currency), the evaluation of the degree of adaptation or localization carried out was hindered by the fact that currency was not present in 84% of the sample (21 SMEs). This is related, amongst other aspects, to the fact that the majority of SME websites in the sample do not provide an e-commerce service. Further, nearly half of the sample websites (48%) do not offer specific news for the target country (indicator 2) and, when they do, only 20% adapt it to the target country.

Table 3. Assessment results of cultural element adaptation in sample websites

Indicators	Yes/sufficient	No/insufficient	Not present
1. Customer care	100% (25)	0% (0)	0% (0)
2. News specific to the target country	20% (5)	32% (8)	48% (12)
3. Volume of information	100% (25)	0% (0)	0% (0)
4. Localized games and competitions	0% (0)	4% (1)	96% (24)
5. Only products available in the target country are offered	8% (2)	8% (2)	84% (21)
6. Links to websites in the target language	4% (1)	56% (14)	40% (10)
7. Adapted currency	12% (3)	4% (1)	84% (21)
8. Guided navigation	16% (4)	84% (21)	0% (0)
9. Scroll length	96% (24)	4% (1)	0% (0)
10. Localized graphics	8% (2)	0% (0)	92% (23)

On a positive note, as regards aspects relating to the availability of customer care in various languages, the volume of information and scroll length (indicators 1, 3 and 9, respectively), nearly all of the corporate websites obtained positive ratings. However, a mere 4 SMEs (16%) make correct use of the HTML "alt" attribute on images compared to 21 (84%) that do not employ it, an aspect referred to by indicator 8 (Guided navigation).

Concerning the existence of localized graphics (indicator 10), the sample SMEs also obtain a low rating as they fail to make use of them in the majority of cases. Only 2 SMEs had graphics on their website, accounting for 8% of the total, although it is true that both carry out an appropriate localization of these. Lastly, regarding the localized games and competition indicator (indicator 4), only one website offers them, against 96% that do not, which complicated the evaluation of this aspect. Besides, the only SME to show this resource does not subject it to any sort of translation or localization.

Frequency of Errors in the Localization of Cultural Elements

As can be seen in Table 3, the indicator that obtained the most positive results is the one that evaluates the existence of unnecessary information for the target language audience (indicator 2). In consonance with what has been observed, none of the websites in the sample offers information unnecessary for the final user. In contrast, a higher number of errors were found in the translation/localization of the fields in which users input their personal information (indicator 5). These were particularly problematic as they often included areas like *state* and *province* that are often included, whose completion should not be compulsory as they may not match the administrative divisions of the users' country of residence. Only half of the SMEs in the sample (52%) adapt these fields appropriately in their corporate websites, whereas the rest commit errors on 1-2 occasions (32%) or 3-4 occasions (16%).

About indicator 4 (Errors in the translation/localization of forms), other types of errors were considered, such as grammar and spelling, the presentation the elements in drop-down menus in the source language and the appearance of messages related to file uploads (such as "no file uploaded"). Only 36% of sample SMEs did not make any errors related to this indicator, whereas 32% (8 SMEs) had 1 or 2 errors and 20% (5 SMEs) had 3 or more errors. Three companies had 5 or more errors.

Table 4. Assessment results of frequency of errors in cultural element website localization

Indicators	Never	1-2	3-4	5-6	6+
1. Unnecessary and/or incorrect explicitations	96% (24)	4% (1)	0% (0)	0% (0)	0% (0)
2. Information unnecessary for the target language audience	100% (25)	0% (0)	0% (0)	0% (0)	0% (0)
3. Errors in the adaptation of the basic details of the company	16% (4)	52% (13)	20% (5)	4% (1)	8% (2)
4. Errors in the translation/localization of forms	36% (9)	32% (8)	20% (5)	4% (1)	8% (2)
5. Errors in the translation of personal information relating to names and addresses	52% (13)	32% (8)	16% (4)	0% (0)	0% (0)
6. Problems with interactivity	44% (11)	20% (5)	8% (2)	4% (1)	24%(6)

An even higher number of errors was observed in the adaptation of basic company details (indicator 3), for the evaluation of which the authors took into consideration aspects such as the indication of the international prefix (+34 in the case of Spain), the exploitation of the country in which the company was based in its English and French versions, and the correct translation of the physical address. In this section, the greater part of the companies (52%) committed 1 or 2 errors, whereas only 16% (4 companies) correctly adapted all of their details. Finally, the poorest results were those referring to company interactivity (indicator 6). Compared to 44% of sites that permitted navigation in English or French without at any point returning to the original version, 32% of websites redirected users between 1 and six times to their Spanish version, and this happened on more than 6 occasions for 24%.

Third Evaluation: Application of Transcreation Strategies in the Corporate Field

The final part of this study focused on analyzing the quality and coherence of corporate websites at a linguistic level as well as investigating the frequency of application of transcreation processes and strategies in this domain. As transcreation is an activity that is still starting to be developed both from a conceptual and practical viewpoint, it was hypothesized that companies with greater infrastructures and economic resources would be more prone to apply transcreation processes and strategies. Thus, a sample of 27 large US corporate websites (source websites, hereinafter SW) was extracted from the Fortune 500 Global list (Fortune, 2018) along with their corresponding 27 versions adapted for the Spanish market (target websites, hereinafter TW) were examined. A checklist was developed including indicators for the evaluation of formal and content elements based on previous studies on localization (Olvera-Lobo & Castillo-Rodríguez, 2019; Olvera-Lobo, Gutiérrez-Artacho & Díaz-Millón, 2019) and advertising language (Theocharous, 2015). Particular attention was given to the analysis of the verbal communicative style employed in both languages and the creative adaptation of slogans and other website texts.

Evaluation of SW Linguistic Quality and Coherence

In the first stage of this part of the study, the indicators of Table 5 were applied to evaluate the linguistic quality and coherence of the sample TW and, in this way, have preliminary data available on the degree of professionalism of the adaptation processes to which the websites have been subjected. With this aim, as a starting point, the number of TWs whose texts had only been partially translated were counted.

The analysis permitted the identification of 5 cases of partially translated TWs (19% of the sample of the 27 websites comprising it). It can be considered that this type of error is as indicative of defects in one or more stages of the website adaptation process as it is of the absence of a final validation phase (Sandrini, 2008).

Table 5. Indicators for the evaluation of SW linguistic quality and coherence

Indicator	Measurement scale
Partial translation	1: the presence of the indicator, 0: absence
Inconsistencies or orthotypographic errors	1: the presence of the indicator, 0: absence
Register errors	1: the presence of the indicator, 0: absence
Other evidence of scarce linguistic quality	1: the presence of the indicator, 0: absence
Redirects to web pages in English not indicated	1: the presence of the indicator, 0: absence

Regarding the inconsistencies or orthotypographic errors identified in the sample, these have been detected in 21 sites (78%). Among the most frequent errors, attention may be drawn to the abundance of inconsistencies (differences in the punctuation at the end of numbered lists or with bullet points, for example), errors easily detectable with the employment any automatic correction program, orthotypographic errors possibly linked to the segmentation rules of assisted translation tools (use of upper case after colons or punctuation inside brackets) and orthotypographic anglicisms. The frequency of the latter type of error is noteworthy as it has also been observed in those TWs that show evidence of having been produced independently of the Source Website (hereinafter SW) due to the considerable differences between both versions. These errors, as such, may not be related to possible interference of the original in English during translation, rather, to the extensive influence of the English language over the Web in general (Bolaños-Medina, 2003).

The switching between formal and informal treatment is another recurring problem in adapted websites. A total of 15 of the 27 websites in Spanish (44% of TWs) show this error, which could be related to the progressive translation of website texts while they are being produced and updated, which gives rise to the possibility of various professionals intervening in the adaptation of all types of sites in an asynchronous and uncoordinated manner.

In the same vein, another type of evidence of scarce linguistic quality was detected in a total of 17 TWs (63%). Amongst the errors detected are the frequency of lexical, semantic and syntactic calques, the use of a poor or not very natural style and the appearance of ungrammatical and nonsensical statements.

Finally, another error that frequently appears in adapted websites is the existence of links that direct to websites in the source language, in this case, English. Over a third of TWs (16 websites, 41%) contain links that direct the user to the original version of the websites or others in English without any prior warning.

Analysis of Similarities between SWs and TWs

For the analysis of similarities and differences between the websites in English and their Spanish adaptations the indicators that appear in **¡Error! La autoreferencia al marcador no es válida.**6 were employed. In the Likert scale used, 1 is equal to "absence of similarity, high evidence of application of transcreation strategies" whereas 5 is "total similarity, scarce evidence of transcreation strategy application". In this manner, lower values presumably indicate a better adaptation to the target website.

Table 6. Indicators for the evaluation of similarity between SWs and TWs

Indicators			Measurement scale
Formal plan	Visual plan	Home page design	Likert 1-5
		Colors	Likert 1-5
		Images in coinciding sections	Likert 1-5
	Text plan	Verbal communication style	1: the presence of the indicator, 0: absence
		Creative adaptation of slogans and other texts	Likert 1-5
Content plan	Tabs and sections		Likert 1-5
	Site maps		Likert 1-5

Formal plan

As shown in Table 6, the formal analysis of the similarities between the SWs and the TWs includes indicators both for the study of the visual and the text plans of the websites. Within the visual plan, in the analysis of the similarity of the home page design, the sample websites obtained an average score of 2.85 on a Likert scale of 1-5, which reflects an average similarity of the TWs as regards their SWs. Furthermore, the authors have identified a high degree of similarity in the colors employed in the majority of website pairs in the sample, as demonstrated by the average score of 4.48 out of 5 obtained by this indicator. No company in the sample has obtained a score of 1, which would be the equivalent of using a radically different color palette in both sites. These results can be linked, among other factors, to the uniformity of the corporate visual identity used by the companies in all markets, in addition to the relative closeness between the American and Spanish cultures to this aspect of the analysis, in which similar values and connotations are attributed to all colors (McCandless, 2014).

In terms of the degree of similarity of the images used by the companies in each target market, the average score of the sample stands at 1.93 on a Likert scale of 1-5, which in principle reveals considerable differences between the SW and TW images. Despite these quantitative data, throughout the analysis, it has been observed that, although the images used are different in the majority of cases, they are not usually culturally marked and show a very similar aesthetic. Thus, there does not appear to be evidence of the application of a deep adaptation process during the selection of graphic elements employed on the websites, rather, it appears that in many cases there has been a decision to select images that are potentially interchangeable between both cultures.

Within the text plan, the authors carried out an analysis of the verbal communication style used in the 27 websites of the sample and their corresponding 27 versions in Spanish. The methodology proposed by Theocharous (2015) was applied, which includes indicators divided into three main groups for determining the level of persuasion, closeness to user and expressiveness of communicative style. Along general lines, a marked tendency towards the use of the persuasive, personal and expressive style in both languages was appreciated. Notwithstanding, the detailed study of the data unearthed by the different indicators allows for the identification of differentiating features in the communicative style employed in each language.

Within the indicators for the evaluation of the level of persuasion used, it was observed that 44% of the TWs use imperatives to encourage users to try their products or services or convince them of their effectiveness, whereas the presence of this indicator in the SWs is more reduced (33%). Also, in English, connectors, coordination, and subordination are used as expressions to introduce statements on products and services slightly more frequently than in Spanish (52% of the SWs show a tendency towards these elements compared to 41% of TWs). This absence of connectors could be linked to the segmentation applied by the assisted translation tools, which may give rise to texts with shorter sentences and a less cohesive style than in the texts originally written in Spanish. Also, the abundance of data on products and services is greater in English (67%) than Spanish (52%), which would be in line with the studies that point to a greater quantity of objective information in advertising in countries with a low context cultural framework like the United States (Theocharous, 2015).

With regards to the indicators relating to closeness to the user, a greater formality and a slightly more impersonal style in Spanish have been observed, as is characteristic of Spanish websites (Bolaños-Medina, 2003). Furthermore, it has been noted that imperatives appear more frequently in elements such as titles, subtitles, and buttons than in the body of the text, which points to persuasive features being more common in these elements, whereas the function of the rest of the text is predominantly informative. Also, one of the most striking differences of the analysis as a whole is the conversational style (simple and frequent vocabulary, informal register) characterizes 85% of the SWs, whereas a mere 37% of the TWs show features particular to this style, which once again coincides with the greater formality of Spanish in the web sphere.

Lastly, concerning the presence of features associated with an expressive style, the use of creative language resources such as word plays or metaphors has only been identified in 26% of the complete sample of websites. This indicator is, nevertheless, more frequent in English (shown by 37% of SWs) than in Spanish (15% of TWs). In general, the SWs reveal higher indices of expressiveness than the TWs, which points to either a loss of this feature during translation or, in the case of texts originally written in Spanish, it not be considered necessary or appropriate to redact them in a, particularly expressive way, given the greater formality of the Spanish.

Regarding the analysis of the creative adaptation of slogans and other parts of a text, this was possible in those pairs of SWs and TWs that presented text sections with similar content. The pairs in which the content differs completely between them do not allow it to be observed whether or not such creative adaptation has been carried out, to which these were given a score of 0 and they were removed from the sample. Of the 27 companies in the sample, only 15 allowed this analysis.

The average score obtained for these 15 companies was 3.3 out of 5, given that over half (53%) do not implement a creative adaptation of their texts, and 40% only do so poorly. Just one website obtained a score of 1. The great majority of websites in the sample employ texts and slogans that, despite being different from the originals in some cases, are not very idiomatic or effective. In other cases, the texts employed in Spanish are effective but lack a noteworthy level of creativity and separation from the original, to which it can be deduced that they have not been subjected to the rewriting process specific to transcreation.

Content plan

To evaluate the differences in the content offered in English and Spanish, the level of similarity between the sections and tabs of the SWs and TWs and between their corresponding site maps was analyzed. These indicators obtained average scores of 2.9 and 2.7, respectively. Broadly speaking, there are a large variety of cases within the sample analyzed with websites that contain content that is completely different in both languages and others that show identical content. However, the majority of differences identified are mainly due to the lower amount of existing content on the site maps for the TWs.

CONCLUSION

The new information and communication technologies offer numerous advantages for companies, among which particular mention can be made of the breaking of geographical barriers, the possibility of carrying out real-time transactions, and the opportunity of entering into contact with new markets almost immediately. Despite this, the linguistic and cultural differences that exist between the different markets, as well as the lack of similarities in consumer expectations in each region, demand the adaptation of communication processes between companies and target publics. In response to these needs, the language industry has begun to offer new adaptation services that that highlight localization and transcreation, affording several advantages for a relatively reduced cost.

However, there are many companies that even today are not taking advantage of the benefits these tools offer. This study has focused on analyzing three different dimensions of corporate online presence and its adaptation to different markets from the perspective of localization and transcreation. According to the first analysis, although the majority of sample SMEs have localized their sites into a variety of target languages, these localizations present a notable number of defects. Some of the main deficiencies identified include poor linguistic quality of target texts, which occasionally show signs of machine translation; the notable frequency of partial translations –only 36% of SMEs translate all texts on their websites while 38% provide a partial translation– and an abundance of broken links. As regards the use of social media platforms, most sample SMEs had a relatively active presence on social media, as shown in the average number of 3.73 social media profiles per sample SME. However, the greater or lesser popularity of each social media platform in Spain did not seem to match the intensity of the use of the sample SMEs. For instance, Facebook and Twitter are still some of the most frequently used social media platforms by SMEs although these media have suffered a serious loss of followers in the last years (IAB 2017, 2018). Additionally, it was noted that profiles were updated at an irregular rate, being microblogging platforms (Instagram, Twitter) the ones that showed a higher update frequency. It should not be forgotten that the sample analyzed includes companies singled out by a major organization and defined as some of the fastest-growing, most dynamic SMEs in Europe.

The results of the second section of the analysis suggest that the majority of Spanish SMEs fail to carry out a satisfactory adaptation of the cultural elements on their websites. Among the aspects most lacking, particular attention may be drawn to guided navigation in 84% and the presence of interactivity errors in 56% of the websites analyzed. Only 16% of SMEs are the basic information of the company correctly adapted, and 48% reveal errors in the translation of personal information (names, addresses). Furthermore, 96% of the SMEs only carry out a partial translation of their website. In general, Spanish SME websites seem to be characterized by their simplicity and their mainly informative nature, with little hope for interaction.

In general terms, the results of the analysis on the level of use of transcreation in websites belonging to large companies point to a lack of application of transcreation processes and strategies even by the wealthiest companies in the world. There is a general lack of adaptation of pictures and colors used and information is disposed of following a very similar structure to the original. Likewise, the verbal communicative style used in Spanish follows very similar patterns to that used in English, resulting in a less idiomatic, more foreign brand voice with which, likely, Spanish customers do not identify as easily as Americans.

LIMITATIONS AND FUTURE RESEARCH DIRECTIONS

One clear limitation of the present study is the reduced size of the samples analyzed, which does not allow for definite conclusions on the frequency and degree of application of localization and transcreation in the Spanish SME corporate field. Future studies may address the relationship between certain translation, localization and transcreation strategies and their effectiveness in achieving a persuasive effect in the sphere of corporate websites and social media. It would also be appropriate to combine traditional website visualization and comparison with corpus linguistics techniques. Corpus linguistics allows for text analyses at a larger scale and helps identify recurring patterns within certain languages and genres, information that could be highly useful for future transcreation projects. Likewise, the identification of frequent formal and content features incorporate websites depending on SME sectors could also be of great interest.

In general terms, websites can be considered a reflection of the great mobilization of actors and resources that take place in the framework of large corporative communication strategies to attract potential customers from very varied contexts. Therefore, a closer collaboration between all agents involved and the development of localization and transcreation guidelines and workflows for the corporate field seem to be two basic pillars for raising the quality of online corporate presence in the SME area. Only so will it be possible to address the numerous challenges posed by the web environment, such as the development of quality content for both SWs and their adapted versions asynchronously and independently and different communicative frameworks.

PRACTICAL AND THEORETICAL IMPLICATIONS

In the sphere of larger companies, in recent years it has been identified that there has been a tendency towards the production of texts for the Web that are easily translatable through the application of automated translation and post-editing tools (Ferreira 2016: 138). To this end, it is possible that companies that produce large quantities of texts are not always interested in applying transcreation processes as they imply a greater cost, the return of which is not always easy to measure, and they complicate the application of translation memories and automated translation. Additionally, according to Roturier (2015:

184), such companies fear losing brand identity if they give localization or transcreation companies too much room for maneuver.

From a general viewpoint, more awareness needs to be raised about the benefits of a solid online presence as a low-cost tool that can bring about fruitful interactions with users and potential customers. This is particularly true for countries where the economic fluctuations of recent decades have negatively impacted SME performance, as is the case of Spain (CEPYME, 2017). As pointed out by Fuchs-Kittowski, Klassen, Faust, & Einhaus (2009), one of the main obstacles for social media adoption is that cost-benefit analyses yield unclear results. Additionally, McCann & Barlow (2015) signaled the importance of measuring the return of investment (ROI) of social media usage paying attention to both qualitative and quantitative indicators. Future studies contributing to this line of research may help boost and improve SME online presence (both in Europe and other regions) and open up new opportunities for entrepreneurial and technological development in the SME sector.

ACKNOWLEDGMENT

This study forms part of the "TRANSCREAWEB: web transcreation for the dissemination of the corporate information of Spanish SMEs from the healthcare sector", funded by the Ministry of Science, Innovation, and Universities (MCIU), the State Research Agency (AEI) and the European Regional Development Fund (ERDF) (reference: RTI2018-093348-B-I00).

REFERENCES

ADEI. (2017). *El trabajo del futuro*. Retrieved from http://observatorioadei.es/publicaciones/NotaTecnica-El-trabajo-del-futuro.pdf

AENOR. (2015). *Servicios de traducción. Requisitos para los servicios de traducción* (UNE-EN ISO 17100:2015). Retrieved from https://www.aenor.com/normas-y-libros/buscador-de-normas/iso/?c=059149

Ahmed, T., Mouratidis, H., & Preston, D. (2009). Website design guidelines: High power distance and high-context culture. *International Journal of Cyber Society and Education*, *2*(1), 47–60.

Baack, D. W., & Singh, N. (2007). Culture and web communications. *Journal of Business Research*, *60*(3), 181–188. doi:10.1016/j.jbusres.2006.11.002

Ballestero, F., & Pérez, M. (2017). El papel del Estado ante la digitalización de la economía. Estrategia digital y políticas públicas. *Información Comercial Española, ICE. Revista de economía*, *898*, 113–130.

Barber, W., & Badre, A. (1998). Culturability: The merging of culture and usability. In *Proceedings of the 4th Conference on Human Factors and the Web*. AT&T Labs.

Bolaños-Medina, A. (2003). Dificultades y estrategias de la localización de sitios web comerciales del inglés al español. In E. Santiago Posteguillo & J. Ramón Prado (Eds.), Internet in Linguistics, Translation and Literary Studies (pp. 241-262). Castellón de la Plana: Publicacions de la Universitat Jaume I.

CEPYME. (2017). *Informe anual de empleo en las pymes*. Retrieved from http://www.cepyme.es

Dam, H. V., Brøgger, M. N., & Zethsen, K. K. (2018). Introduction. In Moving boundaries in translation studies, (pp. 1-11). London: Routledge.

Davis, C. H., & Vladica, F. (2006). Use of Internet technologies and e-business solutions: A structural model of sources of business value among Canadian micro-enterprises. *Proceedings of the 39th Annual Hawaii International Conference on System Sciences*, 1-10. 10.1109/HICSS.2006.519

De Troyer, O., Mushtaha, A. N., Stengers, H., Baetens, M., Boers, F., Casteleyn, S., & Plessers, P. (2006). On cultural differences in local web interfaces. *Journal of Web Engineering*, *5*, 246–264.

Di Giovanni, E. (2008). Translations, transcreations, and trans representations of India in the Italian media. *Meta: Journal des traducteurs, 53*(1), 26-43.

Dormann, C., & Chisalita, C. (2002). Cultural values in web site design. In *11th European Conference on Cognitive Ergonomics*. ECCE.

European Commision. (2019). *The Digital Economy and Society Index (DESI).* Retrieved from https://ec.europa.eu/digital-single-market/en/desi

European Commission. (2003). *Commission Recommendation of 6 May 2003 concerning the definition of micro, small and medium-sized enterprises*. Brussels: European Union.

Fernández Rodríguez, M. A. (2019). Transcreación: Retórica cultural y traducción publicitaria. *Castilla. Estudios de Literatura*, *10*(10), 223–250. doi:10.24197/cel.10.2019.223-250

Ferreira, A. (2016). *Universal UX Design: Building Multicultural User Experience*. Cambridge, UK: Morgan Kaufmann.

Flavián, C., Gurrea, R., & Orús, C. (2016). Choice confidence in the webrooming purchase process: The impact of online positive reviews and the motivation to touch. *Journal of Consumer Behaviour*, *15*(5), 459–476. doi:10.1002/cb.1585

Fortune. (2018). *Fortune 500 Companies 2018*. Retrieved from http://fortune.com/fortune500/

Fuchs-Kittowski, F., Klassen, N., Faust, D., & Einhaus, J. (2009). A comparative study on the use of Web 2.0 in enterprises. In K. Tochtermann (Ed.), *Proceedings of I-KNOW '09 and I-SEMANTICS '09* (pp. 372-378). Graz: Verlag der TU Graz.

Gaballo, V. (2012). Exploring the boundaries of transcreation in specialized translation. *ESP Across Cultures*, *9*, 95–113.

General Secretariat of Industry and SMEs. (2018). *Cifras PYME. Datos febrero 2018*. Retrieved from http://www.ipyme.org/Publicaciones/CifrasPYME-%0Afebrero2018.pdf

Google. (2019). *Shutting down Google+ for consumer (personal) accounts on April 2, 2019*. Retrieved from https://support.google.com/plus/answer/9195133?hl=en

Google Consumer Barometer. (2015). *The smart shopper. Research & purchase behavior (ROPO)*. Retrieved from https://www.consumerbarometer.com/en/

Gutiérrez-Artacho, J., & Olvera-Lobo, M. D. (2017a). Web localization of Spanish SMEs: The case of study in the chemical sector. *Journal of Information Systems Engineering & Management*, *2*(3), 1–8. doi:10.20897/jisem.201715

Gutiérrez-Artacho, J., & Olvera-Lobo, M. D. (2017b). El uso del método Delphi como herramienta de evaluación consensuada en la didáctica de la traducción: el perfil del traductor-localizador. In M. E. del Valle (Ed.), *Nuevos Contenidos Innovadores En Ciencias y Humanidades* (pp. 226–240). Madrid: CUICIID.

Hofstede, G. (1980). *Culture's consequences: International differences in work-related values*. Beverly Hills, CA: Sage Publications.

Hofstede, G. (1991). *Cultures and organizations: Software of the mind*. New York: McGraw-Hill.

IAB Spain. (2017). *Estudio Anual Redes Sociales 2017*. Retrieved from: https://iabspain.es/wp-content/uploads/iab_estudioredessociales_2017_vreducida.pdf

IAB Spain. (2018). *Estudio Anual de Redes Sociales 2018*. Retrieved from https://iabspain.es/wp-content/uploads/estudio-redes-sociales-2018_vreducida.pdf

INE (Instituto Nacional de Estadística). (2017). *Encuesta sobre el uso de TIC y comercio electrónico en las empresas*. Retrieved from: http://www.ine.es

INE (Instituto Nacional de Estadística). (2019). *Encuesta sobre el uso de TIC y comercio electrónico en las empresas*. Retrieved from: http://www.ine.es

Iqbal, Q., Hassan, S. H., & Ahmad, N. H. (2018). The assessment of perceived information pollution in banking sector: A scale development and validation study. *Business Information Review*, *35*(2), 68–76. doi:10.1177/0266382118772891

Iqbal, Q., & Nawaz, R. (2019). Rife information pollution (infollution) and virtual organizations in industry 4.0: within reality causes and consequences. In *Big Data and Knowledge Sharing in Virtual Organizations* (pp. 117–135). IGI Global. doi:10.4018/978-1-5225-7519-1.ch005

Kuzmenko, O., & Roienko, V. (2017). Nowcasting income inequality in the context of the Fourth Industrial Revolution. *Socioeconomic Challenges*, *1*(1), 5–12. doi:10.21272ec.2017.1-01

LISA. (2003). *The localization industry primer*. Geneva: LISA.

London Stock Exchange Group. (2017). *1000 Companies to Inspire Europe - 2017 Report*. Retrieved from https://www.lseg.com/resources/1000-companies-inspire/2017-report-1000-companies-europe

London Stock Exchange Group. (2018). *1000 Companies to Inspire*. Retrieved from https://www.lseg.com/resources/1000-companies-inspire

Lopes, L. A., & Melão, N. F. (2016). Website content and design in SME: Insights from Portugal. *International Journal of Electronic Business*, *13*(1), 70. doi:10.1504/IJEB.2016.075343

Luna, D., Peracchio, L. A., & De Juan, M. D. (2002). Cross-cultural and cognitive aspects of web site navigation. *Journal of the Academy of Marketing Science*, *30*(4), 397–410. doi:10.1177/009207002236913

Marcus, A., & Gould, E. W. (2000). Crosscurrents: Cultural dimensions and global Web user-interface design. *Interaction*, *7*(4), 32–46. doi:10.1145/345190.345238

Marín Dueñas, P. P., & Lasso de la Vega González, M. (2017). La efectividad de las páginas web en la comunicación empresarial de las pequeñas y medianas empresas. Un estudio en PYMES de la provincia de Cádiz. *ZER. Revista de Estudios de Comunicación*, *22*(42), 53–71. doi:10.1387/zer.17797

Mbatha, B. (2013). Exploring the potential of electronic commerce tools in South African SME tourism service providers. *Information Development*, *29*(1), 10–23. doi:10.1177/0266666912452270

McCandless, D. (2014). *Knowledge is Beautiful*. London: HarperCollins.

McCann, M., & Barlow, A. (2015). Use and measurement of social media for SMEs. *Journal of Small Business and Enterprise Development*, *22*(2), 273–287. doi:10.1108/JSBED-08-2012-0096

Michelidou, N., Siamagka, N. T., & Christodoulides, G. (2011). Usage, barriers, and measurement of social media marketing: An exploratory investigation of small and medium B2B brands. *Industrial Marketing Management*, *40*(7), 1153–1159. doi:10.1016/j.indmarman.2011.09.009

Morón, M., & Calvo, E. (2018). Introducing transcreation skills in translator training contexts: A situated project-based approach. *The Journal of Specialised Translation*, *29*, 126–148.

Nantel, J., & Glaser, E. (2008). The impact of language and culture on perceived website usability. *Journal of Engineering and Technology Management*, *25*(1-2), 112–122. doi:10.1016/j.jengtecman.2008.01.005

Nobre, H., & Silva, D. (2014). Social network marketing strategy and SME strategy benefits. *Journal of Transnational Management, 19*(2), 138–151. doi:10.1080/15475778.2014.904658

Observatorio Vodafone. (2019). *III Estudio sobre el estado de digitalización de las empresas y Administraciones Públicas españolas.* Retrieved from https://tinyurl.com/txm9ajt

OECD. (2017a). *Increasing productivity in small traditional enterprises: programs for upgrading management skills and practices*. Paris: OECD Publishing.

OECD. (2017b). *Small, medium, strong. Trends in SME performance and business conditions*. Paris: OECD Publishing.

Olvera-Lobo, M. D., & Castillo-Rodríguez, C. (2019). Website localization in the corporate context: A Spanish perspective. *Journal of Digital Information Management, 17*(1), 34–43. doi:10.6025/jdim/2019/17/1/34-43

Olvera-Lobo, M. D., & Gutiérrez-Artacho, J. (2017). Web localization: the Spanish SMEs as a case of study. In *Proceedings of 12th Iberian Conference on Information Systems and Technologies (CISTI)*. IEEE. 10.23919/CISTI.2017.7975872

Olvera-Lobo, M. D., Gutiérrez-Artacho, J., & Díaz-Millón, M. (2019). Web transcreation in the Spanish business context: the case of healthcare SMEs. In M. Kefalaki (Ed.), *ICCM2019: 5th Annual International Conference on Communication and Management*. Athens: ICCM.

Papadopoulos, G., Rikama, S., Alajääskö, P., & Salah-Eddine, Z. (2019). *Statistics on small and medium-sized enterprises*. Retrieved from https://ec.europa.eu/eurostat/statistics-explained/index.php/Statistics_on_small_and_medium-sized_enterprises#General_overview

Rike, S. M. (2013). Bilingual corporate websites — from translation to transcreation? *The Journal of Specialised Translation, 20*, 68–85.

Roturier, J. (2015). *Localizing apps: a practical guide for translators and translation students*. Oxon, UK: Routledge.

Sandrini, P. (2008). Localization and translation. In H. Gerzymisch-Arbogast, G. Budin & G. Hofer (Eds.), MuTra Journal, Vol 2. LSP Translation Scenarios. Selected Contributions to the EU Marie Curie Conference Vienna 2007 (pp.167-191). Saarbrücken: ATRC.

Seeba, M. (2016). Foreword. In C. Lee (Ed.), *Multilingualism online*. London: Routledge.

Singh, N., Zhao, H., & Hu, X. (2003). Cultural adaptation on the Web: A study of American companies' domestic and Chinese websites. *Journal of Global Information Management, 11*(3), 63–80. doi:10.4018/jgim.2003070104

Sixto García, J., Aguado Domínguez, N., & Riveiro Castro, R. (2017). Presencia 2.0 de las pymes gallegas: niveles de participación y engagement con los usuarios. *Revista Latina de comunicación social, 72*(1), 47-68.

Sun, H. (2001). Building a culturally-competent corporate web site: an exploratory study of cultural markers in multilingual web design. In M. J. Northrop, & S. Tilley (Eds.), *Proceedings of the 19th annual international conference on Computer documentation - SIGDOC '01. Santa Fe, New Mexico, 21-24 October* (pp. 95-102). 10.1145/501516.501536

Telefónica, & Red.es. (2014). *Desarrollo empresarial y redes sociales. El caso de las microempresas españolas*. Barcelona: *Ariel.*

Theocharous, A. (2015). Food advertising as a mirror of intercultural differences: The case of the UK and Greece. *British Food Journal, 117*(4), 1256–1272. doi:10.1108/BFJ-01-2014-0038

Translator's Studio. (2019). *The price difference between transcreation and translation explained.* Retrieved from https://translatorstudio.co.uk/price-difference-transcreation-translation/

Ureña, A., Ballestero, M. P., & Prieto, E. (2017). *Informe e-Pyme 2017 de análisis sectorial de la implantación de las TIC en las empresas españolas*. Retrieved from https://www.ontsi.red.es/ontsi/sites/ontsi/files/Informe ePyme 2017.pdf

World Economic Forum. (2016). *The future of job employment, skills and workforce strategy for the Fourth Industrial Revolution*. Growth Strategies. Retrieved from https://tinyurl.com/yx2z42yq

Yamazaki, A. K. (2011). Web pages of small and medium-sized manufacturing companies in Tokyo and their global business needs. In *2011 IEEE International Professional Communication Conference* (pp. 1–3). Los Alamitos, CA: IEEE. 10.1109/IPCC.2011.6087241

ADDITIONAL READING

Agorni, M. (2018). Translating, transcreating or mediating the foreign? The translator's space of maneuver in the field of tourism. In C. Spinzi, A. Rizzo, & M. L. Zummo (Eds.), *Translation or transcreation? Discourses, texts, and visuals* (pp. 87–105). Cambridge: Cambridge Scholars Publishing.

Jiménez-Crespo, M. Á. (2011a). A corpus-based error typology: Towards a more objective approach to measuring quality in localization. *Perspectives: Studies in Translatology, 19*(4), 315–338. doi:10.1080/0907676X.2011.615409

Jiménez-Crespo, M. Á. (2011b). To adapt or not to adapt to web localization: A contrastive genre-based study of original and localized legal sections in corporate websites. *Jostrans: The Journal of Specialized Translation, 15*, 1–27.

Katan, D. (2016). Translation at the cross-roads: Time for the transcreation turn? *Perspectives: Studies in Translatology, 24*(3), 365–381. doi:10.1080/0907676X.2015.1016049

Okazaki, S. (2006). Searching the web for global brands: How American brands standardize their web sites in Europe. *European Journal of Marketing, 39*(1-2), 87–109.

Opreana, A., & Vinerean, S. (2015). A new development in online marketing. *Expert Journal of Marketing, 3*(1), 29–34.

Pedersen, D. (2014). Exploring the concept of transcreation - transcreation as 'more than translation'? *Cultus: The Journal of Intercultural Mediation and Communication*, *27*, 57–71.

Singh, N., & Pereira, A. (2014). *The culturally customized web site*. Oxford: Elsevier Butterworth-Heinemann.

Wang, Q., & .... (2016). Website location strategies review under Hofstede's cultural dimensions. In F. H. Nah & C. H. Tan (Eds.), *HCI in Business, Government, and Organizations: eCommerce and Innovation* (pp. 258–269). Lecture Notes in Computer Science Cham: Springer. doi:10.1007/978-3-319-39396-4_24

KEY TERMS AND DEFINITIONS

Locale: The target country and the language in which a product subjected to a localization process will be used and sold.

Localization: The process of taking a product and making it linguistically, culturally and technically appropriate for a locale.

Register: A variety of language used for a particular purpose or in a particular communicative situation.

Source Text: A text that a translator, localization/transcreation specialist or another language specialist is given to translate into another language or languages.

Target Text: The text that the translator, localization/transcreation specialist or another language specialist produces from the source text; for example, the product of the translation.

Transcreation: A reinterpretation of a text to adapt it to the readers of a target language taking into account conceptual, linguistic and cultural differences. This process takes into account numerous aspects that go well beyond a translation or cultural adaptation, since it also considers the expectations of the target audience or the need to maintain the company's brand voice across markets in the case of corporate texts, among other elements.

Usability: The ease with which a specific product can be used by its intended users to achieve a specific purpose.

Webrooming: The process of searching for information on a product online and purchasing it in a physical store to reduce uncertainty and increase the level of trust with which the decision to purchase is made.

Section 4

Strategic Management in Industry 4.0

Chapter 11
Strategic Management in SMEs in the Context of Clustering

Mustafa Atilla Arıcıoğlu
Necmettin Erbakan University, Turkey

Büşra Yiğitol
Konya Food and Agriculture University, Turkey

ABSTRACT

Nowadays, the effects of global dynamics are directive on enterprises. Competitiveness is triggered by these dynamics and determine the efficiency of enterprises. Therefore, not only the local and national dimension, but also the global actors have a say on the viability of enterprises and their competitiveness. In such an ecological environment, it is possible to come across many strategies for gaining competitiveness and skills. Porter points out that the national resources should be used optimally and that each country should specialize in specific areas and build clusters through these areas and thus use the resources effectively. Therefore, it draws attention to "the importance of clustering," which is one of the instruments effective in competitiveness with global dynamics. In this study, strategic management processes of small and medium-sized enterprises in the context of clustering will be discussed. In addition, the contribution of cluster studies to SMEs in Industry 4.0 digitalization process will be briefly mentioned.

DOI: 10.4018/978-1-7998-2577-7.ch011

INTRODUCTION

Drucker (2014) underlines that global competition should become a strategic goal for every organization and that it cannot be successful or survive without the standards set by the leaders in their respective fields. Therefore, global dynamics and global competition are the main factors that should be taken into consideration in the sustainability of enterprises. In other words, it is important to define the concept of competition as good and correct and to determine the most suitable position for the company within this context. Another point to know is that the concept of competition differs according to the structure in which it is scaled. While the competition among the enterprises within the country is defined as micro-level, competition between regions/sectors is considered as a mezzo level and competition among countries is considered as macro-level (Arıcıoğlu et al., 2013).

When the development of competition is analyzed, it is seen that production-based or price-based understanding is now far away. Also, in recent years, with the concepts of Industry 4.0 and digitization, the situation of businesses, especially SMEs, creates questions from a strategic point of view. Because this digital environment also plays an active role in changing the dynamics of competition. Another information about the competition that goes far away from what is known is that big fish eat small fish. Size is no longer what matters, it is better to be small and fast for competition. Now that small fish come together and act with the right relationship and in common direction, this cooperation turns them from being bait into rivals. Therefore, the situation in SMEs is changing. Being a large-scale company is no longer a pioneering condition for competition. SMEs also have the potential and dynamism to compete with large-scale companies with various techniques.

In the context of all these points, it is thought that the concept of strategy and strategic management should be discussed again in terms of SMEs. In particular, the inadequacy of the ability of small scale enterprises to reach strategic management individually triggers a new model search. In other words, instead of constructing strategic management on their own, small-sized enterprises should either follow the strategy of the adults or come together and have the ability to produce strategies with a common mind and collective leadership. Clustering is perhaps the best known and effective one of these models.

STRATEGIC MANAGEMENT IN SMEs IN THE CONTEXT OF CLUSTERING

In addition to its re-enactment with Porter as well as its history extending to Marshall, the successful implementation of the cluster as regional development and cooperation model in many countries, especially the EU, has gradually increased the reputation of the cluster. In this section, the concept of clustering and the benefits of clusters to enterprises will be discussed and what kind of facilities can be provided to SMEs in terms of strategic management will be discussed.

What is the Concept of Clustering?

It is possible to find many definitions in the literature about clusters. While some of these definitions look at clusters from a narrow perspective, some give a broad definition. According to Schmitz (1999), clustering means economic geography and sectoral unity. For OECD, the cluster includes a commitment and network of experienced suppliers, value-added production, interconnected businesses, and closely linked stakeholders from university to research institutions supporting them (OECD, 1999). Porter (1998) defines the cluster as the geographical concentration of companies that are both competing and cooperating in the same field of activity, suppliers specialized in a particular field, service providers, companies in the relevant sectors and related institutions. For UNIDO (2019), it is concentrated on the sectoral and geographical basis of the organizations that produce and sell products that are related or complementary to each other. Sölvell et al. (2003), who understood clustering as an organized effort to increase growth and competitiveness, preferred an approach related to growth and competitiveness. Harvard Business Scholl Strategic and Competitive Institutes add the concept of efficiency into this concept (Anonymous, 2019). Clustering can be defined as a geographic density where there is a high dependency relationship among the firms in the same region, triggering regional specialization, increasing the productivity of firms and competitiveness in the national market (Long and Zhang, 2012).

As can be seen, no common definition has been made yet. However, the clusters are generally evaluated based on two dimensions. Some studies consider clusters as geographical communities of firms that produce the same product or service (Arthur, 1990; Sorenson and Audia, 2000) and in some studies, Porter (1998) defines geographically similar groups formed by interrelated industries (Brookfield, 2008).

Although it cannot go to a common definition of the concept in general, it can be said that there is a consensus on the concepts used in defining the concept. Therefore, it would be appropriate to specify the concepts in which clustering is associated to understand the essence of the concept. In this respect, clustering is associated with the following concepts (Arıcıoğlu et al., 2018);

- **Space/location/region:** space, location and region can be geographically limited to the activities of the clusters or they can be decisive for clusters.
- **Firm:** the firm's capabilities and core competence limit the scope of the clusters, making the value chain healthier.
- **Stakeholder:** stakeholders make sense in clusters in terms of team-mates and complementarity.
- **Collaboration:** what clusters say and involve is particularly important for clusters, especially in terms of sustainability. In particular, trust among these actors will also trigger the effectiveness and efficiency of the cluster.
- **Competition:** competition points to several games in the context of clustering.
- **Concentration**
- **Relationship**
- **Social capital and trust**
- **Innovation**

When we evaluate the clusters in terms of formation, it is possible to see that they contain many actors. The clusters may include producers of complementary products, other manufacturers or companies in the relevant sector, public and private institutions such as universities, professional and specialized educational institutions, non-governmental organizations, and trade unions. In other words, it can be defined as a network of cooperation and relations formed by producers or service providers of interconnected activities throughout the value chain. A cluster can be defined as a system of interconnected companies and institutions whose value as a whole is greater than the sum of its parts (Porter, 1998). In other words, a synergy-based structure is mentioned with the concept of clustering. In cluster environments, there is often a solidarity-oriented relationship that is mainly based on quality and efficiency, mostly small and medium-sized enterprises specialized in specific sectors. The basis of solidarity lies in the sense of trust. In addition to the relationship of interest between the actors in the clusters, trust is the main binding element that holds the actors together, makes the relationship sustainable and directs them towards the common goal.

The cluster has two main characteristics (Alüftekin et al., 2012);

a) The orientation of local production to international markets and access to competitiveness
b) Inventive and creative capacity

With the clustering, businesses can strengthen their regional relations while providing access to the goods and services they need easily thanks to the network they establish with other companies. One of the most important details in this process is the transfer of information between actors. With this information flow, synergies between cluster actors can be created, promotes organizational learning and innovative approaches can be developed while increasing both cluster productivity and efficiency and individual productivity and efficiency (Braun et al., 2005). Therefore, it would not be wrong to say that clusters see a center for innovation production. This innovative approach is critical to the development of competitiveness. Porter (1998) stated that the competitive advantage in a global economy is based on local knowledge, networking, and motivation that cannot be developed or enhanced by global partnerships. The importance of clusters in building competitiveness is thus emphasized once again.

The Benefits of Clusters to Firms

Unfortunately, companies can't continue their activities independently of their environment and actors in this environment, even if they try to maintain their existence individually. Not all resources needed in routine activities or innovative steps may be in-house. In such a case, there is dependence on external sources and companies. Conducting this dependency relationship within the framework of cooperation is important to enable the economic activities of the enterprises. To make this relationship a trade-oriented and trust-oriented network, clustering studies have recently become one of the most prominent approaches in regional and organizational fields.

Clustering can provide organizations with better or cheaper access to (private) inputs such as land, components, machinery, commercial services, or personnel, better or cheaper access to information, faster and cheaper access to institutions and public goods, new technological opportunities (Oerlemans et al., 2001). Also, the presence of the enterprises in the same sector, even in the production of complementary products required to produce a product in the production sector will facilitate the production and commercial operations of enterprises so that productivity and efficiency can be increased easily. Developing a common understanding of problems and solutions with clustering greatly facilitates communication and further learning (Brown and Duguid, 1991; Powell et al., 1996).

Clustering activities may apply to all scales, especially in SMEs. Clustering activities are collaborations that complement the interests of each other through the relationship that SMEs come together and establish through a network and feed it by generating social capital. Even though their convergence is interest-based, sharing and preserving this interest in an equitable manner provides five main benefits to each actor in the cluster:

- Development of the business mind regarding the way of doing business jointly through **information sharing,**
- Initiative to make the **cost and benefit of R & D** by joint investment and management,
- **Your competitors in the domestic market are your allies in out**
- For the increased competition, **joint purchasing** establishes an easy-to-maintain relationship of interest, and
- The common mind of how to act together for the **future of the sector,**

The concept of information sharing, as stated in the study of Social Capital by Field (2005), reminds you that it is important that not what you know but who you know. Knowledge sharing is the basis of the cluster. According to Schilling and Phelps, 2007, the benefits of clusters are listed below;

- Clusters increase the capacity of a network to transfer information,
- Clusters enable information presented to a cluster to quickly reach other companies in the cluster,
- Clusters multiple paths between firms improve the quality of the information received,
- Thanks to Clusters, firms can compare information from multiple partners,
- Clusters help to detect distortions or omissions.

In general, the information transfer process starts with ideas and experiences of what actors in the sector and companies with complementary roles should do based on products or services. It then continues with the transfer of information with the equivalent of the output in the context of the market, supplier, and customer.

Although the information transfer process seems to be simple in general terms, it is not so easy to transfer the accumulation acquired and gained over the years for the enterprises. The main element of this process is trust. This trust is reinforced by the productivity and efficiency obtained through the outputs after the sharing of information. Firms and others become aware of increased activity as they share, and sharing continues to increase effectively. The most important part of the common mind and the most important infrastructure of the strategy lies in the success of the sharing process. A cluster allows an enterprise to benefit like a large scale company or formally united with companies - without sacrificing its flexibility (Timurçin, 2010).

When small and medium-sized enterprises are evaluated in terms of their structures and existence missions, they take attention in terms of their position about making renovations or improvements (in the other words “location of R & D activities). However, their structural problems make them difficult to focus on these activities and even prevent them from being away from their mission. Since clustering studies provide the opportunity to realize an investment that cannot be realized by a single enterprise with the common self-sacrifice and resources of more than one enterprise, SMEs can have the opportunity to realize innovation studies by sharing their costs and benefits with the help of the common mind.

Collaborations between cluster actors facilitate the opening up of the sector. Even though they are in competition with each other in the internal market conditions, the integrated movement of the companies in the foreign market provides a competitive advantage and guarantees their place in terms of market entry-promotion activities. This situation is also a hope for the future of the sector.

In the literature, there are many studies on clusters and indicating the innovative aspects of the clusters and their diffusions and drawbacks to the firms. Among these studies, Porter (2003) lists the benefits of clusters as follows;

- Clusters increase productivity/efficiency
  - § Effective access to private inputs, services, employees, information, institutions and "public goods (eg training programs)
  - § Ease of coordination and transactions between firms
  - § Fast deployment of best practices
  - § Ongoing, visible performance comparisons and strong incentives to improve against local competitors
- Clusters encourage and enable innovation.
  - § Improved ability to detect innovation opportunities
  - § Existence of multiple suppliers and institutions to help in creating information
  - § Ease of testing given locally available resources
- Clusters facilitate commercialization.
  - § Opportunities for new companies and new businesses
  - § Commercialize new products and establish new companies are easier because of existing skills, suppliers and so on.

In another study, the benefits of the cluster to firms are listed as follows (Alüftekin et al., 2012);

- thanks to clusters, companies reach the community of specialized and experienced workers and reduce costs in recruitment. Clusters offer job opportunities and reduce the risk of employee turnover because it attracts more skilled workers, this is an important advantage for some industries (Porter, 1998: 145).
- Being a part of a cluster enables companies to work more efficiently in finding input sources, accessing information, technology, and necessary institutions, coordinating with related companies, measuring and motivating development.
- Thanks to the complementary features of the companies that are together, production is realized on time. All processes accelerate from order to shipment

In the early 2000s, during our visit to the IHK Chemnitz Regional Chamber Zwickau and the Über MERGE-MERGE-TU Chemnitz Cluster Center, the speaker gave to us an example about the R & D activities of Audi. This example is given below:

"Audi designs and develops automobiles (for the years the 2010s, 20s) together with the sub-industry and their engineers. This makes it possible to benefit from a wider pool of information, to reach the customer more easily and to manage the cost accurately."

As can be understood from this speech, customer-oriented R&D is now seen as the work of the main industries and everyone with a vision for the future. Every company is listening to the features and demands of customers to continue their activities in the sector they are affiliated with. Companies are moving away from the approach that we can sell what we produce and they adopt the approach that we should produce what customers want. Consequently, businesses began to realize that efficiency is more accurate than growth, and they learned to use the concepts of research and development together. This is generally valid for almost every company in the sector. In other words, this expensive power is now available to the company of all sizes. And also R&D is increasingly described as a useful tool. Of course, one of the main sources of this ground is the clusters. Clusters seem to be the most important tool and relationship form in acquiring R&D infrastructure and mentality and presenting them to enterprises.

A Competitive Perspective: How Clusters Affect Competition for SMEs

In today's economic order, the interdependence of the economies beyond each other, technological advances and uncertainty increases affect the lives of many dynamic enterprises and change their future visions. As Kotler and Caslione (2011) note, there are now two main economic order; normal economy and economics of new normality. It is no longer possible to speak of a foreseeable future as in the normal economic order. Classical conjectural fluctuations not only have been replaced with sudden and large fluctuations but also these sudden and large fluctuations affect many actors that are dependent on each other. The definition of competition in this economic order has also changed. In its simplest form, the concept of competition can be expressed as the efforts of two or more people and / or parties to prevail over each other (Timurçin, 2010). However, in today's competitive environment, this definition has changed and included different dynamics within its context.

Contrary to old knowledge, the concept of competition is no longer a static concept based on cost minimization. The concept of competition is a dynamic and innovative process that develops based on strategic differences. Dominating the market alone is no longer sufficient competition power. The environment in which the enterprises are located is called the hyper-competition environment. In other words, new dynamics are effective in competition.

According to Porter (1998), the main reasons for changing the mentality of evaluating the definition of competition through factor inputs are as follows;

- More countries join the global economic network and consequently increase in input supply
- More efficient national and international factor markets;
- Decreasing factor density of competition.

Çağlar (2008) tried to put forward the change in conditions in the competitive environment with a distinction as in Table 1. The change in the dynamics of the competitiveness of enterprises can be understood more clearly.

Table 1. The changes in the conditions of the competitive environment (Former and new environment) (Çağlar, 2008)

Former environment	New environment
Competition power	**Competition power**
Cheap labor-based Based on cost and price Limited R & D Passive marketing	Skilled workforce Based on quality and knowledge More investment in R & D Marketing innovations

Although large-scale companies in the variable competition environment have a more advantageous position than small scales companies in terms of keeping pace, it is thought that in many business areas, small-scale enterprises are a better economic solution (MUSİAD, 2005). Because SMEs are the basic building blocks of a country's competitiveness level and they also have a motor role in creating employment (Bayülken, 2007). In other words, the competitiveness of SMEs in the economic order is an important question mark for the development and progress of the national economy, especially countries where the majority of the economy is evaluated through small and medium-sized enterprises such as Turkey.

Small and medium-sized enterprises (SMEs) are enterprises with a maximum of 250 employees according to the definition of the European Union. this limit is 200 employees in some countries, while the number of employees in the United States is less than 500 (OECD, 2005). According to Turkey's definition of SMEs (Table 2), Small and medium-sized enterprises (SMEs) are companies with less than 250 employees and an annual turnover not exceeding 125 Million TL.

Table 2. Comparison of the Turkey SME Definitions (Small and Medium Enterprises Development Organization of Turkey, 2005)

Size Category	Staff headcount	Turnover
Medium-sized	50-250	≤ 125 Million TL
Small	10-49	≤ 25 Million TL
Micro	1-9	≤ 3 Million TL

The concepts commonly used in the definition of SMEs are related to the qualitative and quantitative characteristics of SMEs such as their share in the sector, their degree of expertise, manager-owner relations, managerial problems, quantity of capital, production amount, total assets, sales volume (Arıcıoğlu and Yiğitol, 2019; Özgener, 2003).

Considering that small and medium-sized enterprises are the basic elements of a country's industrial and business life, it is understood how important increasing the competitiveness of small and medium-sized enterprises is for the power of the country's industry. Increasing the competitiveness of SMEs not only depends on the way companies react and behave but also success in competition depends on SMEs' capacity building and positioning themselves in the economy (MUSİAD, 2005). SMEs must cooperate in this process and develop a common behavior. In other words, cluster studies are important in terms of improving the competitiveness of SMEs and coping with variable competition dynamics. Because in an international environment where competition is intensified, taking part in the clusters that form a strong and productive base for innovation offers advantages to SMEs (Bacak, 2019).

The three factors determine the competitiveness of clusters (Timurçin, 2010);

- Basic factors (natural resources and quality of workforce)
- Advantageous factors (material and intangible infrastructures such as transport and traffic system, functional training system, communication structure)
- Special factors (Factors that can be referred to as innovators and provide competitive advantage such as high-precision software companies, sensitive optics that can change the position of competition in world markets)

Clusters are geographical concentrations of competing but also collaborative, interconnected companies, specialized suppliers, service providers, companies in related industries and related organizations (eg universities, agencies and trade associations) (Porter, 1998). With the help of clusters, the practices in the sector become decentralized and all processes and relations related to production can be carried out with a participatory policy by gathering local competitors. The common point in the success of all competitive industrial zones is the existence of clusters formed between enterprises that are located on the same value chain as customer-centric (customer-oriented - demand-driven) (Humphrey and Schmitz, 1995). Therefore, clustering is a critical factor of competition in a particular area and is one of the outstanding features of the country-level in the local, regional and national economies (Porter, 1998).

The clustering process affects competition in three ways (Benneworth and Hospers, 2007; Porter, 1998):

§ Increasing the efficiency of the firms or industries in the cluster,
§ By influencing the direction and speed of innovations that support increased productivity in the future and increase their capacity
§ By encouraging new business formation that supports innovation and broadens the cluster.

This has enabled the cluster approach to be used to learn and measure the economies' regional development, competition perception, increase the competitiveness of companies, and to learn competencies and competitive values of countries (Arıcıoğlu et al., 2013).

The presence of clusters shows that most of the competitive advantage remains outside the industry residing in a particular company or even in the locations of business units (Porter, 1998). With clusters, companies can also benefit from the presence of local competitors. In other words, while they can compete regionally with each other, at the same time, they can establish unity against the external environment and gain competitiveness as a single body through the cooperation they create.

The proposition that the cluster supports competition has two implications. The first is explained by the increased competition in the domestic market (micro or mezzo market). In this way, while R&D studies and collaborations increase, companies develop themselves. For the second, the definition area is foreign markets. And the cluster learns its real strength (what it does in the domestic market) in foreign markets. Some questions (such as what is the level of power of unity and how does the effectiveness of collaborative reason work against other competitors) test themselves for every customer and in the struggle to win every market. SMEs that cannot be included in the supplier list of importing countries and companies can overcome this obstacle by cooperating and form bilateral or multilateral relationship-based power unions by establishing sectoral clusters (MUSİAD, 2005).

How can small scale enterprises benefit from the economies of scale used by large scale enterprises? The answer is written on the same concept: Clustering as a collaborative approach. Because of some advantage (such as that clusters adapt better with quality of competition and sources of competitive advantage, that clusters provide significant links, complementarities, and spans that reduce technology, skills, knowledge, marketing and customer requirements between companies and sectors), such links are essential for competition, efficiency, and in particular for the direction and pace of new business creation and innovation (Porter, 1998). Players that create strong synergies reduce transaction costs and trigger innovation employing communication with the clustering approach, buyer-seller relationship, joint marketing, R & D, training and association, etc. (Timurçin, 2010). Therefore, clusters provide an opportunity for small scale enterprises to take advantage of economies of scale.

A concrete example of how small scale enterprises can take advantage of the economies of scale can be given as follows: In the beginning, the number of members of the automotive industry cluster in Konya located in central Anatolia in Turkey was at a relatively low rate. Although the number of firms increased from the twenty to the thirty, the collective power of the joint movement did not provide sufficient bargaining power within the market. A protocol was signed with the Central Anatolian Machinery Exporters Union, which has a larger structure. With this protocol, this power was increased from the 30s to 430s. We protected the interests of the cluster members by providing an advantage for a certain period from fuel to raw material input. Subsequently, we continued to benefit from the existence of the benefits provided by large scale enterprises by independent joint acquisitions as a cluster. The effect of inputs on cost management is always a noteworthy benefit and increases the ability of fast fish to move.

LITERATURE REVIEW

The studies in the literature on clusters are briefly summarized. Since the studies are considered to be important for understanding the role of clusters in providing a competitive advantage for SMEs, they support the results of this study.

There are many studies on the effects of clusters on competitiveness in the world. Porter (1998), one of the most important of these studies, wanted to reveal the impressive role of clusters in competition. The effectiveness of the clusters in the distancing of competition from a centralized policy and the benefits of the firms are explained.

Isaksen (1997) examines some of the claims made in the international literature regarding the regional clustering of small and medium-sized enterprises. In particular, research has been conducted on the growth and competitiveness of firms. The research was conducted in Norway. The study reveals that regional clusters are generally internationally competitive and, with some important exceptions, experience a positive trend in employment compared to relevant sectors across the country.

Albaladejo (2001) attempts to identify the main determinants of competitiveness in SME clusters. Empirical evidence strongly suggests that joint action of clusters may not be sufficient to face new competitive pressures, and suggests that inter-firm links must go beyond the promotion of SME clusters to improve their competitiveness.

Oyelaran-Oyeyinka (2005) examines the dynamics of cooperation between two clusters of small and medium-sized enterprises (SMEs) in the shoe industry in Southeast Nigeria in the face of local and global competition. The study showed that although the two clusters are structurally different from each other, cooperation between enterprises is largely triggered by competitive forces and grows over time.

Venkataramanaiah and Parashar (2007) report on the experience of three car clusters in three main regions of India. They highlighted some important issues that SMEs have faced and concluded by proposing appropriate cluster interventions to improve the competitiveness and sustainability of the SME sector.

Karaev et al. (2007) reviewed the impact of the Clustering approach on the competitiveness of SMEs. The primary objective is to explore the clustering approach among SMEs as a means of overcoming the challenges of globalization and trade liberalization, as well as factors that contribute to the process of improving their competitiveness. The results of the study provided strong evidence that the cluster policy had an additional positive impact on the current SMEs policy in industrialized economies.

In Jardon and Susana Martos (2012) studies, it is aimed to analyze the relationships between the components of intellectual capital in clusters formed by small and medium-sized enterprises (SMEs), a different competitive advantage model. The study suggests that resources affect organizational capabilities in the competitive advantage model in SME clusters; regional and organizational capabilities influence strategic factors that improve performance. One of the most important conclusions is that human capital affects structural capital and structural capital constitutes relational capital and that SMEs need material resources and relational capital to improve their organizational capabilities.

Dasanayaka (2019) aimed to reveal the effects of cluster formation on the growth and competitiveness of SMEs in Sri Lanka. As a result of the study, it is emphasized that encouraging cluster formation and networking is a very good start in improving and increasing the competitiveness of SMEs. Besides, it was stated that the right policy initiative, incentive, business development services, common facilities, and infrastructure activities should be improved.

The studies on clusters conducted in Turkey is also possible to find.

Timurçin (2011) examines the subject of clustering in keeping up with changing competition conditions and maintaining the competitiveness of SMEs that have an important place in Turkey's economy. The studies related to clustering in Turkey are presented in the form of a literature review.

Oğuztürk and Sarıçoban (2013) discussed the concepts of clustering and innovation theoretically and gave place to the clustering samples from the world and Turkey. Also, the effects of clustering and innovation policies on competitiveness were examined. As a result of the study, it was stated that the support of regional clusters could have positive contributions to the regional economy, the emergence of new job opportunities, entrepreneurship and the increase of employment, and more importantly, it would affect the competitiveness of the countries at the international level positively.

The main purpose of Ekinci and Emsen (2014) studies is to determine the effects of the cluster in the competition context and to provide a preliminary study on what can be done for successful policy implementations. For a successful cluster to emerge, it is underlined that support from all segments of society should be provided and this support should be continuous. it is emphasized that Turkey should reach a competitive structure in the long term, to survive in internationally competitive markets, which will be exacerbated in the long term and it should be triggered with the right directions following the clustering logic.

Karadeniz ve Kulaksız (2018) evaluated clustering policies, and currently supports the clusters in Turkey in the light of literature to determine the impact of the cluster on the competitiveness of enterprises. In the study, which was examined through the Çorum Agricultural Food Processing Machinery Cluster, it is stated that the clusters made significant contributions in terms of innovation, internationalization, specialized workforce and access to suppliers and producers.

Strategic Management in SMEs in the Context of Clustering

The prediction of the future of a small-scaled enterprise can only be defined depending on the talent and vision of the manager. Even though those who sometimes have very good perspectives appear, it is not possible to transfer the vision to strategy and turn it into action. The difficulties of sustaining the life make the formation/management of the strategy difficult due to some reasons such as the small number of daily jobs, especially being made this jobs by the owner/manager, not being able to employ competent human resources adequately and the manager having a wide variety of workloads. Businesses that exceed this challenge can scale up and set sail for the international market. For businesses that cannot overcome this challenge, there is an obligation to choose one of two options: to share a common mind or vision and to share a common strategy. another option is to support it as a stakeholder of the strategy of the nearest large business. The choice is naturally related to the awareness of the strategy.

The perceived benefits in eternity are expected to mobilize people, institutions and organizations. It is possible to see much concrete, applied and successful examples of the recognition of the benefits of sharing a common mind, common vision and a common strategy and making the right action with this awareness. With the awareness of the listed benefits, large examples such as Silicon Valley, Sophia Antipolis, Northern Italy, Bavaria, Route 128, the M4 area, and Tokyo (Enright, 2003), as well as many more influential examples from Austria to Korea can be given. These cluster examples illustrate a remarkable way out for SMEs and provide an assessment of the work through two key concepts: specificity for the sector and core competence.

To give priority to the second point (core competence) as everyone knows, small scale enterprises do everything to live. They produce everything and try to be sustainable with a flexible structure. But this is also true for thousands of small scale enterprises. So flexible abilities give rise to flexible opponents. Therefore, being flexible is not enough for sustainability alone. It is necessary to be different, to be innovative, or to do whatever is better than the others. In spite of doing a job very well and being original is more demanding, it is a more accurate formula. Small scale enterprises should be like the story of a Judo child based on the doctrine "Don't worry, you make the only movement you have learned". To this end, the implicit knowledge of businesses and managers will guide them. Expertly acquired or the result achieved by R & D will teach the SMEs what it does better. This doctrine will be the ability of the SMEs to outperform others. This doctrine will be the ability of the SMEs to outperform others. The emphasis on core competence should be understood as implicit knowledge and doing what others cannot.

This result is a guide for the first (specificity for the sector). When SMEs with core competencies are no longer doing everything but doing the right thing, sector definitions will be more specific. When this situation is considered in the context of the sector, the scale type can be evaluated in terms of the sector-product relationship (such as the types of sub-industry manufacturers in the automotive sub-industry sector), the core competencies of the firms, and the future and position of the sector in the geographical context. Thus, the structure and competitiveness of the sector in the region (micro or mezzo) will become clear. This is because the picture of complementary-relationships and stakeholders in the context of the cluster becomes apparent. In this way, the Specificity of the sector emerges.

As can be seen, the most obvious way to achieve a competitive advantage is now through the teachings of networking, sharing, common mind and collective leadership. Clusters are an important model which is developed for competitive advantage. The model is not only a nationally superior interregional competitive advantage, but also a proposed and applied model for achieving international superiority. While SMEs included in this model provide success by integrating sector and regional strategies, they also learn to produce projects for sustainability or to become active as partners in projects.

In particular, clusters do not only contribute to SMEs in developing relations with the main industry and increasing bargaining power against the main industry. It also provides tool kits for strategy determination. In broader terms, clusters offer SMEs the following benefits:

- Providing common use/learning and dissemination of knowledge as Porter (1998) says.
- Use of various techniques and tools that enable the understanding and application of concepts such as productivity and efficiency within the enterprise
- Learning and application of cost management
- Learning and applying international customer and supplier

- Financing facilities and accessibility
- Learning, participating and managing innovation
- Increasing awareness of knowledge with the sector
- Learning the way of doing business jointly
- Qualitative acquisitions of human management

Considering the headings listed above, it is possible to define them as a shortlist of the advantages of association (Clusters).

It can also be argued that these are a common step for new time and innovation. Particularly, because of a new world with a digital transformation (Industry 4.0), and components of new balances in competition, and sustainability concerns of labor-intensive sectors/enterprises, all of these become obvious questions for SMEs. sustainability concerns of the labor-intensive sectors/enterprises become obvious questions for SMEs. The position taken within the framework of the cooperation must also apply to the answers to the new questions. In the most general sense, Industry 4.0 or the fourth industrial revolution represents embedded and connected systems, which in most general sense erases the boundaries between the Cyber-Physical System (CPS) and the real and virtual factory represented by the Internet of Things (Machadoa et al., 2019). According to the classification of BCG (2019), Industry 4.0 technologies consists of 9 parts; big data and analysis, autonomous robots, simulation, horizontal and vertical system integration, Internet of Things, cybersecurity, cloud, additive production, augmented reality. Big data refers to ever increasing linearly quality information and exponentially polluted information (Iqbal, Yang, Nawaz, & Iqbal., 2019). *Big data and analysis* are important to obtain and analyze large scale data from machines related to production processes in real-time and also to make ready for use when it is needed. Storing large scale data provides less space and cost with *Cloud technologies*. Data management related to critical production processes also makes *Cybersecurity* Systems compulsory. Industry 4.0 envisages the incorporation of intelligent factory systems and *Autonomous robots* into production systems and the realization of human-robot production (Li et al., 2017). Not also these robots but also devices can communicate with each other thanks to *The internet of things*. *Simulation* technologies and *Augmented Reality* provide an opportunity for a company about reflecting the production process into a virtual platform (BCG, 2019), So companies make try and perform all activities of production without setup. With *Horizontal and vertical system integration*, companies make corporation with other firms on sharing materials and know-how and enable structured flexible production systems (Manogaran et al., 2017). With *additive manufacturing* technologies, companies can easily perform complex production processes. In briefly, the Industry 4.0 concept encompasses a broad digital transformation involving contemporary automation systems and data-driven manufacturing technologies. With industry 4.0, companies will provide production ecosystems produced by intelligent systems with self-structured, self-monitoring and self-healing autonomous features (Thames and Schaefer, 2017). More efficient business models will emerge as this revolution will allow each data to be collected and well monitored in the production environment.

The 4th industrial revolution, characterized as the digital age, is a process that requires destructive innovations, many structural changes and paradigm shifts in production processes (Castelo-Branco et al., 2019). This technological transformation drives companies to invest heavily in production systems, data acquisition, storage, and analysis. Therefore, this transformation is not a process to be completed at once. It requires both time and funding. Clustering business models can play an active role in firms' effectively completing this process. In particular, cluster studies can be useful in sharing the burden of financing required by large technological investments. With the clustering, network structures are created between the companies with the necessary infrastructure and the companies are strengthened both among themselves and in the sector. The heavy burden of the transformation process has been alleviated by actors such as universities, R & D institutions, standardization institutions, think tanks, public institutions and private institutions providing technical support to vocational education institutions. Because of the structural and financial problems of SMEs, it is the most difficult these companies to provide the necessary products and services for Industry 4.0 and robot systems and to create the infrastructure. For easy adaptation to this process, clustering can be one of the best solutions.

Looking at the possible consequences of Industry 4.0 from the SMEs perspective:

- A more planned business life
- To learn expert business forms
- In Labor-intensive areas, cost advantage turns to technology advantage
- Obligation to register
- Difficulty in acquiring data habit
- More efficient time and production management for deadlines
- From a supplier role perspective, some reasons such as the transfer of the main industries to unmanned factories and outsourcing and logistics costs will lead to a narrower / regional selection of the supply network. This is inherently at risk of expulsion/withdrawal of SMEs within supply networks.
- The effectiveness, use, and security of the technology will set important investment steps.

It is seen that a new way of doing work is developing from the transfer of technology to the use of technology and from labor to process management. The differentiation in the structure of the competition and the scales/classification of enterprises is another possible development.

This will not only improve new forms of cooperation but may also enhance the areas of cooperation. Because while the main industry is now producing in unmanned factories, the competition of the supplier industry in terms of cost and price will gain a new dimension. Or the real question arises as follows: Is there a need for a sub-industry, and if so, what kind of a definition of a sub-industry emerges?

One of the most important inferences that SMEs, which are the main actors of the cluster, learned in the clustering process is to determine their core competencies and to participate in the process in line with these core competencies. The gain provided is becoming more pronounced with Industry 4.0. This gain may also include new areas of risk with the transformation in the production and may require these enterprises to re-perform the risk analysis. In this context, business forms must be correctly understood and re-analyzed for each cluster member. It should even find answers to the questions such as how flexible production and time planning should be provided, where to be just in time, how the new ranges for efficiency measurement and technical equipment should be.

Another very important title concerns everyone: What about humans? Will the technology change, especially in labor-intensive sectors, reveal new sets of solutions in the way of production? It is seen that the new questions will add to these questions since the beginning of the 18th century. This should be questioned with a new mind especially for each member of the cluster be formed by SMEs. The common mind, which is one of the most important features of clusters, has to come up with a collective leadership approach and produce solutions for the cluster.

In the end, it is seen that change or revolution of geometric growth addresses the speed and agility of small-scale enterprises as well as the minds and financial power of large-scale enterprises. Large-scale businesses seem to understand this point. However, small businesses need to act quickly without rushing. Clustering, which is the formula of holding common intelligence, collective leadership, and cooperative power, seems to be an effective tool or method of this process for SMEs. While each process resulting in Industry 4.0 demonstrates how much the importance of the collaboration of SMEs is, it shows that the forms of cooperation will change, and a form, production and management change will occur for SMEs. Therefore, it is necessary to establish awareness that it is the right way to prepare together in the context of industry 4.0 as in all other subjects.

SOLUTIONS AND RECOMMENDATIONS

In this study, it is aimed to discuss the strategic management processes of SMEs in the context of clustering. Besides, the contribution of cluster studies to SMEs in industry 4.0 digitalization process has been briefly mentioned. In the context of the aim of the study, the recommendations of SMEs regarding the future are as follows;

- SMEs should either share a common mind, a shared vision, and a common strategy or support it as a stakeholder of the strategy of large scale enterprise.
- When evaluated in the context of the first one, clusters and the benefits of clustering practices appear.
- Clustering activities for SMEs can be evaluated from two perspectives: providing clarity and core competence for the sector.
- Key skills will not only make the distinction between smes clear but will allow them to do the right thing, not do everything.
- The specificity of the sector covers the structure and competitiveness of the sector. Thus, it will provide an opportunity to know the sector and know its requirements and to recognize its competitors both nationally and internationally.

FUTURE RESEARCH DIRECTIONS

This study aimed to discuss the strategic management processes of SMEs in the context of clustering. In this context, a discussion for SMEs has been tried to be supported by the studies in the literature. Within the scope of the study, the benefits of clustering activities for SMEs are listed and the successes of clustering studies are tried to be demonstrated with concrete examples from the application. However, the change in the dynamics of competition of enterprises will bring many new applications in the era called a new economic environment. This is a process that involves uncertainty within SMEs as well as for large enterprises and causes to ask any question. Therefore, it is still unclear what tools will be effective in predicting the future of enterprises shortly as an industry 4.0 digitalization process. Of course, this will not only develop new forms of cooperation but may also enhance the areas of cooperation. Therefore, it is a matter of curiosity which tools can emerge in the new studies. In particular, the proposal for new tools for SMEs or an assessment of existing tools will be a guide for adaptation to this process.

CONCLUSION

Although large-scale enterprises in the variable competition environment have a more advantageous position than small firms in terms of keeping pace, it is thought that in many business areas, small-scale enterprises are a better economic solution (MUSİAD, 2005). Because SMEs are the basic building blocks of a country's competitiveness level and they also have a motor role in creating employment (Bayülken, 2007). However, SMEs cannot respond to competitive pressure individually and to form factors for expansion and innovation (Dasanayaka, 2019). Therefore, it seems difficult for them to cope with the changing environmental dynamics alone. They should cooperate to gain competitiveness especially in international markets and to overcome the obstacles in entering these markets. SMEs, which are competitors in the regional economy, is important in terms of strengthening their competitive aspects to act as a single body in the national and international economy. In this case, one of the most suitable tools is clusters. Thanks to being part of clusters, companies can create synergies that will come together in line with the common purpose and unity in the applications that they cannot overcome alone. Clusters that benefit in many ways, such as information sharing, the common use of resources, cost advantage, productivity, and efficiency increase, are critical to competitiveness for SMEs. In this study, the importance of clustering practices in strategic management processes in SMEs is discussed and the advantages that clusters can provide to SMEs in the competition are discussed.

The benefits presented in this context are as follows.

- Providing common use/learning and dissemination of knowledge as Porter (1998) says.
- Use of various techniques and tools that enable the understanding and application of concepts such as productivity and efficiency within the enterprise
- Learning and application of cost management
- Learning and applying international customer and supplier
- Financing facilities and accessibility
- Learning, participating and managing innovation
- Increasing awareness of knowledge with the sector
- Learning the way of doing business jointly
- Qualitative acquisitions of human management

Another issue that was evaluated in terms of SMEs is Industry 4.0 applications, which may make itself felt more shortly. With digitalization, a new dimension awaits businesses. The course of competition in this dimension cannot be predicted yet. However, even if the adaptation process seems to be difficult for large-scale enterprises, the main focus of this process will be on the SMEs who try to survive with structural problems. In this study, the future of industry 4.0 was evaluated in the context of SMEs.

Looking at the possible consequences of Industry 4.0 from the SME perspective:

- A more planned business life
- To learn expert business forms
- In Labor-intensive areas, cost advantage turns to technology advantage
- Obligation to register
- Difficulty in acquiring data habit
- More efficient time and production management for deadlines

- From a supplier role perspective, some reasons such as the transfer of the main industries to unmanned factories and outsourcing and logistics costs will lead to a narrower / regional selection of the supply network. This is inherently at risk of expulsion/withdrawal of SMEs within supply networks.

In light of all these discussions, the summary evaluations revealed as a result of the study are given below.

- SMEs with core competencies will now be able to do the right thing, not do everything.
- Identification of core competencies can be assessed on issues such as the future and position of the sector in the geographical context. thus, the specificity of the sector is revealed.
- Clusters are an important model that is developed for competitive advantage.
- Clusters are not only a nationally superior interregional competitive advantage but also a proposed and applied model for achieving international superiority.
- Clusters play an active role in developing relations with the main industry and increasing bargaining power against the main industry.
- Especially in the context of industry 4.0, business forms must be correctly understood and re-analyzed for each cluster member.
- It should even find answers to the questions such as how flexible production and time planning should be provided, where to be just in time, How the new ranges for efficiency measurement and technical equipment should be.
- Another question that comes to mind in this process is related to the future of human factors. Therefore, SMEs should be questioned about this problem with a new mind.
- The common mind, which is one of the most important features of clusters, has to come up with a collective leadership approach and produce solutions for the cluster.

Therefore, it is necessary to establish awareness that it is the right way to prepare together in the context of industry 4.0 as in all other subjects.

REFERENCES

Albaladejo, M. (2001). *Determinants and policies to foster the competitiveness of SME clusters: Evidence from Latin America.* Oxford, UK: Queen Elizabeth House.

Alüftekin, N., Yüksel, Ö., Taş, A., Çakar, G., & Bayraktar, F. (2012). Küresel krizden çıkışta kümelenme modeli: Tekstil ve hazır giyim sektörü örneği. *Uluslararası Yönetim İktisat ve İşletme Dergisi, 5*(10), 1–19.

Anonymous. (2019). Retrieved from http://www.isc.hbs.edu/competitiveness-economic development/frameworks-and-key-concepts/pages/clusters.aspx

Arıcıoğlu, M. A., Gökçe, Ş., & Koraş, M. (2013). Kümelenme ve rekabet analizi için bir uygulama. *Selçuk Üniversitesi Sosyal Bilimler Enstitüsü Dergisi*, (30), 2-18.

Arıcıoğlu, M. A., Yiğitol, B., & Yilmaz, A. (2018). Kümelenmenin anlamı: akademik bakış açılarının çözümlenmesi üzerine bir deneme. Kastamonu University Journal of Economics & Administrative Sciences Faculty, 20(4).

Arthur, W. B. (1990). 'Silicon Valley' locational clusters: When do increasing returns imply monopoly? *Mathematical Social Sciences, 19*(3), 235–251. doi:10.1016/0165-4896(90)90064-E

Bacak, Ç. (2019). *Kümelenmenin kobi'lere sağladığı avantajlar ve kobi'lerin finansmana erişim kolaylıkları.* Retrieved from https://anahtar.sanayi.gov.tr/tr/news/kumelenmenin-kobilere-sagladigi-avantajlar-ve-kobilerin-finansmana-erisim-kolayliklari/107

Bayülken, Y. (2007). KOBİ'ler Nasıl Rekabet Edecek? *Mühendis ve Makina Dergisi, 48*(570), 10-14.

BCG. (2019). *Embracing industry 4.0 rediscovering growth.* Retrieved from https://www.bcg.com/capabilities/operations/embracing-industry-4.0-rediscovering-growth.aspx

Benneworth, P., & Hospers, G. J. (2007). The new economic geography of old industrial regions: Universities as global—local pipelines. *Environment and Planning. C, Government & Policy, 25*(6), 779–802. doi:10.1068/c0620

Braun, P., McRae-Williams, P., & Lowe, J. (2005). Small business clustering Accessing knowledge through local networks. *Journal of New Business.*

Brookfield, J. (2008). Firm clustering and specialization A study of Taiwan's machine tool industry. *Small Business Economics, 30*(4), 405–422. doi:10.100711187-007-9047-0

Brown, J. S., & Duguid, P. (1991). Organizational learning and communities-of-practice: Toward a unified view of working, learning, and innovation. *Organization Science, 2*(1), 40–57. doi:10.1287/orsc.2.1.40

Çağlar, E. (2018). *Kümelenmeler ve Rekabet Gücü.* Retrieved from https://www.tepav.org.tr/upload/files/haber/1255437510r3578.Kumelenmeler_ve_Rekabet_Gucu.pdf

Castelo-Branco, I., Cruz-Jesus, F., & Oliveira, T. (2019). Assessing Industry 4.0 readiness in manufacturing: Evidence for the European Union. *Computers in Industry, 107*, 22–32. doi:10.1016/j.compind.2019.01.007

Dasanayaka, S. W. S. B. (2019). *Enhancing the competitiveness of small and medium scale enterprises through clusters*. Retrieved from http://dl.lib.mrt.ac.lk/handle/123/14013?show=full

Drucker, P. F., Bahçıvangil, İ., & Gorbon, G. (2014). *21. Yüzyıl için yönetim tartışmaları*. Epsilon.

Ekinci, A. P. D. E. D., & Emsen, Ö. S. (2014). *Teorik perspektifte rekabet ve kümelenme ilişkileri: bölgesel kalkınmaya etkileri The relations between competition and cluster in the theoretical perspective: the effects on regional development*. Retrieved from https://www.avekon.org/papers/1031.pdf

Enright, M. J. (2003). *Regional clusters: what we know and what we should know. In Innovation clusters and interregional competition* (pp. 99–129). Berlin: Springer. doi:10.1007/978-3-540-24760-9_6

Field, J. (2005). *Social capital and lifelong learning*. Policy Press.

Humphrey, J., & Schmitz, H. (1995). *Principles for promoting clusters & networks of SMEs* (Vol. 1). Vienna: UNIDO.

Iqbal, Q., Yang, S., Nawaz, R., & Iqbal, K. (2019). A multi-dimensional construct of perceived information pollution in the era of rife infollution. *VINE Journal of Information and Knowledge Management Systems*, *49*(2), 162–180. doi:10.1108/VJIKMS-10-2018-0093

Isaksen, A. (1997). Regional clusters and competitiveness: The Norwegian case. *European Planning Studies*, *5*(1), 65–76. doi:10.1080/09654319708720384

Jardon, C. M., & Susana Martos, M. (2012). Intellectual capital as competitive advantage in emerging clusters in Latin America. *Journal of Intellectual Capital*, *13*(4), 462–481. doi:10.1108/14691931211276098

Karadeniz, K., & Kulaksız, S. (2018). İşletmelerin rekabet gücüne katkısı açısından kümelenme modelinin değerlendirilmesi: Çorum tarımsal gıda işleme makineleri kümesi. *Finans Ekonomi ve Sosyal Araştırmalar Dergisi*, *3*(4), 714–730.

Karaev, A., Lenny Koh, S. C., & Szamosi, L. T. (2007). The cluster approach and SME competitiveness: A review. *Journal of Manufacturing Technology Management*, *18*(7), 818–835. doi:10.1108/17410380710817273

Kotler, P., & Caslione, J. A. (2011). *Kaos Yönetimi (Çev. Kıvanç Dündar)*. İstanbul: Optimist.

Li, G., Hou, Y., & Wu, A. (2017). Fourth Industrial Revolution: Technological drivers, impacts and coping methods. *Chinese Geographical Science*, *27*(4), 626–637. doi:10.100711769-017-0890-x

Long, C., & Zhang, X. (2012). Patterns of China's industrialization Concentration, specialization, and clustering. *China Economic Review*, *23*(3), 593–612. doi:10.1016/j.chieco.2011.09.002

Machadoa, C. G., Winrotha, M., Carlssonb, D., Almströma, P., Centerholtb, V., & Hallin, M. (2019). *Industry 4.0 readiness in manufacturing companies: challenges and enablers towards increased digitalization. way*. Academic Press.

Manogaran, G., Thota, C., Lopez, D., & Sundarasekar, R. (2017). Big data security intelligence for healthcare industry 4.0. In *Cybersecurity for Industry 4.0* (pp. 103–126). Cham: Springer. doi:10.1007/978-3-319-50660-9_5

MUSİAD. (2005). *Kobi'ler için rekabet ve büyüme stratejileri*. Retrieved from https://www.musiad.org.tr/download/Yayinlar/Cep%20Kitaplar%C4%B1/KOB%C4%B0'ler%20%C4%B0%C3%A7in%20Rekabet%20ve%20B%C3%BCy%C3%BCme%20Stratejileri/KOB%C4%B0'ler%20%C4%B0%C3%A7in%20Rekabet%20ve%20B%C3%BCy%C3%BCme%20Stratejileri.pdf

OECD. (1999). *Boosting innovation: The cluster approach, OECD publishing*, Retrieved from http://www.oecd.org/sti/inno/boostinginnovationtheclusterapproach.htm

OECD. (2005). *OECD SME and Entrepreneurship Outlook: 2005*. OECD. Retrieved from https://stats.oecd.org/glossary/detail.asp?ID=3123

Oerlemans, L. A., Meeus, M. T., & Boekema, F. W. (2001). Firm clustering and innovation: Determinants and effects. *Papers in Regional Science*, *80*(3), 337–356. doi:10.1007/PL00013637

Oğuztürk, B. S., & Sarıçoban, K. (2013). Küresel rekabette kümelenme ve inovasyonun rolü. *Sosyal ve Beşeri Bilimler Dergisi*, *5*(1), 94–104.

Oyelaran-Oyeyinka, B. (2005). Inter-firm collaboration and competitive pressures: SME footwear clusters in Nigeria. *International Journal of Technology and Globalisation*, *1*(3-4), 343–360. doi:10.1504/IJTG.2005.008747

Porter, M. (2003). Clusters and regional competitiveness: Recent learnings. In *International Conference on Technology Clusters* (*Vol. 7*, pp. 2007-2013). Academic Press.

Porter, M. E. (1998). Clusters and competition. *On Competition, 7*, 91.

Porter, M. E. (1998). Clusters and the new economics of competition: Vol. 76. *No. 6*. Boston: Harvard Business Review.

Porter, M. E. (2000). Location, competition, and economic development: Local clusters in a global economy. *Economic Development Quarterly*, *14*(1), 15–34. doi:10.1177/089124240001400105

Powell, W. W., Koput, K. W., & Smith-Doerr, L. (1996). Interorganizational collaboration and the locus of innovation: Networks of learning in biotechnology. *Administrative Science Quarterly*, *41*(1), 116–145. doi:10.2307/2393988

Schilling, M. A., & Phelps, C. C. (2007). Interfirm collaboration networks: The impact of large-scale network structure on firm innovation. *Management Science*, *53*(7), 1113–1126. doi:10.1287/mnsc.1060.0624

Schmitz, H., & Nadvi, K. (1999). Clustering and Industrialization: Introduction. *World Development*, *27*(9), 1503–1514. doi:10.1016/S0305-750X(99)00072-8

Small and Medium Enterprises Development Organization of Turkey. (2005). *Küçük ve Orta Büyüklükteki İşletmelerin Tanımı, Nitelikleri ve Sınıflandırılması Hakkında Yönetmelik*. Retrieved from https://www.kosgeb.gov.tr/Content/Upload/Dosya/Mevzuat/KOBI%CC%87%E2%80%99lerin_Tan%C4%B1m%C4%B1,_Nitelikleri_ve_S%C4%B1n%C4%B1fland%C4%B1r%C4%B1lmas%C4%B1_Hakk%C4%B1nda_Yo%CC%88netmelik.pdf

Sölvell, Ö., Lindqvist, G., & Ketels, C. (2003). *The cluster initiative green book*. Stockholm: Ivory Tower.

Sorenson, O., & Audia, P. G. (2000). The social structure of entrepreneurial activity: Geographic concentration of footwear production in the United States, 1940–1989. american. *Journal of Sociology (Melbourne, Vic.)*, *106*(2), 424–462.

Thames, L., & Schaefer, D. (2017). Industry 4.0: an overview of key benefits, technologies, and challenges. In *Cybersecurity for Industry 4.0* (pp. 1–33). Cham: Springer. doi:10.1007/978-3-319-50660-9_1

Timurçin, D. (2010). *Türkiye'de KOBI'lerin rekabet gücü ve rekabet üstünlüğü sağlamada kümelenmenin etkisi* (Doctoral dissertation). İstanbul Üniversitesi SBBF.

Timurçin, D. (2011). Kümelenme Kavramı ve KOBİ\'lerde Rekabet Gücüne Etkisi. Çankaya University. *Journal of the Humanities and Social Sciences*, *8*(1), 21–56.

UNİDO. (2019). *What are Clusters.* Retrieved from http://www.clustersfordevelopment.org/

Venkataramanaiah, S., & Parashar, S. P. (2007). Enhancing the competitiveness of SMEs through industrial clusters: The Indian experience. *International Journal of Technology Management & Sustainable Development*, *6*(3), 227–243. doi:10.1386/ijtm.6.3.227_1

KEY TERMS AND DEFINITIONS

Clustering: It is a working model that brings together the companies and the supporting firms and institutions operating in the same or similar line of business, geographically close to each other, cooperating and competing with each other.

SMEs: SMEs are defined as enterprises that employ less than 250 employees annually and whose annual net sales revenue or financial balance does not exceed amount specified in the law.

Strategic Management: It is the management philosophy that analyzes the goals that an organization wants to achieve in the future and how it is achieved.

Chapter 12
Strategic Management in SMEs in Industry 4.0

Mustafa Atilla Arıcıoğlu
Necmettin Erbakan University, Turkey

Büşra Yiğitol
Konya Food and Agriculture University, Turkey

ABSTRACT

It is envisioned that the fourth industrial revolution contains many concepts such as modern automation and production systems, data collection, data processing, analysis, and data transfer and consists of intelligent factory applications such as augmented reality, the internet of things, cyber physical, and cyber security systems. It reveals the fact that a new era awaits enterprises in the relationship between technology and production due to these predictions for future changes. SMEs are one of the important segments that these triggers, which are the precursors of structural change, will affect. So how will SMEs experience the Industry 4.0 process? What do unmanned factories mean for SMEs? Which countries/SMEs will have the Industry 4.0 technology and Industry 4.0 infrastructure which require high capital, Which of them will create opportunities? In this chapter, the problems that SMEs will face in the digital transformation process and the political and strategic approaches that can be developed to deal with these problems will be evaluated.

DOI: 10.4018/978-1-7998-2577-7.ch012

INTRODUCTION

Toffler describes his book "Shock" (1970-p.10-12), "This book tells what happens to people who are changing". It focuses on our reasons for adopting or failing to adapt to the future. Much has been written about the future. Nevertheless, much of what is written about the world of the future is the product of a simple and rigid approach. However, Toffler (1970) says that the following pages are about the humane and "soft" side of tomorrow and the speed of change in our age is a fundamental force in itself. Furthermore, Toffler (1970) continues his words "this accelerating impulse has personal and psychological consequences as well as sociological consequences ". These words are not said by targeting at any time. In other words, Toffler (1970) explains how the strategy should be learned and taught and explains that if the more accurate the concept of the future is learned in the dynamic structure of time, the more harmonious it will be.

Toffler's words and a significant part of his writings in 1970 are meaningful before and after the time he wrote. It reminds us that the concept that will govern the change in the future is a strategy, and when the existence of the strategy is considered, it is a combination of a strong plan and smart application beyond being a prediction. Or strategy is change management itself. This issue is not clear whether this change is humanistic and soft as Toffler said, or is rigidity as Taylor said. The Industry 4.0 process or concept introduced by Hannover 2011 raises more new questions than the increasing amount of discussions and inferences in the constantly renewed scientific literature.

The efforts to understand and answer the questions are carried out through large scale enterprises rather than small scale enterprises. When the concepts are tried to be understood or executed, the concepts that will come up are: the fourth industrial revolution or digital transformation, modern automation and production systems, data collecting, data processing, analysis, and data transfer, augmented reality, Internet of Things, cyber-physical and cybersecurity systems, and integration of intelligent factory applications.

In this case, it will be inevitable to discuss what strategy should be developed for SMEs in the context of Industry 4.0.

INDUSTRY 4.0

Bringing together energy, raw materials, technology, and human beings forms the basis of the theoretical structure of industrialization. Although human beings are more binding and governing rather than being a component, he constantly seeks space for himself in the existence of the first three elements.

In the theories of organization, while pioneers of classics see man as a part of the machine, Bourdie considered production as a broad conceptual basis from the capital to strategy, and Galbraith thinks that making human beings ordinary and absentaneous in the development of the industry is as "the age of doubt". The privatization and naming of the space include a new perspective with the development of the industry. the rationale for scaling and valuation also emerged with industrialization. This process led to emerging of workshops and then the factories and then the existence of integrated facilities in the rapidly future. electricity, sheet metal, motor and the story of engineer/technician/worker develops through these readings. The existence of speed is a time measurement for large-scale enterprises, whereas for small-scale enterprises, it means the limit between asset and absence is narrowed. SMEs who have survived with the first three revolutions thanks to their curvature, adaptability, and mobility, are preparing for a new but perhaps more difficult test.

What is the Concept of Industry 4.0?

When the concept of industry 4.0 is searched in the literature, the followings can be seen;

§ Big Data and Analytics
§ Autonomous Robots
§ Simulation
§ Internet of Things (IoT)
§ CyberSecurity
§ Augmented Reality
§ Cloud Computing
§ Additive Manufacturing
§ Horizontal and Vertical System Integration

The definition of the fourth technological revolution is based on the general concepts and technologies such as the above concepts

- *Big data*: including data collection, storage, analysis, and data collection
- *Robots;* autonomous, flexible and highly efficient machines capable of working in collaboration with people in their production processes)
- *Simulation:* enactment of the production system in a virtual environment, identification and forecasting of behaviors and movements.
- *Internet of Things*: RFID, Wi-Fi, such as Bluetooth, technological applications through the technologies within the manufacturing process to communicate with each other and to be able to work in a coordinated state.
- *Cybersecurity*: technologies that involve data collection, storage, and security that are becoming more important with digital transformation.
- *Augmented reality*: technologies that allow products to be produced and tested in a virtual environment.
- *Cloud computing*: technology where data is stored and transformed into information when needed.
- *Additive production*: production can be done with the help of three-dimensional (3D) printers.

It is possible to summarize the story of the process until this conceptual flow: I. industrial revolution is a process that began in England in 1763 with the discovery of the steam engine by James Waat and the invention of vehicles and then spread to Europe and the United States. With this process, mechanization has started to spread rapidly, there has been a radical change in production and it has affected both the economic world and the social structure. This process lasted until the 1830s. The period of the II Industrial Revolution, which coincided with the years 1840 to 1870, was called the technology revolution. With the development and use of electrical technology in machinery, machines were developed and production started in large quantities. The foundations of III. Industrial Revolution was laid in the 1950s when digital technology developed. During this period, computer and communication technologies developed and these technologies gradually started to be included in human life. IV. The Industrial Revolution, also known as Industry 4.0, was first introduced by Bosch at the Hannover Fair in 2011, and the machine-machine and machine-human knowledge are discussed through the relationship between numbers and artificial intelligence.

Figure 1. Historical overview of industrial development (Kesayak, 2019)

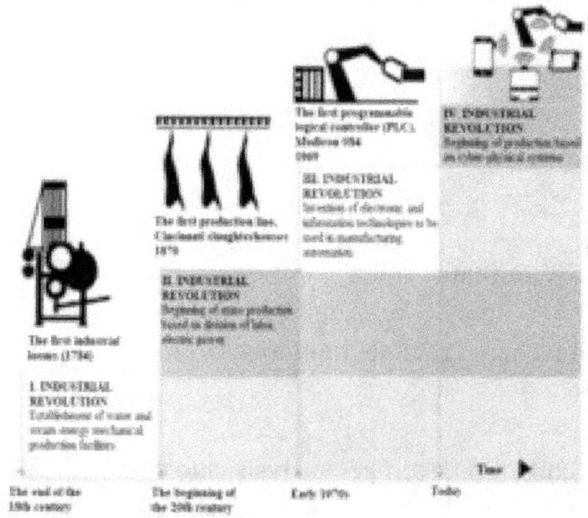

In the report prepared by TUSIAD and Boston Consulting Group (BCG), The radical change in the paradigms of the business world is explained through environmental factors and it is suggested that we should understand this change with four main trends (TUSIAD and BCG, 2016):

- § Regional trends - Increase in social interaction and trade between countries
- § Economic trends - Rising new strong economies and increasing globalization with financial resource flows
- § Technological trends - Increased connectivity and development of platform technologies
- § Meta trends - increasingly scarce resources, increasing concerns about the environment and safety

Figure 2. Trends shaping the future of the world (TUSIAD and BCG, 2016)

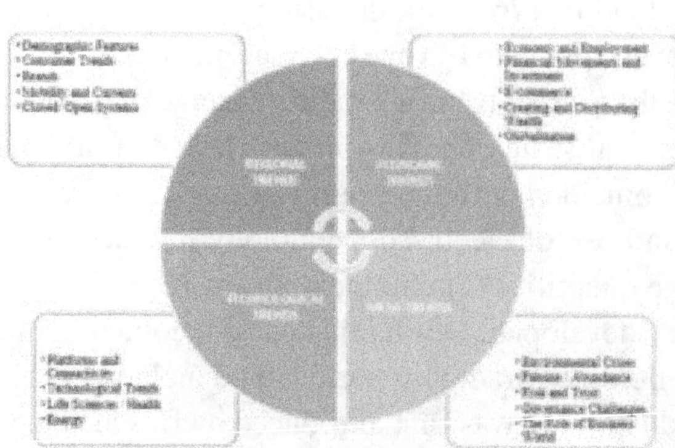

For the question of what these reasons teach for Industry 4.0, it is first necessary to ask the opposite question: For who? For what? These two questions are valuable. Because the Industry 4.0 process is not only an increase in productivity, it is a journey that creates higher value-added, creates its economy, fundamentally changes the established value chains and most importantly, it reaches a much more important point in the need of qualified manpower (TUSIAD and BCG, 2016).

In other words, the objectives of Industry 4.0 are to provide a higher level of operational efficiency and productivity and also to achieve a higher level of automation (Thames and Schaefer, 2016). The system accommodates fewer people, allows shorter production times and it allows the factory areas to shrink. However, in contrast to this shrinkage, the variety of products produced, the quality and quantity of production increased and new products are introduced to the market rapidly. It takes into account revolutionary developments in the design and manufacturing processes, operations and services of manufacturing and product systems (Tjahjono et al., 2017These features are not only closely related to internet technologies and advanced algorithms but also show that Industry 4.0 is an industrial value-added and knowledge management process (Lu, 2017).

In other words, Industry 4.0 technologies enable continuous interaction and exchange of information not only between people but also between people and machines, even between machines (Cooper and James, 2009) and continuous communication over the internet. The following 5 main features are mentioned in industry 4.0 (Roblek et al., 2016; Posada et al., 2015);

- Digitization, optimization, and privatization of production
- Automation and adaptation
- Human-machine interaction
- Value-added services and businesses
- Automatic data exchange and communication.

In this context, while discussing the components of Industry 4.0, a common definition has not yet been reached. Drath and Horch (2014) refer to the fourth industrial revolution and It is understood as the application of general concepts of cyber-physical systems (CPSs) on industrial production systems (cyber-physical production systems).

In some sources, the concept of industry 4.0 is defined as the use of advanced data analytics for transformational business results, and as the term used for the internet of things, machines, computers, people involving the realization of intelligent industrial processes (IIC, 2015). There is vital application of data analytics in the era of industry 4.0 where polluted information is prevalent in nature (Iqbal & Nawaz, 2019). According to Iqbal & Nawaz (2019), drawback of industry 4.0 is rising quantity of polluted information. Tjahjono et al. (2017) define industrial 4.0 as a global transformation of the manufacturing industry with the introduction of digitalization and the Internet. On the other hand, Müller et al. (2018) approached industry 4.0 from a technical, economic, ecological and social framework and included the concept of industry 4.0 as an economic process in which processes are transparent and interconnected, enabling optimization by increasing efficiency, flexibility, quality and personalization.

Beyond a common definition, if we discuss concepts that created a definition and the content of the process, we find ourselves amid the actual debate. The theme of this is what has been said about the expected positive and negative aspects of Industry 4.0. The features that Müller et al. (2018) have compiled from various articles are summarized in Table 1.

Table 1. Positive and negative aspects of Industry 4.0 (Müller et al., 2018)

Possible Opportunities	Possible Threats
New business models with Industry 4.0	Existing business models at stake
New value proposals for improved competitiveness	Loss of flexibility
Increasing productivity	Standardization
Reduce costs	Transparency
Higher quality	High implementation efforts such as costs and standardization
More speed and flexibility	Employee Fears and Concerns
Load balancing and inventory reduction	Lack of expertise
Reduction of monotonous studies	
Reducing environmental impact	

In general, apart from this summary table, it is possible to explain the positive and negative characteristics of industry 4.0 in the following items.

- Industry 4.0 enables the innovation of existing business models (Arnold et al., 2016). Not only does it increase global competitiveness, but it also enables strategic differentiation in new business models (Laudien et al., 2017). Therefore, it poses a threat to existing business models. It is also an opportunity to create new business models with a change in the business strategy of the enterprise.
- Industry 4.0 not only provides enterprises with innovation on competitiveness business strategies but also enables them to gain strategic value in global competition (Brettel et al., 2014). businesses gain the opportunity to create value for the customer through data tracking and analysis and the active use of this information in the improvement of production processes.
- While Human-machine cooperation and even communication and coordination between machines ensure speed and flexibility in production processes (Stock and Seliger, 2016), the quality of products produced (Meyer et al., 2011) and productivity increase is expected. In this case, also it requires less manpower and provides cost advantage as it allows a reduction in error rate.
- The inclusion of information and communication systems in the industrial network also leads to a sharp increase in the degree of automation (Sanders et al., 2016). Intelligent and self-optimizing machines on the production line can synchronize themselves with the entire value chain, from ordering from supplier to receipt and delivery of goods to customers (Spath, et al., 2013).
- Providing automation in production processes provides ease of balancing in terms of production planning. Based on the fact that Industry 4.0 is a radical change process, it provides real-time production planning based on dynamic optimization in contrast to conventional forecasting based production planning (Sanders et al., 2016). Since manufacturers have the advantage of calculating the number of products produced per unit time at a rate close to zero error, they can perform production rapidly according to the demand situation and reduce their product stocks (Oettmeier and Hofmann, 2017) and carry out resource planning effectively.
- Thanks to devices and processes such as artificial intelligence, internet of things, cloud computing and 3-d technology provided by Industry 4.0, employees' motivation and work efficiency increases (Hirsch-Kreinsen, 2014). Accordingly, there are no focus and satisfaction problems in

getting rid of monotonous and uniformity. Intelligent and autonomous production systems provide higher employee satisfaction and motivation for paying more attention to monotonous and repetitive tasks (Müller et al., 2018). Besides, environmental sustainability can be achieved through production processes that reduce environmental hazards to a lesser extent, particularly reducing the carbon footprint (Peukert et al., 2015).

- The disadvantages of Industry 4.0 in general under current conditions and in the future for enterprises and employees are the lack of validity of the existing system and thus the endangering of the assets of the existing systems. Digitization and data monitoring and recording, as well as automation and communication technologies, increase the risk of eternal cyber attacks. Transparency of each business activity through online platforms increases the risk of attack and causes them to become open targets for external threats (Müller et al., 2018). Therefore, the necessity of data security applications increases.
- In terms of cost, the digitalization process requires new technological structuring in industrial production processes. Conducting activities through adaptation through the existing system is both a challenging and cost-increasing situation for enterprises (Müller et al., 2018).
- Industry 4.0 and the digitalization and mechanization lead to the most questionable questions in terms of employment. Personnel competencies and competencies required for the use of new technology, such as data, network technologies, data analysis and processing (Erol et al., 2016), can be alarming for employees and increase the concern for a job loss of existing personnel. The fact that employers are not able to provide qualified personnel or do not provide the necessary training to existing personnel can lead to a complex situation (Kiel et al., 2017).
- Industry 4.0 enables companies to gain important information about the methods to be applied in their internal processes and thus to increase added value for companies (Safar et al., 2018). However, as in any system or the process of change, the age of digitalization contains opportunities and threats. Therefore, companies need to analyze how and what the impact and opportunities will be on the sector and business models in which they operate in this transformation journey and to follow a technological roadmap and draw a strategic roadmap.

SMEs in Industry 4.0

While being demand medium-high technology investment for a new period based on technology and production relationship, this prerequisite will lead to the difference between companies and countries. In other words, while the management and production of technology lead to geometric growth, it is the harbinger of structural change.

*Concept of SMEs

According to Turkey SME Definitions, Small and medium-sized enterprises (SMEs) employ less than 250 workers annually and have an annual financial balance not exceeding TL 250,000,000 (two hundred and fifty million) and are classified economic unit as micro-sized enterprises, small-sized enterprises and medium-sized enterprise (Wikipedia, 2019). Small and medium-sized enterprises (SMEs) are generally owned and controlled by an entrepreneur and a significant portion of the hierarchical decision-making and executive bodies in SMEs are family members (Arıcıoğlu and Yiğitol, 2019).

Table 2. Comparison of the Turkey SME Definitions (Small and Medium Enterprises Development Organization of Turkey, 2005)

Size Category	Staff headcount	Turnover
Medium-sized	50-250	≤ 125 Million TL
Small	10-49	≤ 25 Million TL
Micro	1-9	≤ 3 Million TL

Table 3. Comparison of the EU SME Definitions (European Commission, 2019)

Company category	Staff headcount	Turnover
Medium-sized	< 250	≤ € 50 m
Small	< 50	≤ € 10 m
Micro	< 10	≤ € 2 m

The concepts commonly used in the definition of SMEs are related to the qualitative and quantitative characteristics of SMEs such as their share in the sector, their degree of expertise, manager-owner relations, managerial problems, quantity of capital, production amount, total assets, sales volume (Arıcıoğlu and Yiğitol, 2019; Özgener, 2003).

Small and medium-sized enterprises (SMEs) are considered as the backbone of the economy because they are strong as employers; therefore, they attract the attention of both policymakers and scientists (Safar et al., 2018).

Table 4. SWOT analysis results of SMEs (Kalpande et al., 2010)

Opportunities	Threats
Expert market Support of government Raising the ceiling for SMEs. Government reserves of material items.	Financial tightness. Technological obsolescence. Ignoring the mechanic preparation Increase in the cost of information resources Political peace and instability.
Strengths	**Weaknesses**
Flexibility Owner manager Low labor Low costs Simple structuring Cooperation with employees	Lack of quality consciousness. Lack of financial strength. Lack of correct business culture. The lack of educated workers. Lack of technology superiority Lack of proper management tendency. High score of key personnel. Missing planning. Lack of long-term strategic focus.

The fact that SMEs have various structural problems makes it difficult for them to keep up with the change. Especially when changes in information and communication technologies, complex business life, new business models and globalization are added to the environmental dynamics, the insufficiency of the knowledge and skills of the owner and family members becomes more difficult to adapt to the transformation process. SMEs may experience some problems, especially in the application of new technologies and adaptation of these technologies to business models compared to large enterprises. Some of these problems are the lack of resources, skills and time (Anonymous, 2018). In the report that prepared for SMEs by The Interreg North Sea Region (NSR) project GrowIn 4.0 (2018 shows the barriers to SMEs in general;

- Lack of commercial support,
- Be cautious about investments in Industry 4.0,
- Lack of correct qualifications,
- Lack of digital standards,
- Threats due to cybersecurity,
- Lack of funding
- Lack of the right business tools.

Opportunities mentioned in the report (Anonymous, 2018);

- Efficiency increasing effect
- Increase competitiveness and support global competitiveness
- Growth support

SMEs are again attracting the most attention in the Industry 4.0 digitalization process and are asking questions about the process. So how will SMEs experience the Industry 4.0 process? What do unmanned factories mean for SMEs? Which countries/SMEs would have opportunities thanks to the Industry 4.0 technology and Industry 4.0 infrastructure that require high capital? Will new developments require a new model of cooperation? Does Industry 4.0 have a different sectoral transformation foresight?

The answers to all these questions highlight five points for SMEs:

- Firstly, the trend and preference of unmanned factories (especially some countries such as the USA, Germany, Japan, Korea prefer this way while being competition with China which uses the cheap labor argument) are likely to lead to changes in the SME scale and classification. In particular, the micro-scale and the small-scale are referred to together, while the medium-scale seems to be considered as a separate class.
- It is inevitable that SMEs, which are an important supplier and support element for the main industry in international competition, will turn to new technology-based collaborations.
- The risk areas of the medium-sized companies that seek to achieve global adaptation by producing their technology independently from their countries or transferring them from the international market will expand.
- A new type of network-oriented and innovative technology / SMEs will emerge.
- Ultimately, the digital transformation will change the way SMEs do business and organizational structures, and those who cannot adapt to change will accelerate and gradually disappear.

It is not surprising to anticipate that SMEs will have a challenging test with industry 4.0 based on these expected developments. In this context, SMEs need to make their positions regarding the digital transformation process especially according to their position in the supply chain. Solidarity from the increased competition is a necessity for the successful management of the industry 4.0 process.

While the high cost of using and transferring technology through solidarity/collaboration is minimized, S and M synchronism in the regional context can be an important opportunity for competitive advantage. It should be noted that the adaptation process required for SMEs should also be discussed through new business models that will emerge, and that sectors must perceive this change in different ways. In particular, the change in production-based works and the privilege of the service sector in this context should be monitored more carefully. It can even be foreseen that the change process related to agriculture should be monitored more carefully. Because the distribution of countries and concrete outputs related to the transformation of the manufacturing sector are seen more clearly, in the service and agricultural sector, it will not facilitate the harmonization of country differences and transformation between countries or companies. In the service and agricultural sector, it will not facilitate the harmonization of country differences and transformation between countries or companies. While the emergence of employment policies in labor-intensive agricultural areas and increasing political concerns are some of the barriers, the difference in farmer's asset level in agriculture is an important obstacle to the globalization of investment in this field. It is expected that the transformation in the services sector will be faster in developed economies and slower in others.

In the context of Industry 4.0, it is possible to list the triggering forces and restrictive factors as follows (Anonymous, 2018);

Triggering forces;

§ The power of in-house triggers, such as reducing production costs, improving the quality of products and services, increasing employee productivity and reducing production time
§ The power to increase the efficiency of the production system and to provide the advantage of timely production differentiation in the market
§ The power of the legal requirements of sectors such as construction and health, and the power of legal triggers for environmental and sustainability
§ The power of the market due to the changing needs of the market; meeting the changing demands, reduction in waste amounts, the success of intelligent automation systems in mass production
§ The power of technological changes; increased access to digital technologies, especially in recent times, makes the implementation of industry 4.0 more accessible

Restrictive factors;

§ Lack of support in adapting to new technologies
§ Excessive prudence on investment
§ Lack of talent in the workforce
§ Slow development of digital standards,
§ Information security / cybersecurity concern
§ The problem of access to finance
§ The low share of technological investments in investments

In this new process that SMEs will face, some factors that play a role in terms of sustainability are preference and promotion of public policies, large/global enterprises' process orientations and pressures, special cases of the sector, competitors' position in this process and ultimately the preference of enterprises to use such investment resources.

Factors affecting the application of Industry 4.0 elements in small and medium-sized enterprises (SMEs) can be grouped as follows (Vrchota et al., 2019);

Table 5. Factors influencing the introduction of Industry 4.0 elements in small and medium-sized enterprises (SMEs) (Vrchota et al., 2019)

Machine	Labor	Technical information (Know-how)	Financial planning	Process management	External factors
Services	Recruitment	Opinions	Resources	Personal Characteristics of Managers	Development
Product and Machine Quality	Development	Market Opportunities	Risk management	Process Tuning	Market
Access to Services	Qualifications	Integration Opportunities	Productivity	Corporate Social Responsibility	Government
Optimal Location	Workforce Resources			Rewarding System	Competition
Production Chain				Critical Points for Sustainability	Ecology
Security					
Level					

Table 6. SWOT Analysis of SMEs in the context of Industry 4.0 (Created by authors)

Opportunity	Threats
Reduces production costs Easy adaptation to market demands Flexibility Differentiation in the market Increases productivity Increases competitiveness Provides growth	Ability to survive in a new competitive environment due to faster adaptation by large scale firms Information security More financing needs Cost-increasing feature in the installation The threat to the existing order and business models Employee anxiety and concern Failure to take part in the supply network
Strengths	**Weaknesses**
Flexible structures The vision of technological enterprise Easy adaptability Entrepreneur spirit Cost advantage in Industry 4.0 technologies due to their small size Competitive advantage with collaborative structures Ability to work with low labor Ease of internal communication	Lack of resources, skills and time Lack of support in adapting to new technologies Excessive prudence on investment Lack of talent in the workforce Slow development of digital standards, Information security / cybersecurity concern The problem of access to finance The low share of technological investments in investments Lack of vision of managers Unaware of the strategic management process Lack of strategic awareness Access to databases

Literature Review Related to SMEs in the Context of Industry 4.0

Nuroğlu and Nuroğlu (2018a; 2018b) indicated that industry 4.0 transformation is closely related to that SMEs capture the ındustry 4.0 process in countries such as Turkey that the majority of manufacturing industries network consists of SMEs. In general, the appearance in SMEs is described as uneasiness regarding the process. The factors that they deem critical in this process of digitalization; to train consultants to support the digital transformation of SMEs and to open digital transformation centers, to be target-based rather than uneasiness, to be more supportive for SMEs in focus sectors such as chemicals and pharmaceuticals, motor vehicles, machinery and equipment, semiconductors and electronics and food and beverage, and to include Clustering model in support program.

Cevik (2019) evaluated the applicability of Industry 4.0 in SMEs from the managers' perspective. In a study conducted in Turkey, it is stated that SMEs are not ready and will have difficulty in providing the necessary information equipment and technological infrastructure in the context of Industry 4.0. Also, the areas where small/medium-sized enterprises have the highest expectations due to new technology applications are as follows; to gain innovative production concepts and to produce better quality products, to make improvements in non-value added works and to help institutionalization of enterprises.

Üçler and Vayvay (2018) evaluated the application of Simultaneous Engineering Approaches in SMEs. A simultaneous engineering approach is based on the logic of product and process development of experts and managers from different disciplines by creating cross-functional teams working together simultaneously. Therefore, it is stated that it supports Industry 4.0 studies depending on these characteristics. It is noted that it also supports Industry 4.0, especially because it focuses on horizontal collaboration and integration of distributed technologies with digital technologies (Brettel et al., 2014).

Apilioğulları (2018) examined the relationship between the concepts that should be applied to SMEs to be successful in the digital transformation process. In this study, a road map model is tried to be outlined. As a result of this study, it is underlined that a systematic approach and methodology should be followed in the process of digitalization, the importance of strategic approach, that companies should not be involved in the process without examining, interpreting and constructing standard business processes, and that it is necessary to be informed for setting standards and technological change.

The aim of Safar et al., (2018) is to design a business organization model for existing or newly established SMEs considering traditional approaches to business models and Industry 4.0 requirements to guide SMEs in the early stage of industry 4.0 implementation. In the model obtained as a result of the study, it is stated that

- Additional software and cloud information technologies will be required for both existing and new initiatives,
- This planning should be made at the beginning,
- Enterprises should make investments that require a high amount of financing even if they have existing investments,
- Production costs and times will shorten as a requirement of the current notion of the smart world

The study also emphasized the need to adapt to new technologies not only for enterprises but also for other market participants such as banks, tax offices, and other institutions to participate in the global network.

Vrchota et al. (2019) aimed to identify the factors that affect small and medium-sized enterprises (SMEs) in the Industry 4.0 process. In general, the study was carried out concerning the factors that limit the integration of SMEs into Industry 4.0 in contrast to the factors that may be impulsive for SMEs. The results showed that the awareness of Industry 4.0 is related to the size of the enterprise. While the majority of medium-sized enterprises are considering implementing digitalization and robotization technologies over the next 5 years, this has been observed in less than half of the micro-enterprises.

In the report presented by Schröder (2016), it is covered that review of the literature showing the application of Industry 4.0, typical barriers and challenges in the implementation of Industry 4.0, highlighting the importance of engaging employees in increasing the success of innovation processes in the company. The report provides policy recommendations for overall adaptation and improvement of the process.

In their study, Sevinç et al. (2018) analyzed the push forces of Industry 4.0 adopted in small and medium-sized enterprises. By analyzing the difficulties in the transition process of small and medium-sized enterprises (SMEs) to Industry 4.0, it contributes to the determination of strategic steps by considering these results. In the study, a hierarchical structure was established under the four main criteria (innovation, organization, environment and financial aspects) and the relative weight of these criteria and sub-criteria was calculated. The surveys conducted on business managers were evaluated using the analytic hierarchy process and analytical network process and multi-criteria decision-making methods.

Müller et al. (2017), in their work, discuss the cooperation strategies of SMEs to overcome the lack of resources and information. In this context, jointly developing business models as well as commonly purchased technologies are considered appropriate strategies for SMEs in this process. In this study, the advantages of cooperation between SMEs are discussed. With this cooperation, while providing a cost advantage to small and medium-sized companies, it is mentioned that benefits such as facilitating information and data flow, synergy formation between enterprises, resource transfers and technical information transfer can be provided a competitive advantage.

SMEs in Industry 4.0: Strategies and Policy

Effective implementation of strategy and strategic management differs according to many characteristics such as the size of enterprises, sector, organizational structure and managerial capabilities besides strategic awareness or long-term vision in the process (Arıcıoğlu and Yiğitol, 2019). Therefore, when compared to large scale enterprises, the understanding of strategic management in SMEs differs. In particular, SMEs being local-oriented and ownership and management functions being carried out by the owner/entrepreneur are effective in determining the concept of strategy and the scope of strategic management. In this context, it is not wrong to define the concepts of strategy and strategic management in SMEs as an informal character that includes personal qualities, experience, creativity and intuition in a dynamic and heterogeneous work environment (Todorov, 2014). In other words, it is not possible to talk about comprehensive strategic behavior independent of the manager for SMEs. Strategy formation and decision-making are in the hands of the owner/entrepreneur, and this process is usually carried out for individual purposes (Morden, 2007). In short, it is possible to talk about operational activities and efficiency for SMEs, not strategic management for SMEs. Besides, it is possible to talk about a strategic understanding that can be used either as a follower of the strategies of industry leaders (large scale enterprises) in SMEs or by forming partnerships or clusters. Based on these explanations, it is important to discuss which strategic behaviors and policies SMEs will adopt and implement in the industrial 4.0 process and how they can survive in the competitive environment of the digital industry.

Particularly, as the industry tries to build a new world with a digital transformation, the components of new balances in competition and the sustainability concern of labor-oriented sectors/enterprises become obvious hard questions for SMEs.

With Industry 4.0, possible outcomes are seen from the SMEs perspective:

- A more planned business life
- Learning innovative business forms
- Return of cost advantage to technology in labor-intensive areas
- Obligation to register
- Difficulty in acquiring data habit
- More efficient time and production management for deadlines
- From a supplier role perspective, some reasons such as the transfer of the main industries to unmanned factories and outsourcing and logistics costs will lead to a narrower / regional selection of the supply network. This is inherently at risk of expulsion/withdrawal of SMEs within supply networks.

Industry 4.0 is a digitalization based on information technologies and technological investment is required and SMEs need to overcome the lack of resources and information. In this context, in addition to widely purchased technologies, jointly developing business models, ie collaborations, have strategic importance. Successful and trust-based cooperation provides a cost advantage in technological investments as well as the advantage of distributing the possible risk rather than carrying it on one shoulder (Müller et al., 2017). Collaboration facilitates the exchange of ideas and facilitates synergies between SMEs. Mutual exchange can not only benefit one partner but can also provide benefits to all collaborating partners (Müller et al., 2017).

Other advantages of cooperation are applications that can provide strategic advantage such as focusing on core competence, sharing technical knowledge and transferring resources. Briefly, the industrial 4.0 revolution will develop new forms of cooperation and may further develop the areas of cooperation. Besides, while the main/large industry is now producing in unmanned factories, the competition of sub-industry in terms of cost and price will gain a new dimension. Or the real question arises as follows: Is there a need for a sub-industry, and if so, what kind of a definition of a sub-industry emerges?

One of the most important inferences that SMEs, which are the main actors of the economy, learned in the competition process is to determine their core competence and to be involved in this process in line with this core competency. The gains achieved to become more evident with Industry 4.0, but also this may involve new areas of risk with the transformation in production, and this situation makes enterprises necessitate to re-perform risk analysis. In this context, specialized works formats should be correctly understood and re-analyzed for each SMEs. Even, it should find answers to questions such as who saves flexible production, where should I be in the sector's time planning, where should I be just in time, what should be the new ranges and technical equipment for efficiency measurement.

Another very important title concerns everyone. What about humans? Will technology change, particularly in labor-intensive sectors, reveal new sets of solutions in production modes? new questions may be added with these questions asked since the beginning of the 18th century. this should be questioned with a new mind especially for each SME member of the cluster. Naturally, one of the important factors that will determine this can be explained by the direction and preferences that large scale enterprises give to their production styles. Defining the use of machinery through an integrated process and the presence of new mechanical villages consisting of factories open the discussion of the positioning of people again. It is seen that from Taylor to today, business owners and entrepreneurs looking for pure efficiency in factories will seem to pursue a new quest.

One of the important factors at the center of the discussions about Industry 4.0 is the curiosity of what will happen to a human, however in the new system, there are discussions about the quality of employment rather than quantity. With the new system, technical workforce and expertise knowledge emerge as the star shining areas. Therefore, the evolving of the employment structure in this direction is an inevitable necessity.

Several qualitative and quantitative competencies are deemed necessary in the labor force in the Industry 4.0 process. These abilities are indicated in table 5 (Anonymous, 2018)

Table 7. Qualitative and quantitative competencies of labor in the Industry 4.0 process (Anonymous, 2018)

	Competencies that must be definitely	Competencies that should be	Competencies that may be
TECHNICAL	IT knowledge and usability	Knowledge management	Computer programming and coding capability
	Data and information tracking and analysis	General and interdisciplinary knowledge about technology and organization	Knowledge of technological expertise
	Statistical information	Expert knowledge on production activities and processes	Ergonomics awareness
	Organizational and process understanding	Cybersecurity and data protection awareness	Awareness of legal affairs
PERSONAL	Ability to interact with modern interfaces (human-robot, human-machine)	Trust in new technologies	
	Adaptability to change	Conscious of continuous development and lifelong learning	
	Teamwork ability		
	Social skills		
	Communication skills		

One of the important features of SMEs is the habit of keeping some or part of the economic activities off the record. Although there are reasons such as providing cost advantages or reducing the cost burden on sustainability, this preference is problematic in the legal context. However, digital transformation limits or even eliminates it. In this case, it is necessary to prepare for joining the economy and to determine the real profit/profitability targets with in-house transactions.

Being an SME is a pre-growth scale. To know how and why it grows, it is necessary to keep the data record and calculate the magnitude over an accurate time frame. when companies are small scale, the more accurately planned and managed data retention habits, the more effective the power of future projection will be when they grow.

Industry 4.0 now realizes process management through error-free production planning. Since production planning and process management related to production will be done by artificial intelligence at the next level of the production era, the Industry 4.0 process should be understood and adapted for SMEs as soon as possible. This can be overcome with an integrated program or process development that can be achieved through programming that used currently such as Similar to ERP, MRP.

In the final analysis, with this process, it will not be surprising that SMEs will suffer losses within the framework of sectoral and regional factors and some of them will probably come to the final stage of their lives. Structural changes, flexibility advantages, and renewed perspectives are hints of how they can provide sustainability. Some of these will not be very easy in alone and it is possible to say that the collaborations will have life-saving importance in the new period. Even the forms of cooperation will develop and they will try to find a place in a strategic roadmap. Because togetherness has a life-saving feature especially for SMEs.

SOLUTIONS AND RECOMMENDATIONS

Interreg North Sea Region (Nsr) Project GrowınG 4.0 (2018) has prepared the following strategic behavioral recommendations for industrial SMEs;

- § Define which business model will be used for improved or new offers.
- § Create the technological basis such as tool base for analytics.
- § Build the right organizational structure and capabilities.
- § To develop the necessary partnerships in the digital world.
- § Join and shape technological standardization.
- § Improving technological infrastructure such as fixed and mobile broadband services. Infrastructure should be fast, secure and reliable enough for companies to depend on real-time data.
- § Acquire the right skills and therefore adapt the school curriculum, education, and university programs, and strengthen entrepreneurial approaches to increase it-related skills and innovation capabilities of the workforce and improve the existing workforce.

It is seen that a new way of doing business is evolving from transfer to use of technology, from labor to process management. Differentiation in the structure of competition and differentiation İN the scales / classification of enterprises is another possible development. In this context, having these forms of behavior over collective intelligence and collective leadership will provide an advantage in terms of new forms of competition.

It is possible to list the following predictions for new smes or renewed smes;

- While there may be a new scale on SMEs, micro and small scales can be considered as a group and medium-sized enterprises can be considered as a separate group.
- Collaborative structures will be of great importance for SMEs to survive in the foreseeable future. Therefore, clustering studies are an important move in the application of Industry 4.0 technologies and breaking the competitiveness of large scale enterprises. It is a prediction that medium-sized companies will expand their risk areas due to both competition and human resources regarding the process management.

- The new economic order will allow new technology-based SMEs to derive.
- Choosing new business models instead of existing business models will be a necessity.
- When compared to other sectors, the manufacturing sector appears to be the sector that will be most affected and affected by this process. Considering the easier adaptation of the financial and service sectors with this process, it will not be misleading to foresee that online SMEs will become increasingly widespread in these areas.
- It is a very strong possibility that the existing production integrations of the factories will be operated as an internal factory system in the form of SMEs through outsourcing. As a matter of fact, in the existing automotive factories, the cost-oriented way of working as an internal supplier (integrated trials already exist) will become widespread by going one step further than employing the workers of the sub-industry companies
- The agricultural sector will determine the automation-based way of working as a new mode of operation, from crop planting to development, from development monitoring to harvest, the process will be possible with less employment and more technology.
- SMEs, who need to keep up with the change in education areas, will learn to employ flexible ways of employing engineers or foreman integrated into engineering knowledge.

FUTURE RESEARCH DIRECTIONS

Confronting with the future for SMEs goes at a geometric pace. this situation causes enterprises to discuss new process management/methods in the procurement process. Efforts to achieve sustainable success by using new tools of competition-oriented minds are adding new ones to the working areas.

- The fact that the factories gradually draw the supply network into the factory and re-integrate them with artificial intelligence, the operation of the factory units with outsourcing.
- The emergence of new forms of organization,
- Apart from the blue and white-collar in human resources, artificial intelligence users who will take part in the online process will become widespread,
- Online SMEs concept,
- Change of SMEs scales,
- The development of existing forms of cooperation and the emergence of new forms of cooperation, in particular, the use of cluster forms online,
- Fractal market forms of competition

All of these are some of the most important issues to be studied.

CONCLUSION

The concept of Industry 4.0 is a term that describes a process of digitalization of network and computer systems that encompasses the entire production process to the industry. With this digitalization, industrial automation and the production of highly mechanized products emerge as a dreamed or even partially realized future. In the anticipated future manufacturing processes, the equipment, machinery, materials and end products perceive the status of environmental conditions and process through sensors, communicate with embedded software, and thus optimizes the production process in an unprecedented way (Schröder, 2016). In this way, not only efficiency is provided in technological factories, but also it is possible to produce personalized products with higher quality, faster, less costly according to customer needs. Basic fiction is based on big data applications and data analysis. The emerging new business models allow the evaluation of the data provided and the processing and use of this data.

The exchanger power of the new industrial world on enterprises is a deep-scaled and radical change. Therefore, it is not easy for companies to adapt to this process. New strategies for a sustainability need to be developed with the abandonment of existing schemes and the replacement of new business models and technologies. Otherwise, it is unlikely that enterprises that cannot take the right and timely step will be able to survive. The enterprises should take care of transformational dynamics in earlier and adapt business strategies accordingly. Furthermore, they need to have a good political, legal and infrastructural framework to keep up with the Industry 4.0 issue (Schröder, 2016).

In this process, as well as large-scale enterprises, the situations of small and medium-sized enterprises appear as a critical issue. SMEs are an indispensable element for the economies of the country and play an important role in an economic revival, structural change, and adaptation to technological innovations (Cin, 2012). Especially in the process of change in industry 4.0, The role and the attitude of SMEs (due to the most important role as a backbone of the economy of many countries, including Turkey) in the process are important.

However, the structural problems and administrative deficiencies of SMEs make it difficult for them to adapt to the change process. Especially the changes in information and communication technologies, complex business life, new business models and adaptation to environmental dynamics such as globalization are among the main challenges in this the change process. It is possible to summarize possible problems in the context of Industry 4.0 (Kleindienst and Ramsauer, 2016);

Ø Horizontal Integration

Perhaps one of the biggest problems of SMEs related to digitalization is the lack of specialized personnel in information technologies. SMEs generally specialize in basic software. However, to achieve horizontal integration, they need to gain expertise in different software that can interact with each other. The first step is to define special transfer parameters that will allow data exchange between different departments and companies, especially in creating value.

Ø Consistency in Lifelong Engineering Applications

The biggest limiting factor of not spreading models such as simulation, planning and descriptive models among SMEs is low awareness of such systems. Therefore, the possible advantages are often overlooked. SMEs need to be effective in such applications.

Ø Vertical Integration and Cross-Linked Production Systems

Specifically, provision, analysis, and evaluation of real-time data related to production, assembly, logistics or machiner is a situation that increases the flexibility of SMEs in the process of creating value. However, most SMEs do not have the skills to operate and maintain their systems.

As can be seen, industry 4.0 technologies envisage radical changes in manufacturing processes such as the transition from the provision of simple components to complex engineering systems based on Cyber-Physical Systems. It requires real-time production planning as well as optimization. This enables a flexible and fast response to customer needs. thus, it can provide competitive advantages for SMEs. Reducing manufacturing times with Industry 4.0 applications can help them acquire the new skills needed to gain a competitive advantage on a global scale. Therefore, adapting to this process is as profitable as it is difficult to adapt. Both large-scale enterprises and SMEs are required to make an assessment and prepare themselves through the dynamics of this process. Otherwise, it is unlikely that some businesses will survive within the framework of sectoral and regional factors in the new competitive system. Structural changes, flexibility advantages and renewed perspectives are hints of how they can gain a place in the process and how they will provide sustainability. In this process, SMEs should do their strategic positioning well and take some strategic steps in a timely and accurate manner.

Strategic and political steps to be implemented or to be considered;

- Flexible organizational structures and business models should be adopted.
- Areas of expertise should be well defined
- Focus on core competence,
- Collaborative structuring should be given the strategic importance
- The position within the supply network must be maintained
- To be included in the formal economic system not
- Focus on production and process planning.
- The specialist workforce should be employed
- Integrated programs should be included in the production process
- SMEs' owners/managers need to have strategic awareness. Managers should evaluate the dynamics, the opportunities, and threats of changing technology in the context of the structuring of their enterprises. Also, managers should ensure that smart choices and the right business models are selected and implemented.
- Priority should be given to making necessary investments in information technologies and making the recruitment of specialist workforce needed relevant technologies by either internally through training or externally through re-employment.
- Cybersecurity applications, secure interface technologies should be developed or these requirements must be met externally within the framework of the collaborative structure.
- Expertise is required for effective management of the logistics network.
- One of the last and perhaps most critical two factors is the establishment of consultancy centers that can provide planned specialist training to SMEs. Also to the establishment of these centers, these centers should be included in the collaborative network and permanent consultancy services should be provided.
- The other is the need to revise the educational activities to the desired criteria. Besides, the educational activities should be focused on establishing the expert workforce that enterprises can benefit from in their future employment.

REFERENCES

Anonymous. (2018). *Industry 4.0 – opportunities and challenges for SMEs in the North Sea Region.* Retrieved from https://northsearegion.eu/media/7320/growin-40-desk-study.pdf

Apilioğulları, L. (2018). Üretim Endüstrisi Dijital Dönüşüm Süreci Kavramsal İlişki Haritası. *Anemon Muş Alparslan Üniversitesi Sosyal Bilimler Dergisi, 7*(3), 1–1.

Arıcıoğlu, M. A., & Yiğitol, B. (2019). Paradigm Change in Strategic Management. In Handbook of Research on Managerial Thinking in Global Business Economics (pp. 179-195). IGI Global.

Brettel, M., Friederichsen, N., Keller, M., & Rosenberg, M. (2014). How virtualization, decentralization and network building change the manufacturing landscape: An industry 4.0 perspective. *International Journal of Mechanical. Industrial Science and Engineering, 8*(1), 37–44.

Çevik, D. (2019). KOBİ'lerde Sanayi 4.0'ın Uygulanabilirliği ve Yönetici Bakış Açılarının Değerlendirilmesi. *Uluslararası Bilimsel Araştırmalar Dergisi, 4*(2), 277–291.

Cin, A. (2012). *Türkiye'de KOBİ'lerin sorunları ve çözüm önerileri* (Master's thesis). Trakya Üniversitesi Sosyal Bilimler Enstitüsü.

Cooper, J., & James, A. (2009). Challenges for database management in the internet of things. *IETE Technical Review, 26*(5), 320–329. doi:10.4103/0256-4602.55275

Drath, R., & Horch, A. (2014). Industrie 4.0: Hit or hype? *IEEE Industrial Electronics Magazine, 8*(2), 56–58. doi:10.1109/MIE.2014.2312079

Erol, S., Jäger, A., Hold, P., Ott, K., & Sihn, W. (2016). Tangible Industry 4.0: A scenario-based approach to learning for the future of production. *Procedia CIRP, 54*, 13–18. doi:10.1016/j.procir.2016.03.162

European Commission. (2019). Retrieved from https://ec.europa.eu/growth/smes/business-friendly-environment/sme-definition_en)

Hirsch-Kreinsen, H. (2014, June). Smart production systems. A new type of industrial process innovation. In DRUID society conference (pp. 16-18). Academic Press.

IIC. (2015). *The Industrial Internet Consortium, Fact Sheet.* Retrieved from https://www.iiconsortium.org/docs/IIC_FACT_SHEET.pdf

Iqbal, Q., & Nawaz, R. (2019). Rife information pollution (infollution) and virtual organizations in industry 4.0: within reality causes and consequences. In *Big Data and Knowledge Sharing in Virtual Organizations* (pp. 117–135). IGI Global. doi:10.4018/978-1-5225-7519-1.ch005

Kalpande, S. D., Gupta, R. C., & Dandekar, M. D. (2010). SWOT analysis of small and medium scale enterprises implementing total quality management. *International Journal of Business, Management, and Social Science, 1*(1), 59–64.

Kesayak, B. (2019). *Endüstri Tarihine Kısa Bir Yolculuk.* Retrieved from https://www.endustri40.com/endustri-tarihine-kisa-bir-yolculuk/

Kiel, D., Müller, J. M., Arnold, C., & Voigt, K. I. (2017). Sustainable industrial value creation: Benefits and challenges of industry 4.0. *International Journal of Innovation Management, 21*(08), 1740015. doi:10.1142/S1363919617400151

Kleindienst, M., & Ramsauer, C. (2016). SMEs and Industry 4.0–Introducing a KPI based Procedure Model to identify Focus Areas in Manufacturing Industry. *Athens Journal of Business & Economics, 2*(2), 109-122.

Laudien, S. M., Spieth, P., & Clauß, T. (2017). Digitalization as Driver of Business Model Innovation: An Exploratory Analysis. *Proceedings of the 28th International Society for Professional Innovation Management (ISPIM) Conference.*

Lu, Y. (2017). Industry 4.0: A survey on technologies, applications and open research issues. *Journal of Industrial Information Integration, 6*, 1–10. doi:10.1016/j.jii.2017.04.005

Meyer, G. G., Wortmann, J. C., & Szirbik, N. B. (2011). Production monitoring and control with intelligent products. *International Journal of Production Research, 49*(5), 1303–1317. doi:10.1080/00207543.2010.518742

Morden, T. (2007). *Principles of strategic management.* Ashgate Publishing Limited.

Müller, J. M., Kiel, D., & Voigt, K. I. (2018). What drives the implementation of Industry 4.0? The role of opportunities and challenges in the context of sustainability. *Sustainability, 10*(1), 247. doi:10.3390u10010247

Müller, J. M., Maier, L., Veile, J., & Voigt, K. I. (2017). Cooperation strategies among SMEs for implementing industry 4.0. In *Proceedings of the Hamburg International Conference of Logistics (HICL)* (pp. 301-318). Academic Press.

Nuroğlu, E., & Nuroğlu, H. H. (2018a), Endüstri 4.0'ı Türkiye'nin Dış Ticareti İçin Bir Fırsat Penceresine Dönüştürmek. *Yönetim ve Ekonomi Araştırmaları Dergisi, 16*(1), 329-346.

Nuroğlu, E., & Nuroğlu, H. H. (2018b), Türkiye ve Almanya'nın Sanayide Dijital Dönüşümü: Yol Haritaları Ve Şirketlerin Karşılaştırması. *Süleyman Demirel Üniversitesi İktisadi ve İdari Bilimler Fakültesi Dergisi, 23*, 1537-1560.

Oettmeier, K., & Hofmann, E. (2017). Additive manufacturing technology adoption: An empirical analysis of general and supply chain-related determinants. *Journal of Business Economics, 87*(1), 97–124. doi:10.100711573-016-0806-8

Peukert, B., Benecke, S., Clavell, J., Neugebauer, S., Nissen, N. F., Uhlmann, E., & Finkbeiner, M. (2015). Addressing sustainability and flexibility in manufacturing via smart modular machine tool frames to support sustainable value creation. *Procedia CIRP, 29*, 514–519. doi:10.1016/j.procir.2015.02.181

Posada, J., Toro, C., Barandiaran, I., Oyarzun, D., Stricker, D., de Amicis, R., & Vallarino, I. (2015). Visual computing as a key enabling technology for industrie 4.0 and industrial internet. *IEEE Computer Graphics and Applications, 35*(2), 26–40. doi:10.1109/MCG.2015.45 PMID:25807506

Roblek, V., Meško, M., & Krapež, A. (2016). A complex view of industry 4.0. *SAGE Open, 6*(2). doi:10.1177/2158244016653987

Safar, L., Sopko, J., Bednar, S., & Poklemba, R. (2018). Concept of SME business model for industry 4.0 environment. *TEM Journal*, *7*(3), 626.

Sanders, A., Elangeswaran, C., & Wulfsberg, J. P. (2016). Industry 4.0 implies lean manufacturing Research activities in industry 4.0 function as enablers for lean manufacturing. *Journal of Industrial Engineering and Management*, *9*(3), 811–833. doi:10.3926/jiem.1940

Schröder, C. (2016). *The challenges of industry 4.0 for small and medium-sized enterprises*. Bonn, Germany: Friedrich-Ebert-Stiftung.

Sevinç, A., Gür, Ş., & Eren, T. (2018). Analysis of the difficulties of SMEs in industry 4.0 applications by analytical hierarchy process and analytical network process. *Processes*, *6*(12), 264. doi:10.3390/pr6120264

Small and Medium Enterprises Development Organization of Turkey. (2005). *Küçük ve Orta Büyüklükteki İşletmelerin Tanımı, Nitelikleri ve Sınıflandırılması Hakkında Yönetmelik*. Retrieved from https://www.kosgeb.gov.tr/ Content/Upload/Dosya/ Mevzuat/KOBI%CC% 87%E2%80%99lerin_Tan% C4%B1m%C4%B1,_ Nitelikleri_ve_S%C4% B1n%C4%B1fland% C4%B1r%C4%B1lmas% C4%B1_ Hakk%C4% B1nda_Yo% CC%88netmelik.pdf

Spath, D., Gerlach, S., Hämmerle, M., Schlund, S., & Strölin, T. (2013). Cyber-physical system for self-organized and flexible labor utilization. *Personnel*, *50*(22).

Stock, T., & Seliger, G. (2016). Opportunities for sustainable manufacturing in industry 4.0. *Procedia CIRP*, *40*, 536–541. doi:10.1016/j.procir.2016.01.129

Thames, L., & Schaefer, D. (2016). Software-defined cloud manufacturing for industry 4.0. *Procedia CIRP*, *52*, 12–17. doi:10.1016/j.procir.2016.07.041

The Union of Chambers and Commodity Exchanges of Turkey. (n.d.). Retrieved from https://www.tobb.org.tr

Tjahjono, B., Esplugues, C., Ares, E., & Pelaez, G. (2017). What does industry 4.0 mean to the supply chain? *Procedia Manufacturing*, *13*, 1175–1182. doi:10.1016/j.promfg.2017.09.191

Todorov, K. (Ed.). (2014). *Handbook of research on strategic management in small and medium enterprises*. IGI Global. doi:10.4018/978-1-4666-5962-9

Toffler, A. (1970). *Future Schock*. New York.

TUSIAD & BCG. (2016). *Sanayi 4.0 Raporu*. Retrieved from http://www.tusiad.org/indir/2016/sanayi-40.pdf

Üçler, Ç., & Vayvay, Ö. (2018). KOBİ'lerde Eş Zamanlı Mühendislik: Otomotiv Tedarikçi Sektöründe Bir Uygulama. *Uluslararası Mühendislik Araştırma ve Geliştirme Dergisi*, *10*(2), 76–91.

Vrchota, J., Volek, T., & Novotná, M. (2019). Factors Introducing Industry 4.0 to SMES, Social Sciences, MDPI. *Open Access Journal*, *8*(5), 1–10.

Wikipedia. (2019). *Kobi Tanımı*. Retrieved from https://tr.wikipedia.org/wiki/KOBİ.

KEY TERMS AND DEFINITIONS

Industry 4.0: Industry 4.0 is the fourth industrial revolution that envisages the integration of robots, artificial intelligence and simulation technologies into production processes.

SMEs: It refers to small and medium-sized enterprises (SMEs) that employing less than 250 workers and annual financial balance sheet total not exceeding € 43 m.

Strategic Management: It is a process containing planning, monitoring, analysis, and assessment of all that is necessary for an organization to meet its goals and objectives.

Compilation of References

Aboelmaged, M. G. (2014). Linking operations performance to knowledge management capability: The mediating role of innovation performance. *Production Planning and Control*, *25*(1), 44–58. doi:10.1080/09537287.2012.655802

Abor, J., & Quartey, P. (2010). Issues in SME development in Ghana and South Africa. *International Research Journal of Finance and Economics*, *39*(6), 215–228.

Adam, E. E., Jr., & Ebert, R. J. (2007). Production and Operations Management Concepts, Models, and Behaviour (5th ed.). New Delhi, India: Prentice-Hall of India Private Limited.

Adams, A. (2002). Internal organizational factors influencing corporate social and ethical reporting: Beyond current theorizing. *Accounting, Auditing & Accountability Journal*, *15*(2), 223–250. doi:10.1108/09513570210418905

Addo-Tenkorang, R., & Helo, P. T. (2016). Big data applications in operations/supply-chain management: A literature review. *Computers & Industrial Engineering*, *101*, 528–543. doi:10.1016/j.cie.2016.09.023

ADEI. (2017). *El trabajo del futuro*. Retrieved from http://observatorioadei.es/publicaciones/NotaTecnica-El-trabajo-del-futuro.pdf

AENOR. (2015). *Servicios de traducción. Requisitos para los servicios de traducción* (UNE-EN ISO 17100:2015). Retrieved from https://www.aenor.com/normas-y-libros/buscador-de-normas/iso/?c=059149

Agarwal, R., & Dhar, V. (2014). Big data, data science, and analytics: The opportunity and challenge for IS research. *Information Systems Research*, *25*(3), 443–448. doi:10.1287/isre.2014.0546

Agensi Inovasi Malaysia. (2013). National Biomass Strategy 2020: New wealth creation for Malaysia's biomass industry. Cyberjaya. Retrieved from https://docs.wixstatic.com/ugd/43b4fe_00564483596c43d5a1619e82131f1832.pdf

Ahmed, T., Mouratidis, H., & Preston, D. (2009). Website design guidelines: High power distance and high-context culture. *International Journal of Cyber Society and Education*, *2*(1), 47–60.

Akdağ, R. (2011). *Kamu Hastanelerinin Genel Verimlik Değerlendirmesi*. Ankara: Araştırma Raporu, Sağlık Bakanlığı.

Akkaya, B., & Tabak, A. (2017). The impact of dynamic capabilities on firm perceived marketing performance of small and medium-sized enterprises. Transnational Marketing Journal, 5(2), 121–125. doi:10.33182/tmj.v5i2.383

Albaladejo, M. (2001). *Determinants and policies to foster the competitiveness of SME clusters: Evidence from Latin America*. Oxford, UK: Queen Elizabeth House.

Aldrich, H., & Zimmer, C. (1986). Entrepreneurship through a social network. In D. L. Sexton & R. W. Smilor (Eds.), *The Art and Science of Entrepreneurship* (pp. 3–25). Cambridge, UK: Ballinger Publishing.

Alikaj, A., Nguyen, C. N., & Medina, E. (2017). Differentiating the impact of CSR strengths and concerns on firm performance. *Journal of Management Development*, *36*(3), 401–409. doi:10.1108/JMD-04-2016-0058

Ali, S. (2013). The small and medium enterprises and poverty in Pakistan: An empirical analysis. *European Journal of Business and Economics*, *8*(2), 25–30. doi:10.12955/ejbe.v8i2.376

Alqahtani, K. M. (2016). *Challenges of Innovation for Chinese Small and Medium-sized Enterprises: Case Study in Beijing*. DOI: .v9n12p165 doi:10.5539/ibr

Alshamaila, Y., Papagiannidis, S., & Li, F. (2013). Cloud computing adoption by SMEs in the northeast of England: A multi-perspective framework. *Journal of Enterprise Information Management*, *26*(3), 250–275. doi:10.1108/17410391311325225

Alshanty, A. M., Emeagwali, O. L., Ibrahim, B., & Alrwashdeh, M. (2019). The effect of market-sensing capability on the knowledge creation process and innovation evidence from SMEs in Jordan. Management Science Letters, 9(5), 727–736. doi:10.5267/j.msl.2019.1.016

Altinay, L., Brookes, M., Yeung, R., & Aktas, G. (2014). Franchisees' perceptions of relationship development in franchise partnerships. *Journal of Services Marketing*, *28*(6), 509–519. doi:10.1108/JSM-09-2013-0240

Alüftekin, N., Yüksel, Ö., Taş, A., Çakar, G., & Bayraktar, F. (2012). Küresel krizden çıkışta kümelenme modeli: Tekstil ve hazır giyim sektörü örneği. *Uluslararası Yönetim İktisat ve İşletme Dergisi*, *5*(10), 1–19.

Ambrosini, V., Bowman, C., & Collier, N. (2009). Dynamic capabilities: An exploration of how firms renew their resource base. *British Journal of Management*, *20*, 1–41. doi:10.1111/j.1467-8551.2008.00610.x

Aminuddin, A. S. A., & Nawawi, M. K. M. Investigation of the Philosophy Practised in Green and Lean Manufacturing Management International Journal of Customer Relationship Marketing and Management, 4(1), 1-12, January-March 2013. http://www.oecd.org/els/health-systems/health-data.htm

Amui, L. B. L., Jabbour, C. J. C., de Sousa Jabbour, A. B. L., & Kannan, D. (2017). Sustainability as a dynamic organizational capability: A systematic review and a future agenda toward a sustainable transition. *Journal of Cleaner Production*, *142*, 308–322. doi:10.1016/j.jclepro.2016.07.103

Anand, G., Ward, P., Tatikonda, M., & Schilling, D. (2009). Dynamic capabilities through continuous improvement infrastructure. *Journal of Operations Management*, *27*(6), 444–461. doi:10.1016/j.jom.2009.02.002

Anggadwita, G., & Mustafid, Q. Y. (2014). Identification of factors influencing the performance of small-medium enterprises (SMEs). *Procedia: Social and Behavioral Sciences*, *115*, 415–423. doi:10.1016/j.sbspro.2014.02.448

Anna, Y. (2017). The interplay between social capital and international opportunities: A processual study of international "take-off" episodes in Chinese SMEs. *Industrial Marketing Management*. Doi:10.1016/j.indmarman.2017.07.006

Anonymous. (2018). *Industry 4.0 – opportunities and challenges for SMEs in the North Sea Region*. Retrieved from https://northsearegion.eu/media/7320/growin-40-desk-study.pdf

Anonymous. (2019). Retrieved from http://www.isc.hbs.edu/competitiveness-economic development/frameworks-and-key-concepts/pages/clusters.aspx

Apilioğulları, L. (2018). Üretim Endüstrisi Dijital Dönüşüm Süreci Kavramsal İlişki Haritası. *Anemon Muş Alparslan Üniversitesi Sosyal Bilimler Dergisi*, *7*(3), 1–1.

Arıcıoğlu, M. A., & Yiğitol, B. (2019). Paradigm Change in Strategic Management. In Handbook of Research on Managerial Thinking in Global Business Economics (pp. 179-195). IGI Global.

Arıcıoğlu, M. A., Gökçe, Ş., & Koraş, M. (2013). Kümelenme ve rekabet analizi için bir uygulama. *Selçuk Üniversitesi Sosyal Bilimler Enstitüsü Dergisi*, (30), 2-18.

Arıcıoğlu, M. A., Yiğitol, B., & Yilmaz, A. (2018). Kümelenmenin anlamı: akademik bakış açılarının çözümlenmesi üzerine bir deneme. Kastamonu University Journal of Economics & Administrative Sciences Faculty, 20(4).

Artech, T., Lee, D., Nelson, D., & Walker, J. (2010). The determinants of corporate sustainability performance. *Accounting and Finance*, *50*(1), 31–51. doi:10.1111/j.1467-629X.2009.00315.x

Arthur, J. B. (1994). Effects of Human Resource Systems on Manufacturing Performance and Turnover. *Academy of Management Journal*, *37*, 670–687.

Arthur, W. B. (1990). 'Silicon Valley' locational clusters: When do increasing returns imply monopoly? *Mathematical Social Sciences*, *19*(3), 235–251. doi:10.1016/0165-4896(90)90064-E

Aryanto, R., Fontana, A., & Afiff, A. Z. (2015). Strategic Human Resource Management, Innovation Capability, and Performance: An Empirical Study in Indonesia Software Industry. *Procedia: Social and Behavioral Sciences*, *211*(September), 874–879. doi:10.1016/j.sbspro.2015.11.115

Asah, F., Fatoki, O. O., & Rungani, E. (2015). The impact of motivations, personal values, and management skills on the performance of SMEs in South Africa. *African Journal of Economic and Management Studies*, *6*(3), 308–322. doi:10.1108/AJEMS-01-2013-0009

Attar, A. A., Gupta, A. K., & Desai, D. B. (2012). A Study of Various Factors Affecting Labour Productivity and Methods to Improve It. *IOSR Journal of Mechanical and Civil Engineering,* 11-14. Online available at http://www.iosrjournals.org/iosr-jmce/papers/sicete(civil)-volume1/3.pdf

Attia, A. M. (2016). Effect of quality management on supply chain and organizational performance in the Egyptian textile industry. *International Journal of Business Performance Management*, *17*(2), 198–222. doi:10.1504/IJBPM.2016.075549

Atzori, L., Iera, A., & Morabito, G. (2010). The Internet of Things: A survey. *Computer Networks*, *54*(15), 2787–2805. doi:10.1016/j.comnet.2010.05.010

Avolio, B. J., Kahai, S., & Dodge, G. E. (2000). E-Leadership: Implications For Theory, Research, and Practice. *The Leadership Quarterly*, *11*(4), 615–668. doi:10.1016/S1048-9843(00)00062-X

Baack, D. W., & Singh, N. (2007). Culture and web communications. *Journal of Business Research*, *60*(3), 181–188. doi:10.1016/j.jbusres.2006.11.002

Bacak, Ç. (2019). *Kümelenmenin kobi'lere sağladığı avantajlar ve kobi'lerin finansmana erişim kolaylıkları.* Retrieved from https://anahtar.sanayi.gov.tr/tr/news/kumelenmenin-kobilere-sagladigi-avantajlar-ve-kobilerin-finansmana-erisim-kolayliklari/107

Baheti, R., & Gill, H. (2011). Cyber-physical systems. *The Impact of Control Technology*, *12*(1), 161–166.

Bala Subrahmanya, M. H. (2004). Small Industry and Globalization: Implications, Performance, and Prospects. *Economic and Political Weekly*, *39*(18), 1826–1834.

Ballestero, F., & Pérez, M. (2017). El papel del Estado ante la digitalización de la economía. Estrategia digital y políticas públicas. *Información Comercial Española, ICE. Revista de economía*, *898*, 113–130.

Bamber, G. J., Bartram, T., & Stanton, P. (2017). HRM and workplace innovations: Formulating research questions. *Personnel Review*, *46*(7), 1216–1227. doi:10.1108/PR-10-2017-0292

Barber, W., & Badre, A. (1998). Culturability: The merging of culture and usability. In *Proceedings of the 4th Conference on Human Factors and the Web*. AT&T Labs.

Bargal, H., Dashmishra, M., & Sharma, A. (2009). Performance Analysis of Small Scale Industries - A Study of Pre-liberalization and Post-liberalization period. *International Journal of Business and Management*, *1*(2), 17–26.

Barney, J. B. (1991). Firm Resources and Sustained Competitive. *Journal of Management*, *17*(1), 99–120. doi:10.1177/014920639101700108

Barney, J. B. (2001). Resource-based theories of competitive advantage: A ten-year retrospective on the resource-based view. *Journal of Management*, *27*(6), 643–650. doi:10.1177/014920630102700602

Bass, B. M. (1990). From transactional to transformational leadership: Learning to share the vision. Organi. *Organizational Dynamics*, *18*(3), 19–31. doi:10.1016/0090-2616(90)90061-S

Baumgartner, R. (2014). Managing corporate sustainability and CSR: A conceptual framework combining values, strategies, and instruments contributing to sustainable development. *Corporate Social Responsibility and Environmental Management*, *21*(5), 258–271. doi:10.1002/csr.1336

Baumgartner, R. J., & Ebner, D. (2010). Corporate sustainability strategies: Sustainability profiles and maturity levels. *Sustainable Development*, *18*(2), 76–89. doi:10.1002/sd.447

Bayülken, Y. (2007). KOBİ'ler Nasıl Rekabet Edecek? *Mühendis ve Makina Dergisi, 48*(570), 10-14.

BCG. (2019). *Embracing industry 4.0 rediscovering growth*. Retrieved from https://www.bcg.com/capabilities/operations/embracing-industry-4.0-rediscovering-growth.aspx

Bedi, K. (2015). *Production and Operations Management* (3rd ed.). New Delhi, India: Oxford University Press.

Belderbos, R., Carree, M., & Lokshin, B. (2004). Cooperative R&D and firm performance. *Research Policy*, *33*(10), 1477–1492. doi:10.1016/j.respol.2004.07.003

Bell, D. V., & Cheung, Y. K. A. (Eds.). (2009). *Introduction to Sustainable Development-Volume I*. EOLSS Publications.

Ben Salem, C., & Zouaoui, M. (2017). A Taxonomic Approach for the Study of Manufacturing Tunisian SME. *Journal of Organizational Management Studies*, *2017*, 1–11. doi:10.5171/2017.189595

Benetto, E., Becker, M., & Welfring, J. (2009). Life Cycle Assessment of Oriented Strand Boards (OSB): From Process Innovation to Ecodesign. *Environmental Science & Technology*, *43*(15), 6003–6009. doi:10.1021/es900707u PMID:19731710

Benneworth, P., & Hospers, G. J. (2007). The new economic geography of old industrial regions: Universities as global—local pipelines. *Environment and Planning. C, Government & Policy*, *25*(6), 779–802. doi:10.1068/c0620

Bianchi, M., Campodall'Orto, S., Frattini, F., & Vercesi, P. (2010). Enabling open innovation in small and medium-sized enterprises: How to find alternative applications for your technologies. *Research Management*, *40*(4), 414–431.

Bishop, J. (1990). In value-added manufacturing, customer calls the shots. *Forest Industries*, *1990*, 29–31.

Bolaños-Medina, A. (2003). Dificultades y estrategias de la localización de sitios web comerciales del inglés al español. In E. Santiago Posteguillo & J. Ramón Prado (Eds.), Internet in Linguistics, Translation and Literary Studies (pp. 241-262). Castellón de la Plana: Publicacions de la Universitat Jaume I.

Bolman, L. G., & Deal, T. E. (1984). *Modern approaches to understanding and managing organizations*. Jossey-Bass.

Bos-Brouwers, H. (2010). Corporate sustainability and innovation in SMEs: Evidence of themes and activities in practices. *Business Strategy and the Environment*, *19*(7), 417–453.

Bosco, A., Reinartz, B., & Müller, S. (2009). *Differential Reynolds stress model and grid adaptation for hypersonic double wedge simulations.* Paper presented at the ICHMT Digital Library Online. 10.1615/ICHMT.2009.TurbulHeat-MassTransf.650

Bos-Nehles, A., Renkema, M., & Janssen, M. (2017). HRM and innovative work behavior: A systematic literature review. *Personnel Review*, *46*(7), 1228–1253. doi:10.1108/PR-09-2016-0257

Bourgeois, D. W., & Terence, R. (1978). *The effects of different organizational environments upon decisions about organizational structure*. Academic Press.

Bracker, J. (2012). Historical Development of Strategic Management Concept. *Management*, *5*(2), 219–224.

Braun, P., McRae-Williams, P., & Lowe, J. (2005). Small business clustering Accessing knowledge through local networks. *Journal of New Business.*

Brettel, M., Friederichsen, N., Keller, M., & Rosenberg, M. (2014). How virtualization, decentralization and network building change the manufacturing landscape: An industry 4.0 perspective. *International Journal of Mechanical. Industrial Science and Engineering*, *8*(1), 37–44.

Breznik, L., & Hisrich, R. D. (2014). Dynamic capabilities vs. innovation capability: Are they related? *Journal of Small Business and Enterprise Development*, *21*(3), 368–384. doi:10.1108/JSBED-02-2014-0018

Brockhoff, K. (2003). Customers' perspectives on involvement in new product development. *International Journal of Technology Management*, *26*(5-6), 464–481. doi:10.1504/IJTM.2003.003418

Brookfield, J. (2008). Firm clustering and specialization A study of Taiwan's machine tool industry. *Small Business Economics*, *30*(4), 405–422. doi:10.100711187-007-9047-0

Brown, K., & Siri, E. (2012). Sustainable adaptation to climate change: prioritizing social equity and environmental integrity. Routledge. doi:10.4324/9781849776912

Brown, J. S., & Duguid, P. (1991). Organizational learning and communities-of-practice: Toward a unified view of working, learning, and innovation. *Organization Science*, *2*(1), 40–57. doi:10.1287/orsc.2.1.40

Buil, I., Martínez, E., & Matute, J. (2018). The role of identi fi cation, engagement and proactive personality. *International Journal of Hospitality Management Transformational Leadership and Employee Performance.*

Buse, K., & Howkes, S. (2015). Health in the sustainable development goals: Ready for a paradigm shift? *Globalization and Health*, *11*(1), 13. doi:10.1186/s12992-015-0098-8 PubMed

Çağlar, E. (2018). *Kümelenmeler ve Rekabet Gücü.* Retrieved from https://www.tepav.org.tr/upload/files/haber/1255437510r3578.Kumelenmeler_ve_Rekabet_Gucu.pdf

Calantone, R. J., Cavusgil, S. T., & Zhao, Y. (2002). Learning orientation, firm innovation capability, and firm performance. *Industrial Marketing Management*, *31*(6), 515–524. doi:10.1016/S0019-8501(01)00203-6

Çalışkan, A. Ö. (2012). Sürdürülebilirlik Raporlaması. Muhasebe ve Vergi Uygulamalari Dergisi (MUVU). *Journal of Accounting & Taxation Studies*, *5*(1).

Cameron, K. S., & Quinn, R. E. (2011). *Diagnosing and Changing Organizational Culture: Based on the Competing Values Framework.* San Francisco, CA: Jossey-Bass.

Castelo-Branco, I., Cruz-Jesus, F., & Oliveira, T. (2019). Assessing Industry 4.0 readiness in manufacturing: Evidence for the European Union. *Computers in Industry*, *107*, 22–32. doi:10.1016/j.compind.2019.01.007

Cath, C., Wachter, S., Mittelstadt, B., Taddeo, M., & Floridi, L. (2018). Artificial Intelligence and the 'Good Society': The US, EU, and UK approach. *Science and Engineering Ethics*, *24*(2), 505–528. PubMed

Cavagnaro, E., & George, H. (2017). The three levels of sustainability. Routledge. doi:10.4324/9781351277969

Caymaz, E., Soran, S., & Erenel, F. (2014). The Relationship Between Corporate Sustainability And Corporate Social Responsibility In Business: Global Compact Turkey. *Journal of Management, Marketing, and Logistics.*, *1*(3), 208–217.

Çelik, Y. (2006). Sürdürülebilir kalkınma kavramı ve sağlık. *Hacettepe Sağlık İdaresi Dergisi*, *9*(1), 19–37.

CEPYME. (2017). *Informe anual de empleo en las pymes*. Retrieved from http://www.cepyme.es

Certo, S. C., & Certo, S. T. (2006). *Modern Management*. London: Pearson/Prentice Hall.

Çevik, D. (2019). KOBİ'lerde Sanayi 4.0'ın Uygulanabilirliği ve Yönetici Bakış Açılarının Değerlendirilmesi. *Uluslararası Bilimsel Araştırmalar Dergisi*, *4*(2), 277–291.

Chandrakumara, A. (2011). Value of values for practicing managers and leaders. *Problems and Perspectives in Management*, *9*(2), 80–88.

Chang, D. R., & Cho, H. (2008). Organizational memory influences new product success. *Journal of Business Research*, *61*(1), 13–23. doi:10.1016/j.jbusres.2006.05.005

Chang, W. J., Liao, S. H., & Te Wu, T. (2017). Relationships among organizational culture, knowledge sharing, and innovation capability: A case of the automobile industry in Taiwan. *Knowledge Management Research and Practice*, *15*(3), 471–490. doi:10.1057/s41275-016-0042-6

Chaston, I., Badger, B., Mangles, T., & Sadler-Smith, E. (2001). Organizational learning style, competencies, and learning systems in small, UK manufacturing firms. *International Journal of Operations & Production Management*, *21*(11), 1417–1432. doi:10.1108/EUM0000000006224

Chen, D. (2011). *Research on Performance Management of Chinese SME*. DOI: .v6n4p263 doi:10.5539/ijbm

Chen, D. Q., Preston, D. S., & Swink, M. (2015). How the use of big data analytics affects value creation in supply chain management. *Journal of Management Information Systems*, *32*(4), 4–39. doi:10.1080/07421222.2015.1138364

Chen, H., Chiang, R. H. L., & Storey, V. C. (2018). Business Intelligence and Analytics: From Big Data to Big Impact. *Management Information Systems Quarterly*, *36*(4), 1165–1188. doi:10.2307/41703503

Chesbrough, H. (2003b). Open Innovation: The New Imperative for Creating and Profiting from Technology. Harvard Business School Publishing Corporation.

Chesbrough, H. (2003a). *Open innovation*. Boston: Harvard Business School Press.

Chesbrough, H., Vanhaverbeke, W., & West, J. (2006). *Open innovation: Researching a new paradigm*. Oxford University.

Chin, W. W. (2010). How to write up and report PLS analyses. Handbook of partial least squares, 655-690.

Chin, W. W., & Newstead, P. (1999). Structural Equation Modelling Analysis with Small Samples Using Partial Least Squares. In *Statistical Strategies for Small Sample Research* (pp. 307–341). Thousand Oaks, CA: Sage Publications.

Chittithaworn, C., Islam, M. A., Keawchana, T., & Yusuf, D. H. M. (2011). Factors Affecting Business Success of Small & Medium Enterprises (SMEs) in Thailand. *Asian Social Science*, *7*(5), 180–190. doi:10.5539/ass.v7n5p180

Chiva, R., & Alegre, J. (2005). Organizational learning and organizational knowledge: Towards the integration of two approaches. *Management Learning*, *36*(1), 49–68. doi:10.1177/1350507605049906

Choi, S., & Ng, A. (2011). Environmental and economic dimensions of sustainability and price effects on consumer responses. *Journal of Business Ethics*, *104*(2), 269–282. doi:10.1007/s10551-011-0908-8

Chong, W. K., Shafaghi, M., & Tan, B. L. (2011). *Development of a business-to-business critical success factors (B2B CSFs) framework for Chinese SMEs*. Doi:10.1108/02634501111153700

Chtourou, H., & Triki, M. (2017). Commitment to corporate social responsibility and financial performance: A study in the Tunisian context. Social Responsibility Journal, 13(2), 370–389. doi:10.1108/SRJ-05-2016-0079

Cin, A. (2012). *Türkiye'de KOBİ'lerin sorunları ve çözüm önerileri* (Master's thesis). Trakya Üniversitesi Sosyal Bilimler Enstitüsü.

Claudy, M. C., Peterson, M., & Pagell, M. (2016). The Roles of Sustainability Orientation and Market Knowledge Competence in New Product Development Success. *Journal of Product Innovation Management*, *33*, 72–85. doi:10.1111/jpim.12343

Cohen, J. (1988). *Statistical power analysis*. Academic Press.

Cohen, J. (1988). *Statistical power analysis for the behavioral sciences* (2nd ed.). Hillsdale, NJ: Lawrence Erlbaum Associates.

Cohen, W. M., & Levinthal, D. A. (1990). Absorptive capacity: A new perspective on learning and innovation. *Administrative Science Quarterly*, *35*(1), 128–152. doi:10.2307/2393553

Colombo, M. G., Piva, E., & Rossi-Lamastra, C. (2014). Open innovation and within-industry diversification in small and medium enterprises: The case of open source software firms. *Research Policy*, *43*(5), 891–902. doi:10.1016/j.respol.2013.08.015

Combs, J. G., Michael, S. C., & Castrogiovanni, G. J. (2004). *Franchising: A Review and Avenues to Greater Theoretical Diversity*. Academic Press.

Conti, M., & Passarella, A. (2018). *The Internet of People : A human and data-centric paradigm for the Next Generation Internet*. Academic Press.

Cooper, J., & James, A. (2009). Challenges for database management in the internet of things. *IETE Technical Review*, *26*(5), 320–329. doi:10.4103/0256-4602.55275

Crosby, M., Pattanayak, P., Verma, S., & Kalyanaraman, V. (2016). Blockchain technology: Beyond bitcoin. Applied Innovation Review, (2), 6–10.

Culyer, A. J. (2005). Involving stakeholders in health care decisions: The experience of the National Institute for Health and Clinical Excellence (NICE) in England and Wales. *Healthcare Quarterly*, *8*(3), 56–60. doi:10.12927/hcq..17155 PubMed

Da Xu, L., Xu, E. L., & Li, L. (2018). Industry 4.0: State of the art and future trends. *International Journal of Production Research*, *56*(8), 2941–2962. doi:10.1080/00207543.2018.1444806

Dabić, M., Lažnjak, J., Smallbone, D., & Švarc, J. (2018). Intellectual capital, organizational climate, innovation culture, and SME performance: Evidence from Croatia. *Journal of Small Business and Enterprise Development*. doi:10.1108/JSBED-04-2018-0117

Dam, H. V., Brøgger, M. N., & Zethsen, K. K. (2018). Introduction. In Moving boundaries in translation studies, (pp. 1-11). London: Routledge.

Darroch, J., & McNaughton, R. (2003). Beyond market orientation: Knowledge management and the innovativeness of New Zealand firms. *European Journal of Marketing*, *37*(3/4), 572–593. doi:10.1108/03090560310459096

Dasanayaka, S. W. S. B. (2019). *Enhancing the competitiveness of small and medium scale enterprises through clusters*. Retrieved from http://dl.lib.mrt.ac.lk/handle/123/14013?show=full

Das, P. (2017). Micro, Small and Medium Enterprises (MSME) in India: Opportunities, Issues & Challenges. *Great Lakes Herald*, *11*(1), 77–88.

Davies, M. A. P., Lassar, W., Manolis, C., Prince, M., & Winsor, R. D. (2011). A model of trust and compliance in franchise relationships. *Journal of Business Venturing*, *26*(3), 321–323. doi:10.1016/j.jbusvent.2009.09.005

Davila, T. (2000). An empirical study on the drivers of MCS: Design in new product development. *Accounting, Organizations and Society*, *25*(4-5), 383–409. doi:10.1016/S0361-3682(99)00034-3

Davis, G. F., & Cobb, J. A. (2010). *Resource Dependence Theory : Past and future*. Academic Press.

Davis, C. H., & Vladica, F. (2006). Use of Internet technologies and e-business solutions: A structural model of sources of business value among Canadian micro-enterprises. *Proceedings of the 39th Annual Hawaii International Conference on System Sciences*, 1-10. 10.1109/HICSS.2006.519

de Araújo, C. C. S., Pedron, C. D., & Bitencourt, C. (2018). Identifying and assessing the scales of dynamic capabilities: A systematic literature review. Revista de Gestão, 25(4), 390–412. doi:10.1108/REGE-12-2017-0021

De Troyer, O., Mushtaha, A. N., Stengers, H., Baetens, M., Boers, F., Casteleyn, S., & Plessers, P. (2006). On cultural differences in local web interfaces. *Journal of Web Engineering*, *5*, 246–264.

Demircan, N., & Ert, A. (2010). Comparing Innovation Capability of Small and Medium-Sized Enterprises : Examining the Effects of Organizational Culture and Empowerment. *Journal of Small Business Management*, *48*(3), 325–359. doi:10.1111/j.1540-627X.2010.00297.x

Demirkan, H., & Delen, D. (2013). Leveraging the capabilities of service-oriented decision support systems: Putting analytics and big data in the cloud. *Decision Support Systems*, *55*(1), 412–421. doi:10.1016/j.dss.2012.05.048

Dempsey, N., Bramley, G., Power, S., & Brown, C. (2011). The Social Dimension of Sustainable Development: Defining Urban Social Sustainability. *Sustainable Development*, *19*(5), 289–300. doi:10.1002/sd.417

Department of Statistics Malaysia. (2019). Small and Medium Enterprises (SMEs) Performance 2018. Retrieved from https://www.dosm.gov.my/v1/index.php?r=column/cthemeByCat&cat=159&bul_id=R0Vka2RpeVJ0cUlpR3BqdjhudDZhdz09&menu_id=TE5CRUZCblh4ZTZMODZIbmk2aWRRQT09

Dhewanto, W., Prasetio, E. A., Ratnaningtyas, S., Herliana, S., Chaerudin, R., Aina, Q., … Rachmawaty, E. (2012). Moderating Effect of Cluster on Firm's Innovation Capability and Business Performance: A Conceptual Framework. Procedia - Social and Behavioral Sciences, 65(ICIBSoS), 867–872. doi:10.1016/j.sbspro.2012.11.212

Di Giovanni, E. (2008). Translations, transcreations, and trans representations of India in the Italian media. *Meta: Journal des traducteurs, 53*(1), 26-43.

Diaz-Fernandez, M., Bornay-Barrachina, M., & Lopez-Cabrales, A. (2015). Innovation and firm performance: The role of human resource management practices. Evidence-Based HRM, 3(1), 64–80. doi:10.1108/EBHRM-10-2012-0012

Dickey, M. H., Harrison McKnight, D., & George, J. F. (2008). The role of trust in franchise organizations. *The International Journal of Organizational Analysis*, *15*(3), 251–282. doi:10.1108/19348830710880938

Dictionary, C. (2019). Retrieved from Cambridge Dictionary website: https://dictionary.cambridge.org

Dictionary, O. (2019). Retrieved November 12, 2019, from Lexico Powered by Oxford website: https://www.lexico.com/en/definition/data

Didonet, S., Simmons, G., Villavicencio, G. D., Palmer, M., Didonet, S., & Simmons, G. (2012). The relationship between small business market orientation and environmental uncertainty. *Marketing Intelligence & Planning*, *30*(7), 757–779. doi:10.1108/02634501211273841

Dinca, V. M., Dima, A. M., & Rozsa, Z. (2019). Determinants of Cloud Computing Adoption by Romanian SMEs In The Digital Economy. *Journal of Business Economics and Management*, *20*(4), 798–820. doi:10.3846/jbem.2019.9856

Dinh, D. N. (2017). *Medschool 4.0: how to succeed in the smart revolution of healthcare*. Retrieved 26/7/2019 https://europeansting.com/2017/03/18/medschool-4-0-how-to-succeed-in-the-smart-revolution-of-healthcare/

Dinh, J. E., Lord, R. G., Gardner, W. L., Meuser, J. D., Liden, R. C., & Hu, J. (2014). Leadership theory and research in the new millennium: Current theoretical trends and changing perspectives. *The Leadership Quarterly*, *25*(1), 36–62. doi:10.1016/j.leaqua.2013.11.005

Dixit, A., & Pandey, A. K. (2011). SMEs and Economic Growth in India: Cointegration Analysis. *The IUP Journal of Financial Economics*, *9*(2), 41–59.

Doane, D. & MacGillivray, A. (2001). Economic Sustainability: The Business of Staying in Business. The SIGMA Project, R&D Report.

Donkor, J., Donkor, G. N. A., Kankam-Kwarteng, C., & Aidoo, E. (2018). Innovative capability, strategic goals and financial performance of SMEs in Ghana. Asia Pacific Journal of Innovation and Entrepreneurship, 12(2), 238–254. doi:10.1108/APJIE-10-2017-0033

Dormann, C., & Chisalita, C. (2002). Cultural values in web site design. In *11th European Conference on Cognitive Ergonomics*. ECCE.

Døving, E., & Gooderham, P. N. (2008). Dynamic Capabilities As Antecedents Of The Scope Of Related Diversification: The Case Of Small Firm Accountancy Practices. *Strategic Management Journal*, *29*(8), 841–857. doi:10.1002/smj.683

Drath, R., & Horch, A. (2014). Industrie 4.0: Hit or hype? *IEEE Industrial Electronics Magazine*, *8*(2), 56–58. doi:10.1109/MIE.2014.2312079

Drucker, P. F. (1986). *Management: Tasks, Responsibilities, Practices*. New York: Truman Talley Books/ E.P. Dutton.

Drucker, P. F. (2018). *The Effective Executive*. London: Taylor&Francis Group; doi:10.4324/9780080549354.

Drucker, P. F., Bahçıvangil, İ., & Gorbon, G. (2014). *21. Yüzyıl için yönetim tartışmaları*. Epsilon.

du Plessis, N., & Grobler, A. F. (2014). Achieving sustainability through strategically driven CSR in the South\nAfrican retail sector. *Public Relations Review*, *40*(2), 267–277. doi:10.1016/j.pubrev.2013.11.009

Duh, M. (2003). Family enterprises as an important factor in economic development: The case of Slovenia. *Journal of Enterprising Culture*, *11*(2), 111–130. doi:10.1142/S021849580300007X

Duong, D. H., & Swierczek, F. W. (2019). The Impact of Top Management Team and Organizational Culture on Product/Service and Process Innovation in Vietnamese Banks. *Applied Finance and Banking*, *9*(2), 55–68.

Durst, S., & Edvardsson, I. R. (2012). Knowledge management in SMEs: A literature review. *Journal of Knowledge Management*, *16*(6), 879–903. doi:10.1108/13673271211276173

Durst, S., Mention, A.-L., & Poutanen, P. (2015). Service innovation and its impact: What do we know about? *Investigaciones Europeas de Dirección y Economía de la Empresa*, *21*(2), 65–72. doi:10.1016/j.iedee.2014.07.003

Dwyer, O. (1987). *Output Sector Munificence Effects on the Internal Political Economy of Marketing Channels*. Academic Press.

Dyllick, T., & Hockerts, K. (2002). Beyond the business case for corporate sustainability. *Business Strategy and the Environment*, *11*, 130–141.

Edmister, R. O. (1970). *Financial ratios as discriminant predictors of small business failure* (Doctoral dissertation). The Ohio State University, Columbus, OH.

Eisenhardt, K., & Martin, J. (2000). Dynamic Capabilities. What are they. *Strategic Management Journal*, *21*(10-11), 1105–1122. doi:10.1002/1097-0266(200010/11)21:10/11<1105::AID-SMJ133>3.0.CO;2-E

Ekinci, A. P. D. E. D., & Emsen, Ö. S. (2014). *Teorik perspektifte rekabet ve kümelenme ilişkileri: bölgesel kalkınmaya etkileri The relations between competition and cluster in the theoretical perspective: the effects on regional development*. Retrieved from https://www.avekon.org/papers/1031.pdf

Elbanna, S., & Gherib, J. (2012). Miller ' s environmental uncertainty scale : An extension to the Arab world. *International Journal of Commerce and Management*, *22*(1), 7–25. doi:10.1108/10569211211204483

Ellermann, H., Kreutter, P., & Messner, W. (2016). The Palgrave handbook of managing continuous business transformation. In *The Palgrave Handbook of Managing Continuous Business Transformation*. Academic Press.

Emerson, R. W. (2014). Assessing Awuah v. Coverall North America, Inc.: The Franchisee as a Dependent Contractor. *Stanford Journal of Law, Business & Finance, 19*(2), 203–235.

ENDNOTES

Engin, E., & Akgöz, B. E. (2013). Sürdürülebilir Kalkınma ve Kurumsal Sürdürülebilirlik Çerçevesinde Kurumsal Sosyal Sorumluluk Kavramının Değerlendirilmesi. *Selçuk Üniversitesi İletişim Fakültesi Akademik Dergisi*, *8*(1), 85–94.

Enright, M. J. (2003). *Regional clusters: what we know and what we should know. In Innovation clusters and interregional competition* (pp. 99–129). Berlin: Springer. doi:10.1007/978-3-540-24760-9_6

Erol, S., Jäger, A., Hold, P., Ott, K., & Sihn, W. (2016). Tangible Industry 4.0: A scenario-based approach to learning for the future of production. *Procedia CIRP*, *54*, 13–18. doi:10.1016/j.procir.2016.03.162

Esmaeilian, B., Behdad, S., & Wang, B. (2016). The evolution and future of manufacturing: A review. *Journal of Manufacturing Systems*, *39*, 79–100. doi:10.1016/j.jmsy.2016.03.001

European Commision. (2019). *The Digital Economy and Society Index (DESI)*. Retrieved from https://ec.europa.eu/digital-single-market/en/desi

European Commission. (2003). *Commission Recommendation of 6 May 2003 concerning the definition of micro, small and medium-sized enterprises*. Brussels: European Union.

European Commission. (2018). Annual Report on European SMEs 2017-2018. SMEs growing beyond borders.

European Commission. (2019). Retrieved from https://ec.europa.eu/growth/smes/business-friendly-environment/sme-definition_en)

EUSME Centre. (2019). *SMEs in China: Policy Environment Report*. Author.

Farouk, S., Abu Elanain, H. M., Obeidat, S. M., & Al-Nahyan, M. (2016). HRM practices and organizational performance in the UAE banking sector: The mediating role of organizational innovation. *International Journal of Productivity and Performance Management*, *65*(6), 773–791. doi:10.1108/IJPPM-01-2016-0010

Fauziah, W., Yusoff, W., Jia, L. C., Azizan, A. Z., & Ramin, A. K. (2013). *Business Strategy of Small Medium Enterprises (SMEs): A Case Study among selected Chinese SMEs in Malaysia*. Academic Press.

Fayol, H. (1949). *General and Industrial Management*. London: Pitman&Sons Ltd.

Ferdinand, P. (2016). *Westward ho — the China dream and "one belt, one road": Chinese foreign policy under Xi Jinping*. Academic Press.

Fernández Rodríguez, M. A. (2019). Transcreación: Retórica cultural y traducción publicitaria. *Castilla. Estudios de Literatura*, *10*(10), 223–250. doi:10.24197/cel.10.2019.223-250

Ferreira, A. (2016). *Universal UX Design: Building Multicultural User Experience*. Cambridge, UK: Morgan Kaufmann.

Fey, C. F., & Birkinshaw, J. (2005). External sources of knowledge, governance mode, and R&D performance. *Journal of Management*, *31*(4), 597–621. doi:10.1177/0149206304272346

Field, J. (2005). *Social capital and lifelong learning*. Policy Press.

Flavián, C., Gurrea, R., & Orús, C. (2016). Choice confidence in the webrooming purchase process: The impact of online positive reviews and the motivation to touch. *Journal of Consumer Behaviour*, *15*(5), 459–476. doi:10.1002/cb.1585

Fortune. (2018). *Fortune 500 Companies 2018*. Retrieved from http://fortune.com/fortune500/

Fuchs-Kittowski, F., Klassen, N., Faust, D., & Einhaus, J. (2009). A comparative study on the use of Web 2.0 in enterprises. In K. Tochtermann (Ed.), *Proceedings of I-KNOW '09 and I-SEMANTICS '09* (pp. 372-378). Graz: Verlag der TU Graz.

Fu, N. (2015). The role of relational resources in the knowledge management capability and innovation of professional service firms1. *Human Relations*, *68*(5), 731–764. doi:10.1177/0018726714543479

Fu, N., Flood, P. C., Bosak, J., Morris, T., & O'Regan, P. (2015). How do high-performance work systems influence organizational innovation in professional service firms? *Employee Relations*, *37*(2), 209–231. doi:10.1108/ER-10-2013-0155

Gaballo, V. (2012). Exploring the boundaries of transcreation in specialized translation. *ESP Across Cultures*, *9*, 95–113.

Galpin, T., Whittington, L., & Bell, G. (2015). Is your sustainability strategy sustainable? Creating a culture of sustainability. *Corporate Governance*, *15*(1), 1–17. doi:10.1108/CG-01-2013-0004

Gamage, A. (2003). *Small and Medium Enterprises in Sri Lanka: A Review*. Retrieved from http://202.11.2.113/SEBM/ronso/no3_4/aruna.pdf

Gao, Y. (2017). Business leaders' values, organizational culture, and market orientation. *Journal of Strategic Marketing*, *25*(1), 49–64. doi:10.1080/0965254X.2015.1076879

Gassmann, O. (2006). Opening up the innovation process: Towards an agenda. *Research Management*, *36*(3), 223–228.

Gassmann, O., Enkel, E., & Chesbrough, H. (2010). The future of open innovation. *Research Management*, *40*(3), 213–221.

Gavrea, C., Ilieş, L., & Stegerean, R. (2011). Determinants of Organizational Performance: The Case of Romania. *Management & Marketing Challenges for the Knowledge Society*, *6*(2), 285–300.

General Secretariat of Industry and SMEs. (2018). *Cifras PYME. Datos febrero 2018*. Retrieved from http://www.ipyme.org/Publicaciones/CifrasPYME-%0Afebrero2018.pdf

Geyskens, I., & Steenkamp, J. E. M. (2006). *Make, buy, or ally: A transaction cost theory meta- analysis Make, Buy, or Ally : A Transaction Cost Theory*. Academic Press.

Ghaz. (2017). *Industry 4.0: Are Malaysian SMEs Ready?* Academic Press.

Ghobakhloo, M., Aranda, D. A., & Amado, J. B. (2011). Adoption of e-commerce applications in SMEs. *Industrial Management & Data Systems, 111*(8), 1238–1269. doi:10.1108/02635571111170785

Ghose, A. K. (2001). SMEs and environment protection. *Productivity, 42*(2), 101–117.

Global Skill Summit. (2019). *Skill Development for Industry 4.0.* Retrieved 27/11/2019 http://www.globalskillsummit.com/Whitepaper-Summary.pdf

Gnyawali, D. R., & Park, B. J. R. (2009). Co-opetition and technological innovation in small and medium-sized enterprises: A multilevel conceptual model. *Journal of Small Business Management, 47*(3), 308–330. doi:10.1111/j.1540-627X.2009.00273.x

Goel, M. M., & Prakash (2014). Micro Enterprises in Haryana: An Analysis. *Voice of Research, 3*(1). Retrieved from http://www.voiceofresearch.org/doc/Jun-2014/Jun-2014_15.pdf

Gökçe, S. G. (2015). Kamuda İnovasyon ve Türkiye'deki Uygulamaları. *Journal of International Management and Social Researches, 3*(1), 28–37.

Gold, A. H., Malhotra, A., & Segars, A. H. (2001). Knowledge Management: An Organizational Capabilities Perspective. *Journal of Management Information Systems, 18*(1), 185–214. doi:10.1080/07421222.2001.11045669

Gomes, G., & Wojahn, R. M. (2017). Organizational learning capability, innovation, and performance: A study in small and medium-sized enterprises (SMEs). *Revista de Administração (São Paulo), 52*(2), 163–175. doi:10.1016/j.rausp.2016.12.003

Google Consumer Barometer. (2015). *The smart shopper. Research & purchase behavior (ROPO).* Retrieved from https://www.consumerbarometer.com/en/

Google. (2019). *Shutting down Google+ for consumer (personal) accounts on April 2, 2019.* Retrieved from https://support.google.com/plus/answer/9195133?hl=en

Govil, N. (2017). *Smart Healthcare for Smart India || IoT in Healthcare.* Retrieved 27/11/2019 https://iotdunia.com/smart-healthcare-for-smart-india/

Govindan, K., Cheng, T. C. E., Mishra, N., & Shukla, N. (2018). Big data analytics and application for logistics and supply chain management. *Transportation Research Part E, Logistics and Transportation Review, 114*(May), 343–349. doi:10.1016/j.tre.2018.03.011

Greaver, M. F. (1999). *Strategic outsourcing: a structured approach to outsourcing decisions and initiatives.* AMACOM Div American Mgmt Assn.

Griffin, M. A., & Parker, S. K. (2007). A New Model Of Work Role Performance. *Positive Behavior In Uncertain And Interdependent Contexts The University of Queensland, 50*(2), 327–347.

Griffin, R. W. (2012). *Management.* Mason, OH: Cancage Learning.

Grimsholm, E., & Poblete, L. (2010). *Internal and External Factors Hampering SMEs growth: A qualitative case study of SMEs in Thailand.* Retrieved from http://hgo.diva-portal.org/smash/get/diva2:323837/FULLTEXT01

Gubbi, J., Buyya, R., Marusic, S., & Palaniswami, M. (2013). Internet of Things (IoT): A vision, architectural elements, and future directions. *Future Generation Computer Systems, 29*(7), 1645–1660. doi:10.1016/j.future.2013.01.010

Gümüşlüoğlu, L. (2012). Dinamik Yeteneklerin Yeni Ürün Geliştirme Performansı Üzerine Etkileri. *Farklı İş Stratejileri İçin Sonuçlar, İktisat, İşletme ve Finans, 27*(320), 61–90.

Gundry, L., Kickul, J., Welsch, H. P., & Posig, M. (2003). Technological innovation in women-owned firms: Influence of entrepreneurial motivation and strategic intention. *The International Journal of Entrepreneurship and Innovation, 4*(1), 265–274. doi:10.5367/000000003129574324

Gutiérrez-Artacho, J., & Olvera-Lobo, M. D. (2017a). Web localization of Spanish SMEs: The case of study in the chemical sector. *Journal of Information Systems Engineering & Management, 2*(3), 1–8. doi:10.20897/jisem.201715

Gutiérrez-Artacho, J., & Olvera-Lobo, M. D. (2017b). El uso del método Delphi como herramienta de evaluación consensuada en la didáctica de la traducción: el perfil del traductor-localizador. In M. E. del Valle (Ed.), *Nuevos Contenidos Innovadores En Ciencias y Humanidades* (pp. 226–240). Madrid: CUICIID.

Haag, S., & Anderl, R. (2018). Digital twin – Proof of concept. Manufacturing Letters, 15, 64–66. doi:10.1016/j.mfglet.2018.02.006

Hagedoorn, J., Roijakkers, N., & Kranenburg, H. (2006). Inter-firm R&D networks: The importance of strategic network capabilities for high-tech partnership formation. *British Journal of Management, 17*(1), 39–53. doi:10.1111/j.1467-8551.2005.00474.x

Hair, J. F. J. Jr, Sarstedt, M., Hopkins, L., & Kuppelwieser, V. (2014). Partial least squares structural equation modeling (PLS-SEM) An emerging tool in business research. *European Business Review, 26*(2), 106–121. doi:10.1108/EBR-10-2013-0128

Hair, J. F., Hult, G. T. M., Ringle, C., & Sarstedt, M. (2014). *A Primer on Partial Least Squares Structural Equation Modeling*. PLS-SEM.

Hair, J. F., Hult, T. M., Ringle, C. M., & Sarstedt, M. (2017). *A Primer on Partial Least Square Structural Equation Modeling (PLS-SEM).* Sage Publications.

Hair, J. F. Jr, Hult, G. T. M., Ringle, C., & Sarstedt, M. (2014). *A primer on partial least squares structural equation modeling (PLS-SEM).* Sage Publications.

Hair, J. F., Ringle, C. M., & Sarstedt, M. (2011). PLS-SEM: Indeed a silver bullet. *Journal of Marketing Theory and Practice, 19*(2), 139–152. doi:10.2753/MTP1069-6679190202

Hall, R., & Andriani, P. (2003). Managing knowledge associated with innovation. *Journal of Business Research, 56*(2), 145–152. doi:10.1016/S0148-2963(01)00287-9

Hallstedt, S. I. (2017). Sustainability criteria and sustainability compliance index for decision support in product development. *Journal of Cleaner Production, 140*, 251–266. doi:10.1016/j.jclepro.2015.06.068

Hambrick, D., & Mason, P. (1984). Upper Echelons: The organization as a reflection of its top managers. *Academy of Management Review, 9*(2), 193–206. doi:10.5465/amr.1984.4277628

Hamel, G., Doz, Y. L., & Prahalad, C. K. (1989). Collaborate with your competitors and win. *Harvard Business Review, 67*(1), 133–139.

Hamzah, N., Tokimatsu, K., & Yoshikawa, K. (2019). Solid fuel from oil palm biomass residues and municipal solid waste by hydrothermal treatment for electrical power generation in Malaysia: A review. *Sustainability, 11*(1060), 1–23. doi:10.3390u11041060

Harik, R., El Hachem, W., Medini, K., & Bernard, A. (2015). Towards a holistic sustainability index for measuring the sustainability of manufacturing companies. *International Journal of Production Research*, *53*(13), 4117–4139. doi:10.1080/00207543.2014.993773

Harmon, T. R., & Griffiths, M. A. (2008). Franchisee perceived relationship value. *Journal of Business and Industrial Marketing*, *23*(4), 256–263. doi:10.1108/08858620810865834

Harris, J. M. (2003). Sustainability and Sustainable Development. Retrieved from https://www.researchgate.net/publication/23739820

Harrison, J. L., Kelly, S. J., Harrison, J. L., & Kelly, S. J. (2010). Perceived environmental uncertainty ' s effect on commitment in business-to-business channels. *Marketing Intelligence & Planning*, *28*(6), 792–803. doi:10.1108/02634501011078165

Hartog, D. N., Muijen, J. J., & Koopman, P. L. (1997). Transactional versus transformational leadership: An analysis of the MLQ. *Journal of Occupational and Organizational Psychology*, *70*(1), 19–34. doi:10.1111/j.2044-8325.1997.tb00628.x

Hashem, I. A. T., Yaqoob, I., Anuar, N. B., Mokhtar, S., Gani, A., & Khan, S. U. (2015). The rise of "big data" on cloud computing: Review and open research issues. *Information Systems*, *47*, 98–115. doi:10.1016/j.is.2014.07.006

Hashim, M. K. (2000). SMEs in Malaysia: Past, Present, and Future. *Malaysian Management Review*, *35*(2), 22–30.

Hauser, J., Tellis, G. J., & Griffin, A. (2006). Research on innovation: A review and agenda for marketing science. *Marketing Science*, *25*(6), 687–717. doi:10.1287/mksc.1050.0144

Hegge, B. (2010). *SMEs and European Integration*. London: Taylor&Francis Group.

Hehenberger, P., & Bradley, D. (2016). Digital twin—the simulation aspect. In *Mechatronic Futures* (pp. 59–74). Cham, Switzerland: Springer.

Henseler, J., Ringle, C. M., & Sarstedt, M. (2015). A new criterion for assessing discriminant validity in variance-based structural equation modeling. *Journal of the Academy of Marketing Science*, *43*(1), 115–135. doi:10.1007/s11747-014-0403-8

Henseler, J., Ringle, C. M., & Sarstedt, M. (2015). Testing measurement invariance of composites using partial least squares. *International Marketing Review*.

Hervas-Oliver, J. L., Boronat-Moll, C., & Sempere-Ripoll, F. (2016). On Process Innovation Capabilities in SMEs: A Taxonomy of Process-Oriented Innovative SMEs. *Journal of Small Business Management*, *54*, 113–134. doi:10.1111/jsbm.12293

Hirsch-Kreinsen, H. (2014, June). Smart production systems. A new type of industrial process innovation. In DRUID society conference (pp. 16-18). Academic Press.

Hochleitner, F. P., Arbussà, A., & Coenders, G. (2017). Inbound open innovation in SMEs: Indicators, non-financial outcomes, and entry-timing. *Technology Analysis and Strategic Management*, *29*(2), 204–218. doi:10.1080/09537325.2016.1211264

Hofstede, G. (1980). *Culture's consequences: International differences in work-related values*. Beverly Hills, CA: Sage Publications.

Hofstede, G. (1991). *Cultures and organizations: Software of the mind*. New York: McGraw-Hill.

Horlings, L. (2015). Value in place; A value-oriented approach toward sustainable place-shaping. Regional Studies. *Regional Science*, *2*(1), 257–274.

Hudson, M., Smart, A., & Bourne, M. (2001). Theory and practice in SME performance measurement system. *International Journal of Operations & Production Management*, *21*(8), 1096–1115. doi:10.1108/EUM0000000005587

Humphrey, J., & Schmitz, H. (1995). *Principles for promoting clusters & networks of SMEs* (Vol. 1). Vienna: UNIDO.

Hurley, R. F., & Hult, G. T. M. (1998). Innovation, market orientation, and organizational learning: An integration and empirical examination. *Journal of Marketing*, *62*(3), 42–54. doi:10.1177/002224299806200303

Hussain, I., Farooq, Z., & Akhtar, W. (2012). SME Development and Failure Avoidance in Developing Countries through Public-Private Partnership. *African Journal of Business Management*, *6*(4), 1581–1589.

Hussein, A. S. T. T., Singh, S. K., Farouk, S., & Sohal, A. S. (2016). Knowledge sharing enablers, processes, and firm innovation capability. *Journal of Workplace Learning*, *28*(8), 484–495. doi:10.1108/JWL-05-2016-0041

IAB Spain. (2017). *Estudio Anual Redes Sociales 2017*. Retrieved from: https://iabspain.es/wp-content/uploads/iab_estudioredessociales_2017_vreducida.pdf

IAB Spain. (2018). *Estudio Anual de Redes Sociales 2018*. Retrieved from https://iabspain.es/wp-content/uploads/estudio-redes-sociales-2018_vreducida.pdf

Ibarra, D., Ganzarain, J., & Igartua, J. I. (2018). Business model innovation through Industry 4.0: A review. Procedia Manufacturing, 22, 4–10. doi:10.1016/j.promfg.2018.03.002

Ichniowski, C., & Shaw, K. (1999). The Effects of Human Resource Management Systems on Economic Performance: An International Comparison of U.S. and Japanese Plants. *Management Science*, *45*(5), 704–721. doi:10.1287/mnsc.45.5.704

Idris, R. (2019). *Industrial Revolution 4.0: An Overview of Readiness and Potential Economic Effects in Malaysia from Millennial's Perspective*. Academic Press.

IIC. (2015). *The Industrial Internet Consortium, Fact Sheet*. Retrieved from https://www.iiconsortium.org/docs/IIC_FACT_SHEET.pdf

Indarti, N., & Langenberg, M. (2004). Factors affecting business success among SMEs: empirical evidence from Indonesia. *Proceedings of the (19) 20 & 21 September 2004 Second Bi-Annual European Summer University* (pp. 1-14). University of Twente.

Indarti, N., & Langenberg, M. (2005). A Study of Factors Affecting Business Success among SMEs: Empirical Evidences from Indonesia. *Asian Social Science*, *7*(5), 67–86.

India Brand Equity Foundation. (2017). *Healthcare Industry in India*. Author.

INE (Instituto Nacional de Estadística). (2017). *Encuesta sobre el uso de TIC y comercio electrónico en las empresas*. Retrieved from: http://www.ine.es

INE (Instituto Nacional de Estadística). (2019). *Encuesta sobre el uso de TIC y comercio electrónico en las empresas*. Retrieved from: http://www.ine.es

Iqbal, Q., & Hassan, S. H. (2018). Green management matters: Green human resource management as a blue ocean strategy. Firms' Strategic Decisions. Theoretical and Empirical Findings, 3, 214–236. doi:10.2174/9781681086255118030014

Iqbal, Q., & Hassan, S. H. (2018). Green management matters: Green human resource management as blue ocean strategy. Firms' Strategic Decisions. Theoretical and Empirical Findings, 3, 214–236. doi:10.2174/9781681086255118030014

Iqbal, Q., Ahmad, N. H., & Ahmad, B. (2018). Enhancing sustainable performance through job characteristics via workplace spirituality: A study on SMEs. Journal of Science and Technology Policy Management. doi:10.1108/JSTPM-02-2018-0022

Iqbal, Q., Yang, S., Nawaz, R., & Iqbal, K. (2019). A multi-dimensional construct of perceived information pollution in the era of rife infollution. VINE Journal of Information and Knowledge Management Systems, 49(2), 162–180. doi:10.1108/VJIKMS-10-2018-0093

Iqbal, Q. (2018). The era of environmental sustainability: Ensuring that sustainability stands on human resource management. *Global Business Review*, ▪▪▪, 0972150918778967.

Iqbal, Q., Hassan, S. H., & Ahmad, N. H. (2018). The assessment of perceived information pollution in banking sector: A scale development and validation study. *Business Information Review*, *35*(2), 68–76. doi:10.1177/0266382118772891

Iqbal, Q., Hassan, S. H., Akhtar, S., & Khan, S. (2018). Employee's green behavior for environmental sustainability: A case of the banking sector in Pakistan. World Journal of Science. *Technology and Sustainable Development*, *15*(2), 118–130.

Iqbal, Q., & Nawaz, R. (2019). Rife information pollution (infollution) and virtual organizations in industry 4.0: within reality causes and consequences. In *Big Data and Knowledge Sharing in Virtual Organizations* (pp. 117–135). IGI Global. doi:10.4018/978-1-5225-7519-1.ch005

Iqbal, Q., Yang, S., Nawaz, R., & Iqbal, K. (2019). A multi-dimensional construct of perceived information pollution in the era of rife infollution. *VINE Journal of Information and Knowledge Management Systems*, *49*(2), 162–180. doi:10.1108/VJIKMS-10-2018-0093

Irwin, K. C., Landay, K. M., Aaron, J. R., McDowell, W. C., Marino, L. D., & Geho, P. R. (2018). Entrepreneurial orientation (EO) and human resources outsourcing (HRO): A "HERO" combination for SME performance. *Journal of Business Research*, *90*(May), 134–140. doi:10.1016/j.jbusres.2018.05.016

Isaksen, A. (1997). Regional clusters and competitiveness: The Norwegian case. *European Planning Studies*, *5*(1), 65–76. doi:10.1080/09654319708720384

Islam, M. A., Khan, M. A., Obaidullah, A. Z. M., & Alam, M. S. (2011). Effect of Entrepreneur and Firm Characteristics on the Business Success of Small and Medium Enterprises (SMEs) in Bangladesh. *International Journal of Business and Management*, *6*(3), 289–299.

Islam, M. A., Mian, E., & Ali, M. H. (2008). Determinants of Business Success of Small and Medium Enterprises (SMEs) in Bangladesh. *Business Review (Federal Reserve Bank of Philadelphia)*, *4*(2), 45–57.

Jamil, C. M., & Mohamed, R. (2011). Performance Measurement System (PMS) In Small Medium Enterprises (SMEs): A Practical Modified Framework. *World Journal of Social Sciences*, *1*(3), 200–212.

Jardon, C. M., & Susana Martos, M. (2012). Intellectual capital as competitive advantage in emerging clusters in Latin America. *Journal of Intellectual Capital*, *13*(4), 462–481. doi:10.1108/14691931211276098

Jazdi, N. (2014). Cyber-physical systems in the context of Industry 4.0. Proceedings of 2014 IEEE International Conference on Automation, Quality and Testing, Robotics, AQTR 2014, 1–4. doi:10.1109/AQTR.2014.6857843

Jensen, M. C., & Jensen, M. C. (1983). *Organization Theory and Methodology*. Academic Press.

Jiang, Y., Jiang, Y., & Nakamura, W. (2019). Human capital and organizational performance based on organizational innovation: Empirical study on China. *Revista de Cercetare si Interventie Sociala*, *64*, 156–166. doi:10.33788/rcis.64.13

Jiménez-Jiménez, D., & Sanz-Valle, R. (2011). Innovation, organizational learning, and performance. *Journal of Business Research*, *64*(4), 408–417. doi:10.1016/j.jbusres.2010.09.010

Jordan, J., Lowe, J., & Taylor, P. (1998). Strategy and financial policy in UK small firms. *Journal of Business Finance & Accounting*, *25*(1-2), 1–27. doi:10.1111/1468-5957.00176

Kadrizade, R. (1986). *İşletmelerde Büyüme ve Türkiye'deki İşletmelerde Büyüme Büyüklük ve Karlılık İlişkileri*. İstanbul: Yüksek Lisans Tezi, İstanbul Üniversitesi, Sosyal Bilimler Enstitüsü.

Kagermann, H., Helbig, J., Hellinger, A., & Wahlster, W. (2013). *Recommendations for implementing the strategic initiative INDUSTRIE 4.0: Securing the future of the German manufacturing industry; final report of the Industrie 4.0 Working Group*. Forschungsunion.

Kahneman, D. (2011). *Thinking, fast and slow* (1st ed.). New York: Farrar, Straus and Giroux.

Kalpande, S. D., Gupta, R. C., & Dandekar, M. D. (2010). SWOT analysis of small and medium scale enterprises implementing total quality management. *International Journal of Business, Management, and Social Science*, *1*(1), 59–64.

Karadeniz, K., & Kulaksız, S. (2018). İşletmelerin rekabet gücüne katkısı açısından kümelenme modelinin değerlendirilmesi: Çorum tarımsal gıda işleme makineleri kümesi. *Finans Ekonomi ve Sosyal Araştırmalar Dergisi*, *3*(4), 714–730.

Karaev, A., Lenny Koh, S. C., & Szamosi, L. T. (2007). The cluster approach and SME competitiveness: A review. *Journal of Manufacturing Technology Management*, *18*(7), 818–835. doi:10.1108/17410380710817273

Kassel, K. (2012). The circle of inclusion: Sustainability, CSR and the values that drive them. *Journal of Human Values*, *18*(2), 133–146. doi:10.1177/0971685812454482

Kaur, H., & Singh, S. P. (2018). Heuristic modeling for sustainable procurement and logistics in a supply chain using big data. *Computers & Operations Research*, *98*, 301–321. doi:10.1016/j.cor.2017.05.008

Kay, N. (2010). Dynamic capabilities as context: The role of decision, system, and structure. *Industrial and Corporate Change*, *19*(4), 1205–1223. doi:10.1093/icc/dtq028

Kazamia, K. I., & Kafaridou, M. (2018). An Interdisciplinary Approach to Three-Dımensional Sustainable Design. *The International Journal of the Arts in Society*, *11*(1), 35–43.

Kemayel, L. (2015). Success Factors of Lebanese SMEs: An Empirical Study. *Procedia: Social and Behavioral Sciences*, *195*, 1123–1128. doi:10.1016/j.sbspro.2015.06.158

Kennedy, E. H., Beckley, T. M., McFarlane, B. L., & Nadeau, S. (2009). Why we don't 'walk the talk': Understanding the environmental values/behavior gap in Canada. *Human Ecology Review*, *16*(2), 151–160.

Kesayak, B. (2019). *Endüstri Tarihine Kısa Bir Yolculuk*. Retrieved from https://www.endustri40.com/endustri-tarihine-kisa-bir-yolculuk/

Keskin, H. (2006). Market orientation, learning orientation, and innovation capabilities in SMEs: An extended model. *European Journal of Innovation Management*, *9*(4), 396–417. doi:10.1108/14601060610707849

Khaled, M. E., & Remon, F. A. (2014). Factors Influencing Construction Labor Productivity in Egypt. *Journal of Management Engineering*, *30*(1), 1–9. doi:10.1061/(ASCE)ME.1943-5479.0000168

Khan, A. A., & Khan, M. (2010). Pakistan textile industry facing new challenges. *Research Journal of International Studies*, *14*(14), 21–29.

Khanna, R., & Singh, S. P. (2018). Status of MSMEs in India: A Detailed Study. *Journal of Applied Management-Jidnyasa*, *10*(2), 1–14.

Khan, S. J., & Mir, A. A. (2019). Ambidextrous culture, contextual ambidexterity, and new product innovations: The role of organizational slack and environmental factors. *Business Strategy and the Environment*, *28*(4), 652–663. doi:10.1002/bse.2287

Kidwell, R. E., Nygaard, A., & Silkoset, R. (2007). *Antecedents and effects of free riding in the franchisor-franchisee relationship*. Academic Press.

Kiel, D., Müller, J. M., Arnold, C., & Voigt, K. I. (2017). Sustainable industrial value creation: Benefits and challenges of industry 4.0. *International Journal of Innovation Management*, *21*(08), 1740015. doi:10.1142/S1363919617400151

Kinyua, A. N. (2014). Factors Affecting the Performance of Small and Medium Enterprises in the Jua Kali Sector In Nakuru Town, Kenya. *IOSR Journal of Business and Management, 16*(1), 80-93.

Kleindienst, B. M., & Ramsauer, C. (2012). *SMEs and Industry 4 . 0 – Introducing a KPI based Procedure Model to identify Focus Areas in Manufacturing Industry*. Academic Press.

Kleindienst, M., & Ramsauer, C. (2016). SMEs and Industry 4.0–Introducing a KPI based Procedure Model to identify Focus Areas in Manufacturing Industry. *Athens Journal of Business & Economics, 2*(2), 109-122.

Klewes, J., Popp, D., & Rost-hein, M. (2017a). Digital Transformation and Communications: How Key Trends Will Transform the Way Companies Communicate. In Out-thinking Organizational Communications (pp. 7–31). doi:10.1007/978-3-319-41845-2

Kock, N. (2014). Advanced mediating effects tests, multi-group analyses, and measurement model assessments in PLS-based SEM. *International Journal of e-Collaboration*, *10*(1), 1–13. doi:10.4018/ijec.2014010101

Kohli, A. K., & Jaworski, B. J. (1990). Market orientation: The construct, research propositions, and managerial implications. *Journal of Marketing*, *54*(2), 1–18. doi:10.1177/002224299005400201

Koontz, H. (1961). Management Theory Jungle. *The Academy of Management Perspectives*, *4*(3), 174–188.

Kosacka-olejnik, M., & Pitakaso, R. (2019). Industry 4.0: State of the Art and Research Implications. *Log Forum, 15*(4), 475–485.

Kotler, P., & Caslione, J. A. (2011). *Kaos Yönetimi (Çev. Kıvanç Dündar)*. İstanbul: Optimist.

Kowang, T. O., Ying, Y. C., Yew, L. K., Hee, O. C., Fei, G. C., Long, C. S., … Saiful, M. (2019). *Industry 4.0 Competencies for Production Equipment Manufacturers in Malaysia*. Academic Press.

Kozak, A. M., & Doğantan, E. (2017). Dinamik Yeteneklerin Stratejik Planı Aracılığıyla Analizi: Bir Kamu Kurumu Örneği. *Turizm Akademik Dergisi*, *4*(1), 49–63.

Krishnan, V., & Ulrich, K. T. (2001). Product Development Decisions: A Review of the Literature. *Management Science*, *47*(1), 1–21. doi:10.1287/mnsc.47.1.1.10668

Kristiansen, S. (2002). Competition and Knowledge in Javanese Rural Business. *Singapore Journal of Tropical Geography*, *23*(1), 52–70. doi:10.1111/1467-9493.00118

Kristiansen, S. (2004). Social network and business success: The role of sub-cultures in an African context. *American Journal of Economics and Sociology*, *63*(5), 1149–1171. doi:10.1111/j.1536-7150.2004.00339.x

Kristiansen, S., Furuholt, B., & Wahid, F. (2003). Internet cafe entrepreneurs: Pioneers in information dissemination in Indonesia. *The International Journal of Entrepreneurship and Innovation*, *4*(4), 251–263. doi:10.5367/000000003129574315

Kuckertz, A., & Wagner, M. (2010). The influence of sustainability orientation on entrepreneurial intentions-investing the role of business experience. *Journal of Business Venturing*, *25*(5), 524–539. doi:10.1016/j.jbusvent.2009.09.001

Kuo, T. H. (2011). How to improve organizational performance through learning and knowledge? *International Journal of Manpower*, *32*(5), 581–603. doi:10.1108/01437721111158215

Kurzac, K., & Heurich, C. (2015). *Connecting Project Interdependency Management to Dynamic Capabilities: Police Scotland's Transformation*. Academic Press.

Kuşat, N. (2012). Organizational Sustainability For Sustainable Corporations And Its Endogenous Determinants. *Afyon Kocatepe Üniversitesi, İİBF Dergisi*, *14*(2), 227–242.

Kuzmenko, O., & Roienko, V. (2017). Nowcasting income inequality in the context of the Fourth Industrial Revolution. *Socioeconomic Challenges*, *1*(1), 5–12. doi:10.21272ec.2017.1-01

Kwon, H. S., & Park, H. C. (2019). Creating Sustainable and Climate Shared Value in Public Institution: Lessons from a Case of Korea Army Cadet Military School. *Sustainability*, *11*(14), 37–96. doi:10.3390/su11143796

Lafontaine, F. (1992). Agency Theory and Franchising: Some Empirical Results. *The Rand Journal of Economics*, *23*(2), 263–283. doi:10.2307/2555988

Lasi, H., Fettke, P., Kemper, H. G., Feld, T., & Hoffmann, M. (2014). Industry 4.0. *Business & Information Systems Engineering*, *6*(4), 239–242. doi:10.1007/s12599-014-0334-4

Laudien, S. M., Spieth, P., & Clauß, T. (2017). Digitalization as Driver of Business Model Innovation: An Exploratory Analysis. *Proceedings of the 28th International Society for Professional Innovation Management (ISPIM) Conference*.

Laursen, K., & Salter, A. (2006). Open for innovation: The role of openness in explaining innovation performance among UK manufacturing firms. *Strategic Management Journal*, *27*(2), 131–150. doi:10.1002mj.507

Lawson, B., & Samson, D. (2001). Developing Innovation Capability in Organisations: A Dynamic Capabilities Approach. *International Journal of Innovation Management*, *5*(3), 377–400. doi:10.1142/S1363919601000427

Lee, S., Park, G., Yoon, B., & Park, J. (2010). Open innovation in SMEs-An intermediated network model. *Research Policy*, *39*(2), 290–300. doi:10.1016/j.respol.2009.12.009

Li, L. (2018). Technological Forecasting & Social Change China's manufacturing locus in 2025: With a comparison of "Made-in-China'. *Technological Forecasting & Social Change*, *135*, 66–74. Doi:10.1016/j.techfore.2017.05.028

Liang, W. Y., & Huang, C. C. (2006). Agent-based demand forecast in the multi-echelon supply chain. *Decision Support Systems*, *42*(1), 390–407. doi:10.1016/j.dss.2005.01.009

Liao, S. H., Hu, D. C., Chen, C. C., & Lin, Y. L. (2015). Comparison of competing models and multi-group analysis of organizational culture, knowledge transfer, and innovation capability: An empirical study of the Taiwan semiconductor industry. *Knowledge Management Research and Practice*, *13*(3), 248–260. doi:10.1057/kmrp.2013.46

Lichtenthaler, U. (2008). Open innovation in practice: An analysis of strategic approaches to technology transactions. *IEEE Transactions on Engineering Management*, *55*(1), 148–157. doi:10.1109/TEM.2007.912932

Li, G., Hou, Y., & Wu, A. (2017). Fourth Industrial Revolution: Technological drivers, impacts and coping methods. *Chinese Geographical Science*, *27*(4), 626–637. doi:10.100711769-017-0890-x

Lindblom, C. E. (1959). The Science of " Muddling Through. *Public Administration Review*, *19*(2), 79–88. doi:10.2307/973677

Li, S., & Luo, C. (2008). Growth Pattern, Employment, and Income Inequality: What the Experience of the Republic of Korea and Taipei, China Reveals to the People's Republic of China. *Asian Development Review*, *25*(1/2), 100.

LISA. (2003). *The localization industry primer*. Geneva: LISA.

Loebbecke, C., & Picot, A. (2015). Reflections on societal and business model transformation arising from digitization and big data analytics: A research agenda. *The Journal of Strategic Information Systems*, *24*(3), 149–157. doi:10.1016/j.jsis.2015.08.002

Lo, M. C., Wang, Y. C., Wah, C. R. J., & Ramayah, T. (2016). The critical success factors for the organizational performance of SMEs in Malaysia: A partial least squares approach. *Revista Brasileira de Gestão de Negócios*, *18*(61), 370–391. doi:10.7819/rbgn.v18i61.3058

London Stock Exchange Group. (2017). *1000 Companies to Inspire Europe - 2017 Report*. Retrieved from https://www.lseg.com/resources/1000-companies-inspire/2017-report-1000-companies-europe

London Stock Exchange Group. (2018). *1000 Companies to Inspire*. Retrieved from https://www.lseg.com/resources/1000-companies-inspire

Long, C., & Zhang, X. (2012). Patterns of China's industrialization Concentration, specialization, and clustering. *China Economic Review*, *23*(3), 593–612. doi:10.1016/j.chieco.2011.09.002

Lopes, L. A., & Melão, N. F. (2016). Website content and design in SME: Insights from Portugal. *International Journal of Electronic Business*, *13*(1), 70. doi:10.1504/IJEB.2016.075343

Louis, W. (1986). *Interorganizational relations in marketing channels*. Academic Press.

Love, J. H., & Roper, S. (2015). SME innovation, exporting and growth: A review of existing evidence. International Small Business Journal: Researching Entrepreneurship, 33(1), 28–48. doi:10.1177/0266242614550190

Lucke, D., Constantinescu, C., & Westkämper, E. (2008). A smart factory-a step towards the next generation of manufacturing. In *Manufacturing systems and technologies for the new frontier* (pp. 115–118). Springer; doi:10.1007/978-1-84800-267-8_23.

Luco, J., Mestre, S., Henry, L., Tamayo, S., & Fontane, F. (2018). *Industry 4.0 in SMEs : a sectorial analysis*. Academic Press.

Lu, K., Zhu, J., & Bao, H. (2015). High-performance human resource management and firm performance: The mediating role of innovation in China. *Industrial Management & Data Systems*, *115*(2), 553–582. doi:10.1108/IMDS-10-2014-0317

Luna, D., Peracchio, L. A., & De Juan, M. D. (2002). Cross-cultural and cognitive aspects of web site navigation. *Journal of the Academy of Marketing Science*, *30*(4), 397–410. doi:10.1177/009207002236913

Luo, X., & Bhattacharya, C. B. (2009). The debate over doing good: Corporate social performance, strategic marketing levers, and firm idiosyncratic risk. *Journal of Marketing*, *73*(6), 198–213. doi:10.1509/jmkg.73.6.198

Lu, Y. (2017). Industry 4.0: A survey on technologies, applications and open research issues. *Journal of Industrial Information Integration*, *6*, 1–10. doi:10.1016/j.jii.2017.04.005

Lycett, M. (2013). 'Datafication': Making sense of (big) data in a complex world. *European Journal of Information Systems*, *22*(6), 381–386. doi:10.1057/ejis.2013.10

Machadoa, C. G., Winrotha, M., Carlssonb, D., Almströma, P., Centerholtb, V., & Hallin, M. (2019). *Industry 4.0 readiness in manufacturing companies: challenges and enablers towards increased digitalization. way*. Academic Press.

MacInerney-May, K. (2012). The Value of Dynamic Capabilities for Strategic Management (Doctoral dissertation). Universität zu Köln.

Mackenbach, J. P. (2007). Global environmental change and human health: A public health research agenda. *Journal of Epidemiology and Community Health*, *61*(2), 92–94. doi:10.1136/jech.2005.045211 PubMed

Malaysia Industry-Government Group for High Technology (MIGHT). (2013). Malaysian Biomass Industry Action Plan 2020: Driving SMEs towards a sustainable future. Retrieved from http://www.biomass.org.my/files/editor_files/files/Msia Biomass Industry Action Plan 2020.pdf

Malaysian Industry-Government Group for High Technology (MIGHT). (2014). *Biomass Benchmarking Study: Potential Value Creation for Commercial Utilization of Biomass in Malaysia*. Author.

Maldonado-Guzmán, G., Garza-Reyes, J. A., Pinzón-Castro, S. Y., & Kumar, V. (2019). Innovation capabilities and performance: Are they truly linked in SMEs? *International Journal of Innovation Science*, *11*(1), 48–62. doi:10.1108/IJIS-12-2017-0139

Maletic, M., Maletic, D., Dahlgaard, J., Dahlgaard-Park, S. M., & Gomišcek, B. (2015). Do corporate sustainability practices enhance organizational economic performance? *International Journal of Quality and Service Sciences*, *7*(2/3), 184–200. doi:10.1108/IJQSS-02-2015-0025

Malinowski, B. (1960). *A Scientific Theory of Culture* (2nd ed.). New York: Oxford University Press.

Malliari, L., & Sirkeci, I. (2017). Performance of direct mail in building customer loyalty in Greek automotive sector during the financial crisis. *International Journal of Business Performance Management*, *18*(1), 1–24. doi:10.1504/IJBPM.2017.080841

Manner, M. H. (2010). The Impact of CEO Characteristics on Corporate Social Performance. *Journal of Business Ethics*, *93*(S1), 53–72. doi:10.1007/s10551-010-0626-7

Manogaran, G., Thota, C., Lopez, D., & Sundarasekar, R. (2017). Big data security intelligence for healthcare industry 4.0. In *Cybersecurity for Industry 4.0* (pp. 103–126). Cham: Springer. doi:10.1007/978-3-319-50660-9_5

Marcovitz, H. (2013). *The Industrial Revolution*. San Diego, CA: ReferencePoint Press.

Marcus, A., & Gould, E. W. (2000). Crosscurrents: Cultural dimensions and global Web user-interface design. *Interaction*, *7*(4), 32–46. doi:10.1145/345190.345238

Marín Dueñas, P. P., & Lasso de la Vega González, M. (2017). La efectividad de las páginas web en la comunicación empresarial de las pequeñas y medianas empresas. Un estudio en PYMES de la provincia de Cádiz. *ZER. Revista de Estudios de Comunicación*, *22*(42), 53–71. doi:10.1387/zer.17797

Marques, J. P. (2014). Closed versus open innovation: Evolution or combination? *International Journal of Business and Management*, *9*(3), 196. doi:10.5539/ijbm.v9n3p196

Marsden, K. (1992). African Entrepreneurs - Pioneers of Development. *Small Enterprise Development*, *3*(2), 15–25. doi:10.3362/0957-1329.1992.015

Mattoussi, W., & Ayadi, M. (2017). The dynamics of exporting and innovation: Evidence from the Tunisian manufacturing sector. *Journal of African Economies*, *26*(1), 52–66. doi:10.1093/jae/ejw025

Mayhew, H., Saleh, T., & Williams, S. (2016). Making data analytics work for you- instead of the other way around. *The McKinsey Quarterly*, *4*(October), 1–15.

Mazutis, D. D. (2013). The CEO Effect: A Longitudinal, Multilevel Analysis of the Relationship Between Executive Orientation and Corporate Social Strategy. *Business & Society*, *52*(4), 631–648. doi:10.1177/0007650313490510

Mbatha, B. (2013). Exploring the potential of electronic commerce tools in South African SME tourism service providers. *Information Development*, *29*(1), 10–23. doi:10.1177/0266666912452270

McCandless, D. (2014). *Knowledge is Beautiful*. London: HarperCollins.

McCann, M., & Barlow, A. (2015). Use and measurement of social media for SMEs. *Journal of Small Business and Enterprise Development*, *22*(2), 273–287. doi:10.1108/JSBED-08-2012-0096

McDermott, C. M., & Prajogo, D. I. (2012). Service innovation and performance in SMEs. *International Journal of Operations & Production Management*, *32*(2), 216–237. doi:10.1108/01443571211208632

McGill, M. E., & Slocum, J. W. Jr. (1993). Unlearning the organization. *Organizational Dynamics*, *22*(2), 67–79. doi:10.1016/0090-2616(93)90054-5

McMahon, R. G. P. (2001). Growth and performance of manufacturing SMEs: The influence of financial management characteristics. *International Small Business Journal*, *19*(3), 10–28. doi:10.1177/0266242601193001

McWilliams, A., Siegel, D. S., & Wright, P. M. (2006). Corporate social responsibility: Strategic implications. *Journal of Management Studies*, *43*(1), 1–18. doi:10.1111/j.1467-6486.2006.00580.x

Mead, D. C., & Liedholm, C. (1998). The dynamics of micro and small enterprises in developing countries. *World Development*, *26*(1), 61–74. doi:10.1016/S0305-750X(97)10010-9

Meganathan, M., Kumar, P. B., & Saravanan, R. (2015). Sustainable Trends of MSME in India: An Empirical Study. *International Journal of Research in Management. Economics & Commerce*, *5*(2), 42–51.

Mehta, M. (2009). A + E = LEAN. *Industrial Engineering (American Institute of Industrial Engineers)*, *41*, 28.

Meier, R., & Pilgrim, M. (1994). Policy-Induced Constraints on Small Enterprise Development in Asian Developing Countries. *Small Enterprise Development*, *5*(2), 66–78. doi:10.3362/0957-1329.1994.017

Mekhilef, S., Barimani, M., Safari, A., & Salam, Z. (2014). Malaysia's renewable energy policies and programs with green aspects. *Renewable & Sustainable Energy Reviews*, *40*, 497–504. doi:10.1016/j.rser.2014.07.095

Mell, P., & Grance, T. (2011). The NIST-National Institute of Standards and Technology- Definition of Cloud Computing. NIST Special Publication 800-145.

Mendes, L., & Lourenço, L. (2014). Factors that hinder quality improvement programs' implementation in SME: Definition of a taxonomy. *Journal of Small Business and Enterprise Development*, *21*(4), 690–715. doi:10.1108/JSBED-03-2014-0054

Mentzer, J. T., Keebler, J. S., Nix, N. W., Smith, C. D., & Zacharia, Z. G. (2001). Journal of Business Logistics, Vol.22, No. 2, 2001 1. *The Journal of Business*, *22*(2), 1–25.

Meyer, G. G., Wortmann, J. C., & Szirbik, N. B. (2011). Production monitoring and control with intelligent products. *International Journal of Production Research*, *49*(5), 1303–1317. doi:10.1080/00207543.2010.518742

Michael, H., Harrison, D., & Joey, F. (2007). *The role of trust in franchise organizations*. Academic Press.

Michelidou, N., Siamagka, N. T., & Christodoulides, G. (2011). Usage, barriers, and measurement of social media marketing: An exploratory investigation of small and medium B2B brands. *Industrial Marketing Management*, *40*(7), 1153–1159. doi:10.1016/j.indmarman.2011.09.009

Mikalef, P., Pappas, I. O., Krogstie, J., & Giannakos, M. (2018). Big data analytics capabilities: A systematic literature review and research agenda. *Information Systems and e-Business Management*, *16*(3), 547–578. doi:10.1007/s10257-017-0362-y

Miles, J. A. (2012). *Management and Organization Theory. A Jossey-Bass Reader*. John Wiley & Sons.

Min, H. (2010). Artificial intelligence in supply chain management: Theory and applications. *International Journal of Logistics Research and Applications*, *13*(1), 13–39. doi:10.1080/13675560902736537

Ministry of International Trade and Industry (MITI). (2017). International Biomass Conference Malaysia 2017: Biomass Industry Revolution 4.0. Retrieved from https://www.miti.gov.my/index.php/pages/view/4349

Mishra, S., & Suar, D. (2013). Salience and corporate responsibility towards the natural environment and financial performance of Indian manufacturing firms. *Journal of Global Responsibility*, *4*(1), 44–61. doi:10.1108/20412561311324069

Moeuf, A., Pellerin, R., Lamouri, S., Tamayo-Giraldo, S., & Barbaray, R. (2018). The industrial management of SMEs in the era of Industry 4.0. *International Journal of Production Research*, *56*(3), 1118–1136. doi:10.1080/00207543.2017.1372647

Monostori, L. (2014). Cyber-physical production systems: Roots, expectations, and R&D challenges. Procedia CIRP, 17, 9–13. doi:10.1016/j.procir.2014.03.115

Moore, J. E., Mascarenhas, A., Bain, J., & Straus, S. E. (2017). Developing a comprehensive definition of sustainability. *Implementation Science; IS*, *12*(1), 110. doi:10.1186/s13012-017-0637-1 PubMed

Moorman, C., & Miner, A. S. (1997). The impact of organizational memory on new product performance and creativity. *JMR, Journal of Marketing Research*, *34*(1), 91–106. doi:10.1177/002224379703400108

Morden, T. (2007). *Principles of strategic management*. Ashgate Publishing Limited.

Morón, M., & Calvo, E. (2018). Introducing transcreation skills in translator training contexts: A situated project-based approach. *The Journal of Specialised Translation*, *29*, 126–148.

Morreale, J. C., Costa, A., & Villada, M. (2018). *China's rising middle class: A case study of Shanghai college students*. Doi:10.14254/2071-8330.2018/11-2/1

Müller, J. M., Maier, L., Veile, J., & Voigt, K. I. (2017). Cooperation strategies among SMEs for implementing industry 4.0. In *Proceedings of the Hamburg International Conference of Logistics (HICL)* (pp. 301-318). Academic Press.

Müller, J. M., Kiel, D., & Voigt, K. I. (2018). What drives the implementation of Industry 4.0? The role of opportunities and challenges in the context of sustainability. *Sustainability*, *10*(1), 247. doi:10.3390u10010247

Müller, J. M., Maier, L., Veile, J., & Voigt, K.-I. (2017). Cooperation strategies among SMEs for implementing Industry 4.0. *Proceedings of the Hamburg International Conference of Logistics (HICL)*, 301–318. 10.15480/882.1462

Mumdziev, N., & Windsperger, J. (2013). An Extended Transaction Cost Model of Decision Rights Allocation in Franchising. *The Moderating Role of Trust*, *182*(February), 170–182.

MUSİAD. (2005). *Kobi'ler için rekabet ve büyüme stratejileri*. Retrieved from https://www.musiad.org.tr/download/Yayinlar/Cep%20Kitaplar%C4%B1/KOB%C4%B0'ler%20%C4%B0%C3%A7in%20Rekabet%20ve%20B%C3%BCy%C3%BCme%20Stratejileri/KOB%C4%B0'ler%20%C4%B0%C3%A7in%20Rekabet%20ve%20B%C3%BCy%C3%BCme%20Stratejileri.pdf

Nantel, J., & Glaser, E. (2008). The impact of language and culture on perceived website usability. *Journal of Engineering and Technology Management*, *25*(1-2), 112–122. doi:10.1016/j.jengtecman.2008.01.005

Naranjo Valencia, J., Sanz Valle, R., & Jiménez Jiménez, D. (2010). Organizational culture as a determinant of product innovation. *European Journal of Innovation Management*, *13*(4), 466–480. doi:10.1108/14601061011086294

Naranjo-Valencia, J. C., Jiménez-Jiménez, D., & Sanz-Valle, R. (2011). Innovation or imitation? The role of organizational culture. *Management Decision*, *49*(1), 55–72. doi:10.1108/00251741111094437

Narula, R. (2004). R&D collaboration by SMEs: New opportunities and limitations in the face of globalization. *Technovation*, *24*(2), 153–161. doi:10.1016/S0166-4972(02)00045-7

Naudé, W., & Dimitri, N. (2018). The Race for an Artificial General Intelligence: Implications for Public Policy. SSRN Electronic Journal, (0123456789).

Nawab, S., Nazir, T., Zahid, M. M., & Fawad, S. M. (2015). Knowledge Management, Innovation, and Organizational Performance. *International Journal of Knowledge Engineering-IACSIT, 1*(1), 43–48. doi:10.7763/IJKE.2015.V1.7

Ngai, E. W. T., Chau, D. C. K., Lo, C. W. H., & Lei, C. F. (2014). Design and development of a corporate sustainability index platform for corporate sustainability performance analysis. *Journal of Engineering and Technology Management, 34*, 63–77.

Nguyen, T., Zhou, L., Spiegler, V., Ieromonachou, P., & Lin, Y. (2018). Big data analytics in supply chain management: A state-of-the-art literature review. *Computers & Operations Research, 98*, 254–264. doi:10.1016/j.cor.2017.07.004

Nieves, J., & Haller, S. (2014). Building dynamic capabilities through knowledge resources. *Tourism Management, 40*, 224–232. doi:10.1016/j.tourman.2013.06.010

Nkundabanyanga, S. K., Balunywa, W., Tauringana, V., Ntayi, J. M., & Stephen, K. (2014). *Board role performance in service organisations : the importance of human capital in the context of a developing country*. Academic Press.

Nobre, H., & Silva, D. (2014). Social network marketing strategy and SME strategy benefits. *Journal of Transnational Management, 19*(2), 138–151. doi:10.1080/15475778.2014.904658

Nofer, M., Gomber, P., Hinz, O., & Schiereck, D. (2017). GNRL_Blockchain. *Business & Information Systems Engineering, 59*(3), 183–187. doi:10.1007/s12599-017-0467-3

Nonaka, I. (2002). A dynamic theory of organizational knowledge creation. *The strategic management of intellectual capital and organizational knowledge*, 437-462.

Noruzy, A., Dalfard, V. M., Azhdari, B., Nazari-Shirkouhi, S., & Rezazadeh, A. (2013). Relations between transformational leadership, organizational learning, knowledge management, organizational innovation, and organizational performance: An empirical investigation of manufacturing firms. *International Journal of Advanced Manufacturing Technology, 64*(5–8), 1073–1085. doi:10.1007/s00170-012-4038-y

Nuroğlu, E., & Nuroğlu, H. H. (2018a), Endüstri 4.0'ı Türkiye'nin Dış Ticareti İçin Bir Fırsat Penceresine Dönüştürmek. *Yönetim ve Ekonomi Araştırmaları Dergisi, 16*(1), 329-346.

Nuroğlu, E., & Nuroğlu, H. H. (2018b), Türkiye ve Almanya'nın Sanayide Dijital Dönüşümü: Yol Haritaları Ve Şirketlerin Karşılaştırması. *Süleyman Demirel Üniversitesi İktisadi ve İdari Bilimler Fakültesi Dergisi, 23*, 1537-1560.

O'Cass, A., & Sok, P. (2013). Exploring innovation-driven value creation in B2B service firms: The roles of the manager, employees, and customers in value creation. *Journal of Business Research, 66*(8), 1074–1084. doi:10.1016/j.jbusres.2012.03.004

O'Connor, E. (1999). The Politics of Management Thought: A Case Study of the Harvard Business Sc...: Discovery For the University of Southampton. *Academy of Management Review, 24*(1), 117–131. doi:10.5465/amr.1999.1580444

Observatorio Vodafone. (2019). *III Estudio sobre el estado de digitalización de las empresas y Administraciones Públicas españolas.* Retrieved from https://tinyurl.com/txm9ajt

Odening, M., Wagner, C., Narayana, R., & Huettel, S. (2013). Measuring dynamic efficiency under uncertainty: an application to German dairy farms. In Agricultural & Applied Economics Associations AAEA & CAES Joint Annual Meeting, Washington, DC.

OECD, (2018). Health expenditure and financing: Health expenditure indicators. OECD 157 Health Statistics (database). doi:10.1787/data00349-en

OECD. (1999). *Boosting innovation: The cluster approach, OECD publishing*, Retrieved from http://www.oecd.org/sti/inno/boostinginnovationtheclusterapproach.htm

OECD. (2005). *OECD SME and Entrepreneurship Outlook: 2005*. OECD. Retrieved from https://stats.oecd.org/glossary/detail.asp?ID=3123

OECD. (2017). *Small, Medium, Strong. Trends in SME Performance and Business Conditions*. Paris: OECD.

OECD. (2017a). *Increasing productivity in small traditional enterprises: programs for upgrading management skills and practices*. Paris: OECD Publishing.

OECD. (2017b). *Small, medium, strong. Trends in SME performance and business conditions*. Paris: OECD Publishing.

Oerlemans, L. A., Meeus, M. T., & Boekema, F. W. (2001). Firm clustering and innovation: Determinants and effects. *Papers in Regional Science*, *80*(3), 337–356. doi:10.1007/PL00013637

Oettmeier, K., & Hofmann, E. (2017). Additive manufacturing technology adoption: An empirical analysis of general and supply chain-related determinants. *Journal of Business Economics*, *87*(1), 97–124. doi:10.100711573-016-0806-8

Oğuztürk, B. S., & Sarıçoban, K. (2013). Küresel rekabette kümelenme ve inovasyonun rolü. *Sosyal ve Beşeri Bilimler Dergisi*, *5*(1), 94–104.

Oláh, J., Karmazin, G., Pető, K., & Popp, J. (2018). Information technology developments of logistics service providers in Hungary. *International Journal of Logistics Research and Applications*, *21*(3), 332–344. doi:10.1080/13675567.2017.1393506

Ologbo, A. C., & Nor, K. M. (2015). Knowledge management processes and firm innovation capability: A theoretical model. *Asian Social Science*, *11*(18), 10–17. doi:10.5539/ass.v11n18p10

Olvera-Lobo, M. D., Gutiérrez-Artacho, J., & Díaz-Millón, M. (2019). Web transcreation in the Spanish business context: the case of healthcare SMEs. In M. Kefalaki (Ed.), *ICCM2019: 5th Annual International Conference on Communication and Management*. Athens: ICCM.

Olvera-Lobo, M. D., & Castillo-Rodríguez, C. (2019). Website localization in the corporate context: A Spanish perspective. *Journal of Digital Information Management*, *17*(1), 34–43. doi:10.6025/jdim/2019/17/1/34-43

Olvera-Lobo, M. D., & Gutiérrez-Artacho, J. (2017). Web localization: the Spanish SMEs as a case of study. In *Proceedings of 12th Iberian Conference on Information Systems and Technologies (CISTI)*. IEEE. 10.23919/CISTI.2017.7975872

Orlitzky, M., Siegel, D. S., & Waldman, D. A. (2011). Strategic corporate social responsibility and environmental sustainability. *Business & Society*, *50*(1), 6–27. doi:10.1177/0007650310394323

Ouedraogo, N., & Ouakouak, M. L. (2018). Impacts of personal trust, communication, and affective Commitment on Change Success. *Journal of Organizational Change*, *31*(3), 676–696. doi:10.1108/JOCM-09-2016-0175

Oyelaran-Oyeyinka, B. (2005). Inter-firm collaboration and competitive pressures: SME footwear clusters in Nigeria. *International Journal of Technology and Globalisation*, *1*(3-4), 343–360. doi:10.1504/IJTG.2005.008747

Pal, R., Torstensson, H., & Mattila, H. (2014). Antecedents of organizational resilience in economic crises - An empirical study of Swedish textile and clothing SMEs. International Journal of Production Economics, 147(Part B), 410–428. doi:10.1016/j.ijpe.2013.02.031

Pansiri, J., & Temtime, Z. T. (2008). Assessing managerial skills in SMEs for capacity building. *Journal of Management Development, 27*(2), 251–260. doi:10.1108/02621710810849362

Papadopoulos, G., Rikama, S., Alajääskö, P., & Salah-Eddine, Z. (2019). *Statistics on small and medium-sized enterprises*. Retrieved from https://ec.europa.eu/eurostat/statistics-explained/index.php/Statistics_on_small_and_medium-sized_enterprises#General_overview

Papagiannakis, G., & Lioukas, S. (2012). Values, attitudes and perceptions of managers as predictors of corporate environmental responsiveness. *Journal of Environmental Management, 100*, 41–51. doi:10.1016/j.jenvman.2012.01.023 PubMed

Papanek, M. L. (2011). Kurt Lewin and His Contributions to Modern Management Theory. Academy of Management Proceedings, 1973(1), 317–322. doi:10.5465/ambpp.1973.4981410

Pappas, I. O., Mikalef, P., Giannakos, M. N., Krogstie, J., & Lekakos, G. (2018). Big data and business analytics ecosystems: Paving the way towards digital transformation and sustainable societies. *Information Systems and e-Business Management, 16*(3), 479–491. doi:10.1007/s10257-018-0377-z

Parayitam, S., & Guru-Gharana, K. (2010). Economics Of Resource Based And Dynamic Capabilities View: A Contemporary Framework. *Academy of Strategic Management Journal, 9*(1), 83–93.

Parida, V., Westerberg, M., & Frishammar, J. (2012). Inbound open innovation activities in high-tech SMEs: The impact on innovation performance. *Journal of Small Business Management, 50*(2), 283–309. doi:10.1111/j.1540-627X.2012.00354.x

Pavlou, P. a, & Sawy, O. a El. (. (2011). Understanding the Black Box. Decision Sciences, 42(1), 239–273. doi:10.1111/j.1540-5915.2010.00287.x

Pavlou, P. A., & El Sawy, O. A. (2011). Understanding the elusive black box of dynamic capabilities. *Decision Sciences, 42*(1), 239–273. doi:10.1111/j.1540-5915.2010.00287.x

Pesce, M. (2018). *SWOT Analysis of the Application of International Standard ISO 14001 in the Chinese Context: A Case Study of Guangdong Province*. Doi:10.3390u10093196

Peteraf, M., Stefano, G., & Verona, G. (2013). The Elephant In The Room Of Dynamic Capabilities: Bringing Two Diverging Conversations Together. *Strategic Management Journal*, ▪▪▪, 34.

Peukert, B., Benecke, S., Clavell, J., Neugebauer, S., Nissen, N. F., Uhlmann, E., & Finkbeiner, M. (2015). Addressing sustainability and flexibility in manufacturing via smart modular machine tool frames to support sustainable value creation. *Procedia CIRP, 29*, 514–519. doi:10.1016/j.procir.2015.02.181

Philip Chen, C. L., & Zhang, C. Y. (2014). Data-intensive applications, challenges, techniques, and technologies: A survey on Big Data. *Information Sciences, 275*, 314–347. doi:10.1016/j.ins.2014.01.015

Piantoni, M., Baronchelli, G., & Cortesi, E. (2012). The recognition of international opportunities among Italian SMEs: Differences between European and Chinese markets. *International Journal of Entrepreneurship and Small Business, 17*(2), 199. doi:10.1504/IJESB.2012.048847

Pierto, D. (2012). Does internal and external environmental management contribute to the triple bottom line? *International Journal of Operations & Production Management, 32*(3), 265–290. doi:10.1108/01443571211212574

Pindur, W., Rogers, S. E., & Kim, P. S. (2013). The history of management: A global perspective. *Journal of Management History, 1*(1), 59–77. doi:10.1108/13552529510082831

Pisano, G. P., & Verganti, R. (2008). Which kind of collaboration is right for you. *Harvard Business Review, 86*(12), 78–86.

Popkova, E. G., Ragulina, Y. V., & Bogoviz, A. V. (2019). Fundamental differences of transition to industry 4.0 from previous industrial revolutions. In Industry 4.0: Industrial Revolution of the 21st Century. Studies in Systems, Decision, and Control (Vol. 169, pp. 21–29). doi:10.1007/978-3-319-94310-7_3

Porter, M. (2003). Clusters and regional competitiveness: Recent learnings. In *International Conference on Technology Clusters* (*Vol. 7*, pp. 2007-2013). Academic Press.

Porter, M. E. (1998). Clusters and competition. *On Competition, 7,* 91.

Porter, M. E. (1986). Changing Patterns of International Competition. *California Management Review*, *28*(2), 9–40. doi:10.2307/41165182

Porter, M. E. (1998). Clusters and the new economics of competition: Vol. 76. *No. 6*. Boston: Harvard Business Review.

Porter, M. E. (2000). Location, competition, and economic development: Local clusters in a global economy. *Economic Development Quarterly*, *14*(1), 15–34. doi:10.1177/089124240001400105

Posada, J., Toro, C., Barandiaran, I., Oyarzun, D., Stricker, D., de Amicis, R., & Vallarino, I. (2015). Visual computing as a key enabling technology for industrie 4.0 and industrial internet. *IEEE Computer Graphics and Applications*, *35*(2), 26–40. doi:10.1109/MCG.2015.45 PMID:25807506

Powell, W. W., Koput, K. W., & Smith-Doerr, L. (1996). Interorganizational collaboration and the locus of innovation: Networks of learning in biotechnology. *Administrative Science Quarterly*, *41*(1), 116–145. doi:10.2307/2393988

Preacher, K. J., & Hayes, A. F. (2004). SPSS and SAS procedures for estimating indirect effects in simple mediation models. *Behavior Research Methods, Instruments, & Computers*, *36*(4), 717–731. doi:10.3758/BF03206553 PubMed

Preacher, K. J., & Hayes, A. F. (2008). Asymptotic and resampling strategies for assessing and comparing indirect effects in multiple mediator models. *Behavior Research Methods*, *40*(3), 879–891. doi:10.3758/BRM.40.3.879 PubMed

Purchasing Managers Index for November 2019. (2019). *National Bureau of Statistics of China.* Retrieved from: http://www.stats.gov.cn/english/PressRelease/201912/t20191202_1712936.html

Purchasing Managers' Index (PMI). (2019). *Investopedia.* Retrieved from: https://www.investopedia.com/terms/p/pmi.asp

Radanliev, P., Roure, D. C. De, Nurse, J. R. C., Burnap, P., Anthi, E., Ani, U., … Montalvo, R. M. (2017). *Design principles for cyber risk impact assessment from Internet of Things (IoT).* Academic Press.

Radziwon, A., Bilberg, A., Bogers, M., & Madsen, E. S. (2014). The smart factory: Exploring adaptive and flexible manufacturing solutions. *Procedia Engineering*, *69*, 1184–1190. doi:10.1016/j.proeng.2014.03.108

Raemy, P., Beck, D., Hellmueller, L., Raemy, P., Beck, D., & Hellmueller, L. (2018). Swiss Journalists ' Role Performance: The relationship between conceptualized, narrated, and practiced roles. *Journalism Studies*, *0*(0), 1–18.

Rajnoha, R., & Lesníková, P. (2016). Strategic performance management system and corporate sustainability concept-specific parametres in Slovak Enterprises. *Journal of Competitiveness*, *8*(2), 107–124. doi:10.7441/joc.2016.03.07

Rajpal, N. K. (2015). Micro, Small and Medium Enterprises in North East India: Performance and Prospects. *The IUP Journal of Entrepreneurship Development*, *11*(3), 7–21.

Reddy, L., & Thomson, J. (2015). Environmental. In *Social and Economic Sustainability: Implications for Actuarial Science, Actuaries Institute ASTIN, AFIR/ERM, and IACA Colloquia*. Institute of Actuaries of Australia.

Regnér, P. (2008). Strategy-as-practice and dynamic capabilities: Steps towards a dynamic view of strategy. *Human Relations*, *61*(4), 565–588. doi:10.1177/0018726708091020

Resnik, D. B. (2007). Responsibility for health: Personal, social, and environmental. *Journal of Medical Ethics*, *33*(8), 444–445.

Rike, S. M. (2013). Bilingual corporate websites — from translation to transcreation? *The Journal of Specialised Translation*, *20*, 68–85.

Ristuccia, C. (2019). *Industry 4.0: SMEs Challenges and Opportunities in the Era of Digitalization*. Academic Press.

Robinson, M. (1997). *1997_Morrison and Robinson_a model of how psychological contract violation develops.pdf*. Academic Press.

Robinson, M. S. (1993). Beberapa strategi yang berhasil untuk mengembangkan Bank Pedesaan: Pengalaman dengan Bank Rakyat Indonesia 1970-1990. In S. Sugianto, Purnomo & M. S. Robinson (Eds.), Bunga Rampai Pembiyaan Pertanian Pedesaan (pp. 31-224). Jakarta: Institut Bankir Indonesia.

Roblek, V., Meško, M., & Krapež, A. (2016). A complex view of industry 4.0. *SAGE Open*, *6*(2). doi:10.1177/2158244016653987

Rodič, B. (2017). Industry 4.0 and the New Simulation Modelling Paradigm. Organizacija, 50(3), 193–207. doi:10.1515/orga-2017-0017

Rohde, J. (2004). Hierarchical supply chain planning using artificial neural networks to anticipate base-level outcomes. *OR-Spektrum*, *26*(4), 471–492. doi:10.1007/s00291-004-0170-x

Ross, S. A., Westerfield, R. W., & Jaffe, J. (1999). Corporate Finance (5th ed.). Boston, MA: Irwin and McGraw-Hill.

Roturier, J. (2015). *Localizing apps: a practical guide for translators and translation students*. Oxon, UK: Routledge.

Rozhkov, M., Cheung, B. C., & Tsui, E. (2017). Workplace context and its effect on individual competencies and performance in work teams. *International Journal of Business Performance Management*, *18*(1), 49–81. doi:10.1504/IJBPM.2017.080842

Ruggaber, R. (2006). Athena-Advanced technologies for the Interoperability of heterogeneous enterprise networks and their applications. *Interoperability of Enterprise Software and Applications*, *1*, 459–460.

Russom, P. (2011). Big data analytics. Retrieved from https://vivomente.com/wp-content/uploads/2016/04/big-data-analytics-white-paper.pdf

Sabiu, M. S., Ringim, K. J., Tang, S. M., & Joarder, M. H. R. (2019). Relationship between human resource management practices, ethical climates and organizational performance, the missing link. PSU Research Review, PRR-12-2016-0022. doi:10.1108/PRR-12-2016-0022

Sáenz, J., Aramburu, N., & Rivera, O. (2009). Knowledge sharing and innovation performance: A comparison between high-tech and low-tech companies. *Journal of Intellectual Capital*, *10*(1), 22–36. doi:10.1108/14691930910922879

Safar, L., Sopko, J., Bednar, S., & Poklemba, R. (2018). *Concept of SME Business Model for Industry 4.0 Environment*. Academic Press.

Safar, L., Sopko, J., Bednar, S., & Poklemba, R. (2018). Concept of SME business model for industry 4.0 environment. *TEM Journal*, *7*(3), 626.

Sajan, M., Shalij, P., Ramesh, A., & Biju Augustine, P. (2017). Lean manufacturing practices in Indian manufacturing SMEs and their effect on sustainability performance. *Journal of Manufacturing Technology Management*, *28*(6), 772–793. doi:10.1108/JMTM-12-2016-0188

Saleh, A. S., & Ndubisi, N. O. (2006). *An Evaluation of SME Development in Malaysia*. Academic Press.

Salim, I. M., & Sulaiman, M. (2011). Organizational Learning, Innovation and Performance: A Study of Malaysian Small and Medium-Sized Enterprises. *International Journal of Business and Management*, *6*(12), 118–125. doi:10.5539/ijbm.v6n12p118

Sami El-Khasawneh, B. (2012). Challenges and remedies of manufacturing enterprises in developing countries. *Journal of Manufacturing Technology Management*, *23*(3), 328–350. doi:10.1108/17410381211217407

Sánchez-Báez, E. A., Fernández-Serrano, J., & Romero, I. (2019). Organizational culture and innovation in small businesses in Paraguay. Regional Science Policy and Practice, 1–15. doi:10.1111/rsp3.12203

Sanders, A., Elangeswaran, C., & Wulfsberg, J. P. (2016). Industry 4.0 implies lean manufacturing Research activities in industry 4.0 function as enablers for lean manufacturing. *Journal of Industrial Engineering and Management*, *9*(3), 811–833. doi:10.3926/jiem.1940

Sandrini, P. (2008). Localization and translation. In H. Gerzymisch-Arbogast, G. Budin & G. Hofer (Eds.), MuTra Journal, Vol 2. LSP Translation Scenarios. Selected Contributions to the EU Marie Curie Conference Vienna 2007 (pp.167-191). Saarbrücken: ATRC.

Sankaraiah, M., & Mohan, B. (2016). Growth and Development of MSMEs – An Analytical View. *International Journal of Research and Development - A Management Review*, *5*(4), 48-56.

Saravanan, M., & Surendar, G. (2016). Analysis of Various Factors Influencing Labour Productivity in Construction Project. *International Journal of Emerging Technology in Computer Science & Electronics*, *22*(2), 179–181.

Sarker, B. R., & Fitzsimmons, J. A. (1989). The performance of push and pull systems: A simulation and comparative study. *International Journal of Production Research*, *27*(10), 1715–1731. doi:10.1080/00207548908942650

Saunila, M. (2014). Innovation capability for SME success: Perspectives of financial and operational performance. *Journal of Advances in Management Research*, *11*(2), 163–175. doi:10.1108/JAMR-11-2013-0063

Schilling, M. A., & Phelps, C. C. (2007). Interfirm collaboration networks: The impact of large-scale network structure on firm innovation. *Management Science*, *53*(7), 1113–1126. doi:10.1287/mnsc.1060.0624

Schmitz, H., & Nadvi, K. (1999). Clustering and Industrialization: Introduction. *World Development*, *27*(9), 1503–1514. doi:10.1016/S0305-750X(99)00072-8

Schröder, C. (2017). *The Challenges of Industry 4 . 0 for Small and Medium-sized Enterprises*. Academic Press.

Schröder, C. (2016). *The challenges of industry 4.0 for small and medium-sized enterprises*. Bonn, Germany: Friedrich-Ebert-Stiftung.

Schwartz, S. (1996). Value priorities and behavior: applying a theory of integrated value systems. The Psychology of Values: The Ontario Symposium, 8, 1-24.

Seeba, M. (2016). Foreword. In C. Lee (Ed.), *Multilingualism online*. London: Routledge.

Sekaran, U. (2003). *Research Method For Business, a skill-building approach*. Wiley India.

Sekaran, U., & Bougie, R. (2016). *Research Methods For Business: A Skill Building Approach*. Wiley.

Seuring, S., & Muller, M. (2008). Core issues in sustainable chain management- a Delphi study. *Business Strategy and the Environment*, *17*(8), 455–466. doi:10.1002/bse.607

Sevinç, A., Gür, Ş., & Eren, T. (2018). Analysis of the difficulties of SMEs in industry 4.0 applications by analytical hierarchy process and analytical network process. *Processes*, *6*(12), 264. doi:10.3390/pr6120264

Shafer, W. E., & Wang, Z. (2010). *Effects of ethical context on conflict and commitment among Chinese accountants.* Academic Press.

Shah, M. P., Pitroda, J. R., & Bhavsar, J. J. (2014). Analysis of Factors Influencing Productivity: Survey of Construction Projects in Central Gujarat Region of India. *International Journal of Engineering Sciences & Research Technology*, *3*(4), 3082–3087.

Shanock, L. R., & Eisenberger, R. (2006). When Supervisors Feel Supported : Relationships With Subordinates. *Perceived Supervisor Support, Perceived Organizational Support, and Performance*, *91*(3), 689–695.

Shaw, B. (1995). *User/supplier links and innovation. In The handbook of industrial innovation.* Edward Elgar Publishing.

Shrinivasan, S. (2018). *Life Sciences 4.0: transforming health care in India.* Retrieved 27/11/2019, from https://www.ey.com/Publication/vwLUAssets/ey-transforming-health-care-in-india/$File/ey-transforming-health-care-in-india.pdf

Shukla, O. J., & Misra, A. K. (2013). Easily & Economically Feasible Value Analysis &Value Engineering Concepts for Manufacturing Industry. *Engineering Management Reviews*, *2*(3), 81–85.

Singh, N., Zhao, H., & Hu, X. (2003). Cultural adaptation on the Web: A study of American companies' domestic and Chinese websites. *Journal of Global Information Management*, *11*(3), 63–80. doi:10.4018/jgim.2003070104

Singh, R. K., Garg, S. K., & Deshmukh, S. G. (2008). Strategy development by SMEs for competitiveness: A review. *Benchmarking: An International Journal*, *15*(5), 525–547. doi:10.1108/14635770810903132

Singh, R., Verma, O. P., & Anjum, B. (2012). Small Scale Industry: An Engine of Growth. *Zenith International Journal of Business Economics & Management Research*, *2*(5), 210–221.

Sinkula, J. M. (1994). Market information processing and organizational learning. *Journal of Marketing*, *58*(1), 35–45. doi:10.1177/002224299405800103

Sixto García, J., Aguado Domínguez, N., & Riveiro Castro, R. (2017). Presencia 2.0 de las pymes gallegas: niveles de participación y engagement con los usuarios. *Revista Latina de comunicación social, 72*(1), 47-68.

Slater, S. F., & Narver, J. C. (1995). Market orientation and the learning organization. *Journal of Marketing*, *59*(3), 63–74. doi:10.1177/002224299505900306

Ślusarczyk, B. (2018). Industry 4.0: Are we ready? *Polish Journal of Management Studies*, *17*(3), 232–248. doi:10.17512/pjms.2018.17.1.19

Small and Medium Enterprises Development Organization of Turkey. (2005). *Küçük ve Orta Büyüklükteki İşletmelerin Tanımı, Nitelikleri ve Sınıflandırılması Hakkında Yönetmelik.* Retrieved from https://www.kosgeb.gov.tr/ Content/ Upload/Dosya/ Mevzuat/KOBI%CC% 87%E2%80%99lerin_Tan% C4%B1m%C4%B1,_ Nitelikleri_ve_S%C4% B1n%C4%B1fland% C4%B1r%C4%B1lmas% C4%B1_Hakk%C4% B1nda_Yo% CC%88netmelik.pdf

Small and Medium Enterprises Development Organization of Turkey. (2005). *Küçük ve Orta Büyüklükteki İşletmelerin Tanımı, Nitelikleri ve Sınıflandırılması Hakkında Yönetmelik.* Retrieved from https://www.kosgeb.gov.tr/Content/Upload/Dosya/Mevzuat/KOBI%CC%87%E2%80%99lerin_Tan%C4%B1m%C4%B1,_Nitelikleri_ve_S%C4%B1n%C4%B1fland%C4%B1r%C4%B1lmas%C4%B1_Hakk%C4%B1nda_Yo%CC%88netmelik.pdf

Smallbone, D., Leig, R., & North, D. (1995). The characteristics and strategies of high growth SMEs. *International Journal of Entrepreneurial Behaviour & Research*, *1*(3), 44–62. doi:10.1108/13552559510100657

SME Corporation Malaysia. (2019). SME Definitions. Retrieved from http://www.smecorp.gov.my/index.php/en/policies/2015-12-21-09-09-49/sme-definition

Sölvell, Ö., Lindqvist, G., & Ketels, C. (2003). *The cluster initiative green book*. Stockholm: Ivory Tower.

Sørensen, J. B., & Stuart, T. E. (2000). Aging, obsolescence, and organizational innovation. *Administrative Science Quarterly*, *45*(1), 81–112. doi:10.2307/2666980

Sorenson, O., & Audia, P. G. (2000). The social structure of entrepreneurial activity: Geographic concentration of footwear production in the United States, 1940–1989. american. *Journal of Sociology (Melbourne, Vic.)*, *106*(2), 424–462.

Spath, D., Gerlach, S., Hämmerle, M., Schlund, S., & Strölin, T. (2013). Cyber-physical system for self-organized and flexible labor utilization. *Personnel*, *50*(22).

Spithoven, A., Vanhaverbeke, W., & Roijakkers, N. (2013). Open innovation practices in SMEs and large enterprises. *Small Business Economics*, *41*(3), 537–562. doi:10.100711187-012-9453-9

Stearns, P. N. (2013). *Industrial Revolution in World History*. Boulder, CO: Westview Press.

Steel, W. F. (1994). Changing the Institutional and Policy Environment for Small Enterprise Development in Africa. *Small Enterprise Development*, *5*(2), 4–9. doi:10.3362/0957-1329.1994.013

Stehouwer, K. (2014, Dec.). Northwood University Pioneers Undergraduate Major in Franchising Management. *Olive Software*.

Stock, T., & Seliger, G. (2016). Opportunities for sustainable manufacturing in industry 4.0. *Procedia CIRP*, *40*, 536–541. doi:10.1016/j.procir.2016.01.129

Stoicescu, C. (2016). Big Data, the perfect instrument to study today's consumer behavior. *Database Syst. J*, *6*, 28–42.

Strandhagen, J. W., Alfnes, E., Strandhagen, J. O., & Vallandingham, L. R. (2017). The fit of Industry 4.0 applications in manufacturing logistics: A multiple case study. Advances in Manufacturing, 5(4), 344–358. doi:10.1007/s40436-017-0200-y

Stverkova, H., & Pohludka, M. (2018). Business organizational structures of global companies: Use of the territorial model to ensure long-term growth. *Social Sciences*, *7*(6), 98. doi:10.3390/socsci7060098

Sullivan-Taylor, B., & Branicki, L. (2011). Creating resilient SMEs: Why one size might not fit all. *International Journal of Production Research*, *49*(18), 5565–5579. doi:10.1080/00207543.2011.563837

Sun, H. (2001). Building a culturally-competent corporate web site: an exploratory study of cultural markers in multilingual web design. In M. J. Northrop, & S. Tilley (Eds.), *Proceedings of the 19th annual international conference on Computer documentation - SIGDOC '01. Santa Fe, New Mexico, 21-24 October* (pp. 95-102). 10.1145/501516.501536

Swan, M. (2015). *Blockchain Blueprint for a New Economy* (T. McGovern, Ed.). Sebastopol, CA: O'Reilly.

Swierczek, F. W., & Ha, T. T. (2003). Entrepreneurial orientation, uncertainty avoidance and firm performance: An analysis of Thai and Vietnamese SMEs. *International Journal of Entrepreneurship and Innovation*, *4*(1), 46–58. doi:10.5367/000000003101299393

Szamosi, L. T. (2002). *Just what are tomorrow's SME employees looking for?* Academic Press.

Tamer, G. (2018). Sağlık Kuruluşlarında Sürdürülebilirlik; Özel Sağlık Kuruluşlarında Bir Araştırma. Retrieved from gelisim.edu.tr/xmlui/bitstream/handle/11363/1284/17

Tan, C., & Nasurdin, A. (2011). Human resource management practices and organizational innovation: Assessing the mediating role of knowledge management effectiveness. *Electronic Journal of Knowledge Management*, *9*(2), 155–167.

Taşlıyan, M., Eren, A. S., & Yücel, D. K. (2018). Defining the Determinants of Organizational Performance in Turkish Manufacturing Sees. *IOSR Journal of Business and Management, 20*(5), 26-35.

Taylor, F. W. (1913). *The principles of scientific management*. New York: Harpers & Brothers Publisher.

Teece, D. (2007). Explicating dynamic capabilities: The nature and microfoundations of (sustainable) enterprise performance. *Strategic Management Journal, 28*(13), 1319–1350. doi:10.1002/smj.640

Teece, D., Pisano, G., & Shuen, A. (1997). Dynamic Capabilities and Strategic Management. *Strategic Management Journal, 18*(7), 509–533. doi:10.1002/(SICI)1097-0266(199708)18:7<509::AID-SMJ882>3.0.CO;2-Z

Telefónica, & Red.es. (2014). *Desarrollo empresarial y redes sociales. El caso de las microempresas españolas*. Barcelona: *Ariel*.

Terry Kim, T., Lee, G., Paek, S., & Lee, S. (2013). Social capital, knowledge sharing, and organizational performance: What structural relationship do they have in hotels? *International Journal of Contemporary Hospitality Management, 25*(5), 683–704. doi:10.1108/IJCHM-Jan-2012-0010

Terziovski, M. (2010). Research notes and commentaries innovation practice and its performance implications in small and medium enterprises (SMEs) in the manufacturing sector: A resource-based view. *Strategic Management Journal, 31*(8), 892–902. doi:10.1002mj.841

Tether, B. S. (2002). Who co-operates for innovation, and why: An empirical analysis. *Research Policy, 31*(6), 947–967. doi:10.1016/S0048-7333(01)00172-X

Thames, L., & Schaefer, D. (2016). Software-defined cloud manufacturing for industry 4.0. *Procedia CIRP, 52*, 12–17. doi:10.1016/j.procir.2016.07.041

Thames, L., & Schaefer, D. (2017). Industry 4.0: an overview of key benefits, technologies, and challenges. In *Cybersecurity for Industry 4.0* (pp. 1–33). Cham: Springer. doi:10.1007/978-3-319-50660-9_1

The Union of Chambers and Commodity Exchanges of Turkey. (n.d.). Retrieved from https://www.tobb.org.tr

Theocharous, A. (2015). Food advertising as a mirror of intercultural differences: The case of the UK and Greece. *British Food Journal, 117*(4), 1256–1272. doi:10.1108/BFJ-01-2014-0038

Thong, J. Y. L. (2015). An Integrated Model of Information Systems Adoption in Small Businesses. *Journal of Management Information Systems, 15*(4), 187–214. doi:10.1080/07421222.1999.11518227

Thong, J. Y. L., Yap, C. S., & Raman, K. S. (1994). Engagement of external expertise in information systems implementation. *Journal of Management Information Systems, 11*(2), 209–231. doi:10.1080/07421222.1994.11518046

Timurçin, D. (2010). *Türkiye'de KOBI'lerin rekabet gücü ve rekabet üstünlüğü sağlamada kümelenmenin etkisi* (Doctoral dissertation). İstanbul Üniversitesi SBBF.

Timurçin, D. (2011). Kümelenme Kavramı ve KOBİ\'lerde Rekabet Gücüne Etkisi. Çankaya University. *Journal of the Humanities and Social Sciences, 8*(1), 21–56.

Tippins, M. J., & Sohi, R. S. (2003). IT competency and firm performance: Is organizational learning a missing link? *Strategic Management Journal, 24*(8), 745–761. doi:10.1002mj.337

Tıraş, H. H., & Hüseyin, A. (2018). OECD Ülkelerinde Sağlık Harcamaları ve Ekonomik Büyüme İlişkisi: Panel Nedensellik Analizleri. Siyaset, Ekonomi ve Yönetim Araştırmaları Dergisi, 6(4).

Tiwari, S., Wee, H. M., & Daryanto, Y. (2018). Big data analytics in supply chain management between 2010 and 2016: Insights to industries. *Computers & Industrial Engineering*, *115*, 319–330. doi:10.1016/j.cie.2017.11.017

Tjahjono, B., Esplugues, C., Ares, E., & Pelaez, G. (2017). What does industry 4.0 mean to the supply chain? *Procedia Manufacturing*, *13*, 1175–1182. doi:10.1016/j.promfg.2017.09.191

Todorov, K. (Ed.). (2014). *Handbook of research on strategic management in small and medium enterprises*. IGI Global. doi:10.4018/978-1-4666-5962-9

Toffler, A. (1970). *Future Schock*. New York.

Toker, K. (2017). *Tedarik Ağları, Sürdürülebilirlik ve Değer. İşletmelerde Sürdürülebilirlik Dinamikleri*. İstanbul: Beta.

Toker, K., & Çınar, F. (2017). Sağlık Sektöründe Kurumsal Sürdürülebilirlik Yönetimi ve İstanbul Avrupa Yakasında Faaliyette Bulunan Hastanelerde Bir Araştırma [Institutional Sustainability Management in the Health Sector and a Research on the Hospitals in European Side of İstanbul]. *International Conference on Eurasian Economies*.

Translator's Studio. (2019). *The price difference between transcreation and translation explained.* Retrieved from https://translatorstudio.co.uk/price-difference-transcreation-translation/

Tsai, Y., Wang, H., & Yuan, C. (2015). Transformational Leadership and Job Performance. *The Case of SMEs in Taiwan.*, *4*(8), 57–71.

Tsuruta, D. (2018). SME policies as a barrier to the growth of SMEs. Small Business Economics. doi:10.1007/s11187-018-0119-0

Turhan, D. G., Özen, T., & Albayrak, R. S. (2018). Kurumsal Sürdürülebilirlik Kavramı, Stratejik Önemi ve Sürdürülebilirlik Performansı Ölçümü: Literatür Çalışması [Corporate Sustaınabılıty Concept, Strategıcal Importance and Measuring Sustaınability Performance: A Literature Review]. *Ege Stratejik Araştırmalar Dergisi*, *9*(1), 17–37.

TUSIAD & BCG. (2016). *Sanayi 4.0 Raporu*. Retrieved from http://www.tusiad.org/indir/2016/sanayi-40.pdf

Tutar, F., & Kılınç, N. (2007). Türkiye'nin Sağlık Sektöründeki Ekonomik Gelişmişlik Potansiyeli ve Farklı Ülke Örnekleriyle Mukayesesi. Afyon Kocatepe Üniversitesi İ.İ.B.F. *Dergisi*, *9*(1), 31–54.

Ubius, U., Alas, R., & Vanhala, S. (2009). Innovation and corporate social responsibility in Estonian organizations. *Problems and Perspectives in Management*, *7*(1), 135–145.

Üçler, Ç., & Vayvay, Ö. (2018). KOBİ'lerde Eş Zamanlı Mühendislik: Otomotiv Tedarikçi Sektöründe Bir Uygulama. *Uluslararası Mühendislik Araştırma ve Geliştirme Dergisi*, *10*(2), 76–91.

Umrani, A. I., & Johl, S. K. (2020). *How Different Ownership Structures Perform in Industry 4.0: A Case of Malaysian Manufacturing SMEs*. Academic Press.

Umrani, A. I., & Johl, S. K. (2018). *How Different Ownership Structures Perform in Industry 4.0: A Case of Malaysian Manufacturing SMEs*. Academic Press.

Underwood, S. (2016). Blockchain beyond bitcoin. *Communications of the ACM*, *59*(11), 15–17. doi:10.1145/2994581

UNİDO. (2019). *What are Clusters*. Retrieved from http://www.clustersfordevelopment.org/

Ureña, A., Ballestero, M. P., & Prieto, E. (2017). *Informe e-Pyme 2017 de análisis sectorial de la implantación de las TIC en las empresas españolas*. Retrieved from https://www.ontsi.red.es/ontsi/sites/ontsi/files/Informe ePyme 2017.pdf

Uzkurt, C., Kumar, R., Kimzan, H. S., & Eminoğlu, G. (2013). Role of innovation in the relationship between organizational culture and firm performance: A study of the banking sector in Turkey. *European Journal of Innovation Management, 16*(1), 92–117. doi:10.1108/14601061311292878

Vaidya, S., Ambad, P., & Bhosle, S. (2018). Industry 4.0 - A Glimpse. Procedia Manufacturing, 20, 233–238. doi:10.1016/j.promfg.2018.02.034

Valaei, N., & Rezaei, S. (2016). Job satisfaction and organizational commitment. *Management Research Review, 39*(12), 1663–1694. doi:10.1108/MRR-09-2015-0216

Valtakoski, A., & Witell, L. (2018). Service capabilities and serviced SME performance: Contingency on firm age. *International Journal of Operations & Production Management, 38*(4), 1144–1164. doi:10.1108/IJOPM-06-2016-0328

Van de Vrande, V., De Jong, J. P., Vanhaverbeke, W., & De Rochemont, M. (2009). Open innovation in SMEs: Trends, motives and management challenges. *Technovation, 29*(6), 423–437. doi:10.1016/j.technovation.2008.10.001

Venkataramanaiah, S., & Parashar, S. P. (2007). Enhancing the competitiveness of SMEs through industrial clusters: The Indian experience. *International Journal of Technology Management & Sustainable Development, 6*(3), 227–243. doi:10.1386/ijtm.6.3.227_1

Verbano, C., & Crema, M. (2016). Linking technology innovation strategy, intellectual capital and technology innovation performance in manufacturing SMEs. *Technology Analysis and Strategic Management, 28*(5), 524–540. doi:10.1080/09537325.2015.1117066

Verhees, F. J. H. M., & Meulenberg, M. T. G. (2004). Market Orientation, Innovativeness, Product Innovation, and Performance in Small Firms. *Journal of Small Business Management, 42*(2), 134–154. doi:10.1111/j.1540-627X.2004.00102.x

Verma, R., & Jayasimha, K. (2014). Service delivery innovation architecture: An empirical study of antecedents and outcomes. *IIMB Management Review, 26*(2), 105–121. doi:10.1016/j.iimb.2014.03.002

Vermesan, O., Friess, P., Guillemin, P., Gusmeroli, S., Sundmaeker, H., Bassi, A., & Doody, P. (2011). Internet of Things Strategic Research Roadmap. In Internet of things-global technological and societal trends (Vol. 1, pp. 9–52). Retrieved from http://ec.europa.eu/information_society/policy/rfid/documents/in_cerp.pdf

Vidgen, R., Shaw, S., & Grant, D. B. (2017). Management challenges in creating value from business analytics. *European Journal of Operational Research, 261*(2), 626–639. doi:10.1016/j.ejor.2017.02.023

Vincenza Ciasullo, M., & Troisi, O. (2013). Sustainable value creation in SMEs: A case study. *The TQM Journal, 25*(1), 44–61. doi:10.1108/17542731311286423

Vrchota, J., Volek, T., & Novotná, M. (2019). Factors Introducing Industry 4.0 to SMES, Social Sciences, MDPI. *Open Access Journal, 8*(5), 1–10.

Wallach, E. J. (1983). Individuals and organizations: The cultural match. *Training and Development Journal, 37*(2), 28–35.

Waller, M. A., & Fawcett, S. E. (2013). Data science, predictive analytics, and big data: A revolution that will transform supply chain design and management. *Journal of Business Logistics, 34*(2), 77–84. doi:10.1111/jbl.12010

Wamba, S. F., Akter, S., Edwards, A., Chopin, G., & Gnanzou, D. (2015). How 'big data can make a big impact: Findings from a systematic review and a longitudinal case study. *International Journal of Production Economics, 165*, 234–246. doi:10.1016/j.ijpe.2014.12.031

Wamba, S. F., Gunasekaran, A., Akter, S., Ren, S. J., Dubey, R., & Childe, S. J. (2017). Big data analytics and firm performance: Effects of dynamic capabilities. *Journal of Business Research, 70*, 356–365. doi:10.1016/j.jbusres.2016.08.009

Wang, C.-H., Chang, C.-H., & Shen, G. C. (2015). The effect of inbound open innovation on firm performance: Evidence from the high-tech industry. *Technological Forecasting and Social Change*, *99*, 222–230. doi:10.1016/j.techfore.2015.07.006

Wang, D., & Chen, S. (2013). Does intellectual capital matter? High-performance work systems and bilateral innovative capabilities. *International Journal of Manpower*, *34*(8), 861–879. doi:10.1108/IJM-07-2013-0167

Wang, E. T. G., Chueh, N., Lee, A., Wang, E. T. G., & Lee, N. C. (2013). Using power regimes to explore perceived environmental uncertainty. *Industrial Management & Data Systems*, *113*(7), 950–966. doi:10.1108/IMDS-02-2013-0072

Wang, G., Gunasekaran, A., Ngai, E. W. T., & Papadopoulos, T. (2016). Big data analytics in logistics and supply chain management: Certain investigations for research and applications. *International Journal of Production Economics*, *176*, 98–110. doi:10.1016/j.ijpe.2016.03.014

Wang, S., Guidice, R. M., Tansky, J. W., & Wang, Z.-M. (2010). When R&D spending is not enough: The critical role of culture when you want to innovate. *Human Resource Management*, *49*(4), 767–792. doi:10.1002/hrm.20365

Wang, Y., Bhanugopan, R., & Lockhart, P. (2015). Examining the quantitative determinants of organizational performance: Evidence from China. *Measuring Business Excellence*, *19*(2), 23–41. doi:10.1108/MBE-05-2014-0014

Waseem-Ul-Hameed, S. N., Azeem, M., Aljumah, A. I., & Adeyemi, R. A. (2018). Determinants of e-logistic customer satisfaction: A mediating role of information and communication technology (ICT). Int. J Sup. Chain. *Mgt*, *7*(1), 105.

Weber, R. M. (2018). An Advisor's Introduction to Blockchain. *Journal of Financial Service Professionals*, *72*(6), 49. Retrieved from http://search.ebscohost.com/login.aspx?direct=true&db=edb&AN=132685638&lang=de&site=eds-live&authtype=shib

Wei, X. (2016). Error Orientation and Entrepreneurial Decision Making in Chinese Enterprises. *Opportunity Identification as Mediator*, *44*(4), 555–568.

Weng, R.-H., & Huang, C.-Y. (2017). The impact of exploration and exploitation learning on organizational innovativeness among hospitals: An open innovation view. *Technology Analysis and Strategic Management*, *29*(2), 119–132. doi:10.1080/09537325.2016.1210120

Wikipedia. (2019). *Kobi Tanımı*. Retrieved from https://tr.wikipedia.org/wiki/KOBİ.

Windolph, S., Schaltegger, S., & Herzig, C. (2014). Implementing corporate sustainability what drives the application of sustainability management tools in Germany? Sustainability Accounting Management and Policy Journal, 5(4), 378–404. doi:10.1108/SAMPJ-01-2014-0002

Winter, S. (2003). Understanding Dynamic Capabilities. *Strategic Management Journal*, *24*(10), 991–995. doi:10.1002/smj.318

Woldie, A., Leighton, P., & Adesua, A. (2008). Factors influencing small and medium enterprises (SMEs): An exploratory study of owner/manager and firm characteristics. *Banks and Bank Systems*, *3*(3), 5–13.

Woon, B. C., Kei, C. W., May, L. S., Yi, T. Y., & Mei, T. J. (2019). *Reasons Against Audit Exemption Among Sme*. Academic Press.

World Economic Forum. (2016). *The future of job employment, skills and workforce strategy for the Fourth Industrial Revolution*. Growth Strategies. Retrieved from https://tinyurl.com/yx2z42yq

World Energy Council. (2018). World energy issues monitor 2018: Perspectives on the grand energy transition. Retrieved from http://www.im.worldenergy.org/

Wu, B., & Deng, P. (2020). Internationalization of SMEs from emerging markets: An institutional escape perspective. *Journal of Business Research*, *108*, 337–350. Doi:10.1016/j.jbusres.2019.10.037

Wu, L. F., Huang, I. C., Huang, W. C., & Du, P. L. (2019). Aligning organizational culture and operations strategy to improve innovation outcomes: An integrated perspective in organizational management. *Journal of Organizational Change Management*, *32*(2), 224–250. doi:10.1108/JOCM-03-2018-0073

Xu, L. D., & Duan, L. (2019). Big data for cyber-physical systems in industry 4.0: A survey. *Enterprise Information Systems*, *13*(2), 148–169. doi:10.1080/17517575.2018.1442934

Xu, S. (2015). A study on knowledge management capabilities towards new product innovation type and development performance of Chinese businesses. *Acta Oeconomica*, *65*(s2), 145–157. doi:10.1556/032.65.2015.S2.11

Yamazaki, A. K. (2011). Web pages of small and medium-sized manufacturing companies in Tokyo and their global business needs. In *2011 IEEE International Professional Communication Conference* (pp. 1–3). Los Alamitos, CA: IEEE. 10.1109/IPCC.2011.6087241

Yin, Y., & Qin, S.-F. (2019). A smart performance measurement approach for collaborative design. *Advances in Mechanical Engineering*, *11*(1), 1–15. doi:10.1177/1687814018822570

Yli-Renko, H., Autio, E., & Sapienza, H. J. (2001). Social capital, knowledge acquisition, and knowledge exploitation in young technology-based firms. *Strategic Management Journal*, *22*(6-7), 587–613. doi:10.1002mj.183

Youndt, M. A., Snell, S. A., Dean, J. W. Jr, & Lepak, D. P. (1996). Human resource management, manufacturing strategy, and firm performance. *Academy of Management Review*, *39*(4), 836–866.

Yousif Al-Hakim, L. A., & Hassan, S. (2013). Knowledge management strategies, innovation, and organizational performance: An empirical study of the Iraqi MTS. *Journal of Advances in Management Research*, *10*(1), 58–71. doi:10.1108/09727981311327767

Yue, F., & Yu, H. A. N. (2008). Offshore Service Outsourcing: A SWOT Analysis of SMEs in Jiangsu Province. Academic Press.

Yukl, G. (1999). An evaluation of conceptual weaknesses in transformational and charismatic leadership theories. *The Leadership Quarterly*, *10*(2), 285–305. doi:10.1016/S1048-9843(99)00013-2

Zafar, A., & Mustafa, S. (2017). SMEs and its role in the economic and socio-economic development of Pakistan. International Journal of Academic Research in Accounting, Finance and Management Sciences, 6(4).

Zambon, I., Cecchini, M., Egidi, G., Saporito, M. G., & Colantoni, A. (2019). *Development for SMEs*. Academic Press.

Zhang, H., & Lv, S. (2015). Effect of HR practice on NPD performance The moderating role of environmental. *Nankai Business Review International*, *6*(3), 256–280. doi:10.1108/NBRI-03-2015-0008

Zhang, K. Z. K., Benyoucef, M., & Zhao, S. J. (2015). Computers in Human Behavior Consumer participation and gender differences on companies ' microblogs : A brand attachment process perspective. *Computers in Human Behavior*, *44*, 357–368. doi:10.1016/j.chb.2014.11.068

Zhao, R., Liu, Y., Zhang, N., & Huang, T. (2017). An optimization model for green supply chain management by using a big data analytic approach. *Journal of Cleaner Production*, *142*, 1085–1097. doi:10.1016/j.jclepro.2016.03.006

Zhong, R. Y., Newman, S. T., Huang, G. Q., & Lan, S. (2016). Big Data for supply chain management in the service and manufacturing sectors: Challenges, opportunities, and future perspectives. *Computers & Industrial Engineering*, *101*, 572–591. doi:10.1016/j.cie.2016.07.013

Zhu, L., Yu, F. R., Wang, Y., Ning, B., & Tang, T. (2018). Big data analytics in intelligent transportation systems: A survey. *IEEE Transactions on Intelligent Transportation Systems*, *20*(1), 383–398. doi:10.1109/TITS.2018.2815678

Zhu, Q., Sarkis, J., & Lai, K. (2008). Confirmation of a measurement model for green supply chain management practices implementation. *International Journal of Production Economics*, *111*(2), 261–273. doi:10.1016/j.ijpe.2006.11.029

About the Contributors

Qaisar Iqbal is currently pursuing his Ph.D. in organizational behavior at School of Management, Universiti Sains Malaysia. He has published many research papers in international and national journals including VINE Journal of Information and Knowledge management Systems, Business Information Review, Global Business Review, Journal of Science and Technology Policy Management, Administrative Sciences, Global IGI, World Journal of Science, Technology and Sustainable Development, and The Lahore Journal of Business. Currently, he is also the editorial board member of Probe-Business & Management, Insight-Information, Probe-Accounting, auditing, and taxation, International Journal of Economics, Finance, and Management and Journal of Business Administration Research. He had visited Universiti Muhammadiyah Yogyakarta, Indonesia and Minjiang University, China as an invited Guest Speaker in 2018 and 2019.

* * *

Siti Noor Haslina Abd Halim, is currently pursuing her Ph.D. in Organizational Behavior at Universiti Teknologi MARA Malaysia, Malaysia.

Siti Noor Jannah Abd Halim is currently pursuing her Ph.D. in Organizational Behavior at School of Management, Universiti Sains Malaysia, Malaysia.

Hasliza Abdul Halim, Ph.D., is currently an Associate Professor at School of Management, Universiti Sains Malaysia. She received her PhD from University of Malaya, Malaysia. She has been lecturing for many years on subjects such as HRM, Management, Strategic Management, Communication and others. She is also experienced in the use of modeling and application of software such as AMOS and SPSS. She currently serves as an editorial board member of the Asian Academy of Management Journal (AAMJ). She has presented her research works at various international conferences including the Australia and New Zealand Academy of Management (ANZAM), HRM conference and Global Academy of Business and Economics Research. She has also published in high impact journals such as Journal of Business, Economics and Management, Total Quality Management and Business Excellence. Additionally, she also published in various journals including Journal of Human Resource Costing & Accounting, Singapore Management Reviews, Business Strategies Series, International Journal of Economics and Management and Journal of International Business and Entrepreneurship and received a number of best paper awards.Abdullah Al Humaidan is currently pursuing her Ph.D. in organizational behavior at School of management, Universiti Sains Malaysia.

Noor Hazlina Ahmad, Ph.D., is currently DEAN and Professor at the School of Management USM. She joined the university after completing her PhD at the University of Adelaide, Australia. She teaches entrepreneurship and organizational behavior related subjects. She also supervises PhD and MA students in the field of entrepreneurship and SMEs. Currently, she serves as the President of the Asian Academy of Management and sits on the editorial board of the Asian Academy of Management Journal. She is also actively involved with consultation programs and served as a facilitator for community, entrepreneurship and leadership projects. Her research interests are in the areas of Entrepreneurship, SMEs and Organizational Behavior.

Sahrish Ahmad, Ph.D., has received her Doctorate Degree from School of Management, Universiti Sains Malaysia in 2019.

Abdullah Abdulaziz Alhumaidan is currently pursuing her Ph.D. in organizational behavior at School of management, Universiti Sains Malaysia.

Bülent Akkaya received his Bachelor Degree, Faculty of Education / Department of Teaching English/ from Kocaeli University in Turkey in 2006. In 2013, he got MBA, Faculty of Economics and Administrative Sciences / Department Of Business Administration and Management/ Manisa Celal Bayar University /Turkey. He received his PhD, from Faculty of Economics and Administrative Sciences / Department Of Business Administration and Management/ İzmir Katip Çelebi University/İzmir Turkey. He writes and presents widely on issues of industry 4.0, management, leadership, organizational agility, distance education, dynamic capabilities and statistics. He can use SPSS, AMOS and Maxqda programs. He works as Dr. Lecturer in Manisa Celal Bayar University.

Mustafa Atilla Arıcıoğlu got his undergraduate degree in Business Administration at İzmir Dokuz Eylül University, his master's degree and PhD in Department of Management and Organization at Selçuk University. He worked in private sector for 7 years. Then, he worked at Selçuk University until 2012. Now, he is Professor at Necmettin Erbakan University.

Celia Castillo Rodríguez is currently working as technical research support staff at Faculty of Translation and Interpretation, University of Granada, Spain. She has received her master's degree in professional Translation from University of Granada, Spain.

Mohammad Jamal Khan, Ph.D., is currently working as Assistant Professor at College of Health Sciences, Saudi Electronic University, Saudi Arabia. He has received his doctorate degree in international healthcare marketing from school of management, Universiti Sains Malaysia, Penang, Malaysia. His area of interest is medical tourism, healthcare travel, healthcare management, and travel & tourism marketing and consumer behavior.

Mokhalles Mohammad Mehdi is a Ph.D. Research Scholar, Department of Business Administration, Tezpur University, Tezpur, Assam, India and Assistant Professor of Marketing, MIS & IT, School of Business, The Assam Kaziranga University, Jorhat, Assam.

Teoh Ming Fang is currently pursuing full time PhD studies in School of Management, Universiti Sains Malaysia. She holds a Master degree in Business Administration (MBA) from Universiti Sains Malaysia. She was a lecturer in KDU Penang University College (March 2017- Jan 2019) and taught Cambridge A levels, Business. At Disted College (March 2014 until February 2017), she was taught Business Organization, Study Skills, Principle and Practice of Management, Research Methodology, International Business and Human Resource Management. Her main research interests lie on organization performance, digital business model innovation and digital entrepreneurship.

Debasree Mitra was born in October, 11, 1980 in Kolkata, West Bengal (India) and she received the M.Tech in Computer Science & Engineering from Kalyani Govt. Engineering College, Kalyani, West Bengal, India, and B.Tech degree in Information Technology from Govt. College of Engineering and Ceramic Technology, Kolkata, West Bengal, India,. She is currently engaged with JIS College of Engineering as a Asst. Professor after completion of her master. Her research interests include Image Processing and Machine Learning, Soft Computing.

Elena Moya-Molina is currently working as Young Investigative Staff at Faculty of Translation and Interpretation, University of Granada, Spain. She has received her master's degree from Autonomous University of Barcelona in 2018.

Rajendran Muthuveloo is a senior Lecture at Graduate School of Business, Universiti Sains Malaysia, 11800, Penang. He specializes in Corporate Strategy, Strategic Agility and Human Capital Development.

María-Dolores Olvera-Lobo is a Doctor in Documentation, Full Professor at the Department of Information and Communication at the University of Granada (Spain) and teacher at the Faculty of Communication and Documentation, and at the Faculty of Translation and Interpreting. She has taught courses in PhD, Master's and Postgraduate programmes at various universities. She has led research groups and projects, and teaching innovation projects. She has participated in a big number of international conferences. She has written and co-authored books, chapters and dozens of articles published in prestigious specialised journals.

Sebnem Ozdemir received her B.Sc. degree in Mathematics (Yıldız Technical University), as well as the M.A. in Mathematics Education and M.Sc. in Informatics (İstanbul University). She received her Ph.D. degree from İstanbul University (IU), İstanbul Turkey. In 2018, She was a visiting researcher in Electronics and Computing Engineering Department (Worcester Polytechnic Institute- WPI) for her postdoc research, Worcester, MA, USA. She currently holds the position of research collaborator at Massachusetts Institute of Technology (MIT) Computer Science and Artificial Intelligence Lab (CSAIL). She also works as Assistant Professor at the Department of Management Information System, Istinye University, İstanbul, Turkey. With the machine learning-based model, she built, Mrs. Ozdemir has received the "Contribution to Human Development Award" by Koc University UNESCO Chair. Earlier this year (2018), she began to integrate a new and closely-related research stream with her students, which is called "Deep Projects," which involves deep learning algorithms and methodologies. She has many published papers, book chapters and patents related to data science and machine learning. Ozdemir's main interest fields are artificial intelligence, data science, management information systems, decision-making, mathematical modelling.

Tridib Ranjan Sarma, Ph.D. is an Associate Professor at the Department of Business Administration, Tezpur University, Tezpur, Assam, India. His area of interest are Project Management, Operations Management, Quality, and Operations Research.

Hu Shi is currently pursuing her PhD at School of Management, Universiti Sains Malaysia. She belongs to China. Currently she is the PGA (postgraduate alliance) president. Before she had an experience as a lecturer for English teaching in Chinese Aviation Company.

Mustafa Sundu received his degree BS in Management (National Defense University), MS in Business Administration (Yeditepe University), PhD in Management and Organization (Istanbul University), Certificate in System Engineering. He has 30 years in national and international positions of manager with increasing responsibility including the following areas: leadership, coaching, training management, strategic planning and management, project management, reorganization, organizational development, human resources management, performance management, decision support and analysis techniques, business consulting, scientific research, and defense planning. Currently he works as Assistant Professor at the Department of Management Information System, Beykent University, İstanbul, Turkey. He is acting vice dean of Beykent University Faculty of Economics and Administrative Sciences. He has many published papers, book chapters related to management and leadership. Sundu's main interest fields are management, leadership, management information systems, industry 4.0, business intelligence and artificial intelligence.

Sema Üstgörül, Ph.D., is a Lecturer at Faculty of Health Sciences, Manisa Celal Bayar University, Turkey.

Lee Heng Wei, is a first-class business school graduate from University Sains Malaysia (USM) in 2009. He obtained USM Fellowship Award in 2010 and completed his Master degree in Technology Management in 2013. Dr Lee is currently a Head of Department at the school of business in UOW Malaysia KDU Penang University College. He teaches mainly courses in Research Methodology, Business Statistics, E-Commerce, Management, and Economics. Apart from teaching, he is an avid researcher, especially in the areas of technology management and adoption in business, health industry, and agriculture. His publications have appeared in Journal of Medical System (JMS), International Journal of Information Processing and Management (IJIPM), International Journal of Advancements in Computing Technology (IJACT), Information Society (i-Society), Advanced in Computer Science and its Applications, Computing Technology and Information Management (ICCM), International Journal of eBusiness and eGovernment Studies, and many conference proceedings. Having his contributions in research acknowledged, he is constantly invited to serve as a reviewer for many international journals. In addition, Dr Lee has collaborated with noted companies from various discipline through multiple research projects. To date, his research experience includes research conducted for organization like Malaysian Entrepreneurship Development Center (MEDEC), Muda Agriculture Development Agency (MADA), Suratthani Rajabhat University, Thailand (SRU), and etc. As a person who believes in a well-balanced life, Dr Lee is an active sportsman, playing basketball in the varsity team since his freshman years and represented Malaysia in Asean University Games (AUG) in 2010. He is currently the state coach for Penang Basketball Association.

Büşra Yiğitol was born in 1989 in Sakarya, Turkey. She got her undergraduate education in Business Administration at İzmir Dokuz Eylül University, her master's degree in Department of Management and Organization at Sakarya University. She works as research assistant at Konya Food and Agriculture University since 2016. At the same time, she is a PhD student at Necmettin Erbakan University.

Index

A

Artificial Intelligence 2, 8, 16, 22-24, 26-30, 33-35, 66, 85, 96, 105, 159, 208, 220, 227
Assam 123, 127, 129, 134

B

Bias 28-29, 34, 95, 111
Big data 2, 13-14, 16, 24-25, 30, 32-34, 66, 85, 95-97, 159, 195, 222

C

Challenges 1-3, 9, 12-13, 16, 22, 24-25, 44, 46, 66-67, 72, 81, 86, 96, 105, 108, 123, 133-134, 142, 144, 147, 150, 156, 159, 173, 192, 217, 222
Clustering 183-187, 191-193, 195-198, 204, 216
Configuration 32, 63
Corporate Sustainability 48-49, 62
Corporate Websites 156, 160-161, 163, 166-168, 173

D

Dynamic Capabilities 43-44, 52-57, 62-64, 79, 83, 97

E

Economic Sustainability 62
Environmental Sustainability 47, 62
Environmental Uncertainty 140-141, 144, 146-150

F

Financial 3, 8, 15, 23, 32-33, 51, 54, 67-68, 72, 84, 88, 91, 123, 126-127, 132-133, 196-197, 204, 211, 217, 227
Fourth industrial revolution 2, 12-13, 105-106, 140-141, 159, 195, 205-206, 209, 227

G

Gross Domestic Product (GDP) 1, 13, 50-51, 62, 80
Growth 4, 8, 13, 15-16, 44, 48, 50, 53, 62, 80, 82-84, 88, 105-106, 108, 123, 125-127, 129-130, 132-134, 142-143, 157-159, 185, 188, 192-193, 197, 211

H

Health 4.0 104-106, 117
Horizontal technology collaboration 104, 108-110, 112, 115-117
Human Resource Management 5, 79, 81-85, 89-92, 94, 96-97, 125

I

Industry 4.0 1-2, 8, 12-13, 16, 18, 22, 24-25, 29-30, 33-34, 43-44, 55, 65-67, 79-81, 83-85, 87-91, 95-97, 104-105, 140-141, 143, 151, 159, 183-184, 195-199, 205-207, 209-211, 213-223, 227
Information pollution 25, 159

K

Knowledge Management Capabilities 79, 81-83, 87-88, 90, 92, 97

L

Locale 181
Localization 155-158, 160-162, 166-168, 172-174, 181

M

Made-in-China 1-2
Management 5, 12, 17-18, 22, 24-26, 31-33, 44, 46, 54-57, 79, 81-92, 94-97, 125, 132, 134, 141, 146, 158, 183-184, 192-193, 195-198, 204-206, 209, 211, 214, 217, 220-221, 227

micro 3, 25, 65, 69, 72-73, 124, 191, 194
MSMEs 123-124, 126-127, 129-134

N

Non-Financial 91, 123

O

Organizational Culture 26, 32-33, 79, 81-83, 85-86, 89-92, 96-97
Organizational Innovation Capability 79-83, 85-92, 94-97
Organizational Learning 104, 106, 110-112, 115-117, 186
Organizational Performance 79-84, 88-92, 94, 96-97, 127

P

People's Republic of China 1, 3, 15

R

Resource-based View 79, 82
Role Performance 140-141, 143-144, 146-151

S

Seizing 53-54, 63
Sensing 53-54, 63
Small and medium enterprises 1, 12, 14-15, 66, 80, 124
Small and Medium Private Hospitals 104-106, 111-112, 116-117
small enterprises 2, 15, 65
Smart factory 16, 85
Social Media 105, 155-159, 161-162, 164-165, 172-174
Social Sustainability 62, 68
Source Text 160-161, 181
Strategic Management 18, 24, 32, 55, 183-184, 193, 197-198, 204-205, 217, 227
sustainable performance 1, 4, 65-73
SWOT Analysis 1-2, 9

T

Target Text 181
Transcreation 155-156, 160-161, 168, 170, 172-174, 181
Translation 14, 156, 160-163, 167-169, 171-173, 181

U

Usability 157-158, 181

V

Value-Addition 15, 123-125
Vertical technology collaboration 104, 108-109, 111-112, 115-117

W

Web Localization 162
Webrooming 156-157, 181

www.ingramcontent.com/pod-product-compliance
Lightning Source LLC
LaVergne TN
LVHW080527300926
849162LV00007B/1555